THE FUTURE OF HUMAN RIGHTS PROTECTION IN EUROPE

AF734090

THE FUTURE OF HUMAN RIGHTS PROTECTION IN EUROPE

Angelika Nußberger, Cathérine Van de Graaf
and Yannick Schoog (eds.)

INTERSENTIA
LEFEBVRE GROUP

Intersentia
Lefebvre Belgium SA
Avenue Jean Monnet, 4
1348 Louvain-la-Neuve
Belgium
Email: contact@larcier-intersentia.com

Distribution for the UK, Ireland and
Rest of the World (excl. France, Belgium and Luxembourg)
Ingram Publisher Services UK
1 Deltic Avenue, Rooksley
Milton Keynes MK13 8LD
United Kingdom
Tel: +44 1752 202 301 | Fax: +44 1752 202 331
Email: ipsuk.customercare@ingramcontent.com

Distribution for France and Other Countries (excl. Ireland and the UK)
Interforum Editis
92 avenue de France
75013 Paris
France

Distribution for Belgium and Luxembourg (excl. France, Ireland and the UK)
Larcier-Intersentia
Avenue Jean Monnet, 4
1348 Louvain-la-Neuve
Belgium

The Future of Human Rights Protection in Europe
© The editors and contributors severally, 2026

The authors have asserted the right under the Copyright, Designs and Patents Act 1988, to be identified as authors of this work.

No part of this book may be reproduced, stored in a retrieval system, or transmitted, in any form, or by any means, without prior written permission from Intersentia, or as expressly permitted by law or under the terms agreed with the appropriate reprographic rights organisation. Enquiries concerning reproduction which may not be covered by the above should be addressed to Intersentia at the address above.

ISBN : 978-1-83970-441-3
D/2026/06040/0186
NUR 828

British Library Cataloguing in Publication Data. A catalogue record for this book is available from the British Library

TABLE OF CONTENTS

PART I
FUTURE-PROOFING HUMAN RIGHTS

PART II
OPENING PROCEDURAL PATHWAYS TO TACKLE INJUSTICE

LIST OF CONTRIBUTORS

Dr. Yannick Schoog

Academy for European Human Rights Protection (University of Cologne)

Yannick Schoog is a former doctoral researcher at the Academy for European Human Rights Protection. He obtained his PhD from the University of Cologne with a thesis focusing on the on the protection of social benefits in the case law of the European Court of Human Rights, supervised by Professor Angelika Nußberger. He recently completed his legal clerkship with the German second state exam. His research focuses on social rights and discrimination.

Dr. Ezgi Özlü

University of Strasbourg

Ezgi Özlü is a Postdoctoral Researcher at the University of Strasbourg and a former Re:constitution fellow (2024/25) working on international human rights law and legal professions. She holds a PhD from the same university, where her research focused on how procedural costs affect the right of individual application before the European Court of Human Rights. Her dissertation was awarded the 2024 Thesis Prize by the René Cassin Foundation in France and the best doctoral thesis in Public Law at the University of Strasbourg for 2023–24.

Dr. Paula Rhein-Fischer

Academy for European Human Rights Protection (University of Cologne)

Paula Rhein-Fischer is a postdoctoral researcher at the Academy for European Human Rights Protection, University of Cologne. She is a principal investigator of the research consortium 'Mnemonic Reality' (2023–26) and was a postdoctoral researcher of the 'Memocracy' project (2021–25). She holds both German state exams in law and a Maîtrise en Droit from Université Paris I Panthéon Sorbonne. Paula completed her PhD at the Institute for International Peace and Security Law, University of Cologne on the prohibition to use force and factual mistakes. She is a member of the Young College of the North Rhine-Westphalian Academy of Sciences, Humanities and the Arts.

Dr. Samuel White

University of the West of Scotland

Samuel White is a senior lecturer in law at the University of the West of Scotland (UWS) where he is also Law Unit Lead and Director of the Social

Change Through Law research group. Prior to joining UWS, Samuel completed his PhD at the University of Dundee where his research on incorporation of international human rights law in the UK was funded by the Carnegie Trust for the Universities of Scotland and Royal Society of Edinburgh. He is a member of the Scottish Government's Human Rights Incorporation and Implementation Oversight Board and of the Law Society of Scotland's Human Rights and Constitutional Law Sub-Committee.

Dr. Cathérine Van de Graaf

Human Rights Centre (Ghent University) and Academy for European Human Rights Protection (University of Cologne)

Cathérine Van de Graaf is a postdoctoral researcher at the Human Rights Centre (Ghent University) and the Academy for European Human Rights Protection (University of Cologne). Cathérine is an editor at the Strasbourg Observers blog and a principal investigator on the joint project 'Who is the Court for? Bringing the Human (back) into Human Rights Research' funded by the Volkswagen Foundation in which she focuses on the examination of discrimination complaints before the European Court of Human Rights. She obtained her PhD from Ghent University with a thesis focusing on procedural justice theory, perceived discrimination and Islamophobia under the supervision of Prof. Dr. Eva Brems.

Dr. My Hanh Pham

University of Erlangen-Nuremberg

My Hanh Pham is a legal trainee at the Higher Regional Court of Munich. She studied law at the Ludwig Maximilian University of Munich and at the University of Helsinki. She pursued her doctoral research at the University of Erlangen-Nuremberg under the supervision of Professor Patricia Wiater. Her research focused on the Rights of Nature from a normative and comparative law perspective. In this context, she was a visiting scholar with Professor Klaus Bosselmann at the New Zealand Centre for Environmental Law at the University of Auckland. Her article was awarded first prize by the Winter Foundation for the Rights of Nature.

Dr. Francesca Mussi

Francesca Mussi, PhD in International Law from the University of Milano-Bicocca, is an independent scholar. Previously, she was an Assistant Professor in international law at the School of International Studies of the University of Trento, where she has been engaged in the research project 'The New Frontiers of Corporate Social Responsibility: Towards Green, Sustainable, and Inclusive Growth', funded by the European Union FSE REACT-EU, PON Research and Innovation programme 2014–20. Francesca held visiting positions at the Jagiellonian University (Kraków), the University of Copenhagen and the University of Geneva. She has written extensively in the field of business and human rights.

Dr. Sergii Masol

Sergii Masol is an independent scholar specialising in international law, international criminal law and international human rights law. He was a postdoctoral researcher at the University of Copenhagen and a Humboldt Postdoctoral Research Fellow at the University of Cologne. He also completed visiting fellowships at Roskilde University, the University of Copenhagen and the Institute for Human Sciences in Vienna. Sergii obtained his doctorate in law from the European University Institute in Florence, where he also worked as a research assistant. Sergii's research has been published in leading journals, including the *Leiden Journal of International Law* and the *Journal of International Criminal Justice.*

Reza Khabook

Academy for European Human Rights Protection (University of Cologne)

Reza Khabook is a doctoral researcher and research assistant at the Academy for European Human Rights Protection, University of Cologne. He holds a Master's degree in International Security Studies as a scholarship recipient of the joint programme of the Sant'Anna School of Advanced Studies in Pisa and the University of Trento. He also earned both his Bachelor's and Master's degrees in Law and Public Law from Shahid Beheshti University.

His research focuses on the relationship between the rule of law and states of emergency in the context of pandemic diseases. In recent years, he has also been actively involved in policy-making and teaching projects on human rights, constitutional law in Islamic countries, and transitional justice.

Dr. Tomáš Morochovič

University of Edinburgh and Global Governance Centre (Geneva Graduate Institute)

Tomáš Morochovič is a SNSF Postdoc.Mobility Fellow at the University of Edinburgh and a Research Associate at the Global Governance Centre, Geneva Graduate Institute. He is an associate editor at the Journal of International Dispute Settlement and the principal investigator in the project 'Decoding De-Legalisation: Translations of International Law in Global Governance'. He holds a PhD in International Law (*summa cum laude*) from the Geneva Graduate Institute, LLM in International Human Rights Law from the University of Exeter, and LLB in Law from King's College London. His research focuses on transnational legal theory and the evolving dynamics of human rights protection in a globalised context.

Professor Dr. Dr. h.c. Dr. h.c. Angelika Nußberger MA

Academy for European Human Rights Protection (University of Cologne)

Angelika Nußberger is Professor of international law, public law and comparative law at the University of Cologne and founding director of the Academy for European Human Rights Protection, Vice-President of the

Constitutional Court of Bosnia and Herzegovina, member of the Venice Commission of the Council of Europe and the Institut de Droit International. She was a judge at the European Court of Human Rights, elected on behalf of Germany from January 2011 to December 2019, and its Vice-President from February 2017 until the end of her mandate.

INTRODUCTION THE FUTURE OF HUMAN RIGHTS PROTECTION IN EUROPE

Angelika Nußberger, Cathérine Van de Graaf and Yannick Schoog

Human rights protection in Europe today finds itself at a crossroads. The legal systems and institutions developed in the aftermath of war and authoritarianism are increasingly being tested by crises that are both acute and protracted. Climate change, populism, pandemics, digital disinformation and social exclusion each present complex challenges, many of which unfold gradually over time. They are not short-lived events with a clear beginning and an end but rather evolving conditions even if there seems to be a moment of acceleration in the downwards spiral in the third decade of the 21st century. It is obvious that the changes threaten to reshape the normative and institutional architecture of human rights protection.

What makes these challenges particularly delicate and peculiar is their intergenerational nature. The consequences of present-day actions – or inaction – will be borne disproportionately by the younger generation. And yet, within the academic field of human rights, younger voices remain underrepresented. Scholarly discourse continues to be shaped primarily by senior academics,[1] whose experience is invaluable but who are often less directly impacted by the long-term consequences of contemporary crises. This volume responds to that imbalance by deliberately amplifying the perspectives of early-career researchers. It aims to serve not only as a forum for these emerging scholars but also as a testament to the insight and urgency they bring to the most pressing issues in European human rights law.

---

[1] The first part of the opening ceremony of the Academy for European Human Rights Protection in Cologne in 2022 was dedicated to the voices of young researchers whose articles are published in the present volume; for the documentation of the voices of senior researchers, international judges and court presidents see 'The Future of European Human Rights Protection' (2023) 42(1–9) *Human Rights Law Journal* 1 (with contributions from Koen Lenaerts, Robert Spano, Andreas Vosskuhle, Jonathan Mance, Mary Arden, Angelika Nußberger, Matthias Jestaedt and others).

This collection brings together original contributions that examine how legal systems, institutional practices and research methodologies must evolve to meet the demands of the future. Rather than offering utopian visions or abstract speculation, the authors engage in grounded legal analysis. Their work is forward-looking but anchored in current doctrinal debates and institutional constraints. What emerges is a picture of human rights protection that is both challenged and dynamic, capable of adaptation.

The volume is structured in three parts, each focusing on a distinct axis of transformation in the field of human rights. The first part, titled 'Future-Proofing Human Rights', explores how European legal systems might adapt to long-term threats and structural vulnerabilities and projects the existing (unsatisfactory) solutions into the future. One chapter reflects on how future institutional and legal frameworks may influence our collective memory of the past and reshape our understanding of legal responsibility in the present. Another addresses the potential reaccession of the Russian Federation to the Council of Europe, arguing that such a step must be preceded by a process of de-imperialisation and structural transition. A further contribution critically assesses how the experience of the Covid-19 pandemic has revealed the need for more robust judicial oversight in health emergencies, proposing institutional reforms that could mitigate rights-restricting state action in future crises. Finally, a chapter examines the precarious position of social rights within Europe's multi-layered human rights framework, highlighting the systemic obstacles to their meaningful enforcement and imagining a more integrated approach to their protection.

The second part of the volume, 'Opening Procedural Pathways to Tackle Injustice', shifts the focus from substantive rights to questions of access and enforcement. The chapters in this section interrogate how legal procedures can either facilitate or obstruct justice in practice. One contribution critiques the European Court of Human Rights' anthropocentric approach in environment-related cases, arguing that procedural reorientation is necessary to reflect the ecological dimensions of human rights violations. Another chapter examines the challenges claimants face in repetitive cases before the Strasbourg court, particularly in relation to the reimbursement of costs and expenses, and questions whether access to justice is being quietly narrowed through procedural formalism. The final chapter in this part scrutinises the European Union's Directive on Corporate Sustainability Due Diligence,[2] weighing its potential to advance – or instead, undermine – human rights protection across transnational supply chains. Together, these chapters underscore the need for

[2] Council Directive (EU) 2024/1760 of 13 June 2024 on corporate sustainability due diligence and amending Directive (EU) 2019/1937 and Regulation (EU) 2023/2859 [2024] OJ L1760/1.

procedural reform if human rights are to remain accessible and enforceable in the face of new forms of harm and power.

The third and final part, 'Novel Approaches to Human Rights Research', broadens the lens to consider methodological and conceptual innovation in the field. The contributions in this section reflect on how human rights are represented, narrated and studied, offering insights into how legal meaning is produced and contested. One chapter explores the internet as both a tool and a battleground for the right to political expression, showing how digital platforms reshape protest and dissent in contemporary Europe. Another investigates the role of education and public perception in sustaining – or eroding – support for human rights norms, arguing that these soft factors are central to the future legitimacy of the human rights regime. A final chapter provides a detailed case study of *Lachiri v. Belgium*,[3] mapping the actors and procedural strategies that led to an unexpected victory before the European Court of Human Rights. These contributions reveal the importance of looking beyond institutions to understand the broader social and narrative forces shaping the future of rights protection.

What unites all three parts of the volume is a shared commitment to interrogating the current system while imagining its possible futures. This volume stands apart in three key respects. First, it focuses specifically on legal protection mechanisms, avoiding broad theoretical treatments or socio-political generalisations in favour of a more grounded and doctrinally attuned perspective. Second, it applies a distinctly European lens, recognising the specificity – and, in many respects, the strength – of the European human rights framework compared to other regional or international systems. Third, it places early-career scholars at the centre of the conversation, not only to diversify academic discourse but also to ensure that those most affected by the long-term outcomes of present decisions have a say in shaping them.

In sum, *The Future of Human Rights Protection in Europe* does not offer easy answers or predictions. Instead, it provides a space for critical legal inquiry that is at once reflective and anticipatory. The chapters that follow are united in their sense that human rights protection must change – but also that it can. This volume is both a diagnosis and a call to action, and the authors hope it will contribute meaningfully to the debates that will shape the next chapters in European human rights law.

[3] *Lachiri v. Belgium*, no. 3413/09, 18 September 2018.

PART I.

Future-Proofing Human Rights

CHAPTER 1
AHEAD TO THE PAST: HOW THE FUTURE WILL GOVERN MEMORY OF THE PAST AND THE PRESENT

Paula Rhein-Fischer

1 INTRODUCTION

The first quarter of this century has seen a dramatic turn in politics and law towards memory. By various means, including law, states have been shaping the memory of their own national past and that of other states, sometimes seriously aiming to preserve, unravel, or discover historical facts, sometimes deliberately distorting them. This chapter takes a look into the future: what major trends are currently emerging in the landscape of memory laws and what could it look like 20 years from now?

Memory politics and memory laws – understood here as legal means inscribing an official interpretation of a historical event into law[1] – have been booming for years, with states increasingly using history as means for what has been described as 'ontological security seeking'. Thus, states have created and continue to enforce narratives about their own national past in order to establish or stabilise a sense of 'continuous self' and see it confirmed by others.[2] For instance, the incrimination in the Baltics and Ukraine of denying Soviet crimes can be read as emphasising those states' sovereignty and independence from

---

1 See Council of Europe, '"Memory Laws" and Freedom of Expression', Thematic factsheet, July 2018: '"Memory laws" enshrine state-approved interpretations of crucial historical events and promote certain narratives about the past [...]'; generally, on the phenomenon of memory laws see M. Sadowski, *Intersections of Law and Memory. Influencing Perceptions of the Past*, London, Routledge, 2024; U. Belavusau and A. Gliszczyńska-Grabias (eds), *Law and Memory: Towards Legal Governance of History*, Cambridge, Cambridge University Press, 2017; N. Koposov, *Memory Laws, Memory Wars: The Politics of the Past in Europe and Russia*, Cambridge, Cambridge University Press, 2017.

2 See M. Mälksoo, 'Kononov v. Latvia as an Ontological Security Struggle over Remembering the Second World War' in U. Belavusau and A. Gliszczyńska-Grabias (eds), *Law and Memory: Towards Legal Governance of History*, Cambridge, Cambridge University Press, 2017, p. 91 with further references; on this notion in international relations, see B. Steele, *Ontological Security in International Relations: Self-Identity and the IR State*, London, Routledge, 2008.

Russia.[3] Vladimir Putin's distortive use of history in Russia's aggression against Ukraine, outlawing anyone who diverges from the state narrative that Russia is attempting to 'denazify'[4] Ukraine and to reunite two peoples that had been artificially separated by the Bolsheviks,[5] is another example, though extreme, where distortive memory is instrumentalised to realise imperialistic fantasies. Even 'self-inculpatory' memory laws that explicitly acknowledge and aim to protect the memory of past crimes committed by the 'home' nation,[6] such as the Holocaust denial ban in Germany, can be conceptualised in terms of ontological security, since they contain the implicit promise to have become a peaceful state and never to repeat past atrocities.[7] At the same time, memory laws clearly aim to protect domestic legal interests, the exact determination of which is the subject of debate. For example, the suggested legal interests protected by Holocaust denial bans range from the human dignity of the victims and their descendants,[8] their personal honour[9] and the collective memory of victims or of society more generally[10] to the dignity of the nation, historical truth,[11] or public peace.[12]

3 On Latvia, see M. Mälksoo, above n. 2, p. 105; for a historical account of memory laws in Eastern Europe, see N. Koposov, above n. 1, pp. 126 et seq.; for memory laws in Ukraine, see also U. Belavusau, A. Gliszczyńska-Grabias and M. Mälksoo, 'Memory Laws and Memory Wars in Poland, Russia and Ukraine' (2021) 69 *Jahrbuch des öffentlichen Rechts* 95, 113–15.

4 See the English transcript of Putin's speech of 24 February 2022 announcing the aggression against Ukraine: 'Full text of Vladimir Putin's speech announcing "special military operation" in Ukraine', *ThePrint*, 24 February 2002 <https://theprint.in/world/full-text-of-vladimir-putins-speech-announcing-special-military-operation-in-ukraine/845714/>.

5 See the English transcript of Putin's 'speech on history' of 21 February 2022, three days before launching the aggression: 'President Putin's February 21 speech to the nation – full text', *The Rio Times*, 24 February 2022 <https://www.riotimesonline.com/brazil-news/crypto/president-putins-full-text-of-february-21-2022-speech-to-the-nation/>.

6 On this category, see E. Heinze, 'Should governments butt out of history?', *Free Speech Debate*, 12 March 2019 <https://freespeechdebate.com/discuss/should-governments-butt-out-of-history/>.

7 To this extent, the Holocaust denial ban in Germany shares some features with 'outward-looking' memory laws. On this category, see B. Baranowska and P. Rhein-Fischer, 'Outward-looking memory laws: an illiberal feature?', in *Archiv des Völkerrechts* 63 (2025), 99-121.

8 See, e.g. Federal Constitutional Court, Order of 22.6.2006, 2 BvR 1421/05, BeckRS 2006, 24381 on the German Holocaust denial ban; however, public peace is also considered to be protected, see Federal Court of Justice, Order of 3.5.2016, 3 StR 449/15.

9 I. Junge, 'Das Schutzgut des § 130 StGB', University dissertation, Herdecke, GCA-Verlag, 2000, p. 123 on the German Holocaust denial ban.

10 M. Matuschek, *Erinnerungsstrafrecht: Eine Neubegründung des Verbots der Holocaustleugnung auf rechtsvergleichender und sozialphilosophischer Grundlage*, Berlin, Duncker & Humblot, 2012, pp. 102 et seq. on the German Holocaust denial ban; in France, collective memory is more widely considered a protected value, ibid., pp. 95–98.

11 For the Polish Holocaust denial ban, see ibid., pp. 101 et seq.; for the German Holocaust denial ban, see H. Ostendorf, 'Im Streit: Die strafrechtliche Verfolgung der "Auschwitzlüge"' (1985) 38 *Neue Juristische Wochenschrift* 1062.

12 See, e.g. Cons. const., 8 janvier 2016, n°2015-512 QPC, *M. Vincent R.*; and Cons. const., 28 février 2012, n°2012-647 DC, *Loi visant à réprimer la contestation de l'existence des génocides reconnus par la loi*, on public order and individual rights; approving M. Tissier-Raffin, 'La constitutionnalité enfin confirmée de la loi Gayssot: Liberté d'expression et négationnisme

The relationship of memory laws to human rights is complex. It very much depends on the relevant law whether it effectively contributes to protecting human rights such as the aforementioned personal honour of the victims, human dignity or a potential 'human right to truth'. A crucial factor is how close the state-official narrative incorporated in the law is to historical truth and to what extent it acknowledges historical injustice. A Russian memory law making it a criminal offence to 'disseminate knowingly false information on the activities of the USSR' during WWII[13] – meaning to express the historical truth that the Soviet army committed horrendous crimes during that war – does nothing to raise human rights protection. To the contrary, it neglects the victims' suffering, downgrading their personal honour and identity. Unlike laws of this kind, self-inculpatory or otherwise crime-acknowledging laws such as denial bans do contribute to protect certain human rights values. Nevertheless, they interfere with conflicting human rights, namely the freedom of expression, assembly and research. Besides, laws protecting the memory of a particular historical crime often provoke aspirations of the victims of other crimes who also seek to see their suffering recognised. In this respect, even crime-acknowledging memory laws touch upon fundamental questions of equality and justice.

There is reason to believe that the governance of memory is about to undergo some fundamental changes in the coming years. This chapter aims to explore these looming changes and investigate their repercussions for the current legal framework. In doing so, it primarily focuses on memory laws with the strongest mnemonic element: laws dealing with denialism of historical crimes, most importantly, criminal denial bans.[14]

There are three major factors that appear particularly likely to challenge the existing landscape of memory laws in Europe. First, present and future atrocities will challenge the existing European mnemonic scenery, which is still primarily focused on Nazi and Soviet crimes, the former occupying the most prominent position especially in Western Europe (section 2). Second, the entry into the 'post-factual' age – resulting from increasing disinformation due to state propaganda, the speed of online communication across the globe, and artificial intelligence – increases pressure on legislators to protect the memory

(Art. 11 DDHC)', *La Revue des droits de l'homme*, February 2016; others in France have emphasised public order and humanity (D. Bruère Dawson, C. Charrière-Bournazel, A. Couyoumdjian, L. Forster, A. Jakubowicz, B. Jouanneau, C. Korman, J.-L. Lagarde, P. Mairat, M. Stasi and G. Tcholakian, 'Le négationnisme, une infraction', *Le Monde*, 9 October 2006 <https://www.lemonde.fr/idees/article/2006/10/09/le-negationnisme-une-infraction-par-didier-bruere-dawson-christian-charriere-bournazel-avocats_821493_3232.html>).

13 U. Belavusau, A. Gliszczyńska-Grabias and M. Mälksoo, above n. 3, 106.

14 On their mnemonic element, see P. Rhein-Fischer, 'Militant Democracy in the ECtHR Case Law on Genocide Denial Bans' (2022) *European Yearbook on Human Rights* 483, 488.

of past events by legislative means. This trend is likely to fuel the debate on an emerging 'right to memory' (section 3). Third and interrelated to the entry into the post-factual age, an increasing privatisation of memory governance, due to shifts of communication and responsibilities to social platforms, poses challenges to the mnemonic legal order (section 4).

2 MNEMONIC CHALLENGES BY NEW ATROCITIES

This section explores how the existing European focus on Nazi and Communist crimes (sub-section 2.1) may be challenged by new atrocities, making more extensive memory laws more likely (sub-section 2.2). The section's focus lies on investigating how such a more extensive mnemonic legal framework would fit within existing legal standards under European Union (EU) law and the European Convention on Human Rights (ECHR) (sub-section 2.3). Finally, the section evaluates possible future attempts to widen the existing legal standards so as to accommodate more extensive memory laws (sub-section 2.4).

2.1. Existing European Memory Politics Primarily Focusing on Nazism and Communism

As declaratory resolutions of the EU and the Council of Europe (CoE) illustrate, memory politics of both organisations have traditionally been focusing on National Socialism (Nazism) as well as Soviet crimes. The European Communities, formed by Western European countries, originally focused on the recognition of Nazi crimes, first and foremost the Shoah, as did (and, in great parts, still do) Western Member States in their national memory politics and laws. When many Eastern European states joined the EU in 2004, they had already adopted, in the course of their democratisation processes, memory laws centering around the memory of Soviet crimes against their populations. The European Parliament, in an attempt to reconcile the East-West memory divide, soon adopted a dualistic approach, recognising both the crimes of Nazism and Stalinism,[15] and emphasised that the dominant historical experience in Western Europe was Nazism, while in Central and Eastern European countries, it was

[15] European Parliament Declaration on the proclamation of 23 August as European Day of Remembrance for Victims of Stalinism and Nazism (P6_TA(2008)0439) [2008] OJ C8E/57; more recently, see European Parliament Resolution of 19 September 2019 on the importance of European remembrance for the future of Europe (2019/2819(RSP)) [2021] OJ C171/25.

both Communism and Nazism.[16] Efforts to commemorate other historical crimes have also been made; however, they have remained more exceptional.[17]

Similarly, CoE institutions first adopted declarations centering around the remembrance of the Holocaust.[18] With the end of the Soviet Union, Communist crimes became an additional point of reference for CoE memory policies.[19] The explicit recognition of other genocides has remained scarce within the CoE.[20]

This focus on Nazism and Communism, and less on the many other atrocities in the world's and Europe's history books, obviously results from the large (and, with regards to the Holocaust, certainly incomparable) scale of atrocities committed under these two regimes. Both regimes affected a great part of the (joining) Member States of the EU and the CoE. Forming or joining these organisations was part of overcoming that traumatic past: as much as

---

16 European Parliament Resolution of 2 April 2009 on European conscience and totalitarianism (P6_TA(2009)0213); it also explicitly recognised the Holodomor in 1932 and 1933 a 'crime against the Ukrainian people, and against humanity' (European Parliament Resolution of 23 October 2008 on the commemoration of the Holodomor, the Ukraine artificial famine (1932–1933) (P6_TA(2008)0523)).

17 See, e.g. the European Parliament's recognition of the genocide against Armenians (European Parliament Resolution of 18 June 1987 on a political solution to the Armenian question (A2-0033/87) [1987] OJ C190/119 and European Parliament Resolution of 15 April 2015 on the centenary of the Armenian Genocide (2015/2590(RSP)) [2016] OJ C328/2), of the Srebrenica genocide (European Parliament Resolution of 15 January 2009 on Srebrenica (RC-B6-0022/2009)), of the Soviet genocide of the Chechen People in 1944 (European Parliament Recommendation of 26 February 2004 on EU-Russia relations (2003/2230(INI)). The European Parliament has also qualified China's human rights violations against the Uyghurs as a 'serious risk of genocide' (European Parliament Resolution of 9 June 2022 on the human rights situation in Xinjiang, including the Xinjiang police files (2022/2700(RSP)) [2022] OJ C493/96).

18 See, e.g. PACE (Parliamentary Assembly of the Council of Europe) Written declaration No. 190 of 23 September 1989, 'Recrudescence de l'antisémitisme en Europe' as cited by P. Garcia, 'Vers une politique mémorielle européenne? L'évolution du statut de l'histoire dans le discours du Conseil de l'Europe' in R. Frank, H. Kaelble, M.-F. Lévy and L. Passerini (eds), *Building a European Public Sphere – From the 1950s to the Present*, Brussels, Peter Lang, 2010, p. 179, fn. 51; recently, see Recommendation CM/Rec(2022)5 of the Committee of Ministers to member States on passing on remembrance of the Holocaust and preventing crimes against humanity, 17 March 2022.

19 See, e.g. PACE Resolution 1096 (1996) of 27 June 1996, 'Measures to dismantle the heritage of former communist totalitarian systems'; PACE Resolution 1481 (2006) of 25 January 2006, 'Need for international condemnation of crimes of totalitarian communist regimes'; PACE Resolution 1723 (2010) of 28 April 2010, 'Commemorating the victims of the Great Famine (Holodomor) in the former USSR'.

20 E.g. the Armenian genocide has not been formally recognised, but it was mentioned in declarations signed by PACE members, see PACE Written Declaration No. 275 of 24 April 1998, 'Commemoration of the Armenian genocide of 1915' (Doc. 8091), and PACE Written Declaration No. 320 of 24 April 2001, 'Recognition of the Armenian genocide' (Doc. 9056); in 2012, the Chair of the PACE Committee on Political Affairs and Democracy deplored the genocide denial by the president of Serbia ('Chair of PACE committee concerned about denial of Srebrenica genocide', *PACE.coe.int*, 4 June 2012 <https://pace.coe.int/en/news/3989/le-president-d-une-commission-de-l-apce-est-preoccupe-par-le-deni-du-genocide-de-srebrenica>).

dealing with Nazism became the 'founding myth' of the original European Communities,[21] overcoming communism and dealing with the memory of it became the 'joining myth' of the EU Eastern enlargement. Against this background, measures commemorating these historical eras can also be considered to protect the democratic system, rule of law and fundamental rights, as such.

2.2. *Mnemonic Shift to New Atrocities*

However, history has not stopped at this point. Many conflicts could be mentioned, but the ongoing Russian war of aggression against Ukraine is a particularly clear example of the fact that history has already turned the page on another bloody chapter akin to Nazism and Communism, which is likely to entail major shifts in the landscape of memory laws and politics. Not only is Putin's reasoning and mode of operation reminiscent of Nazi fascism in many respects.[22] He has also adopted various laws protecting a specific narrative about the ongoing war against Ukraine.[23] The Russian annexation of Crimea and the full-scale war of aggression, in turn, have led Ukraine to further distinguish its own national memory of the Second World War and communism from former Soviet memory.[24] More importantly, Ukraine and other potential future victims of Putin's aggressive imperialism will, once the war is over, see the need to protect the memory of Russian crimes committed during this war. The EU and the CoE, supporting Ukraine in its aspiration

---

21 See from the Schuman Declaration of 9 May 1950: 'World peace cannot be safeguarded without the making of creative efforts proportionate to the dangers which threaten it' and Schuman's introduction in the press conference: 'Nearly five years to the day after the unconditional surrender of Germany, France is now taking the first decisive step towards the construction of Europe and is associating Germany in this venture. [...] Out of all this will come forth Europe, a solid and united Europe', as cited by L. Probst, 'Founding Myths in Europe and the role of the Holocaust' (2003) 90 *New German Critique* 45, 48.

22 See T. Snyder, 'We Should Say It. Russia Is Fascist', *The New York Times*, 19 May 2022 <https://www.nytimes.com/2022/05/19/opinion/russia-fascism-ukraine-putin.html>; however, this claim has been challenged by others, see R. Coalson; 'Nasty, Repressive, Aggressive – Yes. But Is Russia Fascist? Experts Say "No"', *RadioFreeEurope/RadioLiberty*, 9 April 2022 <https://www.rferl.org/a/russia-repressive-aggressive-not-fascist/31794918.html>.

23 See contributions by G. Bogush ('Putin's Memory Policies in the Context of Military Aggression in Ukraine') and P. Rhein-Fischer ('German Prototype for Memory Laws and Policies in Europe in the Context of Putin's Instrumentalisation of Denazification') in U. Belavusau, A. Gliszczyńska-Grabias, M. Mälksoo and A. Nussberger (eds), *The Politics of Memory Laws: Russia, Ukraine and Beyond*, Oxford and New York, Bloomsbury, 2025.

24 See only the change of date of the Day of Remembrance and Victory over Nazism from 9 to 8 May; for this and other examples see A. Nekoliak, 'Ukrainian Memory Laws and Policies in the Context of 2022 Russian Aggression' in U. Belavusau, A. Gliszczyńska-Grabias, M. Mälksoo and A. Nussberger (eds), above n. 23; see also Y. Yurchuk, 'Rethinking and Remaking Memory in a Time of War', *ENRS*, 1 July 2024 <https://enrs.eu/article/rethinking-and-remaking-memory-in-a-time-of-war>.

for European integration, can be expected to accommodate this concern. This development is compounded by the loss of the United States as Ukraine's and European ally in the Russo-Ukrainian war, the erosion of the transatlantic relationship and the US' disrespect of international law and states' sovereignty under Donald Trump's second administration, fueling the general turn to great-power politics. Hence, the more the Russo-Ukrainian war evolves to a war about values between Europe including Ukraine and the great powers Russia, China, and the US, the more the need for a mnemonic framework to emphasise smaller states' sovereignty and independence is likely to emerge.

Similarly, the Hamas attack on Israel on 7 October 2023 and the following war in Gaza is likely to shift the landscape of memory laws and politics. Polls show that many Israeli Jews draw parallels from 7 October to the Holocaust[25] – comparisons that also influence the way the Holocaust is collectively remembered in Israel. It is also likely that attempts will be made to also protect the remembrance of the events of 7 October as such. The Hamas attacks have also had implications on the memory laws and politics of other countries. In Germany, 7 October has intensified the country's mnemo-historical commitment vis-à-vis Israel: as a response to the Hamas attacks and their repercussions in Germany, including pro-Palestinian demonstrations, various suggestions were made to protect the existence of the state of Israel. They ranged from criminalising those who deny the existence of the state of Israel or call for its abolition[26] to an obligatory commitment to the existence of Israel as a requirement for German citizenship.[27] Ultimately, only a more lenient provision has made it into the German Nationality Act.[28] Again as a reaction to the 7 October attacks and the ensuing conflict, in November 2024, the German parliament adopted a controversial resolution about the protection

25 S. Sokol, 'Poll: Over half of Israeli Jews see comparison between Holocaust and October 7', *Times of Israel*, 6 May 2024 <https://www.timesofisrael.com/poll-over-half-of-israeli-jews-see-comparison-between-holocaust-and-october-7/>.

26 Draft law Bundestag Drucksache 20/9310, see 'Strafrechtsverschärfung überwiegend kritisch bewertet', *Bundestag*, 15 January 2024 <https://www.bundestag.de/dokumente/textarchiv/2024/kw03-pa-recht-antisemitismus-985006>.

27 Bundestag Drucksache 20/9764, 'Antrag der Fraktion CDU/CSU: Den Wert der deutschen Staatsangehörigkeit bewahren', 13 December 2023.

28 The immigrant must acknowledge the 'special historical responsibility of Germany for the National Socialist regime and its consequences, notably for the protection of Jewish life', and acknowledge the peaceful cohabitation of peoples and the prohibition of wars of aggression (§ 10 Sentence 1 (1) No. 1 a of the Nationality Act); also, the law clarifies that antisemitic, racist and other acts motivated by disregard for humans are incompatible with the free democratic order that immigrants must also acknowledge (§ 10 Sentence 1 (1) No. 1, Sentence 3 of the Nationality Act). However, the law has been interpreted by courts as requiring the acknowledgment of the existence of the state of Israel, Administrative court of Regensburg, Judgment of 7.10.2024 – RO 9 K 2.782.

of Jewish life in Germany,[29] which reiterates its commitment to the relatively wide working definition of antisemitism by the International Holocaust Remembrance Alliance (IHRA), including also Israel-related antisemitism.[30]

In other countries, criticism was voiced more loudly that Israel was weaponising Holocaust memory to shield its military from scrutiny.[31] 'Never again – to anyone' became the catchphrase to express the view that Palestinians in the Gaza strip were victims of a genocide committed by Israel.[32] Such language is not without effects for the memory of the Shoah as it reframes this memory in a way that departs from established mnemonic narratives.

These examples show that the course of history continues to add other historical events to the historical record that may shift states' memory cultures, politics and laws. This is likely to change the way Europe remembers Nazi and Soviet crimes, the current main historical reference points.

This raises the question to what extent a more diverse mnemonic legal framework would fit within the current European legal standards on denialism. To make the analysis more tangible, this issue will be examined using the two above-mentioned conflicts as examples.

2.3. A Wider Mnemonic Landscape's Fit within the Current Legal Framework on denialism

The European legal framework on the incrimination of denialism, even in its contemporary contours, is able to accommodate the remembrance of current and future atrocities – however, only under certain circumstances. To demonstrate this flexibility, but also its limits, it is helpful to distinguish between European standards that *oblige*, or call on, Member States to incriminate denialism and those that *limit* Member States in doing so.

2.3.1 Obligation to Incriminate Denial

As regards standards *obliging*, or calling on, Member States to incriminate the denial of historical crimes, both the relevant legal frameworks of the EU

---

29 Bundestag Resolution 'Nie wieder ist jetzt – Jüdisches Leben in Deutschland schützen, bewahren und stärken' (Bundestag Drucksache 20/13627, 'Never ever is now – Protect, preserve and promote Jewish life in Germany'), 7 November 2024.

30 IHRA, 'IHRA non-legally binding working definition of antisemitism, adopted by the IHRA Plenary in Bucharest', 26 May 2016.

31 J.E. Rosenberg, 'Stop comparing Oct. 7th to the Holocaust', *People's World*, 26 October 2023 <https://peoplesworld.org/article/stop-comparing-oct-7th-to-the-holocaust/>.

32 See A. Johnson and A. Omer, 'Student Movement for Gaza on US Campuses', in D. A. Snow, D. McAdam, and D. M. Moss (eds), *Contemporary Social Movements: Historical and Descriptive Accounts*, Wiley, New Jersey 2025, 177-183; D. Abraham, 'Never Again to Us and/or to Anyone', *Verfassungsblog*, 31 July 2024 < https://verfassungsblog.de/never-again-to-us-and-or-to-anyone/>.

and CoE are construed in general terms and not limited to specific historical crimes. It is true that the most relevant EU law instrument, the binding 2008 EU Framework Decision on combating certain forms and expressions of racism and xenophobia by means of criminal law (FD 2008),[33] explicitly highlights the duty to criminalise the public condoning, denial or gross trivialisation of Nazi crimes (FD 2008, Article 1(1)(d)). However, it also extends this duty, more generally, to genocide, crimes against humanity and war crimes as defined under the Statute of the International Criminal Court (ICC Statute). The public condoning, denial or gross trivialisation (not necessarily the historical crime itself)[34] must be 'directed against a group [...] or a member of such a group defined by reference to race, colour, religion, descent or national or ethnic origin'.[35] Besides, the statement must be 'likely to incite violence or hatred against such a group or a member of such group' (FD 2008, Article 1(1)(c)). The FD 2008 allows Member States to punish only conduct that is 'carried out in a manner likely to disturb public order or which is threatening, abusive

---

33 Council Framework Decision 2008/913/JHA of 28 November on combating certain forms and expressions of racism and xenophobia by means of criminal law [2008] OJ L328/55. Precursors were the Council Joint Action 96/443/JHA of 15 July 1996 concerning action to combat racism and xenophobia [1996] OJ L185/5, calling upon states to incriminate public denial of Nazi crimes where it is contemptuous or degrading to a group defined by reference to colour, race, religion or national or ethnic origin (Title 1(A)(c)), and Article 6 of the CoE Additional Protocol to the Convention on Cybercrime, concerning the criminalisation of acts of a racist and xenophobic nature committed through computer systems, Strasbourg, 29 January 2003 (ETS 189), obliging parties to incriminate the public distribution through computer systems of material approving or justifying genocide or crimes against humanity, as defined by the London Charter or any other international court.

34 It is true that the English version of FD 2008, Article 1(1)(c) could also be read as if the *historical crime* must be directed against such a group; certain language versions indeed only allow for this reading (e.g., Polish version). However, most language versions only allow for the *public condoning, denial and gross trivialisation* as reference point (e.g., French, German, Latvian, Spanish, and Hungarian versions). Principle (10) of the preamble supports this reading, as it states that the FD does not prevent a Member State from extending Article 1(1)(c) to 'crimes directed against a group [...] defined by other criteria than race, colour, religion, descent or national or ethnic origin, such as social status or political convictions'. Although 'crimes' is again ambiguous, most other language versions use terms like 'Straftat', 'misdaden' or 'delitos' that rather refer to the statement and not the historical crime). This interpretation also matches better with the requirement that the statement must be likely to incite violence or hatred against these groups.

35 This excludes great parts of communist crimes, which were based on political ideologies rather than on ethnic factors, see A. Kučs, 'The European Union's Framework Decision on the Use of Criminal Law to Combat Specific Types and Manifestations of Racism and Xenophobia and the Implementation of the Decision in the Latvian Law' (2013) 5 *Juridiskā zinātne* 173, 178; see also P. Lobba, 'From introduction to implementation: first steps of the EU Framework Decision 2008/913/JHA against racism and xenophobia' in P. Behrens, N. Terry and O. Jensen (eds), *Holocaust and Genocide Denial: A Contextual Perspective*, London, Routledge, 2017, p. 189, p. 192; in 2010, the Commission refused to extend the FD 2008's scope of application, see European Commission, 'Report from the Commission to the European Parliament and to the Council: The memory of the crimes committed by totalitarian regimes in Europe', 22 December 2010, COM(2010) 783 final, p. 10.

or insulting' (Article 1(2)). Also, Member States may decide to make only punishable the denial or gross trivialisation of crimes that have been established by a court of this state or an international court (Article 1(4)).

Similarly, non-binding standards at the CoE level are not limited to specific historical crimes. PACE Resolution 1563 (2007),[36] para. 12.3 calls on governments to:

> make a criminal offence the public denial, trivialisation, justification or praise, with racist intentions, of crimes of genocide, crimes against humanity or war crimes in accordance with ECRI General Policy Recommendation No. 7.

The relevant recommendation specifies that the act must be committed against a person or group of persons 'on the grounds of their race, colour, language, religion, nationality, or national or ethnic origin' (ECRI Recommendation No. 7, para. 18).[37] PACE Resolution 2106 (2016) repeats this call, although it omits the latter specification and highlights the Holocaust again explicitly (para. 7.1.2.).[38]

These legal requirements to criminalise denial, (gross) trivialisation and condoning of international crimes are potentially able to cover both Russian crimes against Ukrainians and crimes committed in the war between the Hamas and Israel. There is much to suggest that the Russian army is committing crimes against humanity[39] as well as war crimes.[40] The existence of genocide is more controversial.[41] Similarly, the 7 October 2023 attacks by the Hamas

---

36 PACE Resolution 1563 (2007) of 27 June 2007, 'Combating anti-Semitism in Europe'.

37 European Commission against Racism and Intolerance (ECRI), 'General Policy Recommendation No. 7 on National Legislation to Combat Racism and Racial Discrimination', 13 December 2002, amended on 7 December 2017, CRI(2003)8 REV.

38 PACE Resolution 2106 (2016) of 20 April 2016, 'Renewed commitment in the fight against antisemitism in Europe'. See also CM/Rec(2022)5, above n. 18, para. 8(i): public authorities shall 'arm themselves with legal and institutional instruments to prohibit all displays of denialism, racism and conspiracy theories, in which the Internet, in particular, abounds'.

39 At least under the ICC Statute, Article 7 para. 1 lit. a (murder) and lit. d (deportation and forcible transfer).

40 At least under the ICC Statute, Article 8 para. 2 lit. b (i) and (ii) (intentional attacks against civilians and civilian objects). See also Independent International Commission of Inquiry on Ukraine, Investigative report, May 2025, A/HRC/59/CRP.2, para. 54, referring additionally to the war crime of outrages upon personal dignity under Article 8 para. 2 lit. b (xxi), however not to para. 2 lit. b (ii).

41 In favour of qualification as genocide D. Azarov, D. Koval, G. Nuridzhanian, and V. Venher, 'Understanding Russia's Actions in Ukraine as the Crime of Genocide', 21 (2023) *Journal of International Criminal Justice*, 233-264; for the opposite view see W. Schabas, Genocide and Ukraine: Do words mean what we choose them to mean?, 20 (2022) *Journal of International Criminal Justice*, 843-857.

constituted war crimes,[42] crimes against humanity,[43] and probably genocide.[44] The exact legal qualification of Israel's actions in Gaza depends on the difficult qualification of the Gaza war as international or non-international armed conflict. However, even if the conflict was non-international, evidence suggests that Israel possibly committed war crimes.[45] Many international scholars have also affirmed the commission of crimes against humanity.[46] The controversial question whether Israel's actions also amounted to genocide is currently pending before the International Court of Justice (ICJ).[47]

It is also not difficult to imagine circumstances where the denial, trivialisation or condoning of these crimes is 'directed against' one of the groups mentioned in FD 2008, Article 1(1)(c), namely Ukrainians, Jews/Israeli or Palestinians. For this, it is not decisive whether the relevant international *crimes* themselves are primarily directed against these national or ethnic groups or whether they pursue broader objectives (such as the annexation of Ukraine or the destruction of the Hamas) and render the affected groups a means to this end. For even in the latter case, the denial and trivialisation can precisely

---

42 If one assumes a non-international armed conflict, this would be crimes under the ICC Statute, Article 8 para. 2 lit. c (i) (murder and torture) and (iii) (taking of hostages).

43 At least under the ICC Statute, Article 7 para. 1 lit. a (murder), lit. e (imprisonment), lit. f (torture) and lit. i (enforced disappearences). For the application to non-state actors, see W. Schabas, 'Punishment of Non-State Actors in Non-International Armed Conflict' (2002) 26(4) *Fordham International Law Journal* 907, 922; F. Mégret, 'Is the ICC Focusing Too Much on Non-State Actors?' in M.M. deGuzman and D.M. Amann (eds), *Arcs of Global Justice: Essays in Honour of William A. Schabas*, Oxford, Oxford University Press, 2018, p. 173, pp. 185–92.

44 For this crime and the above-mentioned crimes, see A. van Aaken, B. Abtan, M. Adelman, J. Amaya-Castro, K. Ambos and many others, Public Statement by International Law Experts <https://docs.google.com/forms/d/e/1FAIpQLSd4lrsDRg3HbJqoAf0BlAe7BHJuzpQB_Le27Iureq9vpCoBkw/viewform>.

45 Namely, under the ICC Statute, Article 8 para 2 lit. e (i) (intentional attacks against the civilian population) and (iv) (attacks against religious and educational buildings, and hospitals), for evidence, see UN General Assembly, 'Report of the Independent International Commission of Inquiry on the Occupied Palestinian Territory, including East Jerusalem, and Israel', 11 September 2024, UN Doc. A/79/232, paras. 91 et seq. as well as UN General Assembly, 'Report of the Independent International Commission of Inquiry on the Occupied Palestinian Territory, including East Jerusalem, and Israel', 6 May 2025, UN Doc. A/HCR/59/26. Legally, the Commission also affirms other war crimes, assuming implicitly an international-armed conflict, see ibid. paras. 89. International scholars have also pointed to the use of starvation as a method of warfare against civilians, see Joint Statement on Gaza signed by 290 international lawyers (as of 12.2.2026), initiated by Olivier de Frouville and Julian Fernandez, Just Security, 7.11.2025, para 4. On the controversial legal qualification of the war in Gaza, see J. de Hemptinne, Classifying the Gaza Conflict Under Intenrational Humanitarian Law, a Complicated Matter, EJIL: Talk!, 13.11.2023 <https://www.ejiltalk.org/classifying-the-gaza-conflict-under-international-humanitarian-law-a-complicated-matter/>.

46 Joint Statement on Gaza, above n. 45, para. 4; see also UN Doc. A/HRC/56/26, above n. 45, para. 92, affirming the crime against humanity of extermination.

47 ICJ, Application of the Convention on the Prevention and Punishment of the Crime of Genocide in the Gaza Strip (*South Africa v. Israel*).

aim at denying the groups' suffering during the conflict and thus be 'directed' against them. This is even more obvious for the condoning.

Similarly, the denial, trivialisation or condoning of these crimes can be of a kind that is likely to incite violence and hatred against Ukrainians, Jews/Israeli or Palestinians. This is especially the case with statements that condone the relevant crimes as was seen for Russia's crimes during pro-Russian demonstrations in some European countries.[48] But also the denial or trivialisation can incite violence or hatred, for example, where it is combined with the assertion that the relevant crimes were invented by Ukrainians to harm Russia.[49]

The FD 2008 therefore proves apt to cover the denial, trivialisation and condoning of other crimes than the Shoah, including future crimes – with the important reservation that the statement must amount to hate speech. With this, FD 2008 goes already relatively far in obliging states to protect the collective memory of historical crimes, especially if it is interpreted to cover not only the denial of facts, but also the contestation of their legal qualification.[50] The general denial ban has therefore been met with skepticism by Member States, and for many of them, infringement procedures were necessary to ensure compliance with this EU law obligation.[51] Although the ban has now been introduced in some way in most Member States, it has not had a great practical impact so far: for example, in states like Germany where even the government itself avoided to openly name Israeli war crimes,[52] there is no debate about the potential criminal nature of their denial, let alone of the denial of genocide if this crime were to be affirmed. It remains to be seen whether in the future, the FD 2008's general denial ban will be used more extensively to protect the collective memory of future crimes.

---

48 For demonstrations especially in Germany, see P. Rhein-Fischer, 'Z-Symbol, russische Flagge und Georgsband', *Verfassungsblog*, 7 April 2022 <https://verfassungsblog.de/z-symbol-russische-flagge-und-georgsband/>.

49 Indeed, where Holocaust denial was combined with the assertion that it was an invention by Jews, German courts used to affirm a 'qualified' Holocaust denial which was criminal not only as defamation but even as incitement to hatred; this distinction was relevant before a specific Holocaust denial ban was introduced; see for more details P. Rhein-Fischer and S. Mensing, 'Memory Laws in Germany', *TOAEP Occasional Papers Series* No. 14 (2022), pp. 10 et seq.

50 This was indeed the ECtHR's reading of a similarly phrased Swiss genocide denial ban that led to the case *Perinçek v. Switzerland*, no. 27510/08, 15 October 2015, § 156, on this case see below 2.3.2.

51 For country reports of all 27 Member States, see P. Rhein-Fischer, S. Alves-Jesus, M. Rogers et al., Criminalizing Holocaust Denial in the EU, Compendium on 27 Member States, Theya Editores, 2025.

52 See 'Erklärungen des Auswärtigen Amts in der Regierungspressekonferenz vom 06.12.2024', *Auswärtiges Amt*, 6 December 2024 <https://www.auswaertiges-amt.de/de/newsroom/regierungspressekonferenz-2689414>, where government officials contested the existence of genocide and emphasised simply that Germany is calling on Israel to act in accordance with international humanitarian law.

A final noteworthy aspect in the context of the Russo-Ukrainian war is that neither the FD 2008 nor the relevant PACE resolutions oblige, or call on, Member States to criminalise the denial of the elephant in the room, the crime of aggression that Russian leaders have committed and may possibly commit against other states in the future.[53] This gap results from the fact that the relevant texts date from a period where the crime of aggression had not yet entered into force under the ICC Statute, Article 8 *bis*.[54] It is true that the crime of aggression differs from the other crimes covered by the FD 2008's general denial ban in that it primarily protects state sovereignty and territorial integrity, and hence concerns individuals only indirectly. However, the average recipient will not care much about this legal finesse. It is thus possible to imagine statements that deny or condone the Russian aggression and can still be seen as 'directed against' Ukrainians as a national group and likely to incite to hatred or violence agains them. Against this background, it would be consistent to include the crime of aggression in FD 2008 Article 1(1)(c).

2.3.2 Limits to Incriminating Denial

The outlined European (mostly EU) standards *requiring* a wide ban of denial of historical crimes where it can be seen as a form of hate speech are mirrored by CoE standards that *limit* the possibility to criminalise denialism where it cannot be qualified as hate speech. These standards place constraints to possible future legislative attempts to criminalise the denial of current and future atrocities to a wider extent. They primarily stem from the freedom of expression under the ECHR, Article 10,[55] as interpreted by the European Court of Human Rights (ECtHR).

According to the ECtHR, the criminalisation of statements denying a historical crime is in any case 'necessary in a democratic society' within the meaning of ECHR, Article 10(2) when it can be seen as a form of incitement to hatred or intolerance. For the Holocaust denial, the Court has invariably presumed this – 'for historical and contextual reasons' – as this denial generally connotes an anti-democratic ideology and antisemitism, hence

[53] For an early plea for a Special Tribunal for the crime of aggression against Ukraine, see P. Sands, 'Putin's Crimes of Aggression Must be Tried in Court', *The Times*, 29 March 2022 <https://www.thetimes.com/world/russia-ukraine-war/article/putins-crimes-of-aggression-must-be-tried-in-court-2qt67gwjd>; on the violation of Article 2(4) of the UN Charter, see J. Green, C. Henderson and T. Ruys, 'Russia's attack on Ukraine and the *jus ad bellum*' (2022) 9(1) *Journal on the Use of Force and International Law* 4.

[54] For an account of the Kampala compromise, see C. Kress and L. von Holtzendorff, 'The Kampala Compromise on the Crime of Aggression' (2010) 8 *Journal of International Criminal Justice* 1179.

[55] Convention for the Protection of Human Rights and Fundamental Freedoms, 4 November 1950 (ETS 5).

inciting racial hatred, antisemitism and xenophobia.[56] Thus, Holocaust denial is either removed from the sphere of freedom of speech as being abusive under ECHR, Article 17, or this article serves as an aid of interpreting the limits of the freedom of expression under ECHR, Article 10(2). For the denial of other historical crimes than the Holocaust, however, the Grand Chamber, in its *Perinçek* judgment, required positive evidence that the statement promoted a racist and antidemocratic agenda.[57] In the absence of such evidence, it made the possibility to criminalise the denial dependant on a contextual approach, taking into account, among others, the existence of a geographical and historical connection between the state incriminating the denial and the historical event, the lapse of time since the event occurred, and to what extent the statements affected the victim group's rights.[58] The Court found that Switzerland could not punish the applicant for asserting that the crimes against Armenians under the Ottoman Empire could not be qualified as genocide, since Switzerland was missing a sufficient geographical and historical link to these events and some 90 years had passed.[59]

Therefore, under the current interpretation of the ECHR, criminal bans on the denial of current and future crimes such as those committed during the war against Ukraine, the Hamas attacks or the war in Gaza are compatible with Article 10 only where the ban requires an incitement to violence or hatred against Ukainians, Jews/Israeli or Palestinians, or where the legislating state possesses a sufficiently strong link with the crime. For the crimes committed by Russia, for example, such a link could result from a geographic proximity to Russia or Ukraine or the fact that the state has hosted a large number of refugees.

2.4. *A Narrow Legal Framework Increasingly under Pressure*

As has been shown, under the existing interpretation of the ECtHR, the memory of current and future crimes enjoys slightly less protection than that of Nazi crimes. The increasing temporal distance from the latter crimes, present and future large-scale atrocities, growing criticism from a postcolonial perspective

56 See *Perinçek v. Switzerland*, above no. 50, §§ 209, 243.

57 Ibid., § 234, 243, 253; on the relevance of the racist and xenophobic character of the statement, see P. Lobba, above n. 35, p. 208; P. Lobba, 'Testing the "Uniqueness": Denial of the Holocaust vs Denial of Other Crimes before the European Court of Human Rights' in U. Belavusau and A. Gliszczyńska-Grabias (eds), *Law and Memory: Towards Legal Governance of History*, Cambridge, Cambridge University Press, 2017, p. 109, p. 126

58 *Perinçek v. Switzerland*, above n. 50, §§ 229–54.

59 Ibid., §§ 244–50.

against the (Western) European memory culture's focus on Nazi crimes,[60] and first attempts to diversify that culture[61] are likely to put pressure on these differing standards. As it is hard to imagine that legislators will abolish existing memory legislation such as Holocaust denial bans, this pressure may rather lead to a relaxation of existing human rights standards that limit memory laws regarding other historical crimes. Such a possible relaxation cannot be assessed in black-and-white terms but calls for a nuanced evaluation.

There are valid arguments why the ECtHR could, with caution, allow Member States to follow their own diverse approaches and show their solidarity with victims of international crimes by criminalising the denial of said crimes, even where there is no incitement to hatred and no close connection between the state and the conflict. An example could be a French criminalisation of the 'plain' denial of the Russian aggression against Ukraine on the grounds that it is 'necessary in a democracy' to show solidarity with Ukraine and similar victims and protect the rule-based international order.[62]

An important argument in favour of a relaxation of standards that would allow such a memory law is that this would avoid the difficulty to justify differences in the dealing with different historical crimes. It also bears mentioning that evidently false statements of fact, when made in the awareness of their falsity, are of no value to the public discourse. Rather, they undermine the basic requirement of discourse that participants to communication recognise verifiable facts and feel committed to the truth.[63] Fake information hence impairs the trust that is created by this recognition and that reduces complexity.[64] It is true that even banning fake information may have a problematic chilling effect on true statements.[65] However, in the

---

60 These voices are especially strong with regard to the German memory culture, see the debate sparked by D. Moses, 'The German Catechism', *Geschichte der Gegenwart*, 23 May 2021 <https://geschichtedergegenwart.ch/the-german-catechism/>; see S. Neimann and M. Wildt, *Historiker streiten. Gewalt und Holocaust – die Debatte*, Berlin, Propyläen, 2022.

61 They can be seen e.g. in the mnemonic resolutions of parliaments acknowledging past genocides, for Germany, see Rhein-Fischer & Mensing, above n. 49, p. 84 et seq.

62 On the idea of solidarity in the context of denialism, see *Perinçek v. Switzerland*, above n. 50, 'Partly Concurring and Partly Dissenting Opinion of Judge Nußberger', p. 118.

63 On the truthfulness of participants as precondition for his consensus theory of truth, see J. Habermas, *Erläuterungen zur Diskursethik*, Frankfurt (Main), Suhrkamp, 1991, p. 132; M. Matuschek, above n. 10, p. 141; on the dangers of disinformation, see also B. Baade, *Wahrheit und Recht*, Tübingen, Mohr Siebeck, 2023, pp. 409 et seq.

64 See N. Luhmann, *Soziale Systeme: Grundriß einer allgemeinen Theorie*, Berlin, Suhrkamp, 1987, pp. 154–57; N. Luhmann, *Vertrauen: Ein Mechanismus der Reduktion sozialer Komplexität*, 5th ed., Konstanz and Munich, UVK, 2014, p. 21; on the reduction of complexity, ibid., pp. 27–37.

65 A. Park and K. Youm, 'Fake News from a Legal Perspective: The United States and South Korea Compared' (2019) 25(1) *Southwestern Journal of International Law* 100, 106, 118; E. Volokh, 'Fake news and the law, from 1798 to now', *The Washington Post*, 9 December 2016 <https://www.washingtonpost.com/news/volokh-conspiracy/wp/2016/12/09/

present context, this effect would be significantly mitigated by the fact that most, if not all, criminal bans on denialism require intent, which excludes the possibility to be punished for a mistakenly false statement.[66] Besides, a possible requirement that the falsity must be evident and the historical facts clearly established, could help to exclude a chilling effect on true statements. Of course, the question of who is to decide about the clear falsehood is not easy to answer. It is true that limiting bans on denialism to crimes established by domestic or international courts (as FD 2008, Article 1(4) allows) comes with pitfalls, as court decisions usually only have an effect inter partes and it may be due to historical coincidence or power relations whether an international crime is adjudicated or left to impunity. However, with the increasing adjudication of international crimes before the ICC, domestic or hybrid courts,[67] there is hope that the lack of adjudication may be shrinking. In view of the high standards as to the collection and assessment of evidence before courts, their decisions may hence overall provide a useful indication for whether historical facts are 'clearly established'. In any case, criminalisation should be limited to statements about historical facts and not extent to their legal qualification. The current war against Ukraine and the war in Gaza illustrate that the legal qualification of crimes such as genocide can be very controversial. The legal discourse about judicial legal assessments, however, should remain without constraints.

Despite these valid arguments in favour of allowing for more extensive denial bans – beyond cases where the denial incites violence or hatred –, such an extension raises fundamental concerns. Even if calls for the criminalisation of the denial of large-scale historical crimes are understandable when viewed in isolation, each criminalisation makes it more difficult to reject other victims' claims to have their suffering recognised as well – at least if one is to avoid the troubled waters of hierarchising different historical crimes. However, a creeping increase in memory regulation makes the space for the freedom of speech shrink and risks narrowing the legal scope for political discourse that

fake-news-and-the-law-from-1798-to-now/>; U. Belavusau, 'Memory laws and freedom of speech: governance of history in European law' in A. Koltay (ed), *Comparative Perspectives on the Fundamental Freedom of Expression*, Budapest, Wolters Kluwer, 2015, p. 536, p. 556.

66 This is precisely why the German Federal Constitutional Court explicitly excludes deliberately false statements from the scope of the freedom of speech. Federal Constitutional Court, Order of 22.6.1982, 1 BvR 1376/79, BVerfGE 61, 1(8).

67 On these possibilities, see G. Werle, 'Die Zukunft des Völkerstrafrechts' in S. Grundmann, M. Kloepfer, C.G. Paulus, R. Schröder and G. Werle, (eds), *Festschrift 200 Jahre Juristische Fakultät der Humboldt-Universität zu Berlin*, Berlin, De Gruyter, 2010, p. 1219, p. 1234; especially domestic courts are increasingly active, see C. Kress, 'Deutsche Völkerstrafrechtspflege – Betrachtungen aus aktuellem Anlass' (2022) 100 *Deutsche Richterzeitung* 72.

is constitutive for democracy.[68] Generally, it should primarily be for historians and not parliamentarians or judges to establish and assess history.[69]

Criminalising denial even where it is not likely to incite violence or hatred would cut the remaining connection between denial bans and hate speech. However, the gap left by the otherwise protected right to private life of targeted individuals would need to be filled with other legal values. This could be the rule-based and democratic order or the 'collective memory', rooted in human dignity, itself a part of the right to private life[70] – a right the emergence of which will be traced in more detail below.[71] By this, bans on denialism would become a clearer expression of the militant democracy concept according to which democratic freedoms of those who strive to undermine the democratic order can be cut short.[72] However, this would also entail the typical risk of an increasingly militant democracy: to eventually tip into autocracy. Overall, the ECtHR should therefore be prudent to not relax the standards of ECHR, Article 10, too far in the future.

3 MNEMONIC CHALLENGES BY THE PERCEIVED DISAPPEARANCE OF 'TRUTH'

3.1. *Entry in the 'Post-Factual' Era*

The second factor that is likely to alter the landscape of memory laws in the coming years is the vanishing differentiation between truth and untruth in the 'post-factual' era that has dawned.[73] The most visible factor for this change is the general rise of disinformation.[74] The dissemination of fake information is

---

68 Similarly, P. Lobba, above n. 35, pp. 202 et seq.; L. Pech, 'The Law of Holocaust Denial in Europe: Towards a (qualified) EU-wide Criminal Prohibition' in L. Hennebel and T. Hochmann (eds), *Genocide Denials and the Law*, Oxford, Oxford University Press, 2011, p. 185, p. 233.

69 See P. Lobba, above n. 35, p. 206.

70 See *Perinçek v. Switzerland*, above n. 50, § 227.

71 See below section 3.2.

72 The ECtHR has first explicitly recurred to this concept in the context of memory laws in *Perinçek* (2015), above n. 50, §§ 242 et seq., however, in order to justify the distinction between the Holocaust and other genocides. On the relationship between denial bans and militant democracy, see See P. Rhein-Fischer, above n. 14, 489 et seq.

73 The Oxford Dictionaries Word of 2016 was 'post-truth', understood as 'circumstances in which objective facts are less influential in shaping public opinion than appeals to emotion and personal belief', see 'Word of the Year 2016', *Oxford Languages* <https://languages.oup.com/word-of-the-year/2016/>; on this phenomenon, see M. d'Ancona, *Post Truth: The New War on Truth and How to Fight Back*, London, Ebury Press, 2017; critically on this alleged turn B. Baade, above n. 63, pp. 552 et seq.

74 This concept is used here in accordance with the European Commission, 'A multi-dimensional approach to disinformation: Report of the independent High level Group on fake news and online disinformation', 2018, p. 11: 'all forms of false, inaccurate, or misleading

certainly not a new phenomenon,[75] as the prominent removal of Leon Trotsky and Lev Kamenev from a photo with Lenin during his speech on 5 May 1920 illustrates. However, fake news relating to the Brexit referendum, the US election campaigns in 2020 and 2024, the storm of the US Capitol, the Covid-19 pandemic, and the wars in Ukraine and the Middle East indicate that the concern has gained a new quality in recent years and is likely to remain an important phenomenon over the next twenty years.[76]

There are multiple reasons for this increase in disinformation. On the one hand, disseminating fake information has become a strategy of national and international politics. For example, the Kremlin has put considerable efforts in disseminating state propaganda on its 'special operation' in Ukraine, purportedly aiming to save Russian minorities from a 'genocide'.[77] Russia has also made absolute denial and disinformation its primary strategy of international politics and law in order to evade legal discussions on violations of human rights and international humanitarian law.[78] Interestingly, this strategy, as Riepl puts it, is 'not aimed at producing a single, coherent, and credible counter-narrative for an allegation'; it rather uses 'diversion tactics in order to obfuscate the mainstream narrative as much as possible while insisting on the lack of reliable information'.[79] As Pomarentsev writes, '[t]he aim is to confuse rather than convince, to trash the information space so the audience gives up looking for any truth amid the chaos'.[80] Another prominent figure who has made disinformation a central governing strategy is US President Donald Trump. Two particularly striking examples of 2025 are the employment of national guards in various US cities to fight a made-up 'crime emergency'[81] as well as the kidnapping of the then-Venezuelian President Nicolás Maduro

information designed, presented and promoted to intentionally cause public harm or for profit'; for this and other understandings, see B. Baade, above n. 63, pp. 403–08.

75 F. Olan, U. Jayawickrama, E.O. Arakpogun, J. Sulkan and S. Liu, 'Fake News on Social Media: the Impact on Society' (2024) 26 *Information Systems Frontiers* 443; for a historical account, see R.L. Weaver, 'Luncheon Keynote: Fake News: Reflections from History' (2019) 25(1) *Southwestern Journal of International Law* 1.

76 Especially on the US elections, see A. Park and K. Youm, above n. 65, 100 et seq.

77 See the English transcriptions of Putin's speeches, above nn. 4 and 5.

78 M. Riepl, *Russian Contributions to International Humanitarian Law: A contrastive analysis of Russia's historical role and its current practice*, Baden-Baden, Nomos, 2022, pp. 358–82, on attacks on health facilities in Syria, the use of cluster munitions in Syria and Georgia and the shootdown of plane MH17.

79 Ibid., pp. 368 et seq.

80 P. Pomerantsev, 'Inside Putin's Information War', *Politico*, 4 January 2015 <https://www.politico.com/magazine/story/2015/01/putin-russia-tv-113960/>; see also C. Vaccari and A. Chadwick, 'Deepfakes and Disinformation: Exploring the Impact of Synthetic Political Video on Deception, Uncertainty, and Trust in News' (2020) 6(1) *Social Media and Society* 1, 3.

81 See E. Berman, 'Trump's Manufactured Emergencies: A Playbook for Expanding Authoritarian Power', *Verfassungsblog*, 22 August 2025 <https://verfassungsblog.de/trumps-manufactured-emergencies/>.

based on the (not only legally, but also factually) contested justification that drug trafficking from Venezuela posed an imminent threat to the US.[82]

On the other hand, the increase of fake information is fostered by new technologies that improve the quality and persuasiveness of fake information. In particular, artificial intelligence (AI) technology has contributed to 'deepfakes', that is, manipulated videos, relying on machine learning algorithms, where software applications create highly convincing 'face-graft' videos by carefully superimposing expressions of one person onto the head of another or by reverse engineering a person's speech.[83] With the ever increasing speed of social media and messaging platforms, deepfakes are viewed and shared by millions of users within few hours.[84] Again, political deepfakes may not necessarily *deceive* individuals, but they sow uncertainty, which may, in turn, reduce trust in news altogether.[85] Just like state propaganda, deepfakes thus have the effect to 'cultivate the assumption among citizens that a basic ground of truth cannot be established'.[86] Filter bubbles,[87] that is, echo chambers consisting of communities believing the same (false) propositions, may further exacerbate this phenomenon,[88] although scholars have not yet achieved any consensus on their precise effects. Similarly, the practice of microtargeting, which personalises information that is shown to individuals based on their past choices, and bots, i.e. accounts that do (half-)automatic posts, amplify the problem.[89]

It is much more complex – and impossible to answer here – to what extent the prominent contemporary forms of critical theory, namely, critical race theory, feminist and queer legal theory, have and will contribute to the

82 See J. Uriburu and J. Arato, 'Trump's Illegal Attack on Venezuela and Ist Consequences', *EJIL: Talk!*, 5 January 2026 <https://www.ejiltalk.org/trumps-illegal-attack-on-venezuela-and-its-consequences/>.

83 C. Vaccari and A. Chadwick, above n. 80, 2; for the relevance of the speed of information dissemination, see R.L. Weaver, above n. 75, 3.

84 For the examples of a 'kidnapping' video in India and an educational video with Barack Obama, see C. Vaccari and A. Chadwick, above n. 80, 1.

85 C. Vaccari and A. Chadwick, above n. 80, 9; on further consequences, see A. Wenzel, 'To Verify or to Disengage: Coping with "Fake News" and Ambiguity' (2019) 13 *International Journal of Communication* 1977.

86 See C. Vaccari and A. Chadwick, above n. 80, 3.

87 The term was coined in E. Pariser, 'The Filter Bubble: What the Internet is Hiding from You', London, Penguin Books, 2011.

88 See F. Zimmer, K. Scheibe, W.G. Stock and M. Stock, 'Echo Chambers and Filter Bubbles of Fake News in Social Media: Man-Made or Produced by Algorithms?', 8th Annual Arts, Humanities, Social Sciences & Education Conference 2019, p. 17.

89 European Commission, 'Technology and Democracy: Understanding the influence of online technologies on political behaviour and decision-making', 27 October 2020, pp. 29 et seq.; B. Baade, above n. 63, pp. 415 et seq.

relativisation of truth.[90] This reproach is made by critics of these theories who argue that attempts to de-marginalise specific groups, traditionally targets of discrimination and oppression, by destructing pre-existing social categories, would ultimately challenge the idea of the enlightenment that an objective truth exists. Thus, the assumption of these theories that 'reality is socially constructed by the powerful in order to perpetuate their own hegemony',[91] has been accused of moral and epistemological relativism.[92] It is, however, doubtful that critical theory denies that there is such thing as truth. Rather, the argument 'is that the use of reason in contemporary society, and the truths that it proclaims, serves as a mechanism of oppression'.[93] Nevertheless, the concept is sometimes invoked in overly broad terms as if scientific facts themselves – and not only the human perception of, and categories for them – were the object of social construction. At the same time, critics of critical theory also do their share in creating misunderstandings in this debate.[94]

3.2. *Consequences for the Legal Framework: Distinct Value of 'Collective Memory' and an Emerging 'Right to Memory'?*

As Hannah Arendt held, a people robbed of the perception of an existing truth provides fertile ground for fascism, since it is 'deprived not only of its capacity to act but also of its capacity to think and to judge'.[95] National legislators have therefore reacted to disinformation on various levels, including the law on elections, the press, cyber security, the duties of social platforms, and even

---

90 For a good overview of these theories, see R. Celkates and J. Flynn, 'Critical Theory', *Stanford Encyclopedia of Philosophy*, available at <https://plato.stanford.edu/entries/critical-theory/>, especially section 4.

91 D.A. Farber and S. Sherry, *Beyond all Reason: The Radical Assault on Truth in American Law*, Oxford, Oxford University Press, 1997, p. 23.

92 Ibid., pp. 27–33, 95–112, 121.

93 E.L. Rubin, 'Jews, Truth, and Critical Race Theory' (1999) 93 *Northwestern University Law Review* 525, 537, on Horkheimer and Adorno.

94 E.g. a talk by a German PhD student in biology titled 'Geschlecht ist nicht (Ge)schlecht – Sex, gender und warum es in der Biologie zwei Geschlechter gibt' ('Sex is not gender – Sex, gender and why there are two sexes in biology') at Humboldt University Berlin was cancelled and postponed after students protested, which created a violent debate in Germany (see T. Thiel, 'Cancel Culture an der Humboldt-Uni', *Frankfurter Allgemeine Zeitung*, 3 July 2022 <https://www.faz.net/aktuell/feuilleton/debatten/vortrag-von-marie-luise-vollbrecht-cancel-culture-an-der-humboldt-uni-18146758.html>); though one may share the criticism against the university, the title of the talk could be easily misunderstood by laypersons to mean that intersexuality did not exist in biology.

95 H. Arendt, 'Hannah Arendt: From an Interview', *The New York Review*, 26 October 1978 <https://www.nybooks.com/articles/1978/10/26/hannah-arendt-from-an-interview/>.

criminal law.[96] On the EU level, the Digital Services Act[97] contains certain obligations for providers of online platforms regarding disinformation (see below section 4.2); the AI Act,[98] adopted in 2024, among others, regulates deepfakes by introducing transparency obligations (Article 50(4)), and, under specific circumstances, prohibiting AI systems that generate them (Article 5(1)(a)).[99] The Regulation on the transparency and targeting of political advertising, adopted in 2024, addresses, among others, concerns related to information manipulation in elections.[100] Besides, the EU has developed various soft law initiatives to tackle disinformation.[101]

So far, the increasing number of memory laws in recent years does not seem to be a specific reaction to the spread of disinformation. The relevant provisions in Central and Eastern Europe, themselves sometimes criticised for distorting historical truth, can rather be explained by the attempt to emancipate their nations from Soviet influence or, in turn, to feed populist narratives. Other provisions simply aimed to implement the FD 2008, which, as has been shown above, is situated less in the context of fake information than of hate speech, although both phenomena are interconnected.

Nevertheless, it seems that in the long run, the increasing relativisation of truth is likely to put pressure on national and EU legislators to tighten existing memory laws. This is so in view of two potential, and interrelated, legal developments.

First, such pressure may result from the recognition of a *distinct legal value* of 'collective memory',[102] understood here as the state of consciousness

---

96 In particular, criminal law against disinformation was used during the Covid-19 pandemic, with specific statutes being introduced, e.g. in Uzbekistan, South Africa, Tajikistan and Russia: see Law Library of the US Congress, 'Freedom of Expression during COVID-19', September 2020.

97 Council Regulation (EU) 2022/2065 of 19 October 2022 on a Single Market For Digital Services and amending Directive 2000/31/EC (Digital Services Act) [2022] OJ L277/1.

98 Council Regulation (EU) 2024/1689 of 13 June 2024 laying down harmonised rules on artificial intelligence and amending Regulations 300/2008, 167/2013, 168/2013, 2018/858, 2018/1139 and 2019/2144 and Directives 2014/90/EU, 2016/797 and 2020/1828 (Artificial Intelligence Act) [2024] OJ L series.

99 See M.J. Block, 'A Critical Evaluation of Deepfake Regulation through the AI Act in the European Union' (2024) 13 (4) *EuCML* 184, 188.

100 Council Regulation (EU) 2024/900 of 13 March 2024 on the transparency and targeting of political advertising.

101 See, in particular, the 'Strengthened Code of Practice on Disinformation' of June 2022, which was integrated into the Digital Services Act as the 'Code of Conduct on Disinformation' in 2025; the 'European Democracy Shield' of November 2025; for other initiatives, see 'Tackling online disinformation', *European Commission* <https://digital-strategy.ec.europa.eu/en/policies/online-disinformation>.

102 Foundational works on this notion developed in social sciences, cultural anthropology and philosophy include M. Halbwachs, *Les cadres sociaux de la mémoire*, Paris, Félix Alcan, 1925 and M. Halbwachs, *La mémoire collective*, Paris, Presses Universitaires de France, 1950 (posthumous), holding that individual memories are influenced by society

oscillating between the personal memories of multiple different perspectives and the collectively identifiable and communicable symbolic incorporation of the collective memory.[103] With the turn to post-facticity, collective memory could become considered worthy of protection as such, even regardless of any separate violation of dignity resulting from incitement to hatred. This is because the collective memory of mass atrocities strongly relies on their actual occurrence and requires the recognition of an objective truth. A vanishing of the latter hence heavily impairs the collective memory of mass atrocities and demonstrates its need for protection. That it is worthy of protection in the first place, in turn, results from the fact that the collective memory fills the gap torn by the atrocity[104] and forms the basis for the identity of collectives. Removing its foundation – the existence of truth – thus amounts to harming a group's identity,[105] and hence, human dignity as part of the right to private life (ECHR, Article 8(1)).[106] This is not to say that the collective memory could potentially justify the criminal ban of any historical fact. As Judge Nußberger put it, '[t]here is not one historical truth that could remain permanently immutable' and new evidence may always shed new light on what has been deemed an uncontested view.[107] However, where the memory of a past atrocity serves as foundation for a group's identity, as is the case for the Holocaust but possibly also for other genocides, the collective memory may be considered a value worthy to be taken into account when balancing conflicting interests.

Second, the turn to post-truth is likely to fuel the debate about whether and to what extent there is a state '*duty* to protect collective memory', or, even further, a (subjective) 'right to collective memory', which – in their most

---

and that groups can have a distinct memory; J. Assmann, *Das kulturelle Gedächtnis: Schrift, Erinnerung und politische Identität in frühen Hochkulturen*, 1st ed., Munich, C.H. Beck, 1992, distinguishing between the shorter-term and dynamic communicative memory and the longer-term and rigidified cultural memory; A. Assmann, *Erinnerungsräume: Formen und Wandlungen des kulturellen Gedächtnisses*, 1st ed., Munich, C.H. Beck, 1999; P. Nora, *Les lieux de mémoire*, Paris, Gallimard, 1988–92 and P. Nora, 'La mémoire collective' in J. Le Goff (ed), *La nouvelle histoire*, Paris, Retz-CEPL, 1998, pp. 398–401; for a response to critics of this notion see A. Assmann, *Das neue Unbehagen an der Erinnerungskultur: Eine Intervention*, 3rd ed., Munich, C.H. Beck, 2020, pp. 16–33; for the notion's use in law, see only references in J.J. Savelsberg and R.D. King, 'Law and Collective Memory' (2007) 3 *Annual Review of Law and Social Science* 189, 190.

103 For this notion exceeding the idea of collective memory as a sum of individual entities, see J.A. Barash, 'Que'est-ce que la mémoire collective? Réflexions sur l'interprétation de la mémoire chez Paul Ricœur' (2006/2) 50 *Revue de Métaphysique et de morale* 185, 192 et seq.

104 See E. Wiesel, *Ethik und Erinnerung/Ethics and Memory*, Berlin, De Gruyter, 1997, p. 33 on the reviving element of memory.

105 See, e.g. UNESCO, 'History under attack: Holocaust denial and distortion on social media', 2022, p. 19.

106 See *Aksu v. Türkiye*, no. 4149/04 and 41029/04, 15 March 2012, §§ 58–61, on the protection of a group's sense of identity under ECHR, Article 8(1).

107 *Perinçek v. Switzerland*, above n. 50, 'Partly Concurring and Partly Dissenting Opinion of Judge Nußberger', p. 116.

general formulation – would subject the state to certain legal restraints in its attempt to govern memory of the past. This question has already been taken up by some in the context of a 'right to truth'.[108] Stemming from the right of victims' relatives to know the fate and whereabouts of the disappeared, the right to truth has today developed to a more general right to obtain information about the circumstances of serious human rights violations.[109] While the right to truth has been formally recognised by the Inter-American Court of Human Rights (IACtHR) since 2000,[110] the ECtHR has been more hesitant, although it has ultimately recognised its core.[111] However, much uncertainty remains, for example, as to whether it is of a distinct and substantial nature or stems from the right to access to justice, a procedural duty to cooperate with the Court or the procedural limb of the right to life (ECHR, Article 2) and the prohibition of torture and degrading treatment (ECHR, Article 3).[112] Others see their roots mainly in international humanitarian law, in particular, the right of families to know the fate of their relatives and the obligation of parties to armed conflict to search for missing persons.[113] It is also uncertain what it covers precisely,[114] whether it is an individual or a collective right, and if the latter,[115] how it can be invoked.

---

108 See M. van Noorloos, 'A critical reflection on the right to truth about gross human rights violations' (2021) 21(4) *Human Rights Law Review* 874 (especially 892 et seq.); P. Naftali, 'The "Right to Truth" in International Law: The "Last Utopia?"' in U. Belavusau and A. Gliszczyńska-Grabias (eds), *Law and Memory: Towards Legal Governance of History*, Cambridge, Cambridge University Press, 2017, pp. 70–88 (especially pp. 71 et seq., 80, 84).

109 P. Naftali, above n. 108, pp. 70 et seq.

110 See, e.g. *Bámaca-Velásquez v. Guatemala*, IACtHR Judgment (Merits), 25 November 2000, § 201; *Blanko Romero v. Venezuela*, IACtHR Judgment, 28 November 2005, § 62; for more references, see P. Naftali, above n. 108, pp. 78–81.

111 See *Association '21.12.1989' v. Romania*, no. 33810/07, 24 May 2011, § 106, on the right to know about the circumstances of massive fundamental rights violations; see P. Naftali, above n. 108, pp. 81 et seq.

112 The ECtHR, so far, has not considered obstacles to the right to truth a substantial violation; a judgment by the Fifth Section in *Janowiec and Others v. Russia*, no. 55508/07 and 29520/09, 16 April 2012 on the Soviet and Polish authorities' distortion of history on the Katyn massacre in in this sense (§ 156) was reversed by the Grand Chamber in *Janowiec and Others v. Russia*, no. 55508/07 and 29520/09, 21 October 2013, which based the violation on the duty to cooperate (§ 216); for the ECtHR's earlier approaches, see also UN Office of the High Commissioner for Human Rights (OHCHR), 'Study on the right to truth', 8 February 2006, UN Doc. E/CN.4/2006/91, para. 28.

113 UN OHCHR, above n. 112, para. 5.

114 E.g. whether only facts of the particular cases, or also the context of the violations and interpretive assessments, see M. van Noorloos, above n. 108, 886, 891.

115 A collective dimension was recognised both by the Inter-American Commission on Human Rights (IACHR) (IACHR, 'The Right to Truth in the Americas', 13 August 2014, OEA/Ser.L/V/II.152, paras. 15, 19; IACHR, 'Annual Report of the Inter-American Commission on Human Rights 1985–1986', 26 September 1986, OEA/Ser.L/V/II.68, Doc. 8 rev. 1, Chapter V) and the IACtHR (see, e.g. *Myrna Mack Chang v. Guatemala*, IACtHR Judgment (Merits),

The *duty of memory*, in turn, is considered by some courts, soft law instruments and scholars a corollary of the right to truth,[116] or at least of a more general 'right to know',[117] while others argue that both concepts should be kept apart as the duty of memory raises more complex questions.[118] Even those in favour of a 'duty of memory', however, rarely spell out their content. In this respect, it appears useful to distinguish three aspects: one question is whether a state is obliged to refrain from denying certain crimes of the past itself ('duty to refrain'); another is whether this duty may also extend to the horizontal relationship, that is, whether a state can be obliged to prevent citizens from denying or commemorating these crimes in a positive way ('duty to protect'); and a third question is whether the state may be obliged to positively acknowledge and commemorate past crimes ('duty of positive action'). For all three duties, the subsequent question then is whether they are merely objective in nature or also contain a subjective right of the citizens concerned, which could be invoked in front of a court.

Without being able to answer these questions here, these three potential dimensions of a 'right to memory' suggest that the content of this right is necessarily distinct from, and only interrelated with, the right to truth. Unlike the latter, a right to memory would not be about *obtaining* the truth, but about *preserving* it, its specificity lying in protecting the collective memory against obscuration by lies. The right to truth thus appears as a precondition for the right to memory to be enjoyed. At the same time, at least if the right to truth is understood not merely as a procedural but as a substantial right, both rights seem to have a common ground: dignity as part of the right to private life, of which they present specific forms – specific in view of their character as transitional justice rights.[119] This is because dignity is not only apt to explain

25 November 2003, § 274), as well as the ECtHR (*Al Nashiri v. Poland*, no. 28761/11, 24 July 2014, § 495; *Husayn (Abu Zubaydah) v. Poland*, no. 7511/13, 24 July 2014, § 489); M. van Noorloos, above n. 108, 877.

116 *Rodriguez Vera et al. v. Colombia*, IACtHR Judgment, 14 November 2014, §§ 570 et seq.; *Myrna Mack Chang v. Guatemala*, above n. 144, § 286; for further references see M. van Noorloos, above n. 108, 894.

117 See D. Orentlicher, 'Impunity: Report of the independent expert to update the Set of principles to combat impunity', 8 February 2005, UN Doc. E/CN.4/2005/102/Add.1, Part II(A); similarly, L. Joinet, UNCHR, 'Question of the impunity of perpetrators of human rights violations (civil and political)', 2 October 1997, UN Doc. E/CN.4/Sub.2/1997/20, para. 17.

118 M. van Noorloos, above n. 108, 894 et seq.; for the idea of separation, see also UN Human Rights Council, 'Memorialization processes in the context of serious violations of human rights and international humanitarian law: the fifth pillar of transitional justice', 9 July 2020, UN Doc. A/HRC/45/45.

119 See M. Campisi, 'From a Duty to Remember to an Obligation to Memory? Memory as Reparation in the Jurisprudence of the Inter-American Court of Human Rights' (2014) 8(1) *International Journal of Conflict and Violence* 61, 73 who considers the 'obligation to memory' a component of the international obligation to provide reparation for victims.

why victims and their next of kin have the right to know the circumstances of their and at least their relatives' human rights violations, but it also serves as the basis for the collective memory of these violations, and hence a potential right to memory. It fits with this that the ECtHR, in *Perinçek*, weighed the freedom of expression (ECHR, Article 10) against 'the rights of Armenians to respect for their and their ancestors' dignity' as part of the right to private life,[120] though without recognising any specific right to memory. In any case, if such a right with even some of the three dimensions outlined above were to emerge in view of the increasing need to protect collective memory in the age of post-truth, this is likely to fuel the debate on whether existing memory laws should be further expanded.

4 MNEMONIC CHALLENGES BY THE PRIVATISATION OF MEMORY GOVERNANCE

4.1. Increased Importance of Private Measures of Memory Governance

A final challenge to the current mnemonic landscape, closely connected to the phenomenon of post-truth, can be seen in the increasing privatisation of memory governance.

As communication has significantly shifted to social media, run by private companies, and as the internet has become 'a space for proponents of conspiracy theories [...] to spread ideas that [have] little currency in [...] mainstream discourse',[121] the task to tackle denial of past crimes and hate speech has pushed responsibilities to social media providers. As UNESCO finds in a recent report on Holocaust denial and distortion on social media (2022), 16.4% of the investigated content relating to the Holocaust consisted in denial or distortion; on Telegram, it was even 49%.[122] In view of this, it is hardly surprising that many platforms, in their content moderation policies, provide explicit rules on how they deal with specific memory of the past. Thus, Facebook and Instagram (Meta), prohibit, inter alia:

> harmful stereotypes historically linked to intimidation or violence , such as Blackface; Holocaust denial; [...][123]

[120] *Perinçek v. Switzerland*, above n. 50, §§ 227, 196, 198–203, see also above n. 70 and accompanying text.

[121] UNESCO, above n. 105 (hereafter: UNESCO report), p. 32.

[122] Ibid., pp. 26 et seq.

[123] Facebook community standards, 'Hateful conduct, Policy details', 12 February 2025, https://transparency.meta.com/policies/community-standards/hateful-conduct/; for the 2022 version see also UNESCO report, above n. 105, p. 23.

The platform X (formerly Twitter) lists media or text that refers to 'genocides, (e.g., the Holocaust)' as an example of prohibited content that targets individuals or groups with content that references forms of violence where a protected category was the primary target or victim, where the intent is to harass.[124] It also includes 'symbols historically associated with hate groups, e.g., the Nazi swastika' among examples of hateful imagery.[125] Similarly, TikTok does not allow:

> denying or minimizing well-documented historical atrocities against protected groups, such as the Holocaust or the genocide against the Tutsi in Rwanda.[126]

Telegram, on the contrary, leaves content largely unmoderated in order to 'not block anybody who peacefully expresses alternative opinions'.[127]

At the same time, the application of moderation policies within one platform across the globe entails both a globalisation of these private memory laws and a fragmentation of the mnemonic landscape. Globalisation results from the fact that whilst platform providers are obliged to respect the relevant laws of the country in which the content is available, at least the German Federal Court of Justice has explicitly allowed providers to apply a *more* speech-restrictive policy than state law would require to protect the right to private life of individuals or groups.[128] Against this background, a specific mnemonic moderation policy of one platform may be applied across the globe, even if it is not rooted in the relevant country's perception of the past. This is illustrated by the prohibition of Holocaust denial that Facebook, X and TikTok appear to apply even in those countries in which no legal ban on Holocaust denial exists. Fragmentation, on the other hand, results from the varying standards between different social media platforms – as the comparison between Facebook, Instagram, X and TikTok on the one hand, and Telegram on the other, illustrates – as well as from possible differences with the relevant state memory laws, which remain the only relevant standards outside of social media.[129]

---

124 X, 'Hateful Conduct', *X Help Center*, April 2023 <https://help.x.com/en/rules-and-policies/hateful-conduct-policy>; for the 2022 version see UNESCO report, above n. 134, p. 23.

125 X, above n. 124; see also UNESCO report, above n. 105, p. 23.

126 TikTok, 'Community Guidelines: Safety and Civility: Hate Speech and Hateful Behavior', 14 August 2025 <https://www.tiktok.com/community-guidelines/en/safety-civility#2>; for the 2022 version see UNESCO report, above n. 105, p. 23.

127 UNESCO report, above n. 105, p. 23.

128 See BGH, Judgment of 29.7.2021, III ZR 179/20, (2021) *Neue Juristische Wochenschrift*, 3179, para. 78, on a case of hate speech.

129 On the latter fragmentation factor, see U. Saxer in a presentation at the forum 'Ukraine' of the Association of German Public Law Professors, 21 May 2022, see P. Rhein-Fischer, 'Tagungsbericht: Zum bewaffneten Angriff der Russischen Föderation auf die Ukraine' (2022) 77(18) *JuristenZeitung* 890, 891.

Though the cited examples of private memory governance so far do not raise great concerns, with many states prohibiting Holocaust denial themselves, the general possibility for private entities to influence the memory of the past in deviation from the rules adopted by the democratically elected legislator creates obvious problems. If already the legal governance of the past by *states* is in tension with the freedom of speech and historical research, this concern is multiplied when this governance is determined and enforced by private entities without democratic legitimisation (though in a dominant market position) that are difficult for users to avoid. It suffices to imagine Elon Musk introducing a community standard on X that would have prohibited the 'denial' of the made-up 'crime of a hijacking of the 2024 US presidential election', if Kamala Harris had won against Donald Trump.

4.2. *Mnemonic Repercussions of the Digital Services Act*

An instrument that may prove useful to tackle some repercussions of this privatisation, globalisation and fragmentation of memory laws, but that also adds further complexity, is the EU Digital Services Act (DSA), that entered into full force on 17 February 2024.[130] Using as its model the German Network Enforcement Act,[131] the DSA's underlying rationale is that platform providers are liable for illegal content that is not expeditiously removed after the provider obtains knowledge or awareness of the content (see DSA, Article 6(1)). Providers shall put notice and action mechanisms in place to allow individuals to notify content that they consider illegal (DSA, Article 14(1)); notices give rise to actual knowledge or awareness of the platform (DSA, Article 14(3)). 'Illegal content' is defined as:

> any information that, in itself or in relation to an activity [...], is not in compliance with Union law or the law of any Member State [...], irrespective of the precise subject matter or nature of that law.[132]

As the FD 2008 has no direct effect, platforms are hence held to respect and apply the memory laws adopted at Member State level.

This mechanism, enforcing state memory laws more effectively within social media, contributes to regaining some state control over memory governance, which is still better than leaving memory governance to private entities. However, this mitigation of privatisation has its limits. Already apprehending the different memory standards in various Member States

---

130 See above n. 97.

131 'Netzwerkdurchsetzungsgesetz' of 1 September 2017 <https://www.bmjv.de/SharedDocs/Downloads/DE/Gesetzgebung/BGBl/BGBl_NetzDG.html>.

132 DSA, Article 3(h).

presents a considerable challenge, given that, e.g. the formulations of genocide denial bans differ significantly[133] and even where states use the same concepts, their understanding of notions such as 'trivialisation', 'condoning' or 'distortion' of past crimes is not necessarily congruent. Though the European Commission, in its Q&A section on the DSA, holds that in case content is illegal only in a given Member State, 'as a general rule it should only be removed in the territory where it is illegal',[134] such a rule is not reflected in the DSA; the definition of 'illegal content' in DSA, Article 3(h), cited above, is ambiguous. Against this background, it is likely that platform providers, in case of doubt or difference between the relevant memory laws, for reasons of practicality, will align their policies to the most restrictive memory law. By this, singular strict memory laws risk becoming the instigators for globalised private memory policies that might quickly become the determining standard in public discourse, despite being detached from the general perception of the past in the relevant country.

5 CONCLUSION

There is no crystal ball to look into the future. However, it is suggested here that changes of the mnemonic legal landscape in Europe are underway. The major ones are: first, pressure for diversification of the legal framework of denialism in view of new atrocities; second, the emergence of collective memory as a distinct legal value, or even its prolongation, the right to collective memory, as a consequence of the entry into an era of 'post-truth'; and third, the need to deal with challenges resulting from the privatisation of memory laws. The emancipation of memory laws from hate speech, going along with the recognition of the collective memory as a distinct legal value or right, appears as a recurrent theme in all these shifts. Although law, by recognising this emancipation, would catch up with sociology, anthropology and philosophy,[135] this would come with obvious downsides for free discourse. Whether these developments really take hold, therefore, remains to be seen when the future is actually met by the past.

---

[133] See P. Rhein-Fischer, above n. 14, 489 et seq.; P. Rhein-Fischer, S. Alves-Jesus, M. Rogers et al., above n. 51.

[134] Available at 'Questions and answers on the Digital Services Act', *European Commission*, 23 February 2024 <https://ec.europa.eu/commission/presscorner/detail/en/QANDA_20_2348>.

[135] See M. Halbwachs, *La mémoire collective*, above n. 102; J. Le Goff, *Histoire et mémoire*, Paris, Gallimard, 1988; J. Assmann, above n. 102; J. Assmann, 'Kollektives Gedächtnis und kulturelle Identität' in J. Assmann and T. Hölscher (eds), *Kultur und Gedächtnis*, Berlin, Suhrkamp, 1988, pp. 9–19; A. Assmann, *Cultural Memory and Western Civilization: Functions, Media, Archives*, Cambridge, Cambridge University Press, 2011.

CHAPTER 2

DE-IMPERIALISATION OF RUSSIA AND PROSPECTS FOR ITS REACCESSION TO THE COUNCIL OF EUROPE

Sergii Masol*

1 A NIGHTMARE IN THE COMMON EUROPEAN HOME

Following Russia's full-scale invasion of Ukraine, Russia ceased to be a Member State of the Council of Europe,[1] an international organisation that unites nearly all European states. This event marked a milestone, as Article 8 of the Statute of the Council of Europe, which concerns the cessation of membership,[2] was invoked for the first time. In addition, Russia ceased to be a state party to the Convention for the Protection of Human Rights and Fundamental Freedoms (hereinafter, the ECHR),[3] a regional treaty designed to protect human rights throughout Europe.

---

* This chapter was written while the author was a postdoctoral researcher at the University of Copenhagen and forms part of the research project 'Easternisation: Power Shifts and Regionalisation of International Law', funded by the Independent Research Fund Denmark.

1 Resolution CM/Res(2022)2 of the Committee of Ministers of the Council of Europe on the cessation of the membership of the Russian Federation to the Council of Europe, 16 March 2022.

2 Statute of the Council of Europe, 5 May 1949, 87 UNTS 103, Article 8 ('Any member of the Council of Europe which has seriously violated Article 3 may be suspended from its rights of representation and requested by the Committee of Ministers to withdraw under Article 7. If such member does not comply with this request, the Committee may decide that it has ceased to be a member of the Council as from such date as the Committee may determine').

3 Convention for the Protection of Human Rights and Fundamental Freedoms, 4 November 1950, 213 UNTS 221, Article 58; Resolution of the European Court of Human Rights on the consequences of the cessation of membership of the Russian Federation to the Council of Europe in light of Article 58 of the European Convention on Human Rights, 22 March 2022, para. 1; Resolution CM/Res(2022)3 of the Committee of Ministers of the Council of Europe on legal and financial consequences of the cessation of membership of the Russian Federation in the Council of Europe, 23 March 2022, para. 7.

Mikhail Gorbachev's dream of a 'common European home'[4] came to an end and was replaced by what Frank-Walter Steinmeier, the Federal President of Germany, called a 'nightmare'.[5] For a bystander like Germany, the nightmare has exposed the limitations of *Wandel durch Handel* and made further appeasement of Russia untenable.[6] For Ukrainians, the nightmare has been marked by a great many violations of international human rights law and international humanitarian law committed by Russian invaders.[7] The armed conflict has posed an existential threat not only to Ukraine[8] but also to the liberal democratic order in Europe as a whole.[9] Political and military polarisation has culminated in a new Iron Curtain being drawn across the region,[10] with Ukraine resembling 'a new Cold War Germany'.[11]

That said, no political regime is eternal. A new elite in Moscow might reconsider Russia's attitudes towards the rule of law, individual freedom and political liberty, all of which constitute the foundation of true democracy.[12] The Kremlin might even decide to reapply for membership of the Council of Europe in the distant future.[13]

---

4 'Address given by Mikhail Gorbachev to the Council of Europe (6 July 1989)', *Centre virtuel de la connaissance sur l'Europe* <www.cvce.eu/obj/address_given_by_mikhail_gorbachev_to_the_council_of_europe_6_july_1989-en-4c021687-98f9-4727-9e8b-836e0bc1f6fb.html>.

5 'Rede von Bundespräsident Dr. Frank-Walter Steinmeier beim Festakt zum 70-jährigen Jubiläum der Atlantik-Brücke am 13. Oktober 2022 in Berlin', *Bulletin der Bundesregierung* No. 131-1, 18 October 2022.

6 M. Karnitschnig, '12 Germans Who Got Played by Putin', *Politico*, 5 May 2022 <https://www.politico.eu/article/blame-germany-russia-policy/>. On Germany's strategic corruption and its funding of Russia's military efforts to subjugate Ukraine, see S. Dobbert and U. Thiele, *Nord Stream: Wie Deutschland Putins Krieg bezahlt*, Stuttgart, Klett-Cotta, 2025.

7 E.g. Parliamentary Assembly of the Council of Europe (PACE) Opinion 300 (2022) of 15 March 2022, 'Consequences of the Russian Federation's aggression against Ukraine', para. 6; European Court of Human Rights, *Ukraine and the Netherlands v. Russia*, Judgment, nos. 8019/16, 43800/14, 28525/20 and 11055/22, 9 July 2025; Organisation for Security and Co-operation in Europe (OSCE) Office for Democratic Institutions and Human Rights (ODIHR), 'Report on Violations of International Humanitarian and Human Rights Law, War Crimes and Crimes against Humanity Committed in Ukraine (1 April – 25 June 2022)', 14 July 2022, ODIHR.GAL/36/22/Corr.1; OSCE ODIHR, 'Report on Violations of International Humanitarian Law and Human Rights Law, War Crimes and Crimes against Humanity Committed in Ukraine since 24 February 2022', 13 April 2022, ODIHR.GAL/26/22/Rev.1.

8 M. Arden, A. Bodnar, L. Chanturia, A. Nussberger and G. Yudkivska, 'Human Rights for the Future – A Chance for Peace?' (2022) 42 *Human Rights Law Journal* 18, 26; S. Plokhy, *The Russo-Ukrainian War*, London, Penguin, 2023, p. xxi.

9 R. Spano, 'The European Court of Human Rights in 2040: lost utopia or trademark of the 21st century?' (2022) 42 *Human Rights Law Journal* 5, 6; 'Reykjavík Declaration: United Around Our Values', 4th Summit of Heads of State and Government of the Council of Europe, 16–17 May 2023 (Reykjavík Declaration), p. 9.

10 See e.g. M. Arden, A. Bodnar, L. Chanturia, A. Nussberger and G. Yudkivska, above n. 8, 20, 24; S. Hedlund, 'Europe's New Iron Curtain', *Geopolitical Intelligence Services*, 17 September 2024 <www.gisreportsonline.com/r/new-iron-curtain/>.

11 S. Plokhy, above n. 8, p. 302.

12 Statute of the Council of Europe, above n. 2, preamble.

13 Cf. A. Nussberger, 'The Future of European Human Rights Protection – On the Question of the *status quo* in Twenty Years' Time' (2022) 42 *Human Rights Law Journal* 1, 4 (no return 'in the short term'); A. Drzemczewski and R. Lawson, 'Exclusion of the Russian Federation

In fact, a somewhat similar situation has already taken place in European history. In 1969, following the leaking of a report by the now-defunct European Commission of Human Rights, the Greek Government withdrew from the Council of Europe, a decision effective from 1 January 1971.[14] In 1974, after the fall of the military junta and the restoration of democracy, Greece again joined this international organisation and ratified the ECHR.

As in the case of Greece, the doors behind Russia have not been shut for good. Michael Higgins, the President of Ireland, has unequivocally stated that the exclusion of Russia from the Council of Europe does not – and should not – mean permanent ostracism.[15] Gleb Bogush, a Russian legal scholar in exile, has expressed no doubt that his homeland will come back to Strasbourg, adding, however, that a reaccession process would require significant effort.[16] In academic publications, this subject has also been briefly broached as something that can, at least, be imagined.[17] Indeed, the history of international relations and law demonstrates that periods of Russia's self-inflicted isolation have alternated with returns to Europe.[18]

However, commentators have not outlined any conditions for Russia's potential reaccession to the Council of Europe. On the one hand, such a topic may seem premature amidst the ongoing Russo-Ukrainian war, with mass atrocities demanding immediate attention and action. Currently, it is imperative to safeguard European security and values from the recalcitrant state.[19] On the other hand, the nightmare will end sooner or later. Given the volume and scale of human rights-related problems that have accumulated in Russia and in foreign territories under its effective control, it is essential

---

from the Council of Europe and the ECHR: An Overview' (2022) 21 *Baltic Yearbook of International Law* 38, 58 (no return 'in the foreseeable future').

14 For details, see A. Kiss and P. Végléris, 'L'affaire grecque devant le Conseil de l'Europe et la Commission européenne des droits de l'homme' (1971) 17 *Annuaire français de droit international* 889.

15 '"Reasserting the Moral Weight of the Council of Europe", Speech by H.E. President of Ireland, Michael D. Higgins, Council of Europe Parliamentary Assembly, Strasbourg, Tuesday, 11th October 2022', *Council of Europe* <https://rm.coe.int/pace-october-plenary-address-president-michael-d-higgins/1680a91a51>.

16 I. Kupryakhina, 'Расплатная ведомость: Законна ли конфискация русских денег во всем мире из-за войны? Интервью юриста, эксперта по международному праву Глеба Богуша', *Новая газета*, 30 April 2022 <https://novayagazeta.eu/articles/2022/04/30/rasplatnaia-vedomost>.

17 M. Arden, A. Bodnar, L. Chanturia, A. Nussberger and G. Yudkivska, above n. 8, 20; K. Koroteev, 'Non-execution of Strasbourg Judgments against Russia: the Case for a Trust Fund' (2024) 9(1) *Russian Politics* 121, 132; K. Brummer, 'The Council of Europe, Russia, and the future of European cooperation: any lessons to be learned from the past?' (2024) 61 *International Politics* 258, 273; E. Bates, K. Dzehtsiarou and A. Forde, *Russia, the Council of Europe and the European Convention on Human Rights: A Troubled Membership and Its Legacy*, Bristol, Bristol University Press, 2025, pp. 14–15, 128, 160.

18 L. Mälksoo, 'The History of International Legal Theory in Russia: A Civilizational Dialogue with Europe' (2008) 19(1) *European Journal of International Law* 211.

19 K. Brummer, above n. 17, 273.

to initiate a discussion at an early stage. This will allow sufficient time to grasp and implement the necessary changes in Russia, should a request for reaccession be submitted.

In the absence of a crystal ball, looking at the past and present is a good starting point for reflecting on the future relationship between Russia and the Council of Europe.[20] Moreover, it is logical that expulsion procedures mirror accession procedures,[21] and, by extension, reaccession procedures as well.

In view of the above, this chapter is structured in non-chronological order. Section 2 begins by analysing how the Russo-Ukrainian war has impaired the relations between the Council of Europe and Russia, ultimately leading to the formal severance of ties. Section 3 then examines the historical context, focusing on the period of Russia's accession to the Council of Europe. Finally, section 4 looks ahead, outlining the conditions that Russia would need to meet if a new political elite in Moscow were to seek re-entry into the Council of Europe.

2 THE PRESENT

According to the Committee of Ministers of the Council of Europe, the expulsion of Russia on 16 March 2022 was due to Russia's aggression against Ukraine.[22] This aggression amounted to a serious breach by Russia of its obligations under Article 3 of the Statute of the Council of Europe.[23]

Pursuant to Article 3 of the aforesaid treaty, every member of the Council of Europe shall undertake the following obligations: i) to accept the principle of the rule of law; ii) to ensure that all persons within its jurisdiction enjoy human rights; and iii) to 'collaborate sincerely and effectively in the realisation of the aim of the Council'.[24] What does this aim encompass? The Council of Europe strives:

> to achieve a greater unity between its members for the purpose of safeguarding and realising the ideals and principles which are their common heritage and facilitating their economic and social progress.[25]

---

20 See, *mutatis mutandis*, A. Nussberger, above n. 13, 1.

21 K. Dzehtsiarou and D.K. Coffey, 'Suspension and Expulsion of Members of the Council of Europe: Difficult Decisions in Troubled Times' (2019) 68(2) *International and Comparative Law Quarterly* 443, 453.

22 Resolution CM/Res(2022)2, above n. 1.

23 Ibid.

24 Statute of the Council of Europe, above n. 2, Article 3.

25 Ibid., Article 1(a). Cf. J. Jahn, 'The Council of Europe Excludes Russia: A Setback for Human Rights', *EJIL: Talk!*, 23 March 2022 <www.ejiltalk.org/the-council-of-europe-excludes-russia-a-setback-for-human-rights/> (arguing that the logic of expulsion rests on weak premises unlikely to accomplish the goal of Russia ending its violations).

One of these ideals is peace.[26] The third obligation from the list is the only one with an indisputable extraterritorial dimension.[27] Hence, it may be argued that Russia's full-scale invasion of Ukraine constituted, specifically, a serious breach of the obligation of sincere and effective cooperation.[28]

Given that Russia has waged its war of aggression against Ukraine since February 2014,[29] the question arises regarding the justifications for the eight-year delay in severing ties between Russia and the Council of Europe. A plausible legal explanation could be that the magnitude of human rights violations and the occupation of merely 7% of Ukraine's territory until February 2022 did not meet the statutory threshold of seriousness. The term 'serious' is abstract, allowing some leeway in its interpretation and application in cases of expulsion.[30] In the spring of 2022, Luigi Di Maio, then Chair of the Committee of Ministers of the Council of Europe, clarified that the expulsion of Russia 'was made inevitable by the atrocity of the crimes committed in Ukraine'.[31] Similarly, Pascal Dourneau-Josette spoke of a response 'proportionate to [...] the extreme gravity of the facts', adding the factor of Russia's recidivism.[32] The same logic might also shed light on the persistent reluctance of the Council of Europe to expel Russia for its human rights violations in the occupied parts of Moldova (Transnistria) and Georgia (Abkhazia and South Ossetia).

Yet, a more convincing answer lies in the discretionary clause 'may decide' under Article 8 of the Statute of the Council of Europe, indicating a lack of

---

26 Statute of the Council of Europe, above n. 2, preamble. For this argument, see J. Jahn, above n. 25.

27 K.D. Magliveras, 'Legal and Procedural Issues arising from the Expulsion of the Russian Federation from the Council of Europe' (2023) 23(1) *International and Comparative Law Review* 95, 99.

28 Ibid., 99–100.

29 See generally O. Zadorozhnii (ed), *Українська революція гідності, агресія РФ і міжнародне право*, Kyiv, K.I.C., 2014; T.D. Grant, *Aggression against Ukraine: Territory, Responsibility, and International Law*, New York, Palgrave Macmillan, 2015.

30 K. Dzehtsiarou and D.K. Coffey, above n. 21, 452–53; P. Dourneau-Josette, 'L'expulsion de la Fédération de Russie du Conseil de l'Europe' in O. Delas, M. Mondélice, C. Gomez, O. Bichsel and R. Ouellet (eds), *Reconfiguration des relations internationales et modèle européen: Entre valeurs, guerre et enjeux économiques*, Brussels, Bruylant, 2023, p. 537, p. 543. Cf. E. Klein, 'Membership and Observer Status' in S. Schmahl and M. Breuer (eds), *The Council of Europe: Its Law and Policies*, Oxford, Oxford University Press, 2017, p. 40, p. 68 (interpreting this term as 'the violation of a provision essential to the accomplishment of the object or purpose of the treaty', as enunciated in Article 60 of the Vienna Convention on the Law of Treaties, 23 May 1969, 1155 UNTS 331, which addresses a 'material breach' of international treaties).

31 'The Expulsion of Russia from the Council of Europe Was Inevitable, Di Maio Tells PACE', *Council of Europe: Newsroom*, 28 April 2022 <www.coe.int/en/web/portal/-/the-expulsion-of-russia-from-the-council-of-europe-was-inevitable-di-maio-tells-pace> (emphases omitted).

32 P. Dourneau-Josette, above n. 30, pp. 541–42. See also J. Jahn, above n. 25 ('the extent, gravity and persistence of Russia's current violations of international law').

political will to utilise the limited set of available sanctions.[33] Politically, the Council of Europe not only failed to democratise Russia but also tolerated the growing authoritarianism and imperialist aspirations of the biggest Member State.[34]

After Russia occupied the Crimean Peninsula in 2014, the Parliamentary Assembly of the Council of Europe (hereinafter, PACE) stressed that Russia's military action against Ukraine was 'in clear contradiction with the Statute of the Council of Europe, in particular [...] Article 3'.[35] The expression 'serious violation' was not used. In its Resolution, PACE suspended the following rights of the Russian delegation: 'voting rights; right to be represented in the Bureau of the Assembly, the Presidential Committee and the Standing Committee; [and] right to participate in election observation missions'.[36] This suspension was humiliating for Russia, as it perceived itself as a great power.[37] At the same time, PACE did not suspend the credentials of the Russian delegation in order to promote political dialogue.[38] This concession was not appreciated by Russia, who retaliated by refusing to submit the credentials of its delegation and suspending its budgetary contributions, thereby undermining the financial stability of the international organisation.[39] After Russia threatened to leave Strasbourg,[40] senior officials of the Council of Europe lamented that such a scenario would be unfortunate, given the importance of the ECHR and the European Court of Human Rights (hereinafter, the ECtHR) for Russian citizens.[41] In 2019, all rights of the Russian delegation were restored, despite

---

33 For a similar view, see K. Brummer, above n. 17, 259, 265–68, 274.

34 M. Arden, A. Bodnar, L. Chanturia, A. Nussberger and G. Yudkivska, above n. 8, 22.

35 PACE Resolution 1990 (2014) of 10 April 2014, 'Reconsideration on substantive grounds of the previously ratified credentials of the Russian delegation', para. 4.

36 Ibid., para. 15.

37 P. Roter, 'Russia in the Council of Europe: Participation à la carte' in L. Mälksoo and W. Benedek (eds), *Russia and the European Court of Human Rights: The Strasbourg Effect*, Cambridge, Cambridge University Press, 2018, p. 26, p. 53.

38 PACE Resolution 1990, above n. 35, para. 14.

39 S. Schmahl, 'Völker- und europarechtliche Implikationen des Angriffskriegs auf die Ukraine' (2022) 14 *Neue Juristische Wochenschrift* 969, 971; E. Bates, K. Dzehtsiarou and A. Forde, above n. 17, pp. 100–03.

40 'Лавров: РФ сама выйдет из Совета Европы, если будет поднят вопрос об ее исключении', *ТАСС*, 16 October 2018 <https://tass.ru/politika/5681245>.

41 N. Buckley, 'Human Rights Body Fears Russia Withdrawal: Sanctions', *The Financial Times*, 27 November 2017, p. 4; A. Kornya, 'Христос Якумопулос: "Выход России из Совета Европы принесет Европе больше проблем"', *Ведомости*, 17 May 2018 <www.vedomosti.ru/politics/characters/2018/05/17/769827-vihod-rossii-soveta-evropi-prineset-evrope-bolshe-problem>. See also G. Raimondi, 'Opening of the Judicial Year, 25 January 2019' in Council of Europe, European Court of Human Rights, 'Annual Report 2019 of the European Court of Human Rights', 2020, p. 11, pp. 14–15 (positing that the departure of Russia would be a massive setback for human rights across all Member States).

the ongoing war.[42] It was a diplomatic victory for the Kremlin, whereas PACE lost some of its credibility and integrity.[43] According to Olexander Scherba, a Ukrainian diplomat, the shocking Strasbourg betrayal revealed that Ukraine was enamoured with a conception of Europe that was no longer a reality.[44] In essence, a two-tier regional legal order was introduced, with substandard expectations for the biggest Member State, as foreseen and decried by Mark Janis at the time of Russia's accession to the Council of Europe.[45] In light of the foregoing, it sounded overly complacent when, in 2022, Robert Spano, then President of the ECtHR, expressed pride that the Council of Europe had 'reacted with speed, determination and clarity since the *beginning* of the war'.[46] In fact, this response happened only after the full-scale invasion of Ukraine.

For its part, the Moscow officialdom asserts that Russia, on its own initiative, exited the Council of Europe on 15 March 2022,[47] following the procedure enshrined in Article 7 of the Statute of the Council of Europe.[48] Thus, Russia's membership must have ended on 31 December 2022. Based on a textual interpretation of the treaty, this perspective has merit.[49] Pursuant to Article 8, the Committee of Ministers could have expelled Russia only after a request to withdraw had not been complied with by Russia, which was not the case.

---

42 PACE Resolution 2287 (2019) of 25 June 2019, 'Strengthening the decision-making process of the Parliamentary Assembly concerning credentials and voting', paras. 7, 10.

43 E. Bates, K. Dzehtsiarou and A. Forde, above n. 17, pp. 110, 129; L.R. Glas, 'Russia Left, Threatened and Won: Its Return to the Assembly without Sanctions', *Strasbourg Observers*, 2 July 2019 <https://strasbourgobservers.com/2019/07/02/russia-left-threatened-and-has-won-its-return-to-the-assembly-without-sanctions/>.

44 O. Scherba, *Ukraine vs. Darkness: Undiplomatic Thoughts*, Stuttgart, ibidem-Verlag, 2021, p. 129.

45 M. Janis, 'Russia and the "Legality" of Strasbourg Law' (1997) 8 *European Journal of International Law* 93, 98.

46 R. Spano, above n. 9, 7 (emphasis added). For similar misleading statements, see e.g. K.D. Magliveras, above n. 27, 97; N. Weiss and T.A. Lanzl, 'Die wechselvolle Geschichte der Mitgliedschaft Russlands im Europarat' (2022) 82 *Zeitschrift für ausländisches öffentliches Recht und Völkerrecht* 801; E. Demir-Gürsel, 'The Council of Europe's Sharp Turn: Russia's Expulsion and its Possible Implications for Other Member States', *Verfassungsblog*, 25 March 2022 <https://verfassungsblog.de/the-council-of-europes-sharp-turn/>.

47 Ministry of Foreign Affairs of the Russian Federation, 'О выходе России из Совета Европы (справочный материал)', 14 April 2024, information current as of April 2025 <www.mid.ru/ru/foreign_policy/rso/1834254/>.

48 Statute of the Council of Europe, above n. 2, Article 7 ('Any member of the Council of Europe may withdraw [...]. Such withdrawal shall take effect at the end of the financial year in which it is notified, if the notification is given during the first nine months of that financial year').

49 G. Raimondi, 'L'expulsion de la Fédération de Russie du Conseil de l'Europe – Quel impact sur la Convention européenne des droits de l'homme?' in J.F. Kjølbro, S. O'Leary and M. Tsirli (eds), *Liber Amicorum Robert Spano*, Brussels, Anthemis, 2022, p. 571, pp. 575–77; S. Mantilla Blanco, 'A Backdoor Exit from the European Convention on Human Rights: Russia, the Council of Europe and Article 58(3) ECHR', *Verfassungsblog*, 5 April 2022 <https://verfassungsblog.de/a-backdoor-exit-from-the-european-convention-on-human-rights/>.

Nevertheless, the expulsion decision may be rationalised on contextual and teleological grounds owing to the gravity of Russia's breaches of international law and the implied powers of the Committee of Ministers to protect the fundamental values of the international organisation.[50] In any event, contrary to some propositions,[51] the alleged procedural violation by the Council of Europe cannot, in accordance with the maxim *ex injuria jus non oritur*, justify Russia's own misconduct, including its failure to execute final decisions and judgments of the ECtHR.

Commenting on Russia's departure from the Council of Europe, Petr Tolstoy, Deputy Chairman of the State Duma and former Vice-President of PACE, assured that '[a]ll rights of Russian citizens will be guaranteed in our country'.[52] Nevertheless, this declaration is problematic in at least two respects. First, in practice, the Russian state prioritises the protection of the human rights of those defending the Russian culture.[53] Conversely, critics of Russian imperialism, which – as will be discussed below – is an integral part of Russian culture, should expect less protection at the national level. Second, Petr Tolstoy was silent about the millions of foreigners, particularly those in the Russian-occupied territories, who were deprived of an effective remedy before the ECtHR without their explicit or implicit consent. This attitude came as no surprise. The politician denied the statehood of Ukraine,[54] emphasising that Ukrainians would have to pay a high price for their anti-Russian choice.[55] He also lamented that Russia missed out on Ukraine, Armenia, Azerbaijan, Finland, Estonia, Latvia and Lithuania, all of which, according to him, rightfully belong to Russia through the blood and hard work of many generations of Russians.[56]

With his unshakeable belief that these nations would never be able to exist independently of Russia,[57] Petr Tolstoy did not even try to free himself from the

[50] S. Schmahl, above n. 39, 972 (adding that PACE also considered that Russia could no longer be a member of the Council of Europe); E. Bates, K. Dzehtsiarou and A. Forde, above n. 17, pp. 179–83 (contending that the expulsion procedure under Article 8 may be deemed superior to the withdrawal procedure under Article 7).

[51] M.V. Kuchin, *Прецедентное право Европейского суда по правам человека*, Moscow, Юрайт, 2024, pp. 18–21.

[52] 'Петр Толстой: решение о выходе из Совета Европы принято', *Государственная Дума Федерального Собрания Российской Федерации - Новости*, 15 March 2022 <http://duma.gov.ru/news/53715/>.

[53] A. Nussberger, 'Der "Russische Weg" – Widerstand gegen die Globalisierung des Rechts?' (2007) 53 *Osteuropa Recht* 371, 379.

[54] E.g. P. Tolstoy, *Telegram*, 30 September 2023 <https://t.me/petr_tolstoy/1898>; '"Украины не будет, мы вас уничтожим!" Вице-спикер Госдумы Толстой раскрыл планы Кремля', *YouTube (Denis Kazanskyi)*, 17 October 2021 <https://www.youtube.com/watch?v=9KWIhB-hNcc>.

[55] 'Петр Толстой: Пригожин, Путин, смена пола и ЛГБТ', *Эмпатия Манучи*, 11 September 2023 <https://dzen.ru/video/watch/64fe4d98c450fa1f219d2225>.

[56] Ibid.

[57] Ibid.

imperial consciousness deeply embedded in Russian culture. His great-great-grandfather, Leo Tolstoy, who studied at a law faculty, defined international law as:

> the right of Poland, India, Bosnia and Herzegovina to live independently of foreign powers, but only until people in charge of bigger armies decide otherwise.[58]

Aleksandr Pushkin and Mikhail Lermontov also silenced the subalterns and legitimised military conquests of the Russian Empire, notably in the Caucasus.[59] Evidently, international law of the 19th century was beneficial for Russia, as it was for other European empires, since military conquests were accepted.[60] However, those times are gone, and wars of aggression are now prohibited under both international law and, ironically, Russia's own legislation.[61]

In *War and Peace*, Leo Tolstoy contributed to the consolidation of the myth of Russian imperial innocence and failed to acknowledge the nations of Central and Eastern Europe when they were occupied by the Russian army, thereby perpetuating the misconception that the local populations welcomed the occupiers.[62] In 2022, Kremlin-friendly media disseminated the same disinformation about the contentment of residents in the occupied regions of Ukraine.[63] Among the initial actions taken by Russian invaders was the erection of Pushkin billboards, which recast the writer as a symbol of occupation.[64] Moreover, Mikhail Piotrovsky, director of the Hermitage Museum, jingoistically defended Russian imperialism and described recent

---

58 L.N. Tolstoy, *Полное собрание сочинений*, vol. 38, Moscow, Художественная литература, 1936, p. 56.

59 For a postcolonial critique, see E. Thompson, *Imperial Knowledge: Russian Literature and Colonialism*, Westport and London, Greenwood Press, 2000, pp. 57–84.

60 L. Mälksoo, 'International law between universality and regional fragmentation: the historical case of Russia' in A. Orakhelashvili (ed), *Research Handbook on the Theory and History of International Law*, 2nd ed., Cheltenham and Northampton (MA), Edward Elgar Publishing, 2020, p. 373, p. 387.

61 Charter of the United Nations, 26 June 1945, 3 Bevans 1153, 59 Stat. 1031, TS 993, Article 2(4); United Nations General Assembly, Resolution 3314 (XXIX) of 14 December 1974, 'Definition of Aggression', UN Doc. A/RES/3314(XXIX); Уголовный кодекс Российской Федерации (Criminal Code of the Russian Federation), No. 63-ФЗ, 13 June 1996, Article 353.

62 E. Thompson, above n. 59, pp. 87–88, 97–98, 102–03, 110; K. Krzyżanowska and E. Thompson, 'Imperialism in Russian Literature', *Review of Democracy*, 7 June 2022 <https://revdem.ceu.edu/2022/06/07/imperialism-in-russian-literature/>.

63 E.g. 'Жители освобожденных территорий встречают военнослужащих ЛНР слезами радости - Пасечник', *Луганский информационный центр*, 27 February 2022 <https://lug-info.ru/news/zhiteli-osvobozhdennyh-territorij-vstrechayut-voennosluzhashih-lnr-slezami-radosti-pasechnik/>; N. Makarenkov and P. Khanarin, 'Жители Донбасса встречают освободителей со слезами на глазах', *Комсомольская правда*, 1 March 2022 <www.donetsk.kp.ru/daily/27370/4552517/>.

64 O. Mai, 'В Херсоне появились плакаты "Единой России" с Пушкиным и Суворовым', *Культурометр*, 3 June 2022 <https://culturemeter.od.ua/v-hersone-pojavilis-plakaty-edinoj-rossii-s-pushkinym-i-suvorovym-136203/>.

exhibitions abroad as 'a powerful cultural offensive' and 'a kind of "special operation"',[65] alluding to the Kremlin's euphemism for the full-scale invasion of Ukraine. Behind the veil of the so-called great Russian culture, therefore, lies great Russian propaganda and an imperialist *Weltanschauung*, along with murder, destruction, rape, looting and other mass atrocities committed by Russians.[66] While this culture is still admired in various corners of the world, it has received scarce postcolonial critical analysis.

In Ukraine, Russian culture is increasingly dismissed as a non-culture or 'a stillborn set of occasionally truly distinguished works of art that proved to be incapable of transforming biological beings into humans'.[67] Judicial practice reflects this societal shift. For example, the Odesa Circuit Administrative Court has banned the activities of a cultural organisation named after Aleksandr Pushkin, stating that the writer's œuvre, such as *Poltava*, is 'directly related to the glorification and justification of Russian imperial policy' and 'was used in Soviet ideology to demonstrate the greatness of Russian culture and its superiority over the cultures of other peoples of the USSR'.[68]

At the same time, Western academic discourse on Russia's expulsion from the Council of Europe is preoccupied with legal technicalities or criticism of Vladimir Putin's autocratic rule, while largely ignoring Russian imperialism. For example, none of the articles published in a recent special issue of *Russian Politics*, titled 'Authoritarian States in Human Rights Institutions: Russia and the Council of Europe', address or even mention the problem of Russian imperialism.[69]

Over the years, Western scholars have not made significant efforts to counter Russia's *Drang nach Westen* agenda in the Council of Europe. Rather, they have ruminated on the democratisation of Central and Eastern European states as

65 E. Yakovleva, 'Почему необходимо быть со своей страной, когда она совершает исторический поворот и выбор. Отвечает Михаил Пиотровский', *Российская газета*, 22 June 2022 <https://rg.ru/2022/06/22/kartina-mira.html>.

66 V. Rafeyenko, 'Як мертва російська культура вбиває українців' (2023) 3–4 *Критика* 28–33 <https://krytyka.com/ua/articles/iak-mertva-rosiiska-kultura-vbivaie-ukraiintsiv>.

67 Ibid.

68 Odesa Circuit Administrative Court, decision No. 122094428, 3 October 2024, case No. 420/23645/24.

69 K. Koroteev, above n. 17; J. Kahn, 'Russia in the Council of Europe: A Difficult Relationship' (2024) 9(1) *Russian Politics* 1; G. Flikke and D. Slabinski, 'Authoritarian Sovereignization: Russia's Way out of the Council of Europe' (2024) 9(1) *Russian Politics* 11; D. Kurnosov, 'Resisting Strasbourg to Reassure Moscow: the Recent Story of the Russian Constitutional Court' (2024) 9(1) *Russian Politics* 52; M. Muravyeva and Y. Brin, 'Conservative Jurisprudence and Russia's Response to ECtHR Judgements on Cases of Domestic Violence' (2024) 9(1) *Russian Politics* 74; A. Katz Miller, 'Cost of Expulsion, Dissent and Human Rights in Russia' (2024) 9(1) *Russian Politics* 100; A. Kubal and M. Mrowicki, 'Pushback or Backlash against the European Court of Human Rights? A Comparative Case Study of Russia and Democratically Backsliding Poland' (2024) 9(1) *Russian Politics* 135. For the same shortcoming, see J.-P. Costa, 'Les conséquences de la sortie de la Russie du Conseil de l'Europe' (2023) 133(1) *Revue trimestrielle des droits de l'Homme* 3; P. Dourneau-Josette, above n. 30, pp. 537–52.

a possible neocolonial project,[70] or on the extraterritorial application of the ECHR as a form of neo-imperialism.[71] Moreover, leading Western scholars specialising in Soviet and Russian law have looked at Europe through a Russo-centric lens. Some of them have even championed Russian imperialism. In 2007, just one year before the Russo-Georgian war, Ferdinand Feldbrugge agreed with Vladimir Putin that the collapse of the Soviet Union had been a catastrophe.[72] For the Dutch legal academic, Ukraine could not 'claim to have a significant past as an independent state', while Moldova and Belarus were bluntly described as 'bizarre states'.[73] Ferdinand Feldbrugge questioned the territorial integrity of these states and the raison d'être of their existence.[74] In 2013, just one year before the onset of the Russo-Ukrainian war, Bill Bowring shared his 'great sympathy with those who argue [...] that it is essential for the future of global politics that Russia remains a great power'.[75] In 2014, shortly after the occupation of the Crimean Peninsula by Russia, Michael Geistlinger did his best to justify Russia's actions under international law.[76] In 2022, several weeks after Russia's full-scale invasion of Ukraine, John Quigley urged the victim state to give up some of its territories to the aggressor state.[77] For Ferdinand Feldbrugge, it was 'narrow-mindedly legalistic' to view Ukraine as a sovereign state freely deciding on its foreign policy.[78] These examples reflect a deeper problem in the academic fields of Russian law, international law, human rights and international relations, where Russian imperialism continues to be a blind spot.[79]

---

70 O. Melzer, *Der Europarat und Russland 1992–2006: Demokratieförderung in Russland*, Wiesbaden, Springer, 2012, pp. 146–47.

71 P. Arnell, 'Human rights abroad' (2007) 16(2) *Nottingham Law Journal* 1, 17–18; R. Wilde, 'Compliance with human rights norms extraterritorially: "human rights imperialism"?' in L. Boisson de Chazournes and M. Kohen (eds), *International Law and the Quest for its Implementation – Le droit international et la quête de sa mise en oeuvre: Liber Amicorum Vera Gowlland-Debbas*, Leiden and Boston, Brill, 2010, p. 319, pp. 328–48.

72 F. Feldbrugge, 'The Rule of Law in Russia in a European Context' in F. Feldbrugge (ed), *Russia, Europe, and the Rule of Law*, Leiden and Boston, Martinus Nijhoff, 2007, p. 203, p. 215.

73 F. Feldbrugge, 'Russia and the Rule of Law' in K. Malfliet and S. Parmentier (eds), *Russia and the Council of Europe: 10 Years After*, Basingstoke, Palgrave Macmillan, 2010, p. 57, p. 59.

74 Ibid.

75 B. Bowring, *Law, Rights and Ideology in Russia: Landmarks in the Destiny of a Great Power*, Abingdon, Routledge, 2013, p. 207.

76 M. Geistlinger, 'Der Beitritt der Republik Krim zur Russländischen Föderation aus der Warte des Selbstbestimmungsrechts der Völker' (2014) 52(2) *Archiv des Völkerrechts* 175.

77 J. Quigley, 'Crimea: Key to Ending War in Ukraine', *Opinio Juris*, 5 April 2022 <https://opiniojuris.org/2022/04/05/crimea-key-to-ending-war-in-ukraine/>.

78 F. Feldbrugge, 'A few shades of grey in a black and white picture', *leidenlawblog*, 16 March 2022 <https://leidenlawblog.nl/articles/ukraine-the-birth-of-a-state-and-its-relation-with-russia-and-the-west>.

79 M. Mälksoo, 'The Postcolonial Moment in Russia's War against Ukraine' (2023) 25(3–4) *Journal of Genocide Research* 471, 474; S. Masol, 'From Tartu and Bandung: Decolonising the Debates on the Russo-Ukrainian War', *International Law Blog*, 9 October 2023 <https://internationallaw.blog/2023/10/09/from-tartu-and-bandung-decolonising-the-debates-on-the-russo-ukrainian-war/>.

Against the backdrop of such reductionist mental maps of Central and Eastern Europe, it is tempting to attribute all blame to the dictator Vladimir Putin, as articulated by the Russian liberal opposition, particularly in relation to what they call 'Putin's war' against Ukraine.[80] Yet, the Russian liberal narrative, often tolerated in Western Europe,[81] shows reluctance to question Russia's imperial identity and its chauvinistic attitudes towards Ukraine.[82] The underlying political, historical, legal, social, economic and cultural issues go beyond the mere need for Russia's democratisation. If anything, the Russo-Ukrainian war constitutes an imperial war in the era of nation-states.[83] The current situation is part of a larger historical process of the disintegration of Russia as an empire.[84] In this context, internal oppression and attempts at external expansion are, however, interconnected.[85] The bond in question warrants further examination, especially considering the nascent anti-imperial and anti-colonial turn in law-making,[86] judicial practice[87] and legal scholarship[88] regarding the relationship between Russia and Ukraine.

---

80 S. Shuster, '"Путин – мой враг": Интервью Юлии Навальной об убийстве ее мужа и о планах на будущее', *Time*, 17 April 2024 <https://time.com/6967728/yulia-navalnaya-interview-alexei-navalny-russian/>; A. Gurkov, 'Кара-Мурза, Пивоваров и Яшин: "Не путайте Путина с Россией"', *Deutsche Welle*, 3 August 2024 <www.dw.com/ru/karamurza-pivovarov-i-asin-ne-putajte-putina-s-rossiej/a-69846517>.

81 E.g. O. Scholz, *X* (formerly known as *Twitter*), 17 March 2022 <https://x.com/Bundeskanzler/status/1504507511281442819> ('This is Putin's war. He alone is responsible for it').

82 B. Kassymbekova and E. Marat, 'Time to Question Russia's Imperial Innocence', April 2022, PONARS Eurasia Policy Memo No. 771 <www.ponarseurasia.org/wp-content/uploads/2022/04/Pepm771_Marat-Kassymbekova_April2022.pdf>, p. 1; J. McGlynn, *Russia's War*, Cambridge, Polity, 2023, pp. 30–32; E. Thompson, above n. 59, p. 44.

83 M. Mälksoo, above n. 79, 471. See also T. Snyder, 'The War in Ukraine is a Colonial War', *The New Yorker*, 28 April 2022 <www.newyorker.com/news/essay/the-war-in-ukraine-is-a-colonial-war>.

84 S. Plokhy, above n. 8, p. xxi; 'Сергій Плохій: про історичні паралелі між Гітлером та Путіним, розпад Росії та перемогу України', *YouTube (Голос Америки Українською)*, 2 May 2024 <www.youtube.com/watch?v=Sxp6bq3yvnE>.

85 A. Etkind, *Russia Against Modernity*, Cambridge, Polity, 2023, p. 127.

86 E.g. Закон України 'Про засудження та заборону пропаганди російської імперської політики в Україні і деколонізацію топонімії' (Law of Ukraine 'On the condemnation and prohibition of propaganda of Russian imperial policy in Ukraine and on the decolonisation of toponymy'), No. 3005-IX, 21 March 2023, *Відомості Верховної Ради України*, 2023, No. 65, ст. 221; Закон України 'Про засади державної політики національної пам'яті Українського народу' (Law of Ukraine 'On the principles of state policy of the national memory of the Ukrainian people'), No. 4579-IX, 21 August 2025.

87 E.g. Odesa Circuit Administrative Court, above n. 68; Constitutional Court of Ukraine, decision No. 1-р/2021, 14 July 2021, case No. 1-179/2019(4094/19), § 13.8 ('the political construct of the "Russian-speaking population" of Ukraine is instrumentalised [...] [by Russia as] a tool for restoring the empire').

88 E.g. S. Masol, above n. 79; P. Labuda, 'Countering Imperialism in International Law: Examining the Special Tribunal for Aggression against Ukraine through a Post-Colonial Eastern European Lens' (2024) 49(2) *Yale Journal of International Law* 271; L. Tymchenko, 'Деколонізація міжнародно-правової думки: до осмислення наукової спадщини професора О. В. Задорожнього' (2025) 2 *Український часопис міжнародного права* 35.

3 THE PAST

Russia's shift towards authoritarianism was predisposed by the imperial breakup of the late 1980s and early 1990s and shaped by the long-standing association of both the general public and elites with a strong state that held superpower status.[89] Resentment, humiliation and a sense of defeat arose after Moscow's loss of both the outer empire in Central and Eastern Europe and the inner empire within the former Soviet borders.[90] Some Russian legal scholars have bewailed Russia's entry into the Council of Europe as an action sealing its defeat in the Cold War.[91] Notwithstanding the demise of Soviet communism and territorial losses, the idea of empire did not disappear in Russia.[92] As remarked by Andrei Kozyrev, the Russian Minister of Foreign Affairs (1990–96), 'Russia is predestined to be a great power'.[93]

In 1992, the Transnistria war erupted in Moldova. Many members of the Russian 14th Guards Army, which was stationed in the Moldovan region of Transnistria, joined the local armed groups and Russian nationals, including Cossacks, to fight against Moldovan troops. In this regard, Russia invoked the language of human rights, cheekily claiming that Russian Cossacks had come to Moldova while exercising their right to freedom of movement.[94] Furthermore, the separatists obtained weapons and military vehicles from the 14th Guards Army.[95] Alexander Rutskoy, then Vice-President of Russia, publicly urged the Transnistrians to separate from Chişinău.[96] After the declaration of ceasefire, the Russian armed forces remained in Transnistria on a purportedly peacekeeping mission. When considering Russia's request for membership of the Council of Europe, PACE naively noted that Russia intended to continue withdrawing its forces and armaments from the territory

89 S. Plokhy, above n. 8, p. 41.

90 Ibid.

91 A.Y. Novoseltsev and K.V. Stepanyugin, 'Участие России в Европейской конвенции о защите прав человека и основных свобод' (2021) 1 *Московский журнал международного права* 46, 49.

92 L. Mälksoo, *Russian Approaches to International Law*, Oxford, Oxford University Press, 2015, pp. 177–78.

93 A. Kozyrev, 'The Lagging Partnership' (1994) 73(3) *Foreign Affairs* 59, 62.

94 See *Ilaşcu and Others v. Moldova and Russia*, no. 48787/99, 8 July 2004, § 60, ECHR 2004-VII.

95 See ibid., §§ 57, 59. Similarly, Russia, though officially neutral, was reported to have supplied weapons to separatists and carried out attacks against the Georgian military and civilians during the war in the Georgian breakaway region of Abkhazia (1992–93). See K. Anderson and L. Hammond, 'Georgia/Abkhazia: Violations of the Laws of War and Russia's Role in the Conflict', *Human Rights Watch*, 1 March 1995 <www.hrw.org/reports/1995/Georgia2.htm#P621_144134>.

96 See *Ilaşcu and Others*, above n. 94, § 75.

of Moldova within the time limit set by a to-be-ratified agreement.[97] Despite the Kremlin's repeated promises, the withdrawal has still not been completed, constituting a violation of Moldova's sovereignty and territorial integrity.[98]

During the 1993 political crisis between the Russian President and the Russian Parliament, the sprouts of democracy were crushed by tanks in the streets of Moscow.[99] Approximately 150 people were killed as a result of Boris Yeltsin's decision to employ force.[100] Struggling to save the democratic reforms, he subsequently expanded presidential powers under the new Constitution, thereby establishing an institutional basis for authoritarian rule.[101] The constitutional provisions on human rights were – and continue to be – largely declaratory in practice.[102] And yet, the Constitution became the first legal instrument in Russian history in which domestic human rights guarantees were aligned with those under general international law.[103] The Constitution diverged from Soviet approaches to international law by adopting more individualistic concepts, thereby westernising human rights and paving the way for the acceptance of international mechanisms, notably the ECHR's system.[104] At the European level, some of the high-ranking state officials were generous with their promises, proclaiming that Russia intended to democratise, strengthen the rule of law and genuinely protect human rights.[105]

Meanwhile, attempts to halt the centrifugal forces brought about the two armed conflicts in Chechnya and the accompanying militarisation of the state apparatus.[106] Symbolically, the same tank crew members who fired at the White

97 PACE Opinion 193 (1996) of 25 January 1996, 'Russia's request for membership of the Council of Europe', para. 10.9.

98 United Nations General Assembly, Resolution 72/282 of 22 June 2018, 'Complete and unconditional withdrawal of foreign military forces from the territory of the Republic of Moldova', UN Doc. A/RES/72/282.

99 S. Plokhy, above n. 8, p. 35. See also E.A. Lukasheva and N.V. Kolotova, 'Права человека, политика, мораль' in E.A. Lukasheva (ed), *Права человека*, 2nd ed., Moscow, Норма/ИНФРА-М, 2011, p. 254, pp. 282–83.

100 M. Mikhaylov, 'Битва за Конституцию. Что привело к трагедии октября 1993 года?', *Радио Свобода*, 27 September 2024 <www.svoboda.org/a/bitva-za-konstitutsiyu-chto-privelo-k-tragedii-oktyabrya-1993-goda-/33134741.html>.

101 S. Plokhy, above n. 8, p. 40; P. D'Anieri, *Ukraine and Russia: From Civilized Divorce to Uncivil War*, 2nd ed., Cambridge, Cambridge University Press, 2023, pp. 59, 64.

102 B. Bowring, above n. 75, pp. 144–45; M. Antonov, 'Sovereignty and Russian Resistance to Human Rights' (2020) *European Yearbook on Human Rights* 529, 530–33.

103 I.Y. Nikodimov, *История государства и права России*, Moscow, Дашков и К°, 2019, p. 322.

104 A. Lukina, 'Russia and International Human Rights Law: A View from the Past' in P.S. Morris (ed), *Russian Discourses on International Law: Sociological and Philosophical Phenomenon*, New York and London, Routledge, 2019, p. 46, p. 57.

105 'Заявление Б. Ельцина, В. Черномырдина, В. Шумейко и И. Рыбкина' in *Право Совета Европы и Россия*, Krasnodar, Советская Кубань, 1996, p. 25, p. 25.

106 S. Plokhy, above n. 8, p. 41.

House in Moscow in 1993 attacked Grozny a year later.[107] Mass atrocities committed during the first Russo-Chechen war interrupted, although they did not completely derail, the examination of Russia's request for membership of the Council of Europe.[108] In the context of negotiations between the Kremlin and the Chechens, the colonial dimension was, however, absent, and the Council of Europe did not put it on the agenda.[109]

Throughout the 1990s, Russian politicians, including democrats, as well as the general public, did not hesitate to cast doubt on Ukraine's sovereignty, since Russia's national identity, including the imperial status, was believed to be contingent upon its relationship with Ukraine.[110] The fragile bonds uniting Russia's population made Ukraine central to Russia's essentialist vision of itself as a timeless 'historical Russia' – a unique land with a messianic mission to lead others in fostering cultural self-awareness.[111] To position itself as a great power, Russia needed, at a minimum, a foundational myth tracing its lineage to medieval Kyiv and the ability to assert dominance over subaltern neighbours.[112] Without Ukraine, Russia could not claim to be an empire; conversely, by subjugating and controlling Ukraine, it would automatically re-establish itself as an empire.[113] Thus, the Russian Parliament questioned the legality of transferring Crimea from the Russian Soviet Federative Socialist Republic to the Ukrainian Soviet Socialist Republic.[114] In an even more brazen manner, Sevastopol was declared part of Russia by the Russian Parliament.[115] Although the Russian representative to the United Nations Security Council emphasised that the 'emotional and declaratory' resolution of the Parliament

---

107 S. Medvedev, 'Черный октябрь 93-го', *Радио Свобода*, 4 October 2023 <www.svoboda.org/a/chernyy-oktyabrj-1993-go-efir-v-18-05-/32620023.html>.

108 PACE Resolution 1055 (1995) of 2 February 1995, 'Russia's request for membership in the light of the situation in Chechnya', para. 11.

109 A. Merlin, 'Gambling, Misunderstanding or Compromising? The Council of Europe and the War in Chechnya' in K. Malfliet and S. Parmentier (eds), *Russia and the Council of Europe: 10 Years After*, above n. 73, p. 137, p. 154.

110 See e.g. Z. Brzezinski, 'The Premature Partnership' (1994) 73(2) *Foreign Affairs* 67, 74, 80; S. Plokhy, above n. 8, pp. 65–67; P. D'Anieri, above n. 101, pp. 40–43, 54–55, 77–78, 82–83; R. Pipes, 'Шанс России' (1992) 3(69) *Страна и мир* 2, 5.

111 J. McGlynn, above n. 82, pp. 146, 208.

112 Ibid., pp. 146–47, 161–63; P. D'Anieri, above n. 101, p. 11; S. Plokhy, above n. 8, pp. 4–13.

113 Z. Brzezinski, above n. 110, 80.

114 Постановление Верховного Совета Российской Федерации 'О правовой оценке решений высших органов государственной власти РСФСР по изменению статуса Крыма, принятых в 1954 году' (Resolution of the Supreme Council of the Russian Federation 'On the legal assessment of decisions of the highest state authorities of the RSFSR on changing the status of Crimea, adopted in 1954'), No. 2809-I, 21 May 1992.

115 Постановление Верховного Совета Российской Федерации 'О статусе города Севастополя' (Resolution of the Supreme Council of the Russian Federation 'On the status of the city of Sevastopol'), No. 5359-I, 9 July 1993.

diverged from the policy of both the President and the Government,[116] Russia succeeded in keeping a sizeable navy in this city. Ukraine's sovereignty over the Crimean Peninsula, including Sevastopol, was recognised only after the Moscow officialdom concluded that it could keep the whole of Ukraine in its sphere of influence.[117] Russia's pursuit of control over Ukraine also manifested itself in the exertion of political and economic pressure, including gas and trade wars.[118]

Similar imperialistic rhetoric can be detected in the works of various representatives of Russian culture. In this regard, it is worth noting that being critical of the totalitarian communist past does not necessarily equate to opposing the empire.[119] In his poetry, Joseph Brodsky, a Nobel laureate in literature, spitefully mocked the independence of Ukraine and the right of Ukrainians to self-determination.[120] Another Nobel laureate in literature, Aleksandr Solzhenitsyn, did not believe in the existence of Ukrainians as a separate people.[121] Moreover, he was profoundly aggrieved by what he called the 'false' borders of Ukraine, a 'gift' from Vladimir Lenin and Nikita Khrushchev.[122]

Inspired by Aleksandr Solzhenitsyn, Boris Yeltsin tested the waters in diplomatic talks and considered uniting Russia and Ukraine.[123] As asserted by Ukrainian politicians and international lawyers, Russia's imperialist attitudes towards the neighbouring state have been evident throughout the entire period of Ukraine's independence, beginning with Boris Yeltsin's presidency.[124]

Russia's troublesome foreign policy did not go unnoticed in Strasbourg. When considering Russia's request for membership of the Council of Europe, PACE referenced Russia's commitment not only to various democratic and human rights reforms but also to resolving international disputes through

---

[116] United Nations Security Council, 'Provisional Verbatim Record of the 3256th Meeting', 20 July 1993, UN Doc. S/PV.3256, p. 14.

[117] L. Mälksoo, above n. 92, p. 179.

[118] O. Zadorozhnii, *International Law in the Relations of Ukraine and the Russian Federation*, Kyiv, K.I.S., 2016, pp. 104–09, 124–34, 151–61, 201–09.

[119] E. Thompson, above n. 59, p. 34.

[120] J. Brodsky, 'На независимость Украины', *Культура.рф*, 1991 <www.culture.ru/poems/30468/na-nezavisimost-ukrainy>.

[121] A. Solzhenitsyn, *Публицистика*, vol. 1, Yaroslavl, Верхне-Волжское книжное издательство, 1995, pp. 544–46.

[122] Ibid., pp. 686–87, 692.

[123] See M. Zygar, *Война и наказание: как Россия уничтожала Украину*, 2nd ed., Riga, Медуза, 2024, p. 56; P. D'Anieri, above n. 101, pp. 36–37.

[124] V. Vasylenko, *На війні як на війні: tertium non datur*, vol. 2, Kyiv, Темпора, 2020, pp. 11–23; 'Ющенко. Приезд Путина прямо домой, визиты в Москву, война, убийство Качиньского, безголовая нация', *YouTube (Дмитрий Гордон)*, 26 January 2023 <www.youtube.com/watch?v=8Ng0G3nnC8M>.

peaceful means and without any 'threats of force against its neighbours'.[125] Another related commitment was:

> to denounce as wrong the concept of two different categories of foreign countries, whereby some are treated as a zone of special influence called the 'near abroad'.[126]

However, such a denunciation did not occur, not even in a formal sense. On the contrary, in domestic debates about joining the Council of Europe, Russian state officials emphasised the importance of pursuing national interests and shaping international public opinion.[127] At the time, key issues included the protection of Russian-speaking populations abroad, particularly in the Baltic states, and the Russian military presence in Moldova.[128] By the same token, Russian diplomats said that the Council of Europe would serve as a suitable regional platform to protect the rights of Russian-speaking populations and 'our compatriots' in Latvia, Lithuania and Estonia.[129] This reasoning echoed that of Aleksandr Solzhenitsyn. He insisted that Russia ought to demand full compliance from the Baltic states with 'all-European norms on the rights of national minorities'.[130] Put differently, the Russian self-image of victimhood sought to justify the pursuit of an imperialist foreign policy through the instrumentalisation of international human rights law in the notorious 'near abroad'.[131] In states such as Moldova, Belarus and Ukraine this policy helped local elites to become (further) assimilated into Russia's imperial project, whereas the local cultures and languages were, by implication, destined to be seen as a stigma and a sign of backwardness.[132]

Yielding to pressure from Germany and other Western European states, the Council of Europe admitted Russia in 1996, thereby allowing Boris Yeltsin to present this achievement as a success story in his campaign for re-election as

---

125 PACE Opinion 193 (1996), above n. 97, para. 10.7.

126 Ibid., para. 10.11.

127 S. Glotov, 'Совет Европы и Россия: союз состоялся' in *Право Совета Европы и Россия*, above n. 105, p. 5, pp. 15–17; 'Государственная Дума РФ, из стенограммы заседания 16 февраля 1996 года. Обсуждение вопроса "О принятии России в Совет Европы"' in *Право Совета Европы и Россия*, above n. 105, p. 95, p. 113.

128 S. Glotov, 'Совет Европы и Россия: союз состоялся', above n. 127, pp. 16–17; 'Государственная Дума РФ, из стенограммы заседания 16 февраля 1996 года. Обсуждение вопроса "О принятии России в Совет Европы"', above n. 127, p. 113.

129 M. Shurgalin, 'Политика России в Совете Европы на современном этапе' in *Россия и Совет Европы: перспективы взаимодействия*, Moscow, Институт права и публичной политики, 2001, p. 7, pp. 10–11.

130 A. Solzhenitsyn, above n. 121, p. 690. See also G.M. Velyaminov, *Международное право: опыты*, Moscow, Статут, 2015, p. 365 (criticising alleged human rights abuses in the Baltic region, ostensibly committed with the connivance of the Council of Europe).

131 B. Harzl, 'Nativist ideological responses to European/liberal human rights discourses in contemporary Russia' in L. Mälksoo and W. Benedek, above n. 37, p. 355, pp. 373–74.

132 M. Mälksoo, above n. 79, 473–74.

President.[133] To the West, he was regarded as the only prospect for democracy in Russia.[134] Thus, although it was clear that the world's largest state did not meet all the requirements associated with membership,[135] political considerations took precedence. This controversial decision was partly based on the hope that, through socialisation, accession might gradually bring about the necessary positive changes at the domestic level.[136]

Peter Leuprecht, then Deputy Secretary General of the Council of Europe, resigned in protest over the above-mentioned decision. He argued that:

> it is at the pre-accession stage that the Council's representatives have the most leverage and can press for the reforms needed to bring the applicant country into line with the Council's standards.[137]

His concerns appeared to be prescient. The Council of Europe deluded itself into believing that its active support and monitoring activities would contribute to Russia's successful transformation into a well-functioning democracy.[138]

Admittedly, all Central and Eastern European states faced formidable human rights challenges in the 1990s,[139] with the requirements associated with membership of the Council of Europe being future-oriented.[140] In hindsight, it seems that the new Member States succeeded in their transition from a totalitarian communist regime to a democracy with varying degrees of success and with occasional backlashes against human rights.[141] Crucially, unlike Russia, other states in the region have had no imperialist agenda in Strasbourg.

---

133 P. Leuprecht, 'Innovations in the European System of Human Rights Protection: Is Enlargement Compatible with Reinforcement?' (1998) 8 *Transnational Law and Contemporary Problems* 313, 330.

134 P. D'Anieri, above n. 101, pp. 58–59.

135 R. Bernhardt, F. Ermacora, S. Trechsel and A. Weitzel, 'Report on the conformity of the legal order of the Russian Federation with Council of Europe standards', 28 September 1994, Doc. AS/Bur/Russia (1994) 7. See also J. Kahn, 'The Legal Origins of Russian Membership in the Council of Europe and the Seeds of Russia's Expulsion' (2024) 14(1) *Notre Dame Journal of International & Comparative Law* 1, 3, 26; K. Brummer, above n. 17, 260–61.

136 L. Mälksoo, 'Introduction: Russia, Strasbourg, and the paradox of a human rights backlash' in L. Mälksoo and W. Benedek, above n. 37, p. 3, pp. 3–4. See also J. Kahn, above n. 135, 27–34; R. Bindig, 'Russia's accession to the Council of Europe and the fulfilment of its obligations and commitments' in K. Malfliet and S. Parmentier, above n. 73, p. 33, p. 38.

137 P. Leuprecht, above n. 133, 328. See also M. Janis, above n. 45, 98; P. Roter, above n. 37, p. 52.

138 A. Fogelklou, 'Russian legal reforms and the Council of Europe: three steps forward, two steps back' in K. Malfliet and S. Parmentier, above n. 73, p. 83, p. 84.

139 J.-P. Masseret, 'Report on the honouring of commitments entered into by new member states', 7 March 1994, PACE Doc. 7037, para. 9.

140 J. Kahn, above n. 135, 36–37; P. Leuprecht, above n. 133, 328–29.

141 E. Klein, above n. 30, pp. 85–86, 91–92.

After Vladimir Putin came to power, it became unrealistic to believe that Russia could be democratised.[142] Rather, Russia reinforced the advancement of its interests in the international arena, eroding the liberal democratic order in Europe.[143] Misinterpreted in the West as a 'failed transition to democracy', Russia could be more accurately characterised as 'an alternative to democracy' – one that ostensibly adhered to democratic principles while, in its foreign policy, actively sought to undermine more democratic states,[144] such as Georgia and Ukraine, and international organisations promoting democracy, particularly the Council of Europe. Simultaneously, the Kremlin was constructing its own simulacrum of international law.[145] Ultimately, Russia's self-perception as a great power made it a special Member State in Strasbourg, to the detriment of the principle of equality.[146] Over the years, the Council of Europe deified dialogue and diplomacy, which, however, are not objectives in themselves.[147] When Russia and the Council of Europe used different languages of international law – those of the 19th and 21st centuries respectively – such a conversation was doomed to failure.[148]

4 THE FUTURE

Distancing itself institutionally from Europe and normatively from liberal values, Russia does not provide equivalent human rights safeguards to its population, people living in Russian-occupied territories or other residents of what Russia perceives to be its legitimate *Großraum*. In 2017, Ivan Soltanovsky, then Permanent Representative of Russia to the Council of Europe, did not see any viable alternatives to this international organisation in the region.[149] Since 2022, Russia has neither built up a Moscow-friendly regional system of human rights protection nor revived the discarded Commonwealth of Independent

---

142 K. Malfliet and S. Parmentier, 'Russia's membership of the Council of Europe: ten years after' in K. Malfliet and S. Parmentier, above n. 73, p. 7, pp. 8–10.

143 Ibid., pp. 9–10, 26; E. Bates, K. Dzehtsiarou and A. Forde, above n. 17, pp. 41, 55–61, 68, 111–12, 219.

144 'Putin and the Presidents: Timothy Snyder (interview)', *YouTube (Frontline PBS Official)*, 20 February 2023 <www.youtube.com/watch?v=um-SEQDQidM>.

145 L. Mälksoo, above n. 92, pp. 184–85.

146 P. Roter, above n. 37, pp. 44–46, 52–53. See also N. Weiss and T.A. Lanzl, above n. 46, 824; E. Bates, K. Dzehtsiarou and A. Forde, above n. 17, pp. 48, 112, 222.

147 J. Kranz, 'Imperialism, the Highest Stage of Sovereign Democracy: Some Remarks on the Annexation of Crimea by Russia' (2014) 52(2) *Archiv des Völkerrechts* 205, 220.

148 For a critique of Russia's invocation of 19th century practices, see B. Harzl, above n. 131, p. 367.

149 'Интервью Постоянного представителя России при Совете Европы И. Д. Солтановского "Российской газете", опубликованное 14 сентября 2017 года', *Ministry of Foreign Affairs of the Russian Federation*, 15 September 2017 <www.mid.ru/ru/foreign_policy/rso/coe/1552444/>.

States Convention on Human Rights and Fundamental Freedoms, which still lacks operational capacity. In any case, this treaty provides a lower level of protection than the ECHR.[150]

Possible ideological alternatives, such as the mythic concept of the Russian world (*русский мир*),[151] Eurasianism[152] or the obsolete doctrine of sovereign democracy,[153] are deficient in philosophical foundations and coherent meanings.[154] Even if a distinct ideology exists in present-day Russia, it boils down to imperialism in its particular form of revanchism.[155] This can be better conceptualised by the neologism 'ruscism' (*рашизм*), which dates back to the Russo-Georgian war and gained wider popularity after Russia's full-scale invasion of Ukraine.[156] The Ukrainian Parliament has defined ruscism as:

> a type of totalitarian ideology and practices that form the basis of the Russian Nazi totalitarian regime established in the aggressor state, and that are rooted in the traditions of Russian chauvinism and imperialism, as well as in the practices of communist and National Socialist (Nazi) totalitarian regimes.[157]

---

150 PACE Resolution 1249 (2001) of 23 May 2001, 'Co-existence of the Convention on Human Rights and Fundamental Freedoms of the Commonwealth of Independent States and the European Convention on Human Rights', para. 4.

151 Концепция внешней политики Российской Федерации, утверждена Указом Президента Российской Федерации No. 229 (The Concept of the Foreign Policy of the Russian Federation, approved by Decree of the President of the Russian Federation No. 229), 31 March 2023.

152 Ibid.

153 V. Surkov, 'Национализация будущего', *Эксперт*, No. 43(537), 20 November 2006 <web.archive.org/web/20061231154555/http://www.expert.ru/printissues/expert/2006/43/nacionalizaciya_buduschego/>.

154 See e.g. Roundtable of the Petersburg Political Science Expertise, 'О дискуссии вокруг понятия "суверенная демократия"' (2007) 3 *Политэкс* 268; A. Umland, 'Почему "неоевразийство" Александра Дугина не является евразийским', *Гефтер*, 23 May 2018 <https://gefter.ru/archive/25039>; 'A Declaration on the "Russian World" (Russkii mir) Teaching', *Public Orthodoxy*, 13 March 2022 <https://publicorthodoxy.org/2022/03/13/a-declaration-on-the-russian-world-russkii-mir-teaching/>; B. Harzl, above n. 131, p. 383.

155 A. Etkind, above n. 85, p. 13.

156 See e.g. S. Morfinov, '"Рашизм": історія "російського фашизму" від теорій Дугіна до ідеології "Брата-2"', *BBC News Україна*, 1 October 2022 <https://www.bbc.com/ukrainian/features-63072100>; T. Snyder, 'The War in Ukraine Has Unleashed a New Word', *The New York Times*, 22 April 2022 <www.nytimes.com/2022/04/22/magazine/ruscism-ukraine-russia-war.html>.

157 Law of Ukraine 'On the principles of state policy of the national memory of the Ukrainian people', above n. 86, Article 1(11). Cf. Постанова Верховної Ради України 'Про Заяву Верховної Ради України "Про використання політичним режимом російської федерації ідеології рашизму, засудження засад і практик рашизму як тоталітарних і людиноненависницьких"' (Resolution of the Verkhovna Rada of Ukraine 'On the Statement of the Verkhovna Rada of Ukraine "On the use of the ideology of ruscism by the political regime of the russian federation and on the condemnation of the principles and practices of ruscism as totalitarian and misanthropic"'), No. 3078-IX, 2 May 2023 (linking ruscism directly to President Putin).

In its resolutions, PACE has addressed various aspects of ruscism. First, according to PACE, Russia has become a de facto dictatorship due to the consolidation of overwhelming power in the hands of Vladimir Putin and the lack of checks and balances.[158] Second, PACE has linked Russia's acts of aggression to its anti-democratic political regime:

> The Russian Federation employs acts of aggression against sovereign nations as a strategy to enhance the president's domestic image, with the Chechen wars of the late 1990s, the Russian Federation's influence in the Transnistria region of Moldova and its aggression against Georgia in 2008 serving as illustrative examples. Dictatorships also destroy the fundamental rights [...] of their own population. It is therefore in the interest first and foremost of the people of the Russian Federation, but also of Europe and the whole world, that democracy is restored in the Russian Federation.[159]

Third, PACE has tied the practice of ruscism to international crimes.[160] Fourth, numerous violations of the rights of indigenous peoples, along with heavy casualties suffered on the battlefields, have prompted PACE to assert that the decolonisation of Russia is vital to the establishment of democracy in this state.[161] Nevertheless, the Russian liberal opposition, dismayed by such initiatives, reveals its imperialist mindset by invoking the 'shared background and culture' of the peoples living in Russia.[162]

Some commentators hope for a peaceful transition to democracy in Russia.[163] Whether this will happen remains an open question at the time of writing.

---

158 PACE Resolution 2519 (2023) of 13 October 2023, 'Examining the legitimacy and legality of the ad hominem term-limit waiver for the incumbent President of the Russian Federation', para. 4.

159 Ibid., para. 6.

160 PACE Resolution 2556 (2024) of 26 June 2024, 'Legal and human rights aspects of the Russian Federation's aggression against Ukraine', para. 14.15.

161 PACE Resolution 2540 (2024) of 17 April 2024, 'Alexei Navalny's death and the need to counter Vladimir Putin's totalitarian regime and its war on democracy', paras. 17, 26.12, 28. For an appeal by the Ukrainian Parliament to PACE and other entities regarding the right of peoples, including indigenous peoples, in Russia to self-determination, see Постанова Верховної Ради України 'Про Звернення Верховної Ради України до міжнародного співтовариства про підтримку права на самовизначення народів російської федерації' (Resolution of the Verkhovna Rada of Ukraine 'On the Appeal of the Verkhovna Rada of Ukraine to the international community in support for the right to self-determination of the peoples of the russian federation'), No. 2633-IX, 6 October 2022.

162 'Bled Strategic Forum 2024 - BSF Distinguished Partner Award', *YouTube (Bled Strategic Forum)*, 6 September 2024 <https://www.youtube.com/watch?v=R9IHfxAUACk>.

163 I. Risini and A. Forde, 'Parting Paths – Russia's Inevitable Exit From the Council of Europe', *Völkerrechtsblog*, 12 March 2022 <https://voelkerrechtsblog.org/de/parting-paths-russias-inevitable-exit-from-the-council-of-europe/>.

Typically, authoritarian rulers are subverted in an *unconstitutional* manner.[164] The most frequent form of such exits from office is a coup d'état.[165] Yet, the longer a dictator remains in office (in this respect, consider Vladimir Putin's 26 years in power), the less likely it is that a coup d'état will come to fruition.[166] Alternatively, there could be popular uprisings in Russia – something that Ukraine appears to be pursuing under its victory plan.[167]

For authoritarian rulers, the most common *constitutional* exit from office occurs due to poor health or natural death.[168] In early 1996, Ramazan Abdulatipov, a Russian politician, linked Russia's prospective membership of the Council of Europe to obtaining guarantees for democratic elections, because, he continued, Russia had no tradition of a democratic change of power and its rulers, historically, ended up either in prison or at a cemetery.[169] Today, Russia's gerontocracy is visible to the naked eye: Vladimir Putin, Nikolai Patrushev, Alexander Bortnikov, Sergey Naryshkin and Sergey Lavrov, to name but a few, were born in the early 1950s. With the life expectancy of men at birth being 65.6 years,[170] it can be anticipated that the Russian political elite will undergo change in the not-too-distant future. That said, there is no guarantee that democratic, pro-Ukrainian politicians will come to power. Research conducted in 2015, i.e. approximately one year after the start of the Russo-Ukrainian war, revealed that much of Vladimir Putin's support was genuine.[171] According to this research, the principal reason for the weak opposition movement was the popularity of the autocratic leader.[172] Moreover, as previously discussed, Russian liberals struggle to abandon their imperialist worldview, particularly in relation to Ukraine.

---

164 M.W. Svolik, *The Politics of Authoritarian Rule*, New York, Cambridge University Press, 2012, p. 41 (in approximately two-thirds of all cases worldwide from 1946–2008).

165 Ibid.

166 Ibid., pp. 75–77.

167 T. Odnolitok, 'У Зеленського розповіли деталі щодо плану перемоги: РФ може бути "на понтах" за однієї умови', *УНІАН*, 1 October 2024 <www.unian.ua/politics/u-zelenskogo-rozpovili-detali-shchodo-planu-peremogi-rf-mozhe-buti-na-pontah-za-odniyeji-umovi-12773412.html#goog_rewarded>.

168 M.W. Svolik, above n. 164, p. 40 (in approximately 40% of constitutional exits worldwide from 1946–2008).

169 See 'Вместо введения: Как Россия вступала в Совет Европы' in S.A. Glotov (ed), *Россия и Совет Европы: 20 лет вместе на защите прав человека*, Moscow, Международный юридический институт, 2017, p. 6, p. 20.

170 'Russian Federation', *WHO Data* <https://data.who.int/countries/643> (the latest available data are from 2021).

171 T. Frye, S. Gehlbach, K.L. Marquardt and O.J. Reuter, 'Is Putin's popularity real?' (2017) 33(1) *Post-Soviet Affairs* 1, 10.

172 Ibid. See also L. Mälksoo, above n. 92, pp. 187, 193; J. McGlynn, above n. 82, pp. 26–30.

Regardless of which scenario unfolds, the future of Russia is being shaped on the battlefields of Ukraine.[173] Historically, the ideas of European integration and human rights protection materialised after the major European powers had lost their imperialist wars.[174] Hence, Russia's reaccession to the Council of Europe is hardly possible before its defeat in the ongoing imperialist war of aggression against Ukraine.

In the event of defeat, it may be expected that pro-Russian voices across Europe and elsewhere would advocate for Russia's reaccession to the Council of Europe to protect the human rights of Russian citizens – a campaign similar to that against Russia's expulsion several years ago.[175] However, as previously discussed, Russo-centric optics tend to condone or even legitimise Russian imperialism. It is long past time to shift the analytical focus to the oft-neglected agency and interests of the smaller states of Central and Eastern Europe.

It is argued that the key requirement for reaccession should be Russia's de-imperialisation. This condition should be met in advance, in contrast to the myopic approach taken in 1996.[176] In the process of de-imperialisation, the Kremlin would need to deoccupy the foreign territories and repeal the legal norms that either consider these lands Russian[177] or recognise them as independent states.[178] In the Reykjavík Declaration, the leaders of the Member

---

173 O. Orlov, 'Russie: "ils voulaient le fascisme, ils l'ont eu"', *Le Club de Mediapart*, 13 November 2022 <https://blogs.mediapart.fr/russie-les-voix-de-la-dissidence-daujourdhui/blog/131122/russie-ils-voulaient-le-fascisme-ils-lont-eu>.

174 A. Huneeus and M.R. Madsen, 'Between universalism and regional law and politics: A comparative history of the American, European, and African human rights systems' (2018) 16(1) *International Journal of Constitutional Law* 136, 148; E. Konzett, '"Dieser Krieg bringt eine neue Weltordnung mit sich"/ "Der Widerstand der Ukrainer hat die globale Sicherheit gestärkt"', *Falter*, 21 December 2022 <https://www.falter.at/zeitung/20221221/dieser-krieg-bringt-eine-neue-weltordnung-mit-sich>.

175 N. Buckley, above n. 41, p. 4; A. Kornya, above n. 41; Moscow Helsinki Group, 'Addressing the Crisis in Relations Between the Council of Europe and Russia: Uphold the Values and Fulfil the Mission to Protect Rights Across All of Europe', November 2018 <https://mhg.ru/addressing-crisis-relations-between-council-europe-and-russia-uphold-values-and-fulfil-mission>. See also P. Roter, above n. 37, p. 50; A. Katz Miller, above n. 69, 117–20; N. Weiss and T.A. Lanzl, above n. 46, 822; E. Bates, K. Dzehtsiarou and A. Forde, above n. 17, pp. 103–04.

176 For a similar view, see K. Brummer, above n. 17, 273–74. As for the implementation of other conditions, it makes sense to impose specific time limits. For a similar idea, see V.A. Kartashkin, 'Региональное сотрудничество государств в области прав человека' in E.A. Lukasheva, above n. 99, p. 517, p. 519.

177 E.g. Конституция Российской Федерации, принята всенародным голосованием 12 декабря 1993 года с изменениями, одобренными в ходе общероссийского голосования 1 июля 2020 года (Constitution of the Russian Federation, adopted by popular vote on 12 December 1993, with amendments approved during the all-Russian vote on 1 July 2020), Article 65(1).

178 E.g. Указ Президента Российской Федерации 'О признании Республики Абхазия' (Decree of the President of the Russian Federation 'On the recognition of the Republic of Abkhazia'), No. 1260, 26 August 2008; Указ Президента Российской Федерации 'О признании Республики Южная Осетия' (Decree of the President of the Russian Federation 'On the recognition of the Republic of South Ossetia'), No. 1261, 26 August 2008.

States of the Council of Europe called on Russia to honour its obligations under international law and 'immediately withdraw completely and unconditionally its forces from Ukraine, Georgia and the Republic of Moldova'.[179] By the same token, any unequal treaties that Russia has imposed or may impose on other states must be disregarded.

To withdraw one's troops, reform one's laws or disregard unequal treaties is relatively easy. At the same time, as pointed out by PACE, 'it is much more difficult to change traditions and mentalities at all levels of society, particularly [in] administration and [among] officials'.[180] Indeed, judicial interpretation even of seemingly liberal legal instruments, such as the Russian Constitution, could have illiberal outcomes, since domestic courts consider possible reactions from political authorities in high-profile cases.[181] By way of illustration, in its 2022 rulings on the constitutionality of Russia's military conquest of four Ukrainian provinces, the Constitutional Court of the Russian Federation used Orwellian legal language to normalise Russian imperialism and cloak it in the rhetoric of peace and human rights.[182]

During Russia's accession to – and attempted socialisation at – the Council of Europe, the focus was on the acceptance and implementation of European standards on democracy, human rights and the rule of law 'at the level of policy, institutional, and legislative change'.[183] Nevertheless, Russia tried to minimise such socialisation.[184] More problematically, there was no deep socialisation involving a sort of identity change, which is indispensable to the achievement of sustainable results on the ground.[185]

The failed identity change did not simply pertain to a state-centric perspective on sovereignty, which is understood as both 'immunity from any external pressure' and 'justification for virtually unlimited public interventions

179 Reykjavík Declaration, above n. 9, p. 4. See also PACE Opinion 300 (2022), above n. 7, paras. 5, 13.1.

180 PACE Opinion of 20 September 1993, 'Application by Romania for membership of the Council of Europe' (Doc. 6918).

181 M. Antonov, above n. 102, 530–31; E. Bates, K. Dzehtsiarou and A. Forde, above n. 17, pp. 87–89.

182 Constitutional Court of the Russian Federation (CCRF), ruling No. 36-П, 2 October 2022; CCRF, ruling No. 37-П, 2 October 2022; CCRF, ruling No. 38-П, 2 October 2022; CCRF, ruling No. 39-П, 2 October 2022. For a critical analysis, see S. Masol, 'Orwellian Rulings of the Russian Constitutional Court on the Donetsk, Kherson, Luhansk and Zaporizhzhia Provinces of Ukraine', *EJIL: Talk!*, 25 October 2022 <www.ejiltalk.org/orwellian-rulings-of-the-russian-constitutional-court-on-the-donetsk-kherson-luhansk-and-zaporizhzhia-provinces-of-ukraine/>.

183 P. Roter, above n. 37, p. 33.

184 P. Jordan, 'Russia's Accession to the Council of Europe and Compliance with European Human Rights Norms' (2003) 11(2) *Demokratizatsiya* 281, 287; E. Bates, K. Dzehtsiarou and A. Forde, above n. 17, p. 89.

185 P. Roter, above n. 37, p. 33.

into individual liberties'.[186] Nor did the post-2012 rise of 'authoritarian sovereignty' in Russia constitute 'a prime driver' behind its severance of ties with the Council of Europe, as some scholars have suggested.[187] Instead, it was an external factor, namely aggression against another Member State, that played a crucial role in the decision to expel Russia from the international organisation.[188] The underlying problem lies in Russia's great power state-centrism,[189] which questions the sovereignty of smaller states, especially in the so-called 'near abroad'.[190] For example, Vladimir Putin trumpeted that 'Ukraine's true sovereignty is possible only in partnership with Russia'.[191] Importantly, as previously discussed, Russia's aspiration to be recognised as a great power, along with its claims over Ukraine, predates Vladimir Putin's dictatorial regime and is widely supported across the Russian populace.[192] The political elite, intellectuals and a vast majority of ordinary Russians have yet to come to terms with the imperialism ingrained in Russia's history, ideology and culture, notably its territorial conquests, unpunished atrocities and the anachronistic model of a triune Russian nation consisting of Great Russians (Russians), Little Russians (Ukrainians) and White Russians (Belarusians).[193]

One of the pioneering efforts by a Russian writer to confront the imperial identity of his homeland is a recent book by Mikhail Zygar. The main title of this book, *War and Punishment*, contrasts with Leo Tolstoy's *War and Peace*, bringing the issue of accountability to the forefront. At the outset, Mikhail Zygar makes a confession:

> I am guilty [...]. Like my contemporaries and our predecessors, I, too, bear responsibility for the war that Russia is waging against Ukraine. Russian culture is

---

186 M. Antonov, 'Conservatism in Russia and Sovereignty in Human Rights' (2014) 39 *Review of Central and East European Law* 1, 2, 14.

187 G. Flikke and D. Slabinski, above n. 69, 38.

188 See, *mutatis mutandis*, P. Roter, above n. 37, pp. 47–49, 51, 54, 56; E. Bates, K. Dzehtsiarou and A. Forde, above n. 17, pp. 226–27.

189 For a similar view, see E. Fura and R. Maruste, 'Russia's impact on the Strasbourg system, as seen by two former judges of the European Court of Human Rights' in L. Mälksoo and W. Benedek, above n. 37, p. 222, p. 229; N. Weiss and T.A. Lanzl, above n. 46, 827.

190 L. Mälksoo, above n. 92, pp. 102–04.

191 V. Putin, 'Об историческом единстве русских и украинцев', *Президент России*, 12 July 2021 <http://kremlin.ru/events/president/news/66181>. See also 'Memorandum of Conversation. Subject: Meeting with President of Russia', *National Security Archive*, 6 April 2008, NW#: 78134, DocId: 34685227, p. 5 ('Ukraine [...] is not a nation built in a natural manner. It's an artificial country created back in Soviet times').

192 P. D'Anieri, above n. 101, p. 27.

193 See e.g. S. Plokhy, above n. 8, p. 298; B. Kassymbekova and E. Marat, above n. 82; J. Kranz, above n. 147, 205; M. Mälksoo, above n. 79, 476–78; J. McGlynn, above n. 82, pp. 9, 165–66, 202–04, 216; M. Hlazunova, 'Олександра Матвійчук: "Я не побачила в Європі запиту на справедливість. Я побачила запит на мир"', *LB.ua*, 14 December 2022 <https://lb.ua/culture/2022/12/14/539101_oleksandra_matviychuk_ya_pobachila.html>.

guilty [...]. We did not understand how deadly the very idea of Russia as a 'great empire' could be.[194]

If shared by other Russians, this way of thinking could gradually debunk the entrenched myths of Russian victimhood and imperial innocence. It could be a valuable element of a future *Vergangenheitsaufarbeitung* in Russian society – a process that should address the evils of not only the Russo-Ukrainian war but also ruscism in its entirety.

As for international legal forms of accountability, it would be essential to repeal the 2020 constitutional amendment on the non-enforceability of decisions of interstate bodies that contradict the Russian Constitution.[195] Having abandoned its self-perception as a great power, Russia would need to comply with all relevant judicial decisions and pay compensation for damage, loss or injury caused by its aggression. The Register of Damage Caused by the Aggression of the Russian Federation against Ukraine has already been created.[196] PACE has called on Russia to cooperate with the International Court of Justice and the International Criminal Court.[197] The proposal to establish a special tribunal for the crime of aggression against Ukraine has been canvassed as well,[198] culminating in the signing of a bilateral agreement between Ukraine and the Council of Europe.[199] It goes without saying that all decisions and judgments of the ECtHR delivered in respect of Russia must be executed.[200] This requirement concerns 'acts or omissions capable of constituting a violation of the Convention provided that they occurred until 16 September 2022',[201] notwithstanding the Russian legal ban on the execution of the ECtHR's rulings

[194] M. Zygar, above n. 123, p. 9.

[195] Constitution of the Russian Federation, above n. 177, Article 79.

[196] Resolution CM/Res(2023)3 of the Committee of Ministers establishing the Enlarged Partial Agreement on the Register of Damage Caused by the Aggression of the Russian Federation against Ukraine, 12 May 2023.

[197] PACE Opinion 300 (2022), above n. 7, paras. 7, 13.6.

[198] E.g. PACE Recommendation 2231 (2022) of 28 April 2022, 'The Russian Federation's aggression against Ukraine: ensuring accountability for serious violations of international humanitarian law and other international crimes', paras. 2.3, 2.4; PACE Resolution 2436 (2022) of 28 April 2022, 'The Russian Federation's aggression against Ukraine: ensuring accountability for serious violations of international humanitarian law and other international crimes', paras. 8, 11.6, 12.5.1; Ministers' Deputies, 'Consequences of the aggression of the Russian Federation against Ukraine – Accountability for international crimes', 15 September 2022, Decision CM/Del/Dec(2022)1442/2.3, para. 3.

[199] 'Ukraine and the Council of Europe sign Agreement on establishing a Special Tribunal for the Crime of Aggression against Ukraine', *Council of Europe: Newsroom*, 25 June 2025 <www.coe.int/en/web/portal/-/ukraine-and-the-council-of-europe-sign-agreement-on-establishing-a-special-tribunal-for-the-crime-of-aggression-against-ukraine>.

[200] P. Dourneau-Josette, above n. 30, p. 551; E. Bates, K. Dzehtsiarou and A. Forde, above n. 17, pp. 14, 128, 160.

[201] Resolution CM/Res(2022)3, above n. 3, para. 7. See also Reykjavík Declaration, above n. 9, p. 17.

that entered into force after 15 March 2022.[202] Finally, compliance coalitions are of utmost importance for the successful implementation of the ECtHR's rulings.[203] Independent courts and legislatures, civil society and free media are partners in such coalitions at the domestic level and rein in the executive branch of the government.[204] Since these institutions in Russia are not willing or able to take a stand against the strong executive,[205] a new political elite should develop a system of independent courts, foster the work of civil society and guarantee the freedom of expression.

5 CONCLUSIONS

To paraphrase Pierre-Henri Teitgen,[206] democracies do not descend into ruscism in one day. The imperial breakup of the late 1980s and early 1990s offered an opportunity for Russia to consolidate democracy and abandon its great power ambitions. However, the former effort failed and the latter was rejected.[207] At the Council of Europe, Russia not only resisted socialisation, including deep socialisation, but also pursued an imperialist agenda from the beginning of its membership, particularly by instrumentalising international human rights law. In essence, a two-tier regional legal order was set up in Strasbourg, with substandard expectations for the biggest Member State. Ultimately, Russia's imperialist war of aggression against Ukraine resulted in Russia's expulsion from this international organisation.

It is long overdue to recalibrate the analytical lenses used to scrutinise the relations between Russia and the Council of Europe. The prevailing Russo-centric framework has not only condoned but, at times, legitimised the Kremlin's imperialist goals; at best, it has centred on the plight of ordinary Russians, thereby absolving them of accountability. The focus should instead shift to the smaller states of Central and Eastern Europe, placing their agency and interests at the heart of the discussion. After all, the core problem behind Russia's approaches to democracy, human rights and the rule of law lies in its

---

202 Федеральный закон Российской Федерации 'О внесении изменений в Уголовно-процессуальный кодекс Российской Федерации' (Federal Law of the Russian Federation 'On Amending the Criminal Procedure Code of the Russian Federation'), No. 180-ФЗ, 11 June 2022, Article 2(1).

203 C. Hillebrecht, *Domestic Politics and International Human Rights Tribunals: The Problem of Compliance*, New York, Cambridge University Press, 2014, p. 116.

204 Ibid.

205 Ibid.

206 A. Robertson (ed), *Collected Edition of the 'Travaux Préparatoires'*, vol. 1, The Hague, Martinus Nijhoff, 1975, p. 292 (pointing out that democracies do not turn into Nazi states in one day).

207 P. D'Anieri, above n. 101, p. 4.

great power state-centrism, which contests the sovereignty of smaller states, especially in the so-called 'near abroad'.

If a new political elite in Moscow decides to rejoin the Council of Europe, which may happen following Russia's defeat in its war against Ukraine, the key requirement for reaccession should be Russia's de-imperialisation. This process would necessitate the deoccupation of foreign territories: Georgia, Moldova and Ukraine. More fundamentally, dismantling Russia's imperialist ethos would require a broad societal reckoning with the dark chapters of Russia's history, as well as its imperialist culture and ideology. As regards the legal dimension of accountability, Russia would need to comply with all relevant judicial decisions, including those of the ECtHR, and pay compensation, alongside enacting related constitutional amendments and establishing domestic compliance coalitions.

CHAPTER 3

AFTER COVID-19: FUTURE PANDEMICS AS A STATE OF (HEALTH) EMERGENCY AND THE NEED FOR JUDICIAL REVIEW

Reza Khabook

1 INTRODUCTION

In light of the Covid-19 pandemic, as the most significant recent public health emergency, this chapter examines how the European Court of Human Rights (hereafter: ECtHR, the Court, and the Strasbourg Court) applied judicial review on Covid-19 cases. Overall, the Strasbourg Court, like many national courts across Europe, has frequently deferred to public authorities, drawing on its established doctrines of subsidiarity and the margin of appreciation.[1] This judicial approach developed against the international backdrop in which the World Health Organization (WHO) declared Covid-19 a Public Health Emergency of International Concern (PHEIC) in January 2020,[2] and later a pandemic in March 2020.[3] Such deference illustrates the tension between protecting individual rights and granting states the flexibility needed to respond to unprecedented health threats, raising questions about the adequacy of the existing legal framework in safeguarding the rule of law during pandemic health emergencies.

This chapter investigates the modalities of judicial review in public health emergencies in order to better safeguard the rule of law in future pandemics. The chapter asks one central research question: how can judicial review be

1 For more information on the ECtHR judgments, look at: ECtHR, 'COVID-19 health crisis', fact sheet, October 2024 <https://www.echr.coe.int/documents/d/echr/fs_covid_eng>.

2 For more information on the WHO's declaration, look at: WHO, 'COVID-19 Public Health Emergency of International Concern (PHEIC), Global research and innovation forum: towards a research roadmap', 11–12 February 2020 <https://www.who.int/publications/m/item/covid-19-public-health-emergency-of-international-concern-(pheic)-global-research-and-innovation-forum>.

3 S. Moore, 'History of COVID-19', *News Medical*, 2021 <https://www.news-medical.net/health/History-of-COVID-19.aspx>.

effectively applied during a pandemic health emergency to uphold the rule of law? To address this question, two sub-questions are posed. First, what is the relationship between the state of emergency and the rule of law? Second, how does judicial review interact with the rule of law in times of crisis?

Answering these questions is crucial in light of the Covid-19 pandemic and the remaining potential of future health crises. Emergency measures adopted across Europe profoundly affected the exercise of fundamental rights such as freedom of movement, freedom of assembly, and the right to education,[4] while courts often struggled to ensure both public health and adherence to rule of law and human rights standards.[5] The prospect of future pandemics, potentially more severe than Covid-19,[6] makes it critical to (re)consider how judicial review should operate during such crises. Without clear standards, there is a real danger that emergency restrictive measures will be normalised, weakening the protection of rights and eroding the rule of law in the long term.[7]

Given the tendency of courts to defer to the executive and legislative powers in reviewing Covid-19 cases, some legal scholars[8] have suggested that European states should rely on limitation clauses (e.g. Articles 8–11 of the European Convention on Human Rights)[9] rather than derogations under Article 15 when interfering with Convention rights.[10] They argue that judicial review

---

4 For detailed information on European countries' measures to Covid-19, look at: 'Data on country response measures to COVID-19', *European Centre for Disease Prevention and Control (ECDC)*, 25 August 2022 <https://www.ecdc.europa.eu/en/publications-data/download-data-response-measures-covid-19>.

5 P. Popelier, B. Kleizen, C. De Clerck, M. Glavina and W. Van Dooren, 'The Role of Courts in Times of Crisis: A Matter of Trust, Legitimacy, and Expertise' in *The Rule of Law in Europe: Vision and Challenges*, European Court of Human Rights, 2021, pp. 1–2.

6 Look at: K. Feldscher, 'The next pandemic: not if, but when', *Harvard School of Public Health*, 12 September 2024 <https://www.hsph.harvard.edu/news/features/next-pandemic-not-if-but-when/>; D. Heymann and E. Ross, 'The next pandemic – when could it be?', *Chatham House*, 23 February 2022 <https://www.chathamhouse.org/2022/02/next-pandemic-when-could-it-be>.

7 Look at: T. Ginsburg and M. Versteeg, 'The Bound Executive: Emergency Powers During the Pandemic' (2021) 19 *International Journal of Constitutional Law* 1498.

8 Look at: K. Dzehtsiarou, 'Article 15 Derogations: Are They Really Necessary During the COVID-19 Pandemic?' (2020) 4 *European Human Rights Law Review* 359. Also, V.P. Tzevelekos and K. Dzehtsiarou, 'Normal as Usual? Human Rights in Times of COVID-19' (2020) 1(2) *Eropean Convention on Human Rights Law Review* 141. Also, A. Zysset, 'To Derogate or to Restrict? The COVID-19 Pandemic, Proportionality and the Justificatory Gap in European Human Rights Law' (2022) 4 *Jus Cogens* 285. And, A. Spadaro, 'COVID-19: Testing the Limits of Human Rights' (2020) 11 *European Journal of Risk Regulation* 317.

9 Convention for the Protection of Human Rights and Fundamental Freedoms, 4 November 1950 (ETS 5).

10 In general, one can argue that the limitation is more related to the so-called normal time, while derogation only applies to emergencies. For more information, look at: A. Müller, 'Limitations to and Derogations from Economic, Social and Cultural Rights' (2009) 9(4) *Human Rights Law Review* 557.

under limitation clauses allows for a more substantively proportionate review and thus better safeguards the rule of law and human rights than the more deferential and formally permissive derogation route. Moreover, staying within the limitation clauses avoids triggering Article 15's procedural and exceptional thresholds, ensuring that judges focus on the merits of the restriction itself rather than on whether a state of emergency has been properly declared or met derogation-specific criteria. According to these scholars, this approach leads to clearer, rights-protective judicial review and prevents emergency powers from being treated as an unchecked exception to ordinary rights guarantees.

Those who support limitation clauses instead of derogations, as Alan Greene has pointed out, neglect the risk of 'normalising exceptional powers and permanently recalibrating human rights protection downwards'.[11] Limitation clauses, in fact, accommodate 'exceptional powers under the parameters of "normalcy"' and are the outcome of excessive deferential judicial review in times of a crisis.[12] Public health emergencies such as the Covid-19 pandemic should be considered a 'public emergency' in the meaning of the Convention, not only because they threaten the life of the nation'[13] but also due to a lack of information about their nature and the modality of their treatment and prevention. Nevertheless, concerns persist regarding judicial review even after a state of emergency is declared. The Court may continue to defer excessively to national authorities, accepting claims of proportionality without rigorous scrutiny, and treating the exceptional nature of the situation as a reason to relax ordinary rights protections. Without appropriate safeguards, this risk can occur under both limitation clauses and Article 15 derogations, potentially undermining the effectiveness of judicial oversight.

From a broader perspective, this chapter argues that states should declare a state of emergency in response to public health crises similar to the Covid-19 pandemic in order to restrict the 'effect of a *de jure* state of emergency'[14] under limitation clauses. However, the central argument of this chapter goes beyond that and posits that a detailed and structured proportionality test must be developed to review emergency measures adopted during such crises. Drawing on the experience of judicial deference in Covid-19 cases, this chapter contends that judges should reconsider how the proportionality test is applied as their primary tool for reviewing human rights restrictions during pandemic emergencies. In particular, the assessment of legitimacy, suitability, necessity, and *stricto sensu*

11 A. Greene, 'States Should Declare a State of Emergency Using Article 15 ECHR to Confront the Coronavirus Pandemic', *Strasbourg Observers*, 1 April 2020 <https://strasbourgobservers.com/2020/04/01/states-should-declare-a-state-of-emergency-using-article-15-echr-to-confront-the-coronavirus-pandemic/>.

12 Ibid.

13 Look at: ECHR, Article 15 and International Covenant on Civil and Political Rights, 19 December 1966, 999 UNTS 171, Article 4.

14 A. Greene, above n. 11 (emphasis added).

proportionality is the core element of the proportionality test. This assessment must rigorously rely on clear and scientifically grounded evidence while also incorporating human rights and anti-discrimination considerations.

The development of the argument is divided into four sections. Section 2 investigates the relationship between the state of health emergency and the rule of law. This section demonstrates that, despite certain scholars arguing otherwise, the state of health emergency should be considered bound to the rule of law as one category among the general classification of the state of emergency. Besides empirical evidence, the section will elaborate on the approach of Hans Kelsen towards the relationship between the state of emergency and the rule of law based on his *Grundnorm* and identity theses, as they support this argument. Section 3 will demonstrate how considering the state of health emergency within the rule of law would entitle decisions made during the pandemic emergency to be subjected to judicial review. Section 4 turns to the case law of the European Court of Human Rights in Covid-19-related cases. It will demonstrate how the Court applied the proportionality test as the primary tool for assessing human rights derogations during the pandemic, offering a model for its potential approach in future public health emergencies. Finally, section 5 will introduce the elements and factors that courts should consider when the proportionality test is invoked based on the ECtHR approach in cases related to the Covid-19 pandemic.[15]

2 THE STATE OF EMERGENCY AND THE RULE OF LAW

An 'emergency' is a situation that seriously threatens 'public concerns' such as security, the environment, sanitation, or similar concerns.[16] It refers to any unforeseen event[17] that disrupts the normal functioning of a community and poses a threat to its very existence, requiring a rapid and effective response.[18]

---

15 To have an overview of the relevant cases, look at: L. Graham, 'Challenging State Responses to the Covid-19 Pandemic before the ECtHR', *Strasbourg Observers*, 18 October 2022 <https://strasbourgobservers.com/2022/10/18/challenging-state-responses-to-the-covid-19-pandemic-before-the-ecthr/>.

16 R. Geuss, *Public Goods, Private Goods*, Princeton and Oxford, Princeton University Press, 2003, p. 20.

17 D.E. Alexander, 'An Interpretation of Disaster in Terms of Changes in Culture, Society and International Relations' in R.W. Perry and E.L. Quarantelli (eds), *What is a Disaster?*, Philadelphia, Xlibris Press, 2005, pp. 25–38, cited H. Al-Dahash, M. Thayaparan and U. Kulatunga, 'Understanding the Terminologies: Disaster, Crisis and Emergency' in P.W. Chan and C.J. Neilson (eds), *Proceedings of the 32nd Annual ARCOM Conference*, Manchester, ARCOM, 2016, pp. 1191–200, p. 1192.

18 R. Khabook, 'Nexus Between Exceptionalism and Rule of Law in the Light of Governmentality' (2020) 7 *International Journal of Human Rights and Constitutional Studies* 175. And, WHO, 'Disasters and Emergencies: Definitions Training Package',

The 'state of emergency' denotes the legal and institutional modalities through which such a response is implemented.[19]

Since 9/11, discussions around the state of emergency have focused largely on national security crises and so have deliberations on the definition and delineation of the concept. A precise understanding of a state of emergency requires contextual analysis, including categorisation based on the nature and source of the threat. Tom Ginsburg and Mila Versteeg have attempted to categorise the state of emergency based on its sources.[20] In their understanding, a state of emergency can be based on threats to national security, but also financial crises, natural disasters, and pandemics. Considering the state of emergency as a legal-institutional formulation for tackling an emergency, categorising states of emergency is not a semantic exercise but a necessary exercise to determine appropriate legal responses. The modality of the authorities' responses can be differentiated based on the category an emergency situation belongs to.[21] As a consequence, it will be possible to introduce relevant 'social measures'[22] to tackle the situation even when they interfere with protected individual rights and to identify appropriate methods to control the scope of such measures and their impact on these individual rights.

During a pandemic, the state of emergency is usually based on an etiological threat.[23] As Ginsburg and Versteeg discuss, the onset of a pandemic-related crisis is slower compared to other emergencies.[24] Moreover, pandemic emergencies will last longer than national, financial, and natural disaster crises. All the mentioned factors indicate that the modality of responses in emergencies driven by pandemic diseases should differ from those of other types of emergencies. Because such emergencies develop slowly, persist for extended periods, and affect multiple sectors simultaneously, responses such as the distribution of information, the coordination of a united state response, and the provision of tools like diagnostic testing and personal protective equipment

WHO/EHA PanAfrican Emergency Training Centre, 2002, p. 10, cited in H. Al-Dahash, M. Thayaparan and U. Kulatunga, above n. 17.

19 N. Lazar, *State of Emergency in Liberal Democracies*, Cambridge, Cambridge University Press, 2009, pp. 38–39.

20 Look at: T. Ginsburg and M. Versteeg, above n. 7.

21 Ibid., 1498.

22 For understanding the social measures concept, look at: WHO, 'Public health and social measures during health emergencies', *WHO Public Health and Social Measures Initiative* <https://www.who.int/initiatives/who-public-health-and-social-measures-initiative>. Concerning this document by the WHO, one can say that social measures are those acts to tackle an emergency situation through imposing restrictions on the everyday life of citizens.

23 Etiology refers to the cause of a disease. For more information. Look at: 'etiology' in *Taber's Cyclopedic Medical Dictionary*, 24th ed., Philadelphia, F.A. Davis Company, 2021, available at <www.tabers.com/tabersonline/view/Tabers-Dictionary/731440/0/etiology?q=etiology>.

24 T. Ginsburg and M. Versteeg, above n. 7, 1510.

should be more decentralised and implemented at lower administrative levels than in other crises.[25]

The distinctive features of pandemic-related emergencies, as compared to other crises such as armed conflict, natural disasters, or financial instability, suggest the need to rethink how the law regulates states of emergency during pandemics. A reflection on pandemic emergencies highlights a long-standing scholarly tension related to the state of emergency, which focuses on whether the emergency is to be contained within the legal order or understood as a moment in which the sovereign steps 'beyond the law' and assumes unlimited authority.[26] In this sense, the state of emergency can be conceptualised as a 'space beyond law', in which the legal order, and consequently its inherent constraints, including human rights, democratic principles, and the rule of law, can be set aside.[27]

By contrast, this chapter argues that the legal order must govern an emergency. The sovereign, despite arguments advanced by legal scholars such as the Nazi jurist Carl Schmitt,[28] should remain subject to legal limits even in times of crisis. To clarify this position, one should turn to Hans Kelsen's response to Schmitt. For Kelsen, the legal order is a 'unified hierarchy of norms'.[29] In his theory, the validity of each norm stems from a higher valid legal norm.[30] This chain of validity finally ends with an ultimate foundational norm, which Kelsen calls *Grundnorm*.[31] By accepting Kelsen's *Grundnorm* theory, one can demonstrate the non-reductionist nature of the law, which allows distinguishing legal norms from other norms or orders,[32] such as morality or empirical facts.

The *Grundnorm* also leads to another of Kelsen's theories: the identity thesis. The identity thesis rejects the duality between the law and the state, instead regarding them as identical.[33] For those who adopt a dualist view, as Schmitt did, the state cannot be reduced to a 'juridical entity', so any legal

---

25 Ibid.

26 C. Schmitt, *Political Theology: Four Chapters on the Concept of Sovereignty* (G. Schwab trans.), Cambridge (MA), MIT Press, 1988, p. 6.

27 D. Dyzenhaus, 'Schmitt v. Dicey: Are States of Emergency Inside or Outside the Legal Order?' (2008) 27 *Cardozo Law Review* 2005, 2106.

28 For further information on Carl Schmitt's approach, look at: C. Schmitt, above n. 26. Also, A. Greene, *Permanent States of Emergency and the Rule of Law: Constitutions in an Age of Crisis*, Oxford, Hart Publishing, 2018. Also, O. Gross, 'The Normless and Exceptionless Exception: Carl Schmitt's Theory of Emergency Powers and the "Norm-Exception" Dichotomy' (1999) 21(5–6) *Cardozo Law Review* 1825. And, D. Dyzenhaus, above n. 27.

29 A. Greene, above n. 28, p. 67.

30 H. Kelsen, *Pure Theory of Law* (M. Knight trans.), Berkeley, University of California Press, 1967 p. 86.

31 H. Kelsen, *General Theory of Law and State*, New Jersey, The Lawbook Exchange Ltd, 1999, p. 111.

32 Ibid.

33 Ibid., p. 111.

restrictions imposed on the state reflect the state exercising its sovereign power to constrain itself.[34] In such a perspective, political decisions can override the legal order, and the sovereign becomes the goddess of the order and 'who decides on the state of exception'.[35] By contrast, Kelsen's approach, based on the *Grundnorm* and identity thesis, rejects Schmittian extra-legalism. Kelsenians argue that since the law and the state are identical, the state cannot act outside the legal order, even in times of emergency.[36] The Kelsenian approach replaces (political) decisionism with (legal) normativism, arguing that the state's practices should derive legitimacy from the law and maintain the state of emergency within the rule of law.

In conclusion, within a Kelsenian approach, the state of emergency is not an extra-legal situation that implies the application of other means, such as political decision-making rather than the law. For Kelsen, the state of emergency is a 'constitutional *lex specialis*'.[37] Ultimately, Kelsen's approach provides a framework in which the rule of law as a fundamental feature of the legal order retains its primacy even under emergency circumstances – no matter what the source of the emergency is – and reinforces legal continuity in times of emergency.[38] This is especially significant in the context of pandemics, where prolonged crises require stable legal mechanisms to maintain accountability, legitimacy, and coordinated responses.

3 THE RULE OF LAW AND JUDICIAL REVIEW IN TIMES OF EMERGENCY

Kelsen's approach, which emphasises that emergencies cannot justify violations of the rule of law or the grant of unlimited power to the authorities, is reflected in several international and national legal instruments. Article 4 of the International Covenant on Civil and Political Rights (ICCPR)[39] and Article 15 of the ECHR, for instance, restrict the state of emergency to situations that threaten 'the life of the nation' and designate certain rights as non-derogable,

---

[34] S. Baume, 'On Political Theology: A Controversy Between Hans Kelsen and Carl Schmitt' (2009) 35(3) *History of European Ideas* 369, 373.

[35] C. Schmitt, above n. 26, p. 5.

[36] T. Berkmanas, 'Schmitt v. (?) Kelsen: The Total State of Exception Posited for the Total Regulation of Life' (2010) 3(2) *Baltic Journal of Law & Politics* 98, 100.

[37] A. Zwitter, 'The Rule of Law in Times of Crisis: A Legal Theory on the State of Emergency in the Liberal Democracy' (2012) 98(1) *ARSP: Archiv für Rechts- und Sozialphilosophie / Archives for Philosophy of Law and Social Philosophy* 95, 101.

[38] For more information on the discussion between Kelsen and Schmitt on the legal order and its connection with the rule of law in times of emergency, look at: A. Greene, 'States of Emergency and the Rule of Law' in M. Sevel (ed), *Routledge Handbook of the Rule of Law*, London, Routledge, 2024, pp. 211–24.

[39] International Covenant on Civil and Political Rights, above n. 13.

thereby establishing clear legal limits for state authorities during emergencies. Similarly, approximately 90% of national constitutions include provisions on declaring a state of emergency and regulating the exercise of associated powers.[40]

Therefore, the acceptance of the necessity of adhering to legal constraints and consequently the rule of law in times of emergency is widely acknowledged in modern constitutional law. However, the mere existence of a law on a state of emergency within a legal framework does not guarantee that authorities will comply and thus does not ensure the non-violation of the rule of law during crises. It is necessary to impose a mechanism to ensure public authorities' compliance with the rule of law.

As Kelsen mentions, the constitution should 'designate the organ that has to decide whether or not the prescriptions regulating the legislative function were observed'.[41] Therefore, the judicial power can be introduced as the organ responsible for observing the conformity of the regulations to the rule of law.[42] Nevertheless, the functioning mechanism of judicial review in times of emergency is a challenging issue. In this regard, one can name two general approaches to judicial review in times of emergency. One approach is 'deferential judicial review,' and the other can be called 'restraining judicial review'. Each of these approaches can be seen in the light of Adrian Vermeule's models of constitutionalism.[43] According to Vermeule, there are two approaches towards constitutionalism: precautionary constitutionalism and optimising constitutionalism.[44] The difference between these two models of constitutionalism lies in how a constitution will approach the management

---

40 C. Bjørnskov and S. Voigt, 'The architecture of emergency constitutions' (2018) 16(1) *International Journal of Constitutional Law* 101. Among 40 European countries, 38 countries have an article related to the state of emergency. For more information, look at: A. Horváth, 'Emergency Regimes in the European Constitutions – A Comparative Overview' (2025) 16(2) *European Journal of Risk Regulation* 388.

41 H. Kelsen, above n. 31, p. 156.

42 It is worth mentioning that various scholars argue against the authority of the judicial power over the executive and legislative in reviewing their decisions in light of the rule of law. They argue that since the legislature and the executive are democratically elective representations, their decisions mirror the desires of society. Therefore, judges as non-elected authorities should not have power over them. Regarding the limits of the space and lack of direct relevancy of the issue to the topic of this chapter, one follows the overall acceptance of the authority of judges over other powers through judicial review. For further information about the challenge between the judicial review and democratically elected powers, look at: M. Loughlin, *Against Constitutionalism*, Cambridge (MA), Harvard University Press, 2022. Also, J.N. Shklar, 'Political Theory and the Rule of Law' in A.C. Hutchinson and P.J. Monahan (eds), *The Rule of Law: Ideal or Ideology*, Toronto, Carswell, 1987, pp. 1–16. And, D. Feldman, 'Democracy, the Rule of Law and Judicial Review' (1990) 19(1) *Federal Law Review* 1.

43 Look at: A. Vermeule, *The Constitution of Risk*, Cambridge, Cambridge University Press, 2014.

44 Ibid., pp. 27–91.

of first- and second-order risks. First-order risks arise from everyday events, such as technological, economic, or natural threats, while second-order risks are related to the structure and power distribution of institutions.[45] However, a closer analysis reveals a nexus between these risk categories: in an emergency, a second-order risk may emerge while authorities are addressing a first-order risk.

Optimising constitutionalism, by emphasising the necessity of tackling first-order risks, suggests that the potential for second-order risks should be overlooked or mitigated. According to this view, risks related to the structure and power distribution of institutions are not as severe as precautionary constitutionalists claim, and prioritising their avoidance may obstruct the state in achieving its ultimate aim: the public interest. Optimising constitutionalists treat the Constitution as a risk-management tool that must weigh and balance different types of political risks contextually, rather than applying a blanket bias against one type of risk. Therefore, they emphasise the need to trade off 'all relevant political risks, [...] without any systemic skew or bias against any particular type of political risk'.[46]

Optimising constitutionalists argue that overemphasis on preventing government overreach (a second-order risk) can hinder effective responses to emergencies (first-order risks). Consequently, they contend that the executive branch is best equipped to handle crises without restrictive oversight,[47] as it has more institutional capacity to determine emergencies accurately, rapidly, and flexibly compared to legislative and judicial powers.[48] Supporters of optimising constitutionalism somehow echo Schmitt's famous assertion[49] ('Sovereign is he who decides on the state of exception')[50] and oppose holding the executive accountable when declaring emergencies and necessary responses. This standpoint's proponents suggest that legislative and judiciary powers should 'defer to the executive branch'.[51]

In contrast to supporters of optimising constitutionalism and judicial deference, scholars of precautionary constitutionalism highlight the political

---

45 Ibid., pp. 6–8.

46 A. Vermeule quoted in G. Martinico and M. Simoncini, 'Emergency and Risk in Comparative Public Law', *Verfassungsblog*, 9 May 2020 <https://verfassungsblog.de/emergency-and-risk-in-comparative-public-law/>.

47 A. Vermeule, above n. 43, p. 45.

48 E.A. Posner and A. Vermeule, *Terror in the Balance: Security, Liberty, and the Courts*, Oxford, Oxford University Press, 2007, pp. 42–45.

49 Their argument is not exactly the same as Schmitt's argument. Schmitt considers the state of emergency as beyond the law, while the optimising constitutionalists defend the so-called 'legal black holes'. Legal black holes are still part of the legal order but without the restrictions prescribed by the law, such as the rule of law. For further information, look at: D. Dyzenhaus, above n. 27.

50 C. Schmitt, above n. 26, p. 5.

51 E.A. Posner and A. Vermeule, above n. 48, p. 45.

risks of emergencies and the potential for executive power abuse. They seek mechanisms for reviewing executive actions and emergency legislation by employing restraining judicial review. This group maintains that the mere existence of an emergency does not justify human rights restrictions in the name of public interest; any such restrictions must be properly justified before a court.[52]

However, it should be mentioned that the supporters of restraining judicial review among the precautionary constitutionalists should be divided into two groups. A first group of scholars, such as Robert Alexy, support judicial review based on the balancing method. This group classifies human rights and public interests as 'principles' within the broader category of 'constitutional rights'.[53] According to Alexy, constitutional rights 'have a double character, namely they are both rules and principles'.[54] The distinction between rules and principles lies in whether they can be overridden. Rules, Alexy argues, are norms that are either fully adhered to or not,[55] making them 'definitive reasons'.[56] When two rules come into conflict, either an exception must be introduced or one rule must be invalidated.[57] By contrast, principles are 'optimisation requirements'[58] that act as 'prima facie reasons'.[59] Principles can be satisfied to varying degrees, depending on what is factually possible and what is legally possible.[60] In conflicts between principles, it is not necessary to introduce an exception or invalidate one; instead, one principle is 'displaced' by the other. In such situations, the weight of a particular principle allows judges to prioritise it over the other.[61]

Proponents of balancing follow the 'weight formula',[62] which considers three main factors: the intensity of interference, the abstract weight of the principle,

---

52 For example, look at: J. Ferejohn and P. Pasquino, 'The law of the exception: A typology of emergency powers' (2004) 2(2) *International Journal of Constitutional Law* 210. Also, B. Ackerman, 'The Emergency Constitution' (2004) 113 *Yale Law Journal* 1029, 1047–50. Also, T.R.S. Allan, 'Human Rights and Judicial Review: A Critique of "Due Deference"' (2006) 65(3) *Cambridge Law Journal* 671, 676. And C.R. Sunstein, *One Case at a Time: Judicial Minimalism on the Supreme Court*, Cambridge (MA), Harvard University Press, 2001.

53 R. Alexy, *A Theory of Constitutional Rights* (J. Rivers trans.), Oxford, Oxford University Press, 2009, pp. 44–69.

54 P.C. Vasiloyannis, 'Book Review: A Theory of Constitutional Rights' (2004) 55(2) *Northern Ireland Legal Quarterly* 206.

55 R. Alexy, above n. 53, p. 47.

56 Ibid., p. 57.

57 Ibid., p. 49.

58 Ibid., p. 47

59 Ibid., p. 57.

60 Ibid., pp. 47–48.

61 Ibid., p. 50.

62 R. Alexy, 'On Balancing and Subsumption. A Structural Comparison' (2003) 16(4) *Ratio Juris* 433.

and the certainty of underlying assumptions.[63] The first factor, 'intensity', measures how severely a decision affects a principle – greater interference requires stronger justification. Second, the abstract weight reflects a principle's importance within the legal system. Fundamental rights, for example, often hold greater weight due to their central role in the legal order. Finally, certainty assesses the reliability of the decision's empirical and normative basis. High certainty strengthens a principle's weight, while low certainty weakens it. The weight formula thus provides a structured method for determining when one principle should take precedence over another.[64]

The second group among the supporters of restraining judicial review criticises the balancing method as an unduly 'flexible'[65] method, treating the criteria for justifying an act as being on a 'horizontal'[66] level in relation to one another. They argue that, despite attempts to systematise the weighing process, balancing ultimately relies on 'subjective and decisionist evaluations'[67] rather than on 'rational standards',[68] and thus 'takes place arbitrarily or unreflectively'.[69]

In light of these critiques, opponents of the balancing method propose the proportionality test as an alternative approach to conducting judicial review in times of emergency.[70] In the proportionality test, as compared to the balancing method, the judge is not able to choose between alternative solutions[71] but merely tests the proportionality of the chosen means from the perspective of

---

63 For more information look at: R. Alexy, 'Proportionality and Rationality' in M. Tushnet and V.C. Jackson (eds), *Proportionality: New Frontiers, New Challenges*, Cambridge, Cambridge University Press, 2017, pp. 11–12.

64 For more information about balancing, look at: V.A. da Silva, 'Das Abwägen von Prinzipien in einer Welt voller Regeln' in C. Bäcker (ed), *Rechtsdiskurs, Rechtsprinzipien, Rechtsbegriff: Elemente einer diskursiven Theorie fundamentaler Rechte. Symposium zum 75. Geburtstag von Robert Alexy*, Tübingen, Mohr Siebeck, 2022, pp. 217–46.

65 J. Christoffersen, *Fair Balance: Proportionality, Subsidiarity and Primarity in the European Convention on Human Rights*, Leiden, Martinus Nijhoff, 2009, p. 71.

66 Ibid.

67 B. Schlink, 'Der Grundsatz der Verhältnismäßigkeit' in P. Badura and H. Dreier (eds), *Festschrift 50 Jahre Bundesverfassungsgericht*, vol. II, Tübingen, Mohr Siebeck, 2001, pp. 445–65, cited in R. Alexy, above n. 62.

68 J. Habermas, *Between Facts and Norms: Contributions to a Discourse Theory of Law and Democracy* (W. Rehg trans.), Cambridge (MA), MIT Press, 2001, p. 259.

69 Ibid.

70 Virgílio Afonso da Silva mentions that balancing plays three roles in the application of legal rules. These roles are: (1) it may be part of the interpretive process of legal provisions (interpretation); (2) it may be employed as a justification for teleological reduction or analogical extension (correction); and (3) it may be part of a broader procedure – the proportionality test – aimed at reviewing the compatibility of an ordinary rule with a constitutional provision (judicial review). For more information, look at: V.A. Da Silva, above n. 64.

71 V.A. Da Silva, 'Balancing may be everywhere, but the proportionality test is not' (2023) 13(3) *Global Constitutionalism* 519.

the four sub-tests[72] in a vertical relation: legitimacy, suitability, necessity, and proportionality *stricto sensu*[73] or as some scholars say, the balancing.[74]

To understand the difference between the proportionality test and the balancing test, one should go beyond the definition of the weight formula in the balancing test. Advocates of the proportionality test argue against two points in the balancing. First, critics argue that Alexy's balancing method undermines the concept of absolute rights. Since all rights can be weighed against public interests through the weight formula, even non-derogable rights – such as the prohibition of torture or slavery – may be overridden if the public interest is deemed sufficiently strong. This implies that no right is immune from limitation, effectively eliminating the category of absolute rights.[75]

Second, critics reject Alexy's conceptual framework, which treats both human rights and public interests as 'principles' and subjects them to the same balancing logic. Drawing on Ronald Dworkin's distinction between principles and 'policies', [76] they argue that rights function as 'trumps' that cannot be overridden by mere policy considerations.[77] In this view, rights are principles and public interests are policies; therefore, they are fundamentally different

---

72 There is an ongoing debate about the structure and application of the proportionality test, particularly in the jurisprudence of the ECtHR. Although the ECtHR has never provided a comprehensive explanation of its methodology, it frequently invokes the proportionality test to assess whether a measure is 'necessary in a democratic society'. In developing this chapter's argument on the modalities of the proportionality test, one draws on the well-established principles of German administrative and constitutional law. This approach is justified by the notable parallels between the ECtHR's reasoning and the German model, as seen in cases such as *Thlimmenos v. Greece*, no. 34369/97, 6 April 2000. For more information, look at: H.J. Lee, 'Principle of Proportionality in the Case Law of the ECtHR' in H.J. Lee (ed), *Discrimination Based on Sexual Orientation: Jurisprudence of the European Court of Human Rights and the Constitutional Court of Korea*, Cham, Springer, 2022, pp. 121–64. Also, J. Fan, 'Rethinking the Method and Function of the Proportionality Test in the European Court of Human Rights' (2016) 15(1) *Journal of Human Rights* 47. And, A. Barak, 'Proportionality *Stricto Sensu* (Balancing)' in A. Barak, *Proportionality: Constitutional Rights and Their Limitations*, Cambridge, Cambridge University Press, 2012, pp. 340–70.

73 In various research projects and also according to the tradition of the European Court of Human Rights, proportionality is based on three tests. Accordingly, the legitimacy and suitability tests have been conceived as interconnected. Therefore, in such cases, one can see the reference to the three sub-tests, including suitability, necessity, and proportionality, in a narrow sense.

74 Look at: A. Barak, above n. 72.

75 Robert Alexy, in his book, after accepting that there is no absolute principle, by referring to Article 1(1)(1) of the German Basic Law, tries to justify his theory regarding the possibility of violating human dignity. In his argument, he says human dignity has two characteristics as a norm: a rule and a principle. Therefore, when human dignity stands as a rule, it cannot be violated. In other cases, human dignity is a mere principle that can be balanced before other principles, i.e. other rights or public interests. For more information, look at: R. Alexy, above n. 53, pp. 62–64.

76 R. Dworkin (ed), *Taking Rights Seriously*, London, Bloomsbury, 2013, p. 107.

77 Ibid., p. 110.

in nature and cannot be reduced to a shared metric.[78] These scholars do not claim that rights may never be limited, but they maintain that a particularly compelling justification is required to do so.[79] Consequently, they support the proportionality test, which offers a structured method for evaluating the legitimacy of rights limitations in exceptional circumstances.[80]

The preceding discussion has examined how the relationship between the state of emergency and the rule of law necessitates careful consideration of mechanisms that ensure compliance with the rule of law during exceptional circumstances. Drawing on Kelsen's theory and the general practice in European states of establishing judicial review as a safeguard,[81] this section has evaluated the role and structure of judicial oversight in times of emergency. It argued that courts should not adopt a deferential stance toward the executive and legislative branches but should instead assume an active role in constraining the exercise of emergency powers. Crucially, this judicial restraint must go beyond the conventional balancing approach, which merely weighs public interests against individual rights. Rather, a strictly vertical model of review is needed, one that applies the proportionality test through its structured, sequential sub-tests. Given its detailed analytical framework and its stronger orientation toward upholding the rule of law and protecting human rights, this chapter advances the proportionality test as the preferred method for judicial review in emergency contexts.

4 THE STRASBOURG COURT IN THE TIME OF COVID-19 EMERGENCY

The previous sections have established the inclusion of the state of emergency within the rule of law. Moreover, after evaluating various approaches to judicial review in times of emergency, previous sections have concluded that the proportionality test is the most effective approach for judicial review. The evaluation of the Court's judgments in Covid-19 cases sheds light on what could constitute a proportionality-test-based review in future pandemic cases.

The ECtHR's understanding of the proportionality test appears vague and unclear compared to the above-discussed proportionality test based on four sub-tests. In the ECtHR's cases, the proportionality refers to the assessment

---

78 F. Schauer, 'Commensurability and Its Constitutional Consequences' (1994) 45(4) *Hastings Law Journal* 785.

79 R. Dworkin, above n. 76, p. 231.

80 J. Weinrib, 'When Trumps Clash: Dworkin and the Doctrine of Proportionality' (2017) 30(3) *Ratio Juris* 341, 343.

81 Look at: Venice Commission, 'Rule of Law Checklist', 18 March 2016, CDL-AD(2016)007.

of the adopted measures as 'necessary in a democratic society'.[82] The Court, in *Sunday Times v. United Kingdom*, described the proportionality test in further detail as a measure to assess the interference with human rights in line with pursuing a legitimate aim, relevant, and sufficient to the intended aim.[83] In light of the aforementioned case and after further development of the proportionality test in ECtHR judgments, various scholars define the proportionality test based on four sub-tests, including legitimacy, suitability, necessity, and proportionality *stricto sensu*.[84]

It should be noted that the Court, in the application of the proportionality test, often refers to the margin of appreciation doctrine. The margin of appreciation should be seen as a tool in the hands of the ECtHR to defer to the Member States' interpretation in applying the ECHR.[85] The Court, in applying the margin of appreciation, does not follow a consistent method. The scale of the margin of appreciation moves between a 'wide' and 'narrow' margin, which respectively indicate that the Court will apply either light or strict scrutiny.[86]

Regarding the interconnection between the proportionality test and margin of appreciation in the Court's decision-making processes, understanding the degree of margin of appreciation in Covid-19 cases is essential. In light of the WHO's PHEIC declaration and the rapid increase of infections, the Court's Member States adopted far-reaching measures that restrict the exercise of certain rights. While most governments relied on the ordinary limitation clauses of the Convention, a small number formally notified derogations under ECHR, Article 15.[87] In several cases, many citizens decided to bring their

---

82 Look at: ECHR, Articles 6(1), 8(2), 9(2), 10(2), 11(2); ECHR, Protocol No. 1, Article 1; ECHR, Protocol No. 4, Article 2(3); and ECHR, Protocol No. 7, Article 2. And *Handyside v. United Kingdom*, no. 5493/72, 7 December 1976, § 49, Series A no. 24.

83 *Sunday Times v. United Kingdom (No. 1)*, no. 6538/74, 26 April 1979, Series A no. 30.

84 Look at: I. Porat, 'Proportionality' in *Max Planck Encyclopedia of Comparative Constitutional Law*, Oxford, Oxford University Press, 2018. Also, E. Brems and L. Lavrysen, '"Don't Use a Sledgehammer to Crack a Nut": Less Restrictive Means in the Case Law of the European Court of Human Rights' (2015) 15(1) *Human Rights Law Review* 139, 139–68. Also, A.V. Dolzhikov, 'The European Court of Human Rights on the Principle of Proportionality in "Russian" Cases' (2012) 82 *Teise* 215, 215–24. Also, H.J. Lee, above n. 72. Also, J. Fan, above n. 72. And A. Barak, above n. 72.

85 Y. Arai-Takahashi, *The Margin of Appreciation Doctrine and the Principle of Proportionality in the Jurisprudence of the ECHR*, Cambridge, Intersentia, 2002, cited in I. Porat, above n. 84. And, H.J. Lee, above n. 72, p. 125.

86 L. Lavrysen, *Human Rights in a Positive State: Rethinking the Relationship between Positive and Negative Obligations under the European Convention on Human Rights*, Cambridge, Intersentia, 2016, p. 189, cited in H.J. Lee, above n. 72, p. 126.

87 Most derogation measures affected the right to liberty and security (Article 5), the right to a fair trial (Article 6), the right to respect for private and family life (Article 8), the freedom of thought, conscience and religion (Article 9), the freedom of expression (Article 10), the freedom of assembly and association (Article 11), and rights under the First Protocol, particularly the protection of property (Article 1) and the right to education (Article 2). For further information, look at: R. Friedery and G. Kecskés, 'Fundamental (Human)

complaints against these measures during the pandemic before the ECtHR.[88] In those cases where the Court found the applications admissible, it is evident that a wide margin of appreciation was granted.

The application of a wide margin of appreciation in Covid-19 cases can be seen through the lens of the following reasoning. First, as the Court formerly mentioned in *Vavřička and Others v. Czech Republic*, 'in matters of public-health policy and the prevention of the spreading of very serious diseases, the States enjoy a wide margin of appreciation'.[89] References to this case, despite its focus on mandatory child vaccination, appeared in cases related to rights limitation and derogation during the Covid-19 pandemic in order to demonstrate the Court's precedent in granting a wide margin of appreciation in issues related to public health.[90] Moreover, scholars such as Ronagh McQuigg, in line with *Dickson v. United Kingdom*,[91] have pointed out that in the case of a lack of consensus among the Member States on 'the importance of the interest at stake or as to how best to protect it', the Court can impose a wide margin of appreciation.[92] The reference to the lack of consensus and consequently allowing a wide margin of appreciation in finding the best measures to protect the public interest appeared in Covid-19 cases as well.[93] Finally, the ECtHR invokes the wide margin of appreciation in cases related to human rights derogations during emergencies.[94] The Court, in assessing measures under ECHR, Article 15, first determines whether a 'public emergency threatening the life of the nation' exists and whether the measures taken are 'strictly

Rights versus Emergency Measures: Excerpts from the Case-law of the CJEU and ECtHR' (2024) 63(2) *Quarterly on Refugee Problems – AWR Bulletin* 170, 178. Also, H. Keller and V. Gurash, 'Proportionality of the COVID-19 Measures: The European Court of Human Rights' Approach' in N. Biller-Andorno, J. W. März, C. Mouton-Dorey and S. Dagron (eds.), *Proportionality*, Oxford, Oxford University Press, 2025, 222–236. And, R.J.A. McQuigg, *The European Convention on Human Rights and the COVID-19 Pandemic*, Abingdon, Routledge, 2024, p. 41.

88 In order to have an overview of the recent cases, look at: ECtHR, 'COVID-19 health crisis', above n. 1. And, R.J.A. McQuigg, above n. 87. It should be noted that the provided lists in the mentioned references are not exhaustive. Also, a considerable number of cases are ongoing.

89 *Vavřička and Others v. Czech Republic*, nos. 47631/13, 3867/14, 73094/14, 19298/15, 19306, and 43883/15, 8 April 2021, § 212.

90 For instance, look at: the dissenting opinion in *Communauté genevoise d'action syndicale (CGAS) v. Switzerland*, no. 21881/20, 27 November 2023. And, *Pasquinelli and Others v. San Marino*, no. 24622/22, 29 August 2024, § 128.

91 *Dickson v. United Kingdom*, no. 44362/04, 4 December 2007.

92 R.J.A. McQuigg, above n. 87, pp. 15–16.

93 For example, look at: *Communauté genevoise d'action syndicale (CGAS) v. Switzerland*, above n. 90, § 160. And, *Pasquinelli and Others v. San Marino*, above n. 90, § 92.

94 Look at: ECtHR, 'Guide on Article 15 of the Convention – Derogation in time of emergency', October 2024 <https://ks.echr.coe.int/documents/d/echr-ks/guide_art_15_eng>.

required by the exigencies of the situation'.[95] However, the Court's deference in reviewing Article 15 cases is not limited to determining the existence of an emergency. Judges of the Court also consider the national authorities better suited agents to decide 'on the nature and the scope' of measures during an emergency.[96] Therefore, in those cases related to Article 15, in line with the decision on *Ireland v. United Kingdom*[97] and the Council of Europe's Covid-19 toolkit,[98] the Court is entitled to refer to a wide margin of appreciation.[99]

Overall, a cursory glance at the Court's Covid-19 judgments shows that, so far, the ECtHR has decided to consider most cases inadmissible. The few inadmissibility decisions were either because of the applicant's failure to exhaust the domestic remedies or a lack of demonstration of personal concern and significant disadvantage.[100] In the remaining cases that were deemed admissible, the Court's reasoning reveals a clear tendency to defer to states' discretion by granting a wide margin of appreciation.[101]

Nevertheless, the wide margin of appreciation should not be considered as granting a blank cheque to the Member States. In other words, as the Court mentioned in *Brannigan and McBride v. United Kingdom*,[102] the wide margin of appreciation is not equivalent to 'an unlimited power of appreciation'. Therefore, the Court must still apply thorough scrutiny. The importance of not falling for intense judicial deference – a wide margin of appreciation – has been emphasised by Jonas Christoffersen[103] and Janneke Gerards[104] in

---

95 Ibid. It should be noted that in regular rights limitation, the Court evaluates the mere proportionality of the measures. In cases related to Article 15, the Court examines both the legitimacy of the emergency invoked and whether the derogating measures remain necessary and proportionate to the threat.

96 *Brannigan and McBride v. United Kingdom*, nos. 14553/89 and 14554/89, 26 May 1993, § 43, Series A no. 258-B; *Ireland v. United Kingdom*, no. 5310/71, 18 January 1978, § 48, Series A no. 25.

97 *Ireland v. United Kingdom*, above n. 96.

98 Council of Europe, 'Respecting democracy, rule of law and human rights in the framework of the COVID-19 sanitary crisis: A toolkit for member states', 7 April 2020, SG/Inf(2020)11, p. 2.

99 In *CGAS v. Switzerland*, above n. 90, and *Terheş v. Romania* (dec.), no. 49933/20, 13 April 2021, there is only a brief reference to Article 15. In both cases, however, the Court did not assess the claims from the perspective of derogation, as Article 15 was not relevant to the applicants' arguments. At the time of writing this chapter, the communicated case of *Pešić and Others v. Serbia*, nos. 48973/20, 54565/20 and 54676/20, includes a reference to Article 15. However, since no decision has yet been issued, an analysis of the Court's approach remains premature.

100 ECtHR, 'Guide on Article 15 of the Convention – Derogation in time of emergency', above n. 94.

101 Look at: *Pasquinelli and Others v. San Marino*, above n. 90. Also, *Constantin-Lucian Spînu v. Romania*, no. 29443/20, 11 October 2022. And, *Terheş v. Romania*, above n. 99.

102 *Brannigan and McBride v. United Kingdom*, above n. 96, § 44.

103 J. Christoffersen, above n. 65, p. 170.

104 J. Gerards, 'How to improve the necessity test of the European Court of Human Rights' (2013) 11(2) *International Journal of Constitutional Law* 466, 474.

those cases in which the derogation or the relevant curtailed right is essential for a democratic society. The point of taking the proportionality test in such cases seriously, even in the case of a wide margin of appreciation, has been addressed in the Chamber's decision on *Communauté Genevoise d'Action Syndicale (CGAS) v. Switzerland.*[105] In this case, the Chamber, after recognising the margin of appreciation of the Swiss government and acknowledging the exceptional circumstances of Covid-19, nevertheless found a violation of ECHR, Article 11.[106] However, after the request for referral by the Swiss government, the Grand Chamber took a different standpoint on the case compared to the Chamber's decision. Accordingly, the Grand Chamber added this case to the long list of inadmissible Covid-19 cases due to the lack of direct victim status and the non-exhaustion of domestic remedies.

Although the Chamber's decision in *CGAS* offered a glimmer of hope for a more rigorous application of the proportionality test, even within a wide margin of appreciation, it was ultimately overshadowed by the Grand Chamber's final ruling, which dashed those expectations. As noted by the five dissenting judges, the Chamber's approach had opened the door to developing a form of 'crisis law' under the ECHR, which they described as a framework for addressing the vulnerability of democratic principles during emergencies, aiming to limit states' 'margin of improvisation', and reduce 'the risk of abuse' in future crises.[107] Nevertheless, after the decision of the Grand Chamber, a closer examination of how the proportionality test is applied during pandemics remains essential and requires further development to mitigate the risk of power abuse in future public health emergencies.

5 PROPORTIONALITY-TEST-BASED JUDICIAL REVIEW IN TIMES OF PANDEMIC EMERGENCY

The ECtHR's inadmissibility decision in *CGAS* denies 'definitive guidance'[108] on the application of the proportionality test in pandemic-related cases. The following lines develop a detailed instruction to test the proportionality of adopted measures during the Covid-19 pandemic to provide a roadmap for pending cases and future events. Having a detailed instruction for the proportionality test in times of pandemic emergencies prevents the Court from handing states a blank cheque through a deferential approach. Consequently,

---

105 *Communauté genevoise d'action syndicale (CGAS) v. Switzerland*, above n. 90.

106 Ibid., § 90.

107 Ibid., dissenting opinion § 10.

108 R.J.A. McQuigg, 'The COVID-19 Pandemic and the European Court of Human Rights – The Grand Chamber Decision in *Communaute Genevoise D'Action Syndicale (CGAS) v. Switzerland*' in P. Czech, L. Heschl, K. Lukas, M. Nowak and G. Oberleitner (eds), *European Yearbook on Human Rights 2024*, Leiden, Brill, 2025, pp. 169–87.

the arguments on the modalities of sub-tests of the proportionality test should be seen as providing a practical solution to contradict those scholars who support limitations clauses in times of pandemic emergencies and the granting a wide margin of appreciation to the states.

The argument about the need for more detailed instruction is rooted in the International Covenant on Civil and Political Rights (ICCPR)'s General Comment No. 29 on Article 4, a provision that shares important similarities with Article 15 of the ECHR. The General Comment stresses the necessity of a careful justification for derogatory measures, particularly 'in other situations than an armed conflict'. [109] This highlights that public health emergencies, unlike armed conflicts, present distinct challenges that demand specific and detailed justifications for any human rights restrictions. In such contexts, the proportionality test must be applied with greater precision and nuance. Guidance on how this test should be interpreted and operationalised in public health emergencies can be found in instruments such as the WHO guidelines and the International Health Regulations (IHR).[110] What follows is an examination of how the sub-tests of the proportionality principle – suitability, necessity, and proportionality *stricto sensu* – should be applied in the context of pandemic response measures.

5.1. The Legitimacy Test

Under the legitimacy test, the Court should investigate whether the adopted measures serve a lawful objective. Lawfulness requires that the measures pursue a goal recognised as valid under constitutional law or human rights law.[111] In the context of a public health emergency, the legitimacy of derogating from human rights should generally be understood as aiming to 'protect people's lives (preventing death) and health (preventing, in particular, severe cases of COVID-19)'.[112] Such obligations may even fall within the scope of states'

[109] International Covenant on Civil and Political Rights (ICCPR), 'General Comment No. 29: States of Emergency (Article 4)', 31 August 2001, UN Doc. CCPR/C/21/Rev.1/Add.11 (GC29), para. 3.

[110] WHO, *International Health Regulations (2005)*, 3rd ed., Geneva, WHO, 2016. Although the International Health Regulations (IHR) have been amended in the aftermath of the Covid-19 pandemic, this chapter refers to the version that was in force prior to these amendments, as it constituted the applicable regulatory framework during the Covid-19 period.

[111] A. Barak, *Proportionality: Constitutional Rights and Their Limitations*, Cambridge, Cambridge University Press, 2012, pp. 245–51.

[112] K. Möller, 'The proportionality of lockdowns' in P. Sutoris, A. Mendes Borger, S. Murphy and Y. Nehushtan (eds), *Pandemic Response and the Cost of Lockdowns: Global Debates from Humanities and Social Sciences*, 1st ed., Abingdon, Routledge, 2022, pp. 157–70, 159.

positive obligations. Positive obligations refer to the state's responsibility to take necessary measures to safeguard a right.[113]

Accordingly, the ECtHR can interpret derogations during the pandemic as efforts to fulfil positive obligations to protect life and health. However, when evaluating the legitimacy of these derogatory measures, it is important to note that their objective is typically the protection of public health and safety at large, rather than the life or health of a specific individual. These measures, which often apply to the whole population, are designed to serve public interest, even if this means temporarily restricting individual rights.[114]

Understanding derogation as a means of serving the public interest is also critical when applying the proportionality test, which differs fundamentally from a simple balancing of rights and interests. In proportionality analysis, rights are presumed to have a superior normative weight compared to public interests. Therefore, any derogation must be justified through a rigorous, structured assessment, rather than a general or abstract balancing of competing values.

Traces of consideration for the legitimacy of restrictive measures during a public health emergency can be found in *Le Mailoux v. France*,[115] a case that came before the ECtHR during the Covid-19 pandemic. Here, the Court adopted a cautious approach and did not allow the imposition of excessive protective measures in response to a public health emergency. In this case, the Court rejected an application arguing that the French government had failed to impose sufficient restrictions to protect lives and public health. The Court's decision was based on procedural grounds, as the applicant could not establish himself as a direct victim of the government's failure to implement stricter measures. While this demonstrates the Court's strict adherence to the requirement of victim status, it also highlights the procedural barriers to claims that seek broader public interest protections over individual rights.

5.2. The Suitability Test

When considering public health measures as manifestations of states' positive obligations, one can turn to the second sub-test within the proportionality test – suitability. As the ECtHR held in *López Ostra v. Spain*,[116] states must demonstrate the reasonableness and suitability of their measures when

[113] 'Toolkit: Some definitions', *Council of Europe* <https://www.coe.int/en/web/echr-toolkit/definitions>. And, *López Ostra v. Spain*, no. 16798/90, 9 December 1994, Series A no. 303-C.

[114] G.D.L. Machado, 'Health as a Purpose or as a Right – The Principle of Proportionality and the Measures Against the Covid-19 Pandemic' (2022) 16(3) *ICL Journal* 353, 358, 359.

[115] *Le Mailloux v. France* (dec.), no. 18108/20, 3 December 2020.

[116] *López Ostra v. Spain*, above n. 113.

fulfilling positive obligations.[117] While the *López Ostra v. Spain* case concerned environmental harm, its reasoning is readily extendable to public health crises, reinforcing the principle that state responses must be both proportionate and effective in addressing risks to life and health.[118]

The ECtHR's emphasis on the reasonableness and suitability of adopted measures in *López Ostra v. Spain* can be understood as requiring a demonstrable 'causal link between the means and ends'.[119] In this sense, the suitability test functions as an assessment of the effectiveness of the adopted measures.[120]

However, drawing on the ECtHR's jurisprudence, one may argue that the evaluation of suitability is not governed by 'rigid rules'.[121] Instead, the standard of proof required shifts depending on the context, ranging along a spectrum from '*prima facie* evidence, the preponderance of evidence, and beyond a reasonable doubt'.[122] This variability becomes especially relevant in so-called 'hard cases', where the facts are complex, scientific uncertainty is high, and the stakes are significant.[123] In such situations, as discussed in the previous section, the Court typically affords Member States a wide margin of appreciation, recognising their institutional competence and proximity to the facts.[124] As a result, the suitability test in these cases becomes more deferential and less predictable, allowing for flexibility in the face of competing scientific, legal and policy considerations.

Nevertheless, the ECtHR should adopt a more rigorous and structured approach in cases concerning public health emergencies, particularly where such measures affect multiple rights or interests in a democratic society over an extended period, as seen during the Covid-19 pandemic. In developing this approach, the Court should prioritise precise judicial scrutiny, rather than deferring to the absence of scientific consensus or the uncertainty surrounding the justification and effectiveness of restrictive measures.

---

117 *López Ostra v. Spain*, above n. 113, § 51.

118 *López Ostra v. Spain*, above n. 113.

119 J. Gerards, above n. 104, 474.

120 Ibid.

121 J. Christoffersen, above n. 65, p. 174.

122 Ibid.

123 Ibid., p. 163.

124 For example, look at: *Lawless v. Ireland (No. 3)*, no. 332/57, 1 July 1961, Series A no. 3. Also, *Ireland v. United Kingdom*, above n. 96, § 207. Also, *Brannigan and McBride v. United Kingdom*, above n. 96, § 44. And, *A and Others v. United Kingdom*, no. 3455/05, 19 February 2009. It should be mentioned that in a few cases, the ECtHR did not defer to the national authorities and discussed the effectiveness of the measures. For example, look at: *Denmark, Norway, Sweden, and the Netherlands v. Greece*, , nos. 3321/67, 3322/67, 3323/67, and 3344/67, 5 July 1969, Series A no. 8. And, *Soltysyak v. Russia*, no. 4663/05, 10 February 2011. For more information, look at: C. Jing, 'The ECtHR's suitability test in national security cases: Two models for balancing human rights and national security' (2023) 36(2) *Leiden Journal of International Law* 295, 312.

In this regard, Article 43.2 of the IHR 2005 provides that any measure adopted in response to 'specific public health risks or public health emergencies of international concern [(PHEIC)]' must be grounded in 'scientific evidence'.[125] Reference to the IHR is fully justified, as ECHR, Article 15 expressly requires that any derogation must not be inconsistent with a state's other obligations under international law. Among these, the IHR constitute a key normative framework governing state conduct in public health emergencies. Accordingly, public health measures should be based on:

(a) scientific principles;
(b) available scientific evidence of a risk to human health, or where such evidence is insufficient, the available information including from WHO and other relevant intergovernmental organisations and international bodies; and
(c) any available specific guidance or advice from WHO.[126]

Therefore, when applying the suitability test as a means to protect the rule of law, the ECtHR should request scientific evidence from the responsible authorities rather than granting them a wide margin of appreciation. Insisting on such scientific evidence allows for judicial scrutiny of the actual effectiveness of emergency measures and can challenge overly broad derogations. For instance, during the Covid-19 pandemic, some public health lawyers and experts questioned the justification for international travel restrictions, large-scale quarantines, and blanket lockdowns, relying on pre-existing research, WHO pandemic-response guidelines, and early-stage modelling studies, which mainly were in contrast with the states' derogatory measures.[127] Notably, the WHO's own pre-Covid-19 guidelines either ruled out lockdowns or made no mention of them, and past public health experiences, such as the 2003 SARS outbreak in Toronto and the 2014 Ebola response in Sierra Leone, had shown that large-scale quarantines failed to contain viral spread. Additionally, a March 2020 study from Bonn University in Germany found no evidence of transmission in places like supermarkets and salons, suggesting that major outbreaks were more often linked to close social contact and indoor gatherings.[128]

These early critiques were not made solely in hindsight but were based on the scientific understanding available during the initial phase of the pandemic. Some countries, such as Sweden, adopted alternative public health strategies, emphasising targeted distancing rather than lockdowns, which aligned more

---

[125] WHO, above n. 110, Article 43.2.

[126] Ibid.

[127] R. Habibi et al., 'Do not violate the International Health Regulations during the COVID-19 outbreak' (2020) 395(10225) *The Lancet* 664.

[128] Look at: P. Berger, 'Proportionality, Evidence and the COVID-19-Jurisprudence in Germany' (2022) 7 *European Journal for Security Research* 211, 229. And, S. Murphy, 'Stopping the Spread of Health' in P. Sutoris, S. Murphy, A. Mendes Borges, Y. Nehushtan (eds), *Pandemic Response and the Cost of Lockdowns*, Abingdon, Routledge, 2022.

closely with WHO recommendations and yielded outcomes comparable to or better than those of countries that implemented stricter measures.[129]

Nevertheless, two important points about the reliance on scientific evidence should be acknowledged. First, the Court must consider the 'source' of scientific evidence. During the pandemic, although some states, such as Germany, claimed to base their decisions on expert advice, much of this evidence came from government-affiliated research institutes that were already involved in Covid-19 policy-making processes, raising legitimate concerns about independence and impartiality.[130] Therefore, it is essential to identify and include independent researchers who can offer critical and alternative assessments of the measures adopted. Second, the need for scientific evidence should not result in regulatory paralysis.[131] As public health lawyers have observed, states may rely not only on individual studies but also on scientific principles and WHO guidance.[132]

Therefore, regarding the suitability test, which is considered a 'highly technical'[133] assessment in the context of pandemics, the role of the ECtHR is not to replace the scientific judgment of policymakers. Instead, its role is to ensure that states' justifications are grounded in credible, evidence-based reasoning, rather than in untested assumptions or political expediency.

5.3. *The Necessity Test*

The example of Covid-19 shows that, after a while, strict non-pharmaceutical measures during a public health emergency can be considered suitable. Amendments and changes in the WHO's recommendations may provide supporting evidence of their suitability, both during the crisis and in subsequent judicial reviews. However, derogatory measures still have to be evaluated before other sub-tests to see whether they comply with the proportionality test and the rule of law.

The necessity test, as the third sub-test within the proportionality test, in a nutshell, is meant to scrutinise whether the authorities could achieve a similar aim with less intrusive measures against human rights.[134] In other words, the Court should assess the adopted measure and decide whether it 'is the last

---

129 Look at: F.N.G. Andersson and L. Jonung, 'The Covid-19 lesson from Sweden: Don't lock down' (2024) 44 *Economic Affairs* 3.

130 For more information, look at: P. Berger, above n. 128.

131 J. Gerards, above n. 104, 475.

132 R. Habibi et al., above n. 127.

133 E. Brems and L. Lavrysen, above n. 84, 143.

134 S. Braum, 'Pandemic Regulation – Virus in the Rule of Law?' in S. Braum (ed), *Experimental Law: The Rule of Law and the Regulation of the Corona Pandemic in Europe*, Baden-Baden, Nomos, 2023, pp. 11–42, p. 29. And, for more information on the necessity test, look at: E. Brems and L. Lavrysen, above n. 84, 142–45.

resort to prevent the spreading of the diseases'.[135] Similar to the suitability test, the necessity test underscores the importance of grounding policy decisions in factual evidence and reasoned justification,[136] rather than assumptions or political expediency.[137]

The Court should consider two key factors when assessing the necessity of measures adopted in response to a public health emergency. First, it should examine the decision-making process through which the authorities selected a particular measure to address the source of the emergency. This includes evaluating whether less restrictive alternatives were considered and whether the chosen measure was identified as the least intrusive means capable of achieving the intended public health objective.[138] In doing so, the Court should scrutinise whether the measure was genuinely 'strictly required' within the meaning of Article 15 of the ECHR. The second element concerns the temporal relationship between the measure and the duration of its application, namely, how necessity evolves over time and whether the continued enforcement of a measure remains justified as circumstances change.

Regarding the first element of the necessity test, it is not sufficient to deem measures appropriate solely because the WHO or a research-based organisation recommends them; a more substantive assessment is required. As indicated earlier, there is a possibility of mistakenly referring to government-related evidence and the WHO's recommendations, which themselves may change over time as new information emerges. Therefore, the reasoning behind evaluating a measure as suitable should be unpacked.

Article 43.2 of the IHR states that measures taken against PHEICs must be grounded in 'scientific principles'. While the precautionary principle has become one of the dominant scientific approaches in public health decision-making, particularly during the Covid-19 pandemic, its increasing use raises important concerns regarding legal proportionality and the evidentiary standards required to justify emergency measures.[139]

A careful review of WHO recommendations and guidelines reveals a strong, and arguably disproportionate, reliance, both direct and indirect, on the precautionary principle. As the Independent Panel for Pandemic Preparedness

---

135 *Enhorn v. Sweden*, no. 56529/00, 25 January 2005, § 44.

136 E. Brems and L. Lavrysen, above n. 84, 143.

137 S. Braum, abve n. 134, 31.

138 For more information, look at: C. Heri, 'Deference, Dignity and "Theoretical Crisis": Justifying ECtHR Rights Between Prudence and Protection' (2024) 24(1) *Human Rights Law Review* 1, 18.

139 Look at: Independent Panel for Preparedness and Response, 'COVID-19: Make it the Last Pandemic', May 2021. And, WHO, 'Infection prevention and control in the context of COVID-19: a guideline', 21 December 2023 <https://www.who.int/publications/i/item/WHO-2019-nCoV-IPC-guideline-2023.4>. Although the latter document is more recent and related to the later phases of Covid-19, the reference to the precautionary principle within it is visible.

and Response[140] noted in its report, 'future declarations of a PHEIC by the WHO Director-General should be based on the precautionary principle',[141] and 'precautionary action should be taken on a presumptive basis'.[142] This growing emphasis suggests that the precautionary principle will likely play an even more prominent role in justifying derogatory public health measures in future emergencies.

The precautionary principle encourages action even in the absence of complete scientific certainty,[143] distinguishing itself from preventive and preparatory approaches that rely on more robust empirical data and risk calculation.[144] As the Commission of the European Communities explains:

> [T]he precautionary principle is a decision exercised where scientific information is insufficient, inconclusive, or uncertain and where there are indications that the possible effects[...] may be potentially dangerous and inconsistent with the chosen level of protection.[145]

While this approach may appear reasonable in situations of uncertainty, it raises normative and legal concerns, particularly when used to justify restrictions on fundamental rights. Klaus Meßerschmidt highlights that the precautionary principle makes it easier for authorities to assume a causal connection between a potential risk and harm without requiring full scientific proof.[146] In practical terms, this means that decision-makers may rely on suspicion or hypothetical threats rather than on solid evidence and thorough

140 The Independent Panel for Preparedness and Response was established by the WHO Director-General according to the World Health Assembly (WHA) Resolution 73.1. The Independent Panel's mission 'was to provide an evidence-based path for the future' in tackling infectious diseases, particularly Covid-19. For further information, look at: C. McNab, 'About the Independent Panel', *The Independent Panel for Pandemic Preparedness and Response* <https://theindependentpanel.org/about-the-independent-panel/>.

141 Independent Panel for Preparedness and Response, above n. 139, p. 53, cited in H. Doan, J.-B. Nie and E. Fenton, 'The precautionary principle in public health emergency regime: Ethical and legal examinations of Vietnamese and global response to COVID-19' (2024) 38(1) *Bioethics* 11, 12.

142 Independent Panel for Preparedness and Response, above n. 139, p. 52, cited in H. Doan, J.-B. Nie and E. Fenton, above n. 141.

143 United Nations General Assembly, 'Report of the United Nations Conference on Environment and Development (Rio de Janeiro, 3–14 June 1992)', 12 August 1992, UN Doc. A/CONF.151/26 (Vols. I–III).

144 R. Khabook, 'Application of the Precautionary Principle in Dealing with Future Pandemic Diseases: The Dilemma of Legality and Legitimacy Under the Rule of Law' (2024) 20(3) *Utrecht Law Review* 10, 14–15.

145 European Commission, 'Communication from the Commission on the precautionary principle', 2 February 2000, COM(2000) 1 final.

146 K. Messerschmidt, 'COVID-19 legislation in the light of the precautionary principle' (2020) 8(3) *Theory and Practice of Legislation* 267, 282.

evaluation. The principle thus shifts the basis for action from demonstrable facts to speculative assumptions, reducing the burden of justification.

To better assess the legal implications of invoking the precautionary principle, it is useful to distinguish between two formulations: a moderate version and a hard version.[147] This distinction is highly relevant when evaluating whether public health measures meet human rights standards, particularly under the necessity test required by the ECtHR. The moderate formulation incorporates limiting factors that guard against overreach. These include the use of available scientific evidence, respect for legal and ethical standards, a preference for less restrictive alternatives, and mechanisms for ongoing review and adaptation. It seeks to strike a balance between taking timely precautionary action and maintaining proportionality.[148] In contrast, the hard formulation prioritises the need to act over the procedural and evidentiary constraints usually required by law. It justifies measures based on loosely defined or hypothetical risks, shifts the burden of proof onto those affected, and risks bypassing meaningful scrutiny under the necessity test. In this model, the precautionary principle may operate as a blanket justification for expansive government interventions, regardless of their actual effectiveness or legal defensibility.[149]

This distinction has important implications when assessing the ECtHR's approach during the Covid-19 pandemic. However, in the few relevant cases decided on their merits, the Court's stance toward the precautionary principle remains ambiguous. Generally, in cases related to ECHR, Article 15 or those in which the Court granted a wide margin of appreciation, a tendency toward the hard formulation is identifiable. By contrast, in certain cases involving prisoners and detainees, particularly where the applicants invoked the positive obligations of the state, the Court appears to have adopted a more moderate approach.[150]

This brings us back to the second factor: the evolving relationship between a public health emergency and the passage of time. Necessity is not a static concept; it must evolve with the public health situation and advances in scientific understanding. A measure deemed strictly required at the outbreak of a pandemic may no longer be justified once less restrictive alternatives emerge or when better data become available. This temporal dimension is not yet fully reflected in the ECtHR's pandemic-related jurisprudence, largely due to the fact that many cases related to the second and third phases of Covid-19 remain pending. Nonetheless, some early judgments illustrate the tension. In *CGAS v. Switzerland*[151] and

---

147 H. Doan, J.-B. Nie and E. Fenton, above n. 141, 18.
148 Ibid., 18-19.
149 Ibid., 19-21.
150 For example, look at: *Crăciun and Others v. Romania*, nos. 512/21, 57755/21, 59365/21, 61086/21 and 17889/23, 16 May 2024. And, *Feilazoo v. Malta*, no. 6865/19, 11 March 2021.
151 *Communauté genevoise d'action syndicale (CGAS) v. Switzerland*, above n. 90.

Central Unitaria de Trabajadores/as v. Spain,[152] the Court upheld the necessity of restrictive measures such as bans on public assembly, largely because of the lack of scientific data in the early stages of the pandemic. These rulings suggest that the Court's reasoning was closely tied to the uncertainty of the moment. However, as the pandemic progressed and more evidence became available, the continued justification for such measures became increasingly contestable.

It is therefore essential that, in its future case law, the ECtHR develops a context-sensitive necessity test that takes into account the changing factual and scientific landscape. Necessity cannot be frozen in the moment of emergency declaration; it must evolve with the crisis itself. Only by embracing this temporal dimension can the Court ensure that emergency powers remain exceptional, proportionate, and fully accountable under the ECHR.

This dynamic understanding cannot be easily identified in the Court's decisions because of the pending cases related to the second and third phases of the Covid-19 pandemic. However, in the existing judgments such as *CGAS* and *Central Unitaria de Trabajadores/as v. Spain*, the Court, by referring to the lack of scientific data in the early stages of the pandemic, considered the decision of the governments in restricting freedom of assembly and association necessary and consequently lawful. Therefore, as often the Court's approach shows,[153] one can hope that the ECtHR in the upcoming judgments may adjust its necessity test contextually and not merely based on the circumstances at the beginning of the pandemic.

In sum, a principled and structured approach to the necessity test during public health emergencies must address both the decision-making process behind the adoption of restrictive measures and the temporal evolution of their justification. The increasing reliance on the precautionary principle, particularly in its hard formulation, risks undermining the evidentiary and proportionality standards that have developed by the ECtHR interpreting the ECHR. While some degree of flexibility is warranted during periods of acute uncertainty, this cannot justify a blanket suspension of rights or the indefinite extension of emergency measures without rigorous judicial scrutiny. The ECtHR has a vital role to play in ensuring that precautionary reasoning remains grounded in legal principle. By adopting a context-sensitive necessity test that evolves over time and distinguishes between different formulations of the precautionary principle, the Court can better safeguard fundamental rights while still recognising the legitimate imperatives of public health protection.

---

[152] *Central Unitaria de Traballadores/as v. Spain*, no. 49363/20, 17 October 2024, § 72.

[153] For example, in *A and Others v. United Kingdom*, above n. 124, although it accepted the wide margin of appreciation, the Court applied a stricter proportionality test in reviewing the anti-terrorism measures compared to its earlier judgment in *Brannigan and McBride v. United Kingdom*, above n. 96.

5.4. *The Proportionality in Stricto Sensu*

Assuming that the previous stages of the proportionality test have been satisfied with regard to the measures adopted in response to the Covid-19 pandemic, the chapter now turns to the final stage: the application of the *stricto sensu* proportionality test. This stage requires a careful determination of whether the interference with an individual right is justified in light of the benefits gained in protecting a competing public interest.[154]

In line with the Court's jurisprudence, *stricto sensu* proportionality seeks to ensure that any encroachment on a Convention right is not excessive or disproportionate to the aim pursued.[155] The Court often articulates this as the need to 'strike a balance' between the demands of the public interest and the requirements of the protection of individual rights.[156] This stage thus functions as a structured mechanism for assessing whether the societal benefits of a given measure outweigh the burden imposed on the individual right in question.

It should be noted, however, that the ECtHR, in invoking the *stricto sensu* proportionality, does not follow 'a coherent and unified method'.[157] Nonetheless, it may be argued that the Court generally follows three steps in applying this test: 1) assessment of the gravity of the interference with personal freedoms; 2) assessment of the weight of the relevant public interest; and 3) assessment of whether the pursued public interest outweighs the individual rights restriction.[158]

In the context of Covid-19, it is clear that interference with personal freedoms during the pandemic was significant. As discussed earlier under the legitimacy test, the protection of public health and the preservation of life represent compelling interests. However, the proportionality analysis must also focus on balancing these public interests against the rights that have been curtailed.

Derogatory measures during a pandemic usually include a bigger group of individuals rather than those under rights deprivation; the Court, in the evaluation of their proportionality, should adopt an equality-based and non-discriminatory approach. Alain Zysset calls this equality-based and non-discriminatory approach the 'egalitarian' approach.[159] Accordingly, to achieve

---

154 Look at: *Von Hannover v. Germany (No. 2)*, nos. 40660/08 and 60641/08, 7 February 2012. And, *Satakunnan Markkinapörssi Oy and Satamedia Oy v. Finland*, no. 931/13, 27 June 2017, cited in B. Çali, 'Balancing Test: European Court of Human Rights (ECtHR)' in *Max Planck Encyclopedia of International Procedural Law*, Oxford, Oxford University Press, 2018.

155 A. Barak, above n. 111, p. 340.

156 *Otto-Preminger-Institut v. Austria*, no. 13470/87, 20 September 1994, § 44, Series A no. 295-A, cited in B. Çali, above n. 154.

157 B. Çali, above n. 154.

158 K. Möller, above n. 112, p. 160.

159 Look at: A. Zysset, above n. 8.

the legitimate goal of the derogation, it is essential to ensure that the burden of interference is not disproportionately placed on individuals and groups affected by the interfering norm.[160]

In fact, various measures during the Covid-19 pandemic based on the egalitarian approach when applying the *stricto sensu* proportionality test can be categorised as disproportional and against the rule of law. For example, workplace closure can be considered a measure suggested by the WHO and has been considered effective in some cases.[161] However, as the WHO mentions, workplace measures will have serious negative economic consequences. Thus, it can only be imposed when there is 'job and income security for workers',[162] otherwise, it is a disproportionate measure. A very similar argument can be put forward about school closures. As various research projects show, school closures have severe impacts on the mental health of children and also bear socio-economic risks for parents.[163]

Therefore, when applying the proportionality test in its narrow sense, the Court should go beyond simply considering which right is being restricted. It should also examine 'whose right is being restricted'.[164] In this case, if a government disregards solutions such as categorising restrictions or providing remedies for those who will suffer most from the derogation of rights, the Court should deem the adopted measure disproportionate and contrary to the rule of law.

6 CONCLUSION

As this chapter has demonstrated, a state of emergency must operate within the framework of the rule of law.

First, the chapter examined provisions such as Article 4 of the ICCPR and Article 15 of the ECHR, alongside the fact that over 90% of world constitutions impose limits on declaring and managing a state of emergency. This supports the principle that emergencies should be governed by the rule of law. Second, after analysing Kelsen's views on *Grundnorm* and his rejection of a separation between law and state, the chapter treated the state of emergency as a constitutional *lex specialis*, rather than an exception that overrides the constitution or the rule of law.

Building on this foundation, the chapter explored the deeper implications of embedding the state of emergency within the rule of law. In this regard, it

---

160 Ibid., 295.
161 P. Berger, above n. 128, 214–15.
162 Ibid., 215.
163 A. Zysset, above n. 8.
164 Ibid., 299.

underscored the necessity of judicial review as a safeguard to ensure the rule of law remains intact during emergencies. However, recognising the complexities of emergency governance, the chapter examined two key judicial approaches: 'deferential judicial review' and 'restraining judicial review'.

While deferential judicial review was criticised for functioning as a mere rubber-stamping mechanism that legitimises executive actions during emergencies, the chapter favoured restraining judicial review. Yet, as discussed, this approach itself can be divided into two methodologies: balancing and proportionality. Given the critiques of the balancing method, particularly its excessive flexibility and lack of principled constraints, which risk undermining rights in favour of public interests, the chapter ultimately endorsed the proportionality test as the preferred method for reviewing rights derogations in times of emergency.

Later, in order to pave the way for proposing an appropriate model for the ECtHR's application of the proportionality test in future pandemics, this chapter examined the Court's decisions on Covid-19-related cases. In this context, the general approach of the Court in applying the proportionality test, particularly its connection with the margin of appreciation doctrine, was explored. As demonstrated, the ECtHR has thus far shown a tendency to grant a wide margin of appreciation to states in its pandemic-related judgments.

Finally, drawing on ECtHR judgments during Covid-19, WHO guidelines, and the IHR, this chapter proposes a particular model of proportionality-based judicial review framework for future public health emergencies. Each sub-test of the proportionality test was examined in detail, with specific recommendations for ensuring a structured and effective system for overseeing derogatory measures during emergencies. The central argument here was that while judicial review in emergency contexts has historically been deferential to the executive and judiciary, principles enshrined in the ECHR and international (health) law provide a foundation for strengthening judicial oversight. Strengthening such oversight can serve as a safeguard against the abuse of power, uphold the rule of law, and reinforce the ECtHR's role in protecting human rights in future pandemic-related cases.

CHAPTER 4
THE FUTURE OF SOCIAL RIGHTS IN A MULTILAYERED SYSTEM FOR THE PROTECTION OF HUMAN RIGHTS

Yannick Schoog

1 INTRODUCTION

In the past decade, there has been no shortage of – largely political – declarations on the European level underlining the importance of and the commitment to social rights. In 2014, the Council of Europe (CoE) launched the so-called Turin Process aimed at strengthening the European Social Charter (ESC)[1] and its supervisory mechanism, the European Committee of Social Rights (ECSR).[2] A decade later, the Vilnius Declaration did not lead to either significant reform or further commitments by the Member States.[3] Since its *Airey*[4] judgment, the European Court of Human Rights (ECtHR) has regularly transgressed the boundaries of civil and political rights explicitly enshrined in the Convention and ventured into the realm of social rights, arguably leading to the Convention's 'socialization'[5], understood as the process of applying the Convention to subject matters in the social and economic field.

---

1 European Social Charter, 18 November 1961 (ETS 35).

2 See also Council of Europe Steering Committee for Human Rights (CDDH), 'Improving the Protection of Social Rights in Europe, Volume I: Analysis of the legal framework of the Council of Europe for the protection of social rights in Europe', Strasbourg, 2019.

3 Council of Europe, 'Vilnius Declaration', 3–4 July 2024; L.R. Glas, 'The Tide Is Turning for the European Social Charter: the Vilnius Declaration and the Warm-Up Thereto', *Strasbourg Observers*, 19 July 2024 <https://strasbourgobservers.com/2024/07/19/the-tide-is-turning-for-the-european-social-charter-the-vilnius-declaration-and-the-warm-up-thereto/>.

4 *Airey v. Ireland*, no. 6289/73, 9 October 1979, Series A no. 32.

5 I. Leijten, 'Social Security as a Human Rights Issue in Europe – *Ramaer and Van Willigen* and the Development of Property Protection and Non Discrimination under the ECHR' (2013) 73 *Zeitschrift für ausländisches öffentliches Recht und Völkerrecht* 177, 188.

The European Union (EU) on the other hand proclaimed the European Pillar of Social Rights in 2017 in another attempt to overcome the widespread perception of the EU as a project for economic integration only. Already before, social rights had been inserted in Title IV (labelled 'Solidarity'), of the Charter of Fundamental Rights of the EU (CFR; Charter) that entered into force in 2009.[6]

Each European source of social rights comes with its own interpreter: the ECSR, the ECtHR and the European Court of Justice (ECJ). In most cases, national courts play a role as well, especially as interpreters of national constitutions. The protection of social rights in Europe is therefore multilayered: Before the final decision is handed down, multiple courts may already have rendered a decision about the very same case. Why is this relevant? First, the fact that multiple adjudicators of social rights cases exist might prove useful for the interpretation of social rights which have always been criticised as 'too vague to be enforced'.[7] Second, the different arbiters of social rights might cross-reference each other, leading to more consistent argumentation and outcomes. For applicants, this could lead to the application of higher social rights standards, but it cannot be entirely ruled out that lower standards may be applied to their case. In the best-case scenario, the outcome should not depend on the forum applicants have access to or choose to pursue their case.

This chapter aims to analyse recent developments in European social rights protection[8] with an emphasis on the interaction between the different enforcement and supervisory mechanisms and to extrapolate the implications for social rights protection in the future. What conclusions for the future may be drawn from the current state of interactions in the field of social rights? First, the sources and interpreters of social rights are briefly introduced. Second, the chapter focuses on the scope and content of two classic fields of social rights protection (the right to social security and the right to collective bargaining and the right to strike) to identify and illustrate possible divergences and convergences. Third, these findings are synthesised into general methodological insights about the state of multilayered social rights protection in Europe: how do the different actors interact and engage with one another? Finally, the chapter takes a look at the future of social rights protection in Europe.

Methodologically, this chapter uses a dogmatic analysis of case law by the ECSR, ECtHR and ECJ. Cases have been selected with specific regard to their

6 Charter of Fundamental Rights of the European Union [2012] OJ C326/391.

7 See in detail: J. King, *Judging Social Rights*, Cambridge, Cambridge University Press, 2012, p. 5.

8 The focus on Europe leads to the exclusion of both the International Covenant on Economic, Social and Cultural Rights, 19 December 1966, 999 UNTS 171 (ICESCR) as well as the protection offered by International Labour Organization (ILO) treaties and enforcement mechanisms.

references to other interpreters of social rights and do not necessarily include the key or most recent cases on the subject matters concerned. The same is true for the literature examined: it has been chosen with a specific emphasis on the interactions and not necessarily for the most pertinent literature on social rights protection under the different regimes as such.

2 SOURCES AND INTERPRETERS OF SOCIAL RIGHTS

Notwithstanding sources and interpreters of social rights on the national level, European citizens today may rely on three different sources of social rights – and their interpreters – on the European level: the ESC is the classic repository for social rights in Europe. The ESC and its counterpart, the European Convention on Human Rights ("ECHR"),[9] are the cornerstones of CoE human rights protection. Whereas the ESC's potential for social rights protection is obvious, this is not the case for the ECHR: its potential for social rights protection becomes visible only through the jurisprudence of the ECtHR. The CFR is the newest addition to the team: its Title IV ('Solidarity') contains various social rights. It is for the ECJ to have the last say on their interpretation.

2.1. The Revised European Social Charter and the European Committee of Social Rights

The ESC is the CoE's traditional protection regime for economic and social rights. It comprises the ESC as well as the 1996 Revised ESC ("RESC").[10] The ECSR monitors state compliance with both instruments. As of 2024, 35 out of 46 CoE Member States had ratified the RESC. The ECSR is entrusted with two tasks: first and foremost, it reviews state compliance through a reporting system that leads to the adoption of conclusions on the RESC conformity of the legal situation in the Member States. This is supplemented by a collective complaints procedure for trade unions, non-governmental organisations (NGOs) and employer organisations introduced by the ESC 1995 protocol which has been ratified by 16 CoE states only.[11] According to its Article 9, the CoE Council of Ministers recommends the state to take measures to remedy the situation when a violation is found. States then have to submit a follow-up

9 Convention for the Protection of Human Rights and Fundamental Freedoms, 4 November 1950 (ETS 5).

10 Revised European Social Charter, 3 May 1996 (ETS 163).

11 Additional Protocol to the European Social Charter Providing for a System of Collective Complaints, 9 November 1995 (ETS 158). See in detail: N.A. Papadopoulos, 'Strategic litigation before the European Committee of Social Rights: Fit for purpose?' (2022) 40(4) *Netherlands Quarterly of Human Rights* 379.

report on their implementation measures. It is then again for the ECSR to monitor whether the state has properly discharged its obligations under the ESC. Since it leads to the adoption of decisions, this procedure has been labeled 'quasi-judicial'.[12] Nevertheless, it cannot be compared to the binding nature of ECtHR judgments. Individuals lack legal recourse to address ESC violations – a fact that has been criticised by legal scholars.[13]

The ESC contains numerous economic and social rights, such as the right to work (RESC, Article 1), the right to bargain collectively (RESC, Article 6), the right to vocational training (RESC, Article 10), the right to protection of health (RESC, Article 11), the right to social security (RESC Article 12) or the right to housing (RESC, Article 31). It must be noted however, that a system of so-called à la carte-ratification applies to the RESC: Within certain limitations, the states may individually choose the provisions to which they are held.

2.2. The European Convention on Human Rights and the European Court of Human Rights

Compared to the ESC, the ECHR's prima facie potential for social rights protection is less obvious. First and foremost, the Convention is aimed at the protection of classic civil and political rights, such as the right to liberty and security in Article 5, or freedom of expression in Article 10(1). Although there is no consensus on the definition of a social right in general, there are some ECHR guarantees that may be qualified as social rights, e.g. Article 4 (prohibition of slavery and forced labor), Article 11(1) (freedom of assembly and association) or Protocol No.1, Article 2 (right to education). Nevertheless, the ECtHR found as early as in 1979 in its seminal *Airey* judgment that:

> [w]hilst the Convention sets forth what are essentially civil and political rights, many of them have implications of a social or economic nature. The Court therefore considers, [...] that the mere fact that an interpretation of the Convention may extend into the sphere of social and economic rights should not be a decisive factor against such an interpretation; there is no water-tight division separating that sphere from the field covered by the Convention.[14]

---

12 R. Brillat, 'The Supervisory Machinery of the European Social Charter: Recent Developments and Their Impact' in G. de Búrca and B. de Witte (eds), *Social Rights in Europe*, Oxford, Oxford University Press, 2005, p. 32.

13 O. De Schutter, 'The CFREU and its Specific Role to Protect Fundamental Social Rights' in F. Dorssemont, K. Lörcher, S. Clauwaert and M. Schmitt (eds), *The Charter of Fundamental Rights of the European Union and the Employment Relation*, Oxford and Portland, Hart Publishing, 2019, p. 10; C. Warbrick, 'Economic and Social Interests and the European Convention on Human Rights' in M. Baderin and R. McCorquodale (eds), *Economic, Social and Cultural Rights in Action*, Oxford, Oxford University Press, 2007, p. 245.

14 *Airey v. Ireland*, above n. 4, § 26.

Since then, the ECtHR has transgressed further into the field of social interests by using the civil and political rights contained in the Convention. The protection granted by the Court is thus often characterised as 'indirect protection'[15] or 'protection par ricochet'.[16] By interpreting the civil and political rights contained in the Convention in a way that allows it to bring social interests within their purview, it has considerably expanded the scope of the Convention beyond the guarantees expressly included.[17] It has considered various issues in the past, such as the right to health or healthcare,[18] the right to housing[19] or the right to social security.[20] It is important to note that individuals may apply to the ECtHR (cf. Article 34). The Court may then issue binding judgments (Article 46(1)). Nevertheless, the Court has continuously reminded applicants that:

> the Convention does not guarantee, as such, socio-economic rights, including the right to charge-free dwelling, the right to work, the right to free medical assistance, or the right to claim financial assistance from a State to maintain a certain level of living.[21]

Repeated efforts to explicitly include social rights in the Convention have not yielded any fruit to this day.[22]

2.3. *The Charter of Fundamental Rights of the European Union and the European Court of Justice*

The Charter is the first (legally binding) rights text to contain economic, social and cultural rights on an equal footing with civil and political rights. Under the heading 'Solidarity' (Title IV) it assembles, for instance: the right of collective

---

[15] E. Brems, 'Indirect Protection of Social Rights by the European Court of Human Rights' in D. Barak-Erez and A. Gross (eds), *Exploring Social Rights: Between Theory and Practice*, Oxford and Portland, Hart Publishing, 2007, p. 138.

[16] F. Sudre, 'La protection des droits sociaux par la Cour européenne des droits de l'homme: un exercice de «jurisprudence fiction»?' (2003) 55 *Revue trimestrielle des droits de l'homme* 755, 760.

[17] This has also sparked criticism, cf. e.g. M. Bossuyt, 'Should the Strasbourg Court exercise more self-restraint? On the extension of the jurisdiction of the European Court of Human Rights to social security regulations' (2007) 28 *Human Rights Law Journal* 321, 321–32.

[18] E.g. *Nitecki v. Poland* (dec.), no. 65653/01, 21 March 2002.

[19] E.g. *Chapman v. United Kingdom*, no. 27238/95, 18 January 2001, ECHR 2001-I; *O'Rourke v. United Kingdom* (dec.), no. 39022/97, 26 June 2001; *Yordanova and Others v. Bulgaria*, no. 25446/06, 24 April 2012.

[20] E.g. *Stec and Others v. United Kingdom*, 12 April 2006, nos. 65731/01 and 65900/01, ECHR 2006-VI; *Budina v. Russia* (dec.), no. 45603/05, 18 June 2006.

[21] *Pančenko v. Latvia*, no. 40772/98, 28 January 1999; *A.H. and J.K. v. Cyprus*, nos. 41903/10 and 41911/10, 21 July 2015, § 145.

[22] Cf. e.g. PACE Recommendation 1415 (1999) of 23 June 1999, 'Additional protocol to the European Convention on Human Rights concerning fundamental social rights'.

bargaining and action (Article 28); fair and just working conditions (Article 31); social security and social assistance (Article 34); healthcare (Article 35); and environmental protection (Article 37). According to Article 52(3), the Charter rights correspond to the rights guaranteed in the ECHR and their meaning and scope are to be the same as in the Convention. What this entails for the rights contained in Title IV of the Charter remains opaque since the ECHR does not explicitly guarantee any corresponding rights (although they may be guaranteed in substance under other Convention rights). The RESC nevertheless features in the Charter's preamble ('[...] the Social Charters adopted by the Union and by the Council of Europe [...]'). The explanations to the Charter refer to the RESC for almost all of the rights contained in Title IV.[23] Nevertheless, there is no reference to the RESC for the purposes of interpretation of the rights contained in the CFR. The engagement with the rights contained in Title IV is further complicated by some of the articles being construed as mere principles (cf. CFR, Article 51(1)) instead of real rights. Yet, after the adoption of the CFR and it becoming legally binding in 2009, many were hoping that it would lead to greater protection for social rights (the chapter will discuss below whether this hope actually turned into a reality or not).

Until today, the ECJ has not issued many judgments on social rights. Whereas the ESC at least provides for a collective complaints procedure and citizens may file individual applications to the ECtHR, there is no instrument to seize the ECJ – neither collectively or individually – and allege a violation of Charter rights. Instead, it has been the preliminary reference procedure (Article 267 of the Treaty on the Functioning of the EU (TFEU))[24] that prompted the ECJ to adjudicate on social rights related matters.

3 SCOPE AND CONTENT OF SOCIAL RIGHTS IN COMPARISON

In order to understand how and to what extent the ECSR, ECtHR and ECJ protect social rights, a comparative look at different social rights is warranted. This section takes a look at the right to social security and the right to collective bargaining as prototype social rights.[25] They are prime examples for the study of interactions between the different interpreters of social rights focused on in this chapter.

---

23 [2007] OJ C303/26.

24 Consolidated Version of the Treaty on the Functioning of the European Union [2012] OJ C326/47.

25 It is by no means this chapter's objective to provide authoritative and in-depth accounts of these selected social rights. It aims to provide an overview of the rights as they have been interpreted by the ECSR, ECtHR and ECJ to gain comparative insights about their approaches.

3.1. *The Right to Social Security*

The right to social security is the prototypical social right. It features explicitly in the RESC as well as the CFR. Although this is not mirrored in the ECHR, the Strasbourg Court has provided protection via different legal avenues, e.g. through property protection (ECHR, Protocol No. 1, Article 1), the right to a fair trial (ECHR, Article 6(1)) or the prohibition of discrimination (ECHR, Article 14). The Charter does include a provision on social security and social assistance (CFR, Article 34); the ECJ has also provided protection via the right to property (CFR, Article 17).

Article 12 of the RESC contains an explicit right to social security. Interestingly, it is not phrased as an individual right but as a state obligation to: first establish or maintain a social security system; second, keep it at a satisfactory level; third, endeavour to progressively raise the standards to a higher level; and, fourth and finally, coordinate social security systems amongst the CoE states. This is complemented by various other rights.[26] The ECSR has given extensive guidance on the obligations RESC, Article 12 places upon the states.[27] An interesting example in recent years of diverging interpretations are the ECSR's decisions on the Greek austerity measures taken in the wake of the global financial crisis: The ECSR held that many of the measures demanded by the Troika, amongst them the introduction of a new apprenticeship contract[28] as well as pension reforms,[29] violated RESC Article 12. In the decision on the pension reforms, the ECSR engaged extensively with the ECtHR's jurisprudence on the property protection of social security benefits. The ECtHR, relying on the margin of appreciation enjoyed by the states in social policy, later deemed the application inadmissible (on the merits) because it was manifestly ill-founded.[30] The applicants had alleged violations of various

---

26 Namely RESC, Article 13 on the right to social and medical assistance, Article 14 on the right to benefit from social welfare services and Article 30 on the right to protection against poverty and social exclusion.

27 See for an in-depth account of the ECSR case law on Article 12: ESC, 'Digest of the case law of the European Committee of Social Rights', *Council of Europe*, June 2022, pp. 119 et seq. <https://www.coe.int/en/web/european-social-charter/-/updated-digest-of-the-case-law-of-the-european-committee-of-social-rights>.

28 ECSR, Collective Complaint 66/2011 – *General Federation of employees of the national electric power corporation (GENOP-DEI) and Confederation of Greek Civil Servants' Trade Unions (ADEDY) v. Greece*, Decision of 23 May 2012.

29 ECSR, Collective Complaint 76/2012 – *Federation of employed pensioners of Greece (IKA-ETAM) v. Greece*, Decision of 7 December 2012; ECSR, Collective Complaint 78/2012 – *Pensioners' Union of the Athens-Piraeus Electric Railways (I.S.A.P.) v. Greece*, Decision of 7 December 2012; ECSR, Collective Complaint 79/2012 – *Panhellenic Federation of pensioners of the public electricity corporation (POS-DEI) v. Greece*, Decision of 7 December 2012; ECSR, Collective Complaint 80/2012 – *Pensioners' Union of the Agricultural Bank of Greece (ATE) v. Greece*, Decision of 7 December 2012.

30 *Koufaki and ADEDY v. Greece* (dec.), nos. 57665/12 and 57657/12, 7 May 2013, § 31.

Convention articles, amongst them Protocol No. 1, Article 1. The ECtHR made no reference to either the RESC or the ECSR's decision.

The Strasbourg Court has protected social security benefits mainly through property protection (Protocol No. 1, Article 1). In the aftermath of its watershed decision in *Stec and Others v. United Kingdom* that put contributory benefits on par with those financed entirely from taxes,[31] the Court has delivered numerous decisions on the property protection of social security benefits.[32] In many instances, especially in the aftermath of the 2008 global financial crisis, the Court has shown considerable deference to the states and accepted most austerity measures put in place by the states to reduce the public deficit.[33] Nevertheless, in cases of alleged discrimination in social security provision, the Court has also provided stronger protection to applicants as well in certain exceptional circumstances.[34] In any case, the Court has never held that Protocol No. 1, Article 1 included the positive right to receive certain social benefits or put the obligation on the states to put in place a system of social security. However, in the case of asylum seekers, the Court held that the prohibition of torture (ECHR, Article 3) could require the states to guarantee certain material conditions by relying heavily on the applicant's vulnerability as an asylum seeker as well as the EU Reception Directive.[35] The Court has not extended this case law to other vulnerable groups. It has, however, provided procedural protection through the right to a fair trial (ECHR, Article 6(1))[36] as well protection against discrimination[37] in the area of social security. Recently, the Court has arguably weakened discrimination protection for social security benefits in the case of *Savickis v. Latvia* by heavily relying on the element

---

31 *Stec and Others v. United Kingdom*, above n. 20, § 53.

32 Cf. recently *Béláné Nagy v. Hungary*, no. 53080/13, 13 December 2016; *Fábián v. Hungary*, no. 78117/13, 5 September 2017; *Savickis and Others v. Latvia*, no. 49270/11, 9 June 2022.

33 E.g. *Koufaki and ADEDY v. Greece* (dec.), above n. 30; *Da Conceição Mateus and Santos Januário v. Portugal*, nos. 62235/12 and 57725/12, 8 October 2013; *Savickas and Others v. Lithuania*, nos. 66365/09, 12845/10, 29809/10, 29809/10, 29813/10, 30623/10 and 28367/11, 15 October 2013; *Da Silva Carvalho Rico v. Portugal*, no. 13341/14, 1 September 2015; *Mamatas and Others v. Greece*, nos. 63066/14, 64297/14 and 66106/14, 21 July 2016; ECtHR, 'Implementing the European Convention on Human Rights in times of economic crisis', Seminar to mark the opening of the judicial year of the European Court of Human Rights, Strasbourg, 25 January 2013; D. Kagiaros, 'Austerity Measures at the European Court of Human Rights: Can the Court Establish a Minimum of Welfare Provisions?' (2019) 25(4) *European Public Law* 535.

34 E.g. *Béláné Nagy v. Hungary*, above n. 32.

35 Council Directive (EU) 2024/1346 of 14 May 2024 laying down standards for the reception of applicants for international protection [2024] OJ L2024/1346; *M.S.S. v. Belgium and Greece*, no. 30696/09, 21 January 2011.

36 E.g. *Fazia Ali v. United Kingdom*, no. 40378/10, 20 October 2015.

37 E.g. *Fábián v. Hungary*, above n. 32.

of choice.[38] The ECtHR essentially held that the applicants had never even tried to gain Latvian citizenship which would have enabled them to stop the discrimination.[39]

The EU Charter combines both the express recognition of social security and social assistance entitlements in its Article 34. For a long time, the scope and consequences of CFR, Article 34 remained unclear.[40] More than a decade later, this is still the case. Most notably, it does not include 'rights language' but chooses the Union as the point of departure which is obligated to:

> [... recognise] and respect the entitlement to social security benefits and social services providing protection in cases such as maternity, illness, industrial accidents, dependency or old age, and in the case of loss of employment, in accordance with the rule laid down by Union law and national laws and practices.[41]

It is thus hardly surprising, that the Curia database only lists six results under CFR, Article 34. Its role in each of the judgments is negligible: the Court is merely taking notice of the existence of CFR, Article 34 and includes a reference to it.[42] However, it has at least been used to by the Court to guide the interpretation of EU legal acts and to corroborate results in favour of applicants.[43] Yet, it has not been a real game-changer that prompted the Court to arrive at results previously unimaginable in the field of social rights. In parallel, the ECJ has also recently made use of property protection (CFR, Article 17(1)) as a means to protect social security benefits, and engaged rather extensively with ECtHR jurisprudence:

> In those circumstances, it is necessary to examine whether Article 17 of the Charter, in particular paragraph 1 thereof, precludes national legislation such as that at issue in the case in the main proceedings. In order to determine the scope of the fundamental right to peaceful enjoyment of property, it is necessary, having regard to Article 52(3) of the Charter, to take account of Article 1 of Protocol

38 *Savickis and Others v. Latvia*, above n. 32, § 215. Cf. C. Van de Graaf and Y. Schoog, '*Savickis v. Latvia*: the role of immutability and choice in the discrimination analysis in the ECtHR' (2025) 25 *International Journal of Discrimination and the Law* 160.

39 S. Ganty and D.V. Kochenov, 'It's Their Own Fault: The New Non-Discrimination Standard in Savickis v. Latvia is about Blaming Minorities for their State-Mandated Statelessness', *Strasbourg Observers*, 5 August 2022 <https://strasbourgobservers.com/2022/08/05/its-their-own-fault-the-new-non-discrimination-standard-in-savickis-v-latvia-is-about-blaming-minorities-for-their-state-mandated-statelessness/>.

40 J. Tooze, 'Social Security and Social Assistance' in T.K. Hervey and J. Kenner (eds), *Economic and Social Rights under the EU Charter of Fundamental Rights*, Oxford, Hart Publishing, 2003, p. 161.

41 CFR, above n. 6, Article 34(1).

42 E.g. Case C-89/16, *Szoja v. Sociálna poisťovňa*, ECLI:EU:C:2017:538, § 43.

43 Case C-571/10, *Kamberaj v. Istituto per l'Edilizia Sociale della Provincia autonoma di Bolzano (IPES) and Others*, ECLI:EU:C:2012:233, § 92.

No 1 to the European Convention for the Protection of Human Rights and Fundamental Freedoms, signed in Rome on 4 November 1950, which enshrines that right (see, to that effect, judgment of 3 September 2008, *Kadi and Al Barakaat International Foundation v Council and Commission*, C-402/05 P and C-415/05 P, [...], paragraph 356).

In that regard, where legislation provides for the automatic payment of a social benefit, it generates a proprietary interest for persons meeting the requirements thereof falling within the ambit of Article 1 of Protocol No 1 to that convention (ECtHR, 7 July 2011, *Stummer v. Austria*, [...], § 82). The rights resulting from the payment of contributions to a social security scheme thus constitute rights of property for the purposes of that article (ECtHR, 12 October 2004, *Kjartan Ásmundsson v. Iceland*, [...], § 39). However, the right to property enshrined in that article cannot be interpreted as entitling a person to a pension of a particular amount (ECtHR, 12 October 2004, *Kjartan Ásmundsson v. Iceland*, [...], § 39).[44]

This way, the ECJ has grafted the long-standing ECtHR jurisprudence onto its own interpretation of the right to property.

3.2. *The Right to Collective Bargaining (Including the Right to Collective Action and Strike)*

Amongst the rights explored in this chapter, it has probably been the right to collective bargaining including the right to collective action and strike that has sparked the most controversy in European social rights protection.

The RESC contains said right in its Article 6. The controversy ensuing from the *Laval* judgment is easily the most well-known conflict between the spheres of the ESC and EU law. The *Laval* case concerned the posting of workers to Sweden by a Latvian construction service provider. After learning that the working conditions of the Latvian workers were significantly worse than those enjoyed by domestic workers, several Swedish trade unions initiated a blockade of the construction site. The Latvian company was not willing to sign a collective bargaining agreement with the Swedish trade unions and subsequently went bankrupt. In the aftermaths, the ECJ ruled that the collective action undertaken by the Swedish trade unions constituted a restriction on the free provision of services according to TFEU, Article 56.[45] This was despite referring to the ESC as a means of inspiration and recognising the right to collective bargaining as a fundamental right.[46]

The ECSR, on the other hand, found – after the so-called Swedish *lex Laval* bringing the legal situation in line with what the ECJ had prescribed

44 Case C-258/14, *Florescu and Others v. Casa Județeană de Pensii Sibiu and Others*, ECLI:EU:C:2017:448, §§ 49 and 50.

45 Case C-341/05, *Laval un Partneri Ltd v. Svenska*, ECLI:EU:C:2007:809.

46 Ibid., § 90.

had entered into force – that this situation was not in conformity with the rights contained in the ESC.[47] Although the Committee simply interprets the RESC, its decision reads as a critique of the ECJ's reasoning in *Laval*.[48] In its decision, it phrased as follows:

> Consequently, the facilitation of free cross-border movement of services and the promotion of the freedom of an employer or undertaking to provide services in the territory of other States – which constitute important and valuable economic freedoms within the framework of EU law – cannot be treated, from the point of view of the system of values, principles and fundamental rights embodied in the Charter, as having a greater *a priori* value than core labour rights, including the right to make use of collective action to demand further and better protection of the economic and social rights and interests of workers.[49]

Unlike the ECtHR, that has held that compliance with EU law would entail a presumption of compliance with the ECHR,[50] the ECSR has never subscribed to such a statement. Differently put, the ECSR does not suppose that social rights enjoy equal protection on the EU level as they do on the ESC level.[51]

On the Convention level, the judgment in *Demir and Baykara* was equally controversial. According to ECHR, Article 11(1), everyone has the right to freedom of peaceful assembly and to freedom of association with others, including the right to form and join trade unions for the protection of his/her interests. The Strasbourg Court has issued numerous judgments on this article. In *Demir and Baykara v. Turkey*, the ECtHR decided that ECHR, Article 11 included the right for civil servants to form trade unions and that the Turkish ban on this violated the right to associate freely.[52] Not only did the Court mention the right to organise in RESC, Article 5 and the right to bargain collectively in RESC, Article 6 but also the corresponding rights of CFR Articles 12 and 28 in the section on the relevant international law. It further went on to conduct a full-fledged interpretation of ECHR, Article 11 in the light of these international instruments, especially those of the RESC. The judgment was especially controversial because Turkey had not ratified the

---

47 ECSR, Collective Complaint 85/2012 – *Swedish Trade Union Confederation (LO) and Swedish Confederation of Professional Employees (TCO) v. Sweden*, Decision of 3 July 2013.

48 M. Rocca, 'The European Social Charter and the European Union' in S. Angeleri and C. Nivard (eds), *The European Social Charter: A Commentary*, vol. 1, Leiden, Brill, 2022, pp. 375–401, p. 392.

49 ECSR, Complaint 85/2012 – *Swedish Trade Union Confederation (LO) and Swedish Confederation of Professional Employees (TCO) v. Sweden*, above n. 47, § 122.

50 Cf. *Bosphorus Hava Yolları Turizm v. Ireland*, no. 45036/98, 30 June 2005, § 155, ECHR 2005-VI.

51 Council of Europe Steering Committee for Human Rights (CDDH), above n. 2, § 163.

52 *Demir and Baykara v. Turkey*, no. 34503/97, 12 November 2008.

international law provisions relied on by the ECtHR in its interpretation at the time. In this way, the ECtHR held Turkey to stricter standards as it had (legally) entered into by infusing its interpretation of the ECHR with RESC standards. Compared to that, the CFR played only a minor role. It finally held that ECHR, Article 11(1) included the right to form trade unions for civil servants.

In *Enerji Yapı-Yol Sen v. Turkey*, the ECtHR for the first time acknowledged the right to strike as part of ECHR, Article 11.[53] Its legacy remains unclear, however, as the Court recently had no objections to the blanket ban on strike action for German civil servants in the judgment of *Humpert and Others v. Germany*.[54] Interestingly, the judgment again hinges on the element of choice, as the Court underlined that there was no violation of ECHR, Article 11(1) because the civil servants could have also exercised the option of being employed as public sector employees – who do enjoy the right to strike.

4 CONNECTING THE DOTS: DIFFERENCES AND CONVERGENCES, ENGAGEMENT AND INTERACTION

After this veritable tour de force through various social rights, this section will turn now – as far as possible – to connecting the dots.

4.1. Differences and Convergences

The different examples of social rights explored above have, first of all, shown that none of the European actors today outrightly refuse to engage with social rights. Certainly, this is hardly surprising in the case of the ECSR. It is much more in the case of the ECtHR since the ECHR has, since its inception, been aimed at protecting civil and political rights. The ECJ – despite being equipped with a fundamental rights text explicitly guaranteeing social rights – is still grappling with its role. When it comes to protecting social security benefits, it resorts to the right to property – a civil and not a social right. The rights especially in Title IV have not yet played a large role in practice. This leads to the finding that the protection granted to social rights by (quasi-)judicial actors – ironically – does not necessarily depend on their inclusion in the text the respective actor is in charge of interpreting. The ECJ's role is further limited because of the EU's limited competences in the social field: except for the areas of the internal market and asylum seekers, social security and social rights remain the Member States' domains.

53 *Enerji Yapı-Yol Sen v. Turkey*, no. 68959/01, 21 April 2009.

54 *Humpert and Others v. Germany*, nos. 59433/18, 59477/18, 59481/18 and 59494/18, 14 December 2023.

Second of all, the different examples show varying degrees of difference or convergence. There seems to be more convergence in the field of education and health, arguably less contentious issues. Social security and the right to collective bargaining, on the other hand, gave rise to a large degree of difference. It transpires from this that the actors involved have not developed individual consistent theories of how to protect social rights that they would apply across the board but instead proceed on a case-by-case basis. Connecting the dots is thus a difficult endeavour. By far the most problematic divergences are those including EU law because, after all, EU law will prevail.[55]

Third of all – yet again ironically – it is the ECtHR that has achieved a surprisingly high level of social rights protection despite their absence from the ECHR. By holding states accountable to ESC provisions that they had not ratified, it even acted as a catalyst for the ESC:[56] not only does it issue a binding judgment on what are rights covered by the ESC (a competence the ECSR does not have), it also applies stricter standards than the ECSR could have due to the lack of ratification. Further, its extensive interpretation of the ECHR articles has enabled it to provide protection of social interests to a degree much larger than expected when reading the ECHR on its face, especially in the field of social security and trade union rights.

4.2. Engagement and Interaction

As this chapter has also shown, none of the European actors outrightly and fully refuse to engage with social rights contained in other rights documents or – to a certain extent – with the jurisprudence by other actors. Certainly, this engagement and interaction varies in frequency, consistency and quality. It is, however, difficult to identify patterns as the mutual references are often haphazard.

The ECSR seems to be the most open to engage both with the ECHR as well as the CFR. The ECtHR also makes frequent references to the ESC as well as ECSR decisions.[57] One may distinguish two different forms of references: it may either be the fleeting reference to the ESC in the 'Relevant Law' or 'Relevant International Law' sections of the ECtHR's judgments. Nevertheless, they are usually little more than random and haphazard citations illustrating the surrounding legal regimes. Yet, the Court at times conducts a proper and profound analysis of international law instruments, such as that undertaken

---

55 S. Garben, 'The problematic interaction between EU and international law in the area of social rights' (2018) 7(1) *Cambridge International Law Journal* 77, 81.

56 *Demir and Baykara v. Turkey*, above n. 52.

57 C. Deliyanni-Dimitrakou, 'The European Social Charter and the European Convention on Human Rights' in S. Angeleri and C. Nivard (eds), *The European Social Charter: A Commentary*, vol. 1, Leiden, Brill, 2022, pp. 351–74, pp. 362 et seq.

in *Demir and Baykara v. Turkey* or in the realm of the right to education. In *Demir and Baykara*, the Court even advanced the bold argument that since the States Parties to the ESC had expressed their wish to strengthen the ESC, this would also translate into their greater willingness to promote economic and social rights on the ECHR level.[58] This, however, cannot be considered the rule but rather the exception. In recent years, the ECtHR has also been less willing to conduct such in-depth analyses of international law and base its judgments on them. Furthermore, the methodology and extensive interpretation brought forward in *Demir and Baykara* has not been used consequently by the Court in the aftermath.[59] This might suggest that the high time of these social rights-friendly judgments may be over for the time being.

The ECtHR's references to the CFR have, however, only been fleeting. It has, for instance, included CFR, Article 34 (social security and social assistance) in the section of relevant EU law.[60] It does not, however, stop there and includes the reference to CFR, Article 34 as an argument leading it to find that the applicants had to bear an excessive individual burden since the Charter endorses benefits providing protection in the case of loss of employment.[61] When engaging with trade union rights, the ECtHR also refers to CFR, Articles 12 (freedom of association) and 28 (right of collective bargaining and action).[62] All in all, the ECtHR seems more open to engage with international law than the ECJ.[63]

The latter still seems to be stuck in another moment in time: it appears as though it were still grappling with the aftermath of the inclusion of social rights in the CFR and not yet ready to consider significant social rights interpretations by other actors in the field. Certainly, this may also be due to the very cautious phrasing of some of the rights contained in Title IV of the CFR. On the other hand, it has stressed that all EU Member States are members of the ESC or RESC respectively.[64] It has not addressed the issue of whether the RESC were

58 *Demir and Baykara v. Turkey*, above n. 52, § 84.

59 K. Lörcher, 'The New Social Dimension in the Jurisprudence of the European Court of Human Rights (ECtHR): The *Demir and Baykara* Judgment, its Methodology and Follow-up' in F. Dorssemont, K. Lörcher and I. Schömann (eds), *The European Convention on Human Rights and the Employment Relation*, London, Hart Publishing, 2013, p. 46.

60 *N.K.M. v. Hungary*, no. 66529/11, 14 May 2013, § 20; *Gáll v. Hungary*, no. 49570/11, 25 June 2013, § 19; *R.Sz. v. Hungary*, no. 41838/11, 2 July 2013, § 18.

61 *N.K.M. v. Hungary*, above n. 60, § 70; *Gáll v. Hungary*, above n. 60, § 69; *R.Sz. v. Hungary*, above n. 60, § 59.

62 *Demir and Baykara v. Turkey*, above n. 52, §§ 47 and 51.

63 C. Barnard, 'The Protection of Fundamental Social Rights in Europe after Lisbon: a Question of Conflicts of Interests' in S. de Vries, U. Bernitz and S. Weatherill (eds), *The Protection of Fundamental Rights in the EU After Lisbon*, London, Hart Publishing, 2013, p. 44.

64 Case C-116/06, *Kiiski v. Tampereen kaupunki*, ECLI:EU:C:2007:536, § 48; Case C-684/16, *Max-Planck-Gesellschaft zur Förderung der Wissenschaften v. Tetsuji Shimizu*, ECLI:EU:C:2018:874, § 70.

to be covered by 'international agreements to which [...] all the Member States are party' (CFR, Article 53).[65] This has, however, not led it to regard the ESC as a guideline for interpretation in its own judgments – also beyond the CFR.[66]

4.3. *Entangled Rather than Layered Protection?*

Just as the protection granted is often ad hoc, so are differences and convergences identified and so is the degree of regard the actors have to the jurisprudence of their social rights counterparts. Connecting the dots and painting the big picture – as this chapter has set out to do – remains thus a very difficult undertaking, but it is a start. And yet other elements of the title might have to be reconsidered: the image of multiple layers of protection stacked neatly on top of each other. It presupposes that – similar to national judicial proceedings that spiral to ever higher courts – social rights claims would go through different levels and ultimately arrive before their final arbiter. This, however, is not the case. Certainly, for a case to go to the ECtHR, it must comply with the requirement of exhaustion of domestic remedies (ECHR, Article 35(1)). Such a requirement does not exist in the collective complaint procedure before the ECSR. Finally, considering the ECJ, preliminary questions may be referred to Luxembourg by any national court; the ECJ might thus engage with questions relating to the social rights in the CFR at a very early stage already (although it must be conceded that EU law will prevail in most cases of conflict.) The different layers are thus not neatly stacked on top of each other but may be interlaced or entangled.

The ECtHR judgments on social interests in general as well as the recent ECJ judgments on the protection of social security benefits by way of property protection (CFR, Article 17) show yet another tendency: the reliance and continuing attractiveness of walking down the well-entrenched avenues of protecting social rights through civil and political rights. Whereas the ECtHR really has no other choice, the ECJ actively chooses to employ CFR, Article 17 instead of engaging with the CFR provision actually dealing with social security (i.e. Article 34).

5 CONCLUSION

Finally, what are the prospects for future social rights protection in Europe? Against the background of the renewed commitments to social rights on the European level mentioned in the introduction (see above section 1), one could

[65] M. Rocca, above n. 48, p. 379.

[66] Ibid., p. 383.

be led to expect a greater degree of protection in the future. Nevertheless, it seems unlikely that this will be the case. The Turin Process certainly led to improvements within the ESC system, but the number of ratifications of the collective complaints protocol remains low. The European Pillar of Social Rights project has also not brought about significant changes in social rights protection on the EU level. EU accession to the ESC, as endorsed both by the European Parliament and the ECSR, seems highly unlikely after the ECJ already stopped EU accession to the ECHR.[67]

Consequently, one will have to work with what one already has. First and foremost, the different actors are required to engage in more dialogue, a need they have already identified themselves.[68] The stakeholders would do well to pay greater attention to each other as this could improve their reasoning, enrich it and provide synergies. It would further force them to strive for greater convergence in delineating scope and content of social rights. If – for whatever reason – convergence is not an option, the different adjudicating bodies would be compelled to give reasons for their diverging construction of a right. This could profoundly improve legal reasoning in social rights matters where protection is often ad hoc. It remains uncertain, however, if the actors involved are willing to engage in such a reinforced dialogue.

Similar to many other areas of the law, one should expect a greater role to be played by the ECJ. Its social rights jurisprudence on the basis of the CFR has only just kicked off and one should expect to see more judgments dealing with the rights contained in Title IV of the CFR. It will be interesting to see which stance the Luxembourg Court will take in interpreting these rights. It is telling that many commentators on the CFR still write about it as though it were not in force yet.[69] It may, however, very well be possible that the rights contained therein do not go beyond mere lip service although calls have been made for the ECJ to include the ESC to a greater extent in its interpretations of the CFR.[70] Still, at this point, the ECJ is not willing to meaningfully engage with the ESC.[71]

---

67 Cf. Opinion 2/13, *Opinion pursuant to Article 218(11) TFEU*, ECLI:EU:C:2014:2454. See also O. De Schutter, 'L'adhésion de l'Union européenne à la Charte sociale européenne (The Accession of the European Union to the European Social Charter)', 8 July 2014 <https://papers.ssrn.com/sol3/papers.cfm?abstract_id=2475754>.

68 ECSR, The relationship between European Union law and the European Social Charter: Working Document', 15 July 2014, § 4.

69 Cf. F. Dorssemont, 'Article 12(1) – Freedom of Assembly and of Association' in S. Peers, T. Hervey, J. Kenner and A. Ward (eds), *The EU Charter of Fundamental Rights: A Commentary*, Oxford, Hart Publishing, 2021, § 96: '[...] the Charter provision has the potential to be relevant [...]'.

70 O. De Schutter, 'The European Social Charter in the context of the implementation of the EU Charter of Fundamental Rights', 2016, p. 40 <https://op.europa.eu/en/publication-detail/-/publication/5183c21c-c0d3-11e5-9e54-01aa75ed71a1>.

71 M. Rocca, above n. 48, p. 400.

The revolutionary potential of the renewed emphasis on social rights should not be overestimated. Despite renewed emphasis on social rights both by the CoE and the EU in the last decade, the prospects for stronger protection remain low. The ECtHR continues to struggle with social rights post-*Airey*. It seems unrealistic to expect any more from it than minimum social rights protection in hard cases. The RESC's enforcement mechanism, i.e. the ECSR, does not have the power to render binding decisions. The protocol on collective complaints empowering the ECSR to pass judgments on collective complaints by trade unions and employer organisations has been ratified by a handful of states only. After the failed EU accession to the ECHR, its accession to the RESC seems even less likely.[72] Some also caution against it in order not to interfere with the autonomy of the EU legal order.[73] The Charter was hailed for finally putting social rights on an equal footing with civil and political rights. However, its limited scope has prevented it from being the social rights watershed moment. This will most likely also not change as a consequence of the European Pillar of Social Rights. First of all, it is a merely political declaration; it is not legally binding. While this may be seen as a major shortcoming of the document, it has also been hailed because it avoids a potentially harmful duplication of social rights protection regimes.[74] While the European Commission has launched initiatives, strategies and at times even concrete proposals for action on some of the principles of the Pillar, this is not (yet) the case for the rights relevant in this chapter listed in Chapter III, titled 'Social Protection and Inclusion', e.g. social protection or healthcare. Only the future can tell whether the Commission will step up its game and deliver on these principles as well. Accurately phrased by Garben, the Pillar 'will only show its true worth in its implementation'.[75]

Certainly, the protection of social rights in Europe by the different actors involved will continue to be an interesting matter of inquiry for the years to come and demands further attention in the future.

---

72 See for an in-depth account of the question of EU accession to the ESC: O. De Schutter, above n. 67.

73 S. Garben, above n. 55, 90.

74 S. Garben, 'The European Pillar of Social Rights and the European Social Charter' (2020) *Europe of Rights & Liberties/Europe des Droits & Libertés* 65, 67.

75 Ibid., 65.

PART II.

Opening Procedural Pathways to Tackle Injustice

CHAPTER 5
THE ANTHROPOCENTRIC APPROACH OF THE ECTHR IN ENVIRONMENT-RELATED CASES

My Hanh Pham

1 INTRODUCTION

The Anthropocene is an era characterised by humankind's growing impact on the environment.[1] Cross-border environmental problems, such as climate change and the loss of biodiversity, are the greatest global challenges of the 21st century.[2] Based on these rapid developments, the world is currently in the period of:

> growing awareness of human impact on the environment at the global scale and the first attempts to build global governance systems to manage humanity's relationship with the Earth System.[3]

There is agreement that action is needed, but the question of *how* to act remains mostly unanswered or insufficient due to the various interests that need to be considered. International environmental law, for example, is 'stubbornly anthropocentric'[4] in its approach and regularly puts human interests above those of non-human beings and therefore fails to guarantee adequate protection for nature. Against this background, the most advanced and innovative development – considered as one solution to global environmental problems – will be examined: the Rights of Nature (RoN) approach,[5] an idea

1 W. Steffen, J. Grinevald, P. Crutzen and J. McNeill, 'The Anthropocene: conceptual and historical perspectives' (2011) 369 *Philosophical Transactions of the Royal Society A* 842.

2 A. López-Claros, A.L. Dahl and M. Groff, *Global Governance and the Emergence of Global Institutions for the 21st Century*, Cambridge, Cambridge University Press, 2020, pp. 360–78.

3 W. Steffen, J. Grinevald, P. Crutzen and J. McNeill, above n. 1, 842, 856.

4 E. Jones, 'Posthuman international law and the rights of nature' (2021) 12 *Journal of Human Rights and the Environment* 76, 80.

5 The Rights of Nature are sometimes referred to as 'environmental rights', cf. D. Shelton, 'Human Rights, Environmental Rights, and the Right to Environment' (1991) 28 *Stanford Journal of International Law* 103, 117; A. Boyle, 'Human Rights or Environmental Rights? A Reassessment' (2007) 18(3) *Fordham Environmental Law Review* 471, 473.

that recognises that nature has rights just as humans do.[6] In its dogmatic configuration, there is a distinction between the '*sui generis* approach' and the 'integrative approach'. The *sui generis* approach implements RoN in new special regulatory regimes,[7] whereas the integrative approach includes the protection of nature into existing dogmatic structures. Applying the latter approach, this chapter examines whether and how the protection of nature is integrated into the existing European human rights system and whether a RoN approach is necessary. For this purpose, environmental-ethics concepts on the intrinsic value of nature are introduced (section 2.1). They serve as a yardstick for the subsequent analysis of the relevant case law of the European Court of Human Rights[8] on environment-related cases. The analysis shows that the indirect protection of nature due to the strong anthropocentric approach of the ECtHR causes insufficient protection (section 2.2). Therefore, the chapter discusses the integration of nature as human rights subject under the ECtHR based on considerations of the Inter-American Human Rights System[9] (section 2.3). The conclusion gives an outlook on possible follow-up research that goes hand in hand with the future integration of nature as a human rights subject into the European human rights system (section 3).

2 THE INTEGRATIVE APPROACH OF THE ECTHR

2.1. *Environmental Ethics as a Normative Basis*

From a *normative* perspective, the question is whether nature *should* have rights. For those areas of law that have a pronounced ethical orientation, a congruence between law and morality should be established.[10] Thus, nature conservation regulations are subject to a high burden of justification, which can usually be found in environmental ethical considerations. These considerations are suitable for this purpose as they deal with the justification and criticism

---

[6] Definition according to 'What are the Rights of Nature?', *Global Alliance for the Rights of Nature (GARN)* <https://www.garn.org/rights-of-nature/>. All web sources were last accessed on 12 July 2024.

[7] Cf. Constitution of the Republic of Ecuador 2008, Articles 71–74; La Ley de Derechos de la Madre Tierra (Bolivia – Law 071 of 21 December 2010), Article 7; Te Awa Tupua (Whanganui River Claims Settlement) Act 2017 (New Zealand – Public Act 2017 No. 7), Article 14(1) that grants legal personhood to the Whanganui River.

[8] Hereinafter: 'ECtHR' or 'the Court'.

[9] American Convention on Human Rights: 'Pact of San José, Costa Rica', 22 November 1969, 1144 UNTS 123 (hereinafter: ACHR).

[10] M.-C. Gruber, *Rechtsschutz für nichtmenschliches Leben*, Baden-Baden, Nomos, 2006, p. 161; S. Stucki, *Grundrechte für Tiere*, Baden-Baden, Nomos, 2016, p. 78.

of human behaviour towards *nature*.[11] The intersection between legal and environmental ethics encompasses human behaviour towards nature that is or should be reflected in *law*.[12]

2.1.1 Intrinsic Value

To define this intersection, various concepts are available about the *moral status* of nature and thus about the legally and ethically correct way for humans to interact with nature. Having moral status means having an *intrinsic* value. Insofar as an entity has intrinsic value, 'it is valuable *in* and *for* itself'.[13] In contrast to the *extrinsic* value, it 'is not derived from its utility'[14] for human beings. Moral status is the key to being part of the moral community.[15] Within this community, a distinction is made between *moral agents* and *moral patients*.[16] Only human beings are moral agents, they must fulfil moral duties because they can judge morally and can act in the light of moral principles.[17] These moral obligations exist not only towards other moral agents,[18] but also towards moral patients who lack this capacity.[19] All members of the moral community deserve moral consideration.[20] This moral consideration is expressed in *direct* moral duties.[21] *Direct* duties arise from an entity's intrinsic value, whereas *indirect* duties arise from an entity's extrinsic value and from the potential consequences – if damage is caused to the latter – for entities with intrinsic value.[22] The current key question is what kinds

11 J. Nida-Rümelin and D. von der Pfordten, 'Einführung: Auf dem Weg zu einer Ökologischen Rechtstheorie' in J. Nida-Rümelin and D. von der Pfordten (eds), *Ökologische Ethik und Rechtstheorie*, 2nd ed., Baden-Baden, Nomos, 2002, pp. 9, 11.

12 Ibid.

13 J.B. Callicott, 'On the intrinsic value of nonhuman species' in B.G. Norton (ed), *The Preservation of Species*, Princeton, Princeton University Press, 1986, p. 140.

14 Ibid.

15 C.W. Morris, 'The Idea of Moral Standing' in T.L. Beauchamp and R.G. Frey (eds), *The Oxford Handbook of Animal Ethics*, Oxford, Oxford University Press, 2011, pp. 255, 260 et seq.

16 G.J. Warnock, *The Object of Morality*, London, Routledge, 1971, pp. 148–52.

17 W.K. Frankena, 'Ethics and the Environment' in K.E. Goodpaster and K.M. Sayre (ed), *Ethics and Problems of the 21st Century*, Notre Dame, University of Notre Dame Press, 1979, pp. 3–20, pp. 3, 5.

18 T. Regan, *The Case for Animal Rights*, 2nd ed., Berkeley, University of California Press, 2004, p. 152.

19 Ibid., p. 151.

20 Ibid., p. 152; P.W. Taylor, 'The Ethics of Respect for Nature' (1981) 3(3) *Environmental Ethics* 197, 201.

21 This distinction between direct and indirect duties is derived from I. Kant, *Metaphysische Anfangsgründe der Tugendlehre*, Hamburg, Felix Meiner Verlag, 2016, § 16, p. 83.

22 In Kant's anthropocentric reasoning on animal welfare, Kant states that cruelty to animals is not immoral because the animals suffer in the process – he thus denies a direct duty towards animals – but it blunts human compassion, which is 'a natural disposition that is very conducive to morality towards other human beings' and derives from an indirect duty towards animals from it: I. Kant, ibid., § 17, p. 84, own translation.

of beings do moral agents have duties to?[23] The scope of moral duties and thus the extent of moral patients in the moral community is related to the moral status of nature, which is linked to certain criteria depending on the conception of environmental ethics.[24]

2.1.2 Anthropocentric and Physiocentric Concepts

The concepts of environmental ethics can generally be differentiated into anthropocentric and physiocentric concepts. The latter can be further divided into a pathocentric, biocentric and a holistic concept and differs in the scope of natural entities that have intrinsic value.[25] In a nutshell: anthropocentrism attributes intrinsic value only to *rational* beings, usually humans.[26] From this particular moral position, the relationship to nature is always characterised by an *indirect* one, since only extrinsic value is attributed to nature.[27] Pathocentrism extends intrinsic value to *sentient* beings,[28] including higher vertebrates. Biocentrism shifts the criterion for intrinsic value from sentience to *life*[29] and therefore attributes intrinsic value to all animals and plants. Holism, as the broadest form of physiocentrism, attributes intrinsic value to entities due to their *existence*,[30] so that species and ecosystems are also included.[31]

They differ in the scope of entities to which an intrinsic value is assigned, and thus also in the size of the moral community.[32] The scope of humans' direct moral duties towards nature can be derived from this. Thus, while anthropocentrism has the narrowest scope and recognises moral duties only towards humans, holism[33] has the broadest scope, recognising moral duties

---

23 W.K. Frankena, above n. 17, pp. 3, 5.

24 G.J. Warnock, above n. 16, p. 148.

25 This conceptual framework is based on: W.K. Frankena, above n. 17, pp. 3–20.

26 J.B. Callicott, above n. 13, p. 141; B.G. Norton, *Why Preserve Natural Variety?*, Princeton, Princeton University Press, 1987, p. 137.

27 B.G. Norton, above n. 26, p. 135.

28 H. Würbel, 'Ethology applied to animal ethics' (2009) 118 *Applied Animal Behaviour Science* 118, 123. The crucial question 'is not, Can they reason? nor, Can they talk? but, Can they suffer?': J. Bentham, *An Introduction to the Principles of Morals and Legislation*, New York, Hafner, 1948, p. 311.

29 A. Schweitzer, *Kulturphilosophie*, 2nd ed., Munich, C.H. Beck, 2007, p. 330; P.W. Taylor, above n. 20, 197, 206.

30 T. Berry, 'Legal Conditions for Earth Survival' in M. Tucker (ed) and T. Berry, *Evening Thoughts: Reflecting on Earth as Sacred Community*, San Francisco, Sierra Club Books, 2006, pp. 109 et seq.

31 D.R. Boyd, *The Rights of Nature: A Legal Revolution That Could Save The World*, Toronto, ECW Press, 2017, pp. 88 et seq.; H. Rolston III, 'Is There an Ecological Ethic?' (1975) 85(2) *Ethics* 93, 101.

32 M. Gorke, *Eigenwert der Natur: Ethische Begründung und Konsequenzen*, Stuttgart, S. Hirzel Verlag, 2010, p. 21.

33 The following refers to physiocentrism in its holistic form.

towards all non-human entities, including the inanimate ones.[34] The respective extension of moral responsibility thus includes *all* previous concepts, so that physiocentrism 're-envision[s] the balance of interests between human and nonhuman nature'.[35] This also makes it clear that the suffix *-centrism* is misleading and should not mean that either humans or nature should be at the centre.[36] The concepts of environmental ethics presented here serve as a normative benchmark for the subsequent analysis of the jurisprudence of the European human rights system. How does the ECtHR answer the question of the moral status of nature?

2.2. *The Court's Approach to Environment-Related Situations*

A look into the European Convention on Human Rights[37] is sobering: the Convention says nothing about a right to a healthy environment, let alone Rights of Nature.[38] However, the scope of human rights protection is not limited by the written Convention, but is also determined by its interpretation and further development through the case law of the ECtHR.[39] Considering the link between human rights and the environment,[40] the Court has established an extensive 'greening'[41] jurisprudence on environment-related issues since the 1970s.[42]

---

34 H. ROLSTON III, above n. 31, 93, 101.

35 J.M. ANGSTADT and M. HORDEQUIN, 'Taking Stock of the Rights of Nature' in D.P. CORRIGAN and M. OKSANEN (eds), *Rights of Nature: A Re-examination*, New York, Routledge 2021, p. 15.

36 U. ESER, A.-K. NEUREUTHER and A. MÜLLER, *Klugheit, Glück, Gerechtigkeit. Ethische Argumentationslinien in der nationalen Strategie zur biologischen Vielfalt*, Bonn, Bundesamt für Naturschutz, 2011, p. 68.

37 Convention for the Protection of Human Rights and Fundamental Freedoms, 4 November 1950 (ETS 5), p. 221 (hereinafter: ECHR or Convention).

38 This is due to the fact that at the time the ECHR was drafted after World War II, environmental protection was not yet a central concern, M. DEMERIEUX, 'Deriving Environmental Rights from the European Convention for the Protection of Human Rights and Fundamental Freedoms' (2001) 21(3) *Oxford Journal of Legal Studies* 521; O.W. PEDERSEN, 'European Environmental Human Rights and Environmental Rights: A Long Time Coming?' (2008) 21(1) *Georgetown International Environmental Law Review* 73, 84; L. LOUCAIDES, 'Environmental Protection Through the Jurisprudence of the European Convention on Human Rights' (2004) 75(1) *British Yearbook of International Law* 249, 267.

39 J. HUSA, *A New Introduction to Comparative Law*, Oxford, Hart Publishing, 2015, p. 53.

40 J. KNOX, 'Report of the Independent Expert on the issue of human rights obligations relating to the enjoyment of a safe, clean, healthy and sustainable environment', 24 December 2012, UN Doc. A/HRC/22/43, para. 10.

41 E. ZAHRADNIKOVA, 'European Court of Human Rights: Giving the Green Light to Environmental Protection' (2017) 8 *Queen Mary Law Journal* 13, 15; A. BOYLE, above n. 5, 471, 472.

42 The Court has already dealt with more than 300 decisions and judgments in environment-related issues, T. EICKE, '"Human Rights and Climate Change: What Role for the European Court of Human Rights?", Inaugural Annual Human Rights Lecture', *Council of Europe*, 2 March 2021 <https://rm.coe.int/human-rights-and-climate-change-judge-eicke-speech/1680a195d4>.

Basically, according to the environmental-ethics conceptions, two models can be drawn from the Court's jurisprudence. Within Model 1, the environment is protected indirectly, and environmental concerns can have two functions from a substantive perspective: a *limiting* and an *annex* function.[43] The limiting function deals with cases in which state measures for environmental protection conflict with certain rights under the Convention. The annex function protects the environment to some extent through an unwritten 'right to a healthy environment', read into various Convention rights.[44] It reflects the growing recognition of the crucial importance of the environment under human rights law.[45] The following is a selective cross-section of the ECtHR's approach to environment-related cases in the above-mentioned functions. The focus is kept on cases where ECHR, Protocol No. 1, Article 1 (that protects the peaceful enjoyment of possessions), and ECHR, Article 8 (that protects the right to respect private and family life) were invoked, leaving aside the environmental decisions on other provisions of the Convention.[46] Model 2 shows that nature *as such* is not protected (see below section 2.2.2.). *Direct* protection of nature under the Convention is not guaranteed. This is followed by a normative classification and critical appraisal of the Court's approach (see below section 2.2.3.).

2.2.1 Model 1: Indirect Protection of the Environment

2.2.1.1 *Limiting Function – Environmental Concerns as General Interest*

In its *limiting* function, environmental concerns serve as legitimate aims to limit certain rights and freedoms guaranteed by the Convention. This usually entails situations when state measures for environmental protection conflict with landowners' property rights. But property rights under Protocol No. 1, Article 1

---

43 Based on S. Theil, 'Der Umfang des Umweltschutzes in der Rechtssprechung des Europäischen Gerichtshofs für Menschenrechte' (2014) 36 *Natur und Recht* 330, 331.

44 For an overview of the environment-related Convention rights: R. Schmidt-Radefeldt, *Ökologische Menschenrechte – Ökologische Menschenrechte: Ökologische Menschenrechtsinterpretation der EMRK und ihre Bedeutung für die umweltschützenden Grundrechte des Grundgesetzes*, Baden-Baden, Nomos, 1999; N. Kobylarz, 'The European Court of Human Rights: An Underrated Forum for Environmental Litigation' in H. Tegner Anker and B. Egelund Olsen (eds), *Sustainable Management of Natural Resources*, Cambridge, Intersentia, 2018, pp. 102–04.

45 K. Reid, *A Practitioner's Guide to the European Convention on Human Rights*, 5th ed., London, Sweet & Maxwell, 2015, p. 525.

46 H. Müllerová, 'Environment Playing Short-handed: Margin of Appreciation in Environmental Jurisprudence of the European Court of Human Rights' (2015) 24(1) *Review of European Comparative & International Environmental Law* 83, 86. Unfortunately, environmental concerns are addressed too restrictively via ECHR, Article 2 or Article 3, as a violation requires a high threshold of interference, R. Schmidt-Radefeldt, above n. 44, p. 197.

are never absolute or unqualified.[47] According to the second paragraph of Protocol No. 1, Article 1, states are entitled to 'control the use of property in accordance with the general interest' by enforcing such laws as they deem necessary for the purpose. In conflicting situations, the Court has consistently granted the state a wide margin of appreciation in the choice of means and in the assessment of whether the effects of their application are justified by the general interest.[48] In its well-established case law on Protocol No. 1, Article 1,[49] the Court needs to strike a fair balance 'between the demands of the general interest of the community and the requirements of the protection of the individual's fundamental rights'.[50] The Court recognised for the first time in the judgment of *Fredin v. Sweden (No. 1)*[51] that 'in today's society the protection of the environment[52] is an increasingly important consideration'[53] and therefore a 'general interest' under the second paragraph of Protocol No. 1, Article 1. This interpretation gives the provision an *ecological limitation* that allows the guaranteed property right to be restricted in favour of nature conservation interests. It is remarkable that the Court, in balancing environmental protection as a general interest against the right to property as an individual right, assigns great general importance to environmental needs without considering the particularities of the individual case.[54] The Court does this solely for the scale of the individual interest. This is due to the restrained control of the margin of appreciation, which at the same time opens the possibility for states to limit property rights in favour of environmental protection by appropriate laws.

Under these conditions, measures to protect wildlife[55] or uphold national environmental standards, such as the demolition of buildings to protect

---

47 A. Boyle, above n. 5, 471, 493.

48 *Fredin v. Sweden (No. 1)*, no. 12033/86, 18 February 1991, § 51, Series A no. 192.

49 Cf. *Mellacher and Others v. Austria*, nos. 10522/83, 11011/84 and 11070/84, 19 December 1989, § 42, Series A no. 169; *Sporrong and Lönnroth v. Sweden*, nos. 7151/75 and 7152/75, 23 September 1982, § 61, Series A no. 52.

50 *Fredin v. Sweden (No. 1)*, above n. 48.

51 Ibid. This case concerned the revocation of permission to operate a gravel pit on the plaintiff's land. The national authority's decision was based on the Swedish Nature Protection Act 1955 (*naturskyddslagen* 1952:688) and was accepted by the Court. Another leading case in this context, cf.: *Pine Valley Developments Ltd and Others v. Ireland*, no. 12742/87, 29 November 1991, Series A no. 222.

52 The case law sometimes refers to 'nature', which is understood as a subcategory of 'environment', cf. *Turgut and Others v. Türkiye*, no. 1411/03, 8 July 2008, § 90.

53 *Fredin v. Sweden (No. 1)*, above n. 48, § 48.

54 K. Gelinsky, *Der Schutz des Eigentums gemäß Art. 1 des Ersten Zusatzprotokolls zur Europäischen Menschenrechtskonvention*, Berlin, Duncker & Humblot, 2016, p. 183. Cf. e.g. *Pine Valley Developments Ltd and Others v. Ireland*, above n. 51, § 57; *Hamer v. Belgium*, no. 21861/03, 27 November 2007, § 81, ECHR 2007-V.

55 *Matos E Silva, Lda. and Others v. Portugal*, no. 15777/89, 16 September 1996, § 89, ECHR 1996-IV; *Friend and Others v. United Kingdom* (dec.), nos. 16072/06 and 27809/08, 24 November 2009, § 50; *Chassagnou and Others v. France*, nos. 25088/94, 28331/95 and 28443/95, 29 April 1999, § 79, ECHR 1999-III.

a seashore[56] or woodland,[57] the refusal of planning permission to protect a green belt[58] or national park,[59] and fishing bans[60] to protect the marine environment, have been recognised as adequate measures to achieve the legitimate aim and to justify the interference with property rights. Even if these constellations are 'scarce and incidental exceptions[s]',[61] nature conservation is becoming increasingly important in the context of the fair balance test, which can be interpreted as a signal for greater tolerance of Convention restrictions in favour of nature conservation measures in the future.

2.2.1.2 *Annex Function – Environmental Concerns as Individual Interests*

A different situation is where the Court must decide whether disturbances caused by air pollution, water contamination, noise and other nuisances have a serious impact on people's homes. These cases typically deal with industrial nuisances and the state's failure to take adequate preventive measures to regulate private industries.[62] As already mentioned:

> there is no explicit right in the Convention to a clean and quiet environment, but where an individual is directly and seriously affected by noise or other pollution, an issue may arise under Article 8.[63]

Thus, environmental concerns serve as an *annex* to ECHR, Article 8.[64] ECHR, Article 8(2) reads that any interference by a public authority must be in accordance with the law and be necessary in a democratic society in the interests of national security, public safety or the economic well-being of the

56 *Brosset-Triboulet and Others v. France*, no. 34078/02, 29 March 2010, § 84; *Depalle v. France*, no. 34044/02, 29 March 2010, § 81; *N.A. and Others v. Türkiye*, no. 37451/97, 11 October 2005, § 40, ECHR 2005-X.

57 *Hamer v. Belgium*, above n. 54; *Köktepe v. Türkiye*, no. 35785/03, 13 October 2009, § 87; *Şatir v. Türkiye*, no. 36192/03, 10 March 2009, § 33; *Tumeliai v. Lithuania*, no. 25545/14, 9 January 2018, § 75.

58 *Pine Valley Developments Ltd and Others v. Ireland*, above n. 51, §§ 9, 57.

59 *Matczyński v. Poland*, no. 32794/07, 15 December 2015, § 106.

60 *O'Sullivan McCarthy Mussel Development Ltd v. Ireland*, no. 44460/16, 7 June 2018, § 128.

61 N. Kobylarz 'Balancing its way out of strong anthropocentrism: Integration of "ecological minimum standards" in the European Court of Human Rights "fair balance" review' (2022) 13 *Journal of Human Rights and the Environment* 16, 30.

62 A. Boyle, above n. 5, 471, 487.

63 *Hatton and Others v. United Kingdom*, no. 36022/97, 8 July 2003, § 96, ECHR 2003-VIII; see also *Giacomelli v. Italy*, no. 59909/00, 2 November 2006, § 76, ECHR 2006-XII.

64 Cf. e.g. *López Ostra v. Spain*, no. 16798/90, 9 December 1994, Series A no. 303-C; *Fadeyeva v. Russia*, no. 55723/00, 9 June 2005, ECHR 2005-IV; *Di Sarno and Others v. Italy*, no. 30765/08, 10 January 2012; *Dubetska and Others v. Ukraine*, no. 30499/03, 10 February 2011.

country. Like any interferences to property rights, the Court must strike a fair balance between the interests of the individual and of the community.[65]

In its annex function, environmental protection is considered as an interest of the *individual* in the fair balance test. The environmental pollution is inseparably connected to the harm to the individual and the Court does not assess the environmental harm *as such*. The legitimate aim of the interference is given if it serves the interests of the community – usually the economic well-being of a country.[66] This leads to a curious and remarkable situation, revealing the ambiguity of environmental concerns under the fair balance test: the damage to the environment and to the individual share a scale. Both are then weighed against the competing public economic interest, *although* environmental protection as such is certainly[67] also in the public interest.[68]

Apart from this oddity, a violation under ECHR, Article 8 was only affirmed in exceptional cases. This is based on two main reasons: first, within the fair balance test, the Court asserts that it reviews the substantive and procedural steps taken by the respondent state to ensure compliance with the Convention.[69] Nevertheless, the Court tends to review only the procedural guarantees, as the substantive ones allegedly fall within the state's margin of appreciation.[70] The revision of material conclusions of the national authorities are only for 'exceptional circumstances'.[71] It is therefore not surprising that a breach of domestic law necessarily constitutes a violation of ECHR, Article 8.[72] An apparent weakness of this approach is that low environmental standards set by the national legislatures are practically never an issue under the Convention.[73] Even if the Court has made it clear that the mere compliance with domestic law does not per se decide the issue in favour of the state,[74]

---

65 *Powell and Rayner v. United Kingdom*, no. 9310/81, 21 February 1990, § 41, Series A no. 172; *López Ostra v. Spain*, above n. 64, § 51.

66 Cf. e.g. *Hatton and Others v. United Kingdom*, above n. 63, §§ 54, 121; *Çiçek and Others v. Türkiye* (dec.), no. 44837/07, 4 February 2020, § 25; *Giacomelli v. Italy*, above n. 63, §§ 81, 83.

67 *Fredin v. Sweden (No. 1)*, above n. 48.

68 H. Müllerová, above n. 46, 89, 91.

69 *Hatton and Others v. United Kingdom*, above n. 63, § 99.

70 Ibid., § 122.

71 *Fadeyeva v. Russia*, above n. 64, § 105. E.g. for a substantive review: *Kapa and Others v. Poland*, no. 75031/13, 14 October 2021; *Association Burestop 55 and Others v. France*, nos. 56176/18, 56189/18, 56232/18 et al., 1 July 2021; *Kolyadenko and Others v. Russia*, nos. 17423/05, 20534/05, 20678/05, 23263/05, 24283/05 and 35673/05, 28 February 2012.

72 *López Ostra v. Spain*, above n. 64, § 54 (missing municipal licence to build and operate the waste-treatment plant); *Fadeyeva v. Russia*, above n. 64, § 119 (steel plant failed to safeguard a wider sanitary security zone).

73 N.M. De Sadeleer, 'Enforcing EUCHR Principles and Fundamental Rights in Environmental Cases' (2012) 81(1) *Nordic Journal of International Law* 39, 71; H. Müllerová, above n. 46, 83, 90.

74 *Fadeyeva v. Russia*, above n. 64, § 68.

inconsistencies in the approach must be noted. For example, in *Hardy and Maile v. United Kingdom*,[75] a violation of ECHR, Article 8 was negated – since national authorities had met the extensive environmental law standards[76] – although the risk for the marine environment posed an actual threat.[77] The wide margin of appreciation of national authorities in material guarantees is mocked as a 'margin of under-appreciation of the environment'.[78]

The second reason concerns the still rather restrictive interpretation of the Convention, as the Court requires that a human being is directly injured[79] in order to avoid *actio popularis*.[80] To qualify as a victim:

> there must be a sufficiently direct link between the applicant and the harm which they consider they have sustained on account of the alleged violation.[81]

The negative effects of the environmental pollution must therefore attain a certain minimum level of severity, which is determined by the circumstances of the individual case, such as the intensity and duration of the nuisance, and its physical or mental effects.[82] In this regard, the Court places the burden of proof to demonstrate the relevance of the adverse impact on the applicant.[83] Invoking a purely hypothetical risk is not sufficient to trigger a Convention violation.[84]

2.2.1.3 *Conclusion*

The cases have in common that the fair balance test is characterised by its flexibility,[85] which, depending on the margin of appreciation of the state, leaves the ECtHR scope for a 'superficial or a more in-depth proportionality assessment'[86] and significantly determines the outcome of the proceedings. A significant common feature is that the margin of appreciation is equally broad

---

75 *Hardy and Maile v. United Kingdom*, no. 31965/07, 14 February 2012.

76 Ibid., § 223.

77 Cf. O.W. Pedersen, 'Environmental Risks, Rights and Black Swans' (2013) 15 *Environmental Law Review* 55, 57–59.

78 H. Müllerová, above n. 46, 83, 92.

79 *Fadeyeva v. Russia*, above n. 64, § 68.

80 *Centre for Legal Resources on behalf of Valentin Câmpeanu v. Romania*, no. 47848/08, 17 July 2014, § 101, ECHR 2014; *Klass and Others v. Germany*, no. 5029/71, 6 August 1978, § 33, Series A no. 28.

81 *Gorraiz Lizarraga and Others v. Spain*, no. 62543/00, 27 April 2004, § 35, ECHR 2004-III.

82 *Fadeyeva v. Russia*, above n. 64, §§ 69 et seq.

83 *Vearncombe and Others v. Germany and United Kingdom*, no. 12816/87, 18 January 1989, Commission Admissibility Decision, p. 15.

84 *Tauira and Others v. France*, no. 28204/95, 4 December 1995, Commission Admissibility Decision 1995, p. 127; *Segi and Others v. 15 states of the European Union* (dec.), no. 6422/02, 23 May 2002, p. 7, ECHR 2002-V.

85 N. Kobylarz, above n. 61, 16, 30.

86 Ibid., 16, 32.

in both alternatives, regardless of whether the exercise of individual rights is adversely affected by nature conservation measures (see section 2.2.1.1.) or by damage to nature (see section 2.2.1.2.).[87] A significant difference is the legitimate aim pursued in the two constellations. In the context of nature conservation measures, this serves as a legitimate purpose for restricting individual rights, whereas in the case of damage to nature, economic interests are the main legitimate aim. In a nutshell, environmental protection is Janus-faced within the fair balance test, either an individual or general interest. Therefore, the outcome differs: in the limiting function, the Court generously tolerates freedom-restricting measures of state environmental protection. Within the annex function, the environment-friendly approach is not continued, and the judicial self-restraint led to inconsistent standards for environmental protection and human rights protection.[88]

2.2.2 Model 2: No Direct Protection of Nature

Despite its evolutionary approach in Model 1, the limits of the 'greening-process' of the Convention become evident in the case of environmental harm without certainty or evidence of a harm to individual human beings. The Court is not yet able to guarantee a right to a healthy environment in a broader sense of granting rights to parts of the environment. This becomes particularly impressive in the *Kyrtatos v. Greece*[89] case that concerns an illegal building project for urban development. The applicants have complained that the project has destroyed the swamp, which was adjacent to their home and has lost all its scenic beauty and the character as a natural habitat for birds and other species.[90] The Court states that the Convention is not 'specifically designed to provide general protection to the environment as such [...]'.[91]

> Yet the crucial element which must be present in determining whether, in the circumstances of a case, environmental pollution has adversely affected one of the rights safeguarded by paragraph 1 of Article 8 is the existence of a harmful effect

---

87 Ibid., 16 (32, fn. 98).

88 Y. Arai-Takahashi, 'The margin of appreciation doctrine: a theoretical analysis of Strasbourg's variable geometry' in A. Føllesdal, B. Peters and G. Ulfstein (eds), *Constituting Europe: The European Court of Human Rights in a National, European and Global Context*, Cambridge, Cambridge University Press, 2013, pp. 62–105, pp. 62, 80. For a critical overview, see pp. 62, 78–82.

89 *Kyrtatos v. Greece*, no. 41666/98, 22 May 2003, ECHR 2003-VI.

90 Ibid., §§ 46, 51. Similar in: *Ogloblina v. Russia*, no. 28852/05, 26 November 2013, §§ 20–22, 28.

91 *Kyrtatos v. Greece*, above n. 89, § 52. See also: *Şchiopu and Verzescu v. Romania* (dec.), no. 26040/06, 26 November 2013, § 28; *Cordella and Others v. Italy*, nos. 54414/13 and 54264/15, 24 January 2019, § 100.

on a person's private or family sphere and not simply the general deterioration of the environment.[92]

Even if the environment has been severely damaged by urban development, the applicants failed to demonstrate that the alleged harm to the birds and other species living in the swamp was of such a nature as to directly affect their own rights under ECHR, Article 8.[93] Without an individual being directly affected, this is effectively an *actio popularis* complaint, which intends to serve the public interest – namely nature conservation – and lies outside the competence of the ECtHR.[94] This decision points to the heart of the problem: the Court refuses to examine the merits of any case seeking environmental protection in general without specifying that an individual right guaranteed by the Convention or its protocols is at stake.[95]

2.2.3 Protection Gaps

2.2.3.1 *Strong Anthropocentrism*

Although the Convention does not contain explicit rights relating to the environment, the Court's case law clearly demonstrates how much environmental protection can be extracted from existing human rights norms without the need to create specific RoN.[96] From a normative perspective, the crucial question is which entities apart from human beings stand within the core of direct duties or outside in the periphery of indirect duties. Even if the ECtHR has never explicitly stated in its environment-related cases which environmental concept underlies its analyses, a *strong anthropocentric human rights protection* can be identified.[97] This approach is defined by two characteristics: *first*, this strong anthropocentric human rights approach pursues an approach solely focused on the human individual.[98] The protection of the environment is 'solely [...] a side-effect of the protection of other rights'[99] and is therefore not intended

92 *Kyrtatos v. Greece*, above n. 89, § 52.

93 Ibid., § 53. The decision also indicates that the case would probably have been decided differently if the concept of 'home' had been understood more broadly, L. Loucaides, above n. 38, 249, 267.

94 *Klaas and Others v. Germany*, above n. 80, § 33; *Crash 2000 OOD and Others v. Bulgaria* (dec.), no. 49893/07, 17 December 2013, § 84; *Ogloblina v. Russia*, above n. 90, §§ 26, 28.

95 N. Kobylarz, above n. 44, pp. 99, 106.

96 A. Boyle, above n. 5, 471, 504.

97 N. Kobylarz, above n. 61, 16, 33.

98 K. Morrow, 'The ECHR, Environment-Based Human Rights Claims and the Search for Standards' in S.J. Turner, D.L Shelton, J. Razzaque, O. McIntrye and J.R. May (eds), *Environmental Rights: The Development of Standards*, Cambridge, Cambridge University Press, 2019, pp. 41–59, pp. 41, 42; N. Kobylarz, above n. 61, 16, 35.

99 H. Müllerová, above n. 46, 83.

by the Court. Prue Taylor summarises this traditional human rights approach under the term 'environmental human rights'.[100]

From a normative point of view, only human beings have intrinsic value and only towards them exist direct duties. These direct duties are expressed in the fact that the Convention places only the individual under its protection. In this approach, nature enjoys indirect duties due to its extrinsic value. These indirect duties are expressed in the fact that the Court places nature under 'the regime of indirect protection of the environment through the proxy of human rights'[101] and only grants it *if* it serves the well-being of human beings. *Second*, the strongly anthropocentric human rights protection focuses on 'short-term and near-sighted perspectives'.[102] This means that European human rights protection is designed to provide immediate and timely redress for individual rights violations and ignores long-term consequences for both humanity and nature.

2.2.3.2 *Weak Anthropocentrism*

The European human rights system does not stay effectively in the service of the environment. This means that the Court intervenes – sometimes with disastrous environmental consequences – only when the level of environmental protection falls below that required to uphold guaranteed rights, while minor human rights violations do not.[103] Against the background of today's global environmental challenges, this strong anthropocentric approach is not sustainable anymore. However, in its recent *Verein KlimaSeniorinnen*[104] climate ruling, the ECtHR goes one step further by preventing long-term man-made risks to human beings.[105] The ruling brought with it two new developments: on the one hand, associations are entitled to bring a climate action before the ECtHR *even if* the members have not met the victim-status requirements in the climate-change context.[106] In doing so, the ECtHR is creating precisely 'what the judgment repeatedely asserts it wants to avoid, namely a basis for *actio popularis* type complaints',[107] as Judge Tim Eicke explains in his separate

100 Environmental human rights 'refer to the traditional rights approach of granting rights and creating duties and obligations to the environment, at a level sufficient to ensure the continued survival of present and future generations': P.E. Taylor, 'From Environmental to Ecological Human Rights: A New Dynamic in International Law?' (1998) 10(2) *Georgetown International Environmental Law Review* 309.

101 N. Kobylarz, above n. 61, 16, 33.

102 Ibid., 16, 39.

103 N. Kobylarz, above n. 44, p. 99, 112.

104 *Verein KlimaSeniorinnen Schweiz and Others v. Switzerland*, no. 53600/20, 9 April 2024. Other rulings, cf.: *Duarte Agostinho and Others v. Portugal and 32 others* (dec.), no. 39371/20, 9 April 2024; *Carême v. France*, no. 7189/21, 9 April 2024.

105 S. Theil, above n. 43, 330, 334.

106 *Verein KlimaSeniorinnen Schweiz and Others v. Switzerland*, above n. 104, § 502.

107 Ibid., Separate Opinion of Judge Tim Eicke, § 45.

opinion. This is contradictory to his usual approach in Model 2, where the Court does not examine the merits of cases seeking environmental protection or climate change protection in general. On the other hand, the ECtHR derives positive climate change obligations from ECHR, Article 8. With respect to the margin of appreciation, each state is free to establish its own adequate path for reaching carbon neutrality.[108]

> It follows [...] that effective respect for the rights protected by Article 8 of the Convention requires that each Contracting State undertake measures for the substantial and progressive reduction of their respective GHG emission levels, *with a view to reaching net neutrality within, in principle, the next three decades.*[109]

With this decision, the ECtHR adopts a more moderate form of anthropocentrism in climate change cases *alongside* its still strongly anthropocentric approach in other environmental cases.[110] This approach is also known as a *weak* or *immersive anthropocentric approach* that combines the traditional environmental human rights with the recognition of a deep interdependence between humans and nature.[111] Nature conservation in the form of climate protection is therefore in the collective interest and is promoted independently of its individualistic benefits.[112] What both forms of anthropocentrism have in common, however, is that they regard nature as an *object* and not as a subject of rights.[113] Even within the framework of weak anthropocentrism, nature is indirectly protected through human rights. Natalia Kobylarz summarises this human rights approach under the term 'ecological human rights'.[114] Is this new approach sufficient to protect nature and is the debate about the RoN therefore superfluous? Even the weakly anthropocentric approach cannot close the protection gaps of its strong counterpart. One significant argument is that climate protection measures can conflict with measures to protect nature. For example, the expansion of wind energy could fail because the construction of wind farms conflicts with the rights of a neighbouring nature reserve and the endangered bird species living there.[115]

108 *Verein KlimaSeniorinnen Schweiz and Others v. Switzerland*, above n. 104, § 546.
109 Ibid., § 548 (emphasis added).
110 Ibid., § 422.
111 E. Lambert, 'The Environment and Human Rights: Introductory Report to the High-Level Conference *Environmental Protection and Human Rights*', Strasbourg, 27 February 2020, p. 4.
112 D. Shelton, above n. 5, 103, 110; N. Kobylarz, above n. 61, 16, 45.
113 E. Lambert, above n. 111, p. 4.
114 Ecological human rights 'engender considerations of true interests of environmental protection, including interest that lie beyond individual and immediately noticeable material benefits to humans': N. Kobylarz, above n. 61, 16, 39.
115 M. Kramm, ‚Rechte für einzelne Ökosysteme' in M. Kramm (ed), *Rechte für Flüsse, Berge und Wälder: Eine neue Perspektive für den Naturschutz?*, Munich, oekom, 2023, pp. 69, 77.

But should the exclusive circle of moral community for humans be opened to non-human beings in the coming decades? With a physiocentric approach, the intrinsic value of nature would emerge and would no longer be considered as an 'appendix' to human needs. How can *direct* and stronger substantive and procedural protection of natural entities be ensured through the Convention? Alongside the climate judgment of the ECtHR as one mechanism to face the ecological crisis, its counterpart, the Inter-American Court of Human Rights[116] in San José, presents another opportunity: nature as a non-human human rights subject. What is this new legal notion about and is it thinkable for the European human rights system?

2.3. *Nature as a Non-Human Human Rights Subject*

To speak of RoN sounds at first 'odd or frightening or laughable',[117] but it is no longer wishful thinking. The IACtHR presents in its groundbreaking Advisory Opinion OC-23/17[118] an innovative development that is an alternative to the purely anthropocentric approach of the ECtHR. It examines environmental law as a systematic whole separately from single cases of environmental harm.[119] The IACtHR recognises that nature *as such* is an independent human rights subject. It is worth quoting the IACtHR's reasoning at length here:

> The Court considers it important to stress that, as an autonomous right, the right to a healthy environment, unlike other rights, protects the components of the environment, such as forests, rivers and seas, as legal interests in themselves, even in the absence of the certainty or evidence of a risk to individuals. This means that it protects nature and the environment, not only because of the benefits they provide to humanity or the effects that their degradation may have on other human rights, such as health, life or personal integrity, but because of their importance to the other living organisms with which we share the planet that also merit protection in their own right. In this regard, the Court notes a tendency, not only in court judgments, but also in Constitutions, to recognize legal personality and, consequently, *rights to nature*.[120]

---

[116] Hereinafter: IACtHR.

[117] C.D. Stone, 'Should Trees have Standing? – Toward Legal Rights for Natural Objects' (1972) 45 *Southern California Law Review* 450, 445.

[118] IACtHR Advisory Opinion OC-23/17 of 15 November 2017, 'The Environment and Human Rights' (hereinafter: the Advisory Opinion). In general, advisory opinions are judicial interpretations of provisions of the Inter-American Convention on Human Rights (IACHR) or other treaties that are binding in their nature, ACHR, Article 64.

[119] P. Siwior, 'The Inter-American Court of Human Rights Advisory Opinion OC-23/17 on the Relationship between Human Rights and the Environment' (2021) 46(3) *Review of European and Comparative Law* 177, 185; M. Feria-Tinta and S. Milnes, 'The Rise of Environmental Law in International Dispute Resolution: Inter-American Court of Human Rights Issues a Landmark Advisory Opinion on Environmental and Human Rights' (2016) 27(1) *Yearbook of International Environmental Law* 64, 65.

[120] Advisory Opinion, above n. 118, § 62 (emphasis added).

It represents a hybrid model, combining physiocentric and anthropocentric approaches. In a physiocentric sense, it recognises that the right to a healthy environment is an *autonomous* right under ACHR, Article 26[121] – an economic, social, and cultural right – and grants rights to the components of the environment, which means that an interference with human rights is not required.[122] With this innovative approach, the IACHR expands the exclusive circle of human rights holders and recognises nature as such with an individual protection claim as a non-human human rights subject.[123] In an anthropocentric sense, it determines that the right to a healthy environment has an individual and collective dimension. In its individual dimension, this right is linked to the enjoyment of other human rights, particularly the right to life, personal integrity, and health.[124] In its collective dimension, the right constitutes a universal value that is owed to present and future generations.[125] Thus, it is a *fundamental* right that serves as a mechanism to protect the existence of humankind from environmental degradation. The significance of the Advisory Opinion is evident; '[it] go[es] beyond the interests of the States parties [...] and [is] important for all the States of the planet'.[126]

This historic Advisory Opinion has already influenced the subsequent case law. In *Indigenous Communities of the Lhaka Honhat (Our Land) Association v. Argentina*,[127] the IACtHR applied the rights to a healthy environment as an enforceable right under ACHR, Article 26 to indigenous peoples and communities for the first time in a contentious case.[128] Even though reference was made to the Advisory Opinion[129] and expert evidence was available that

121 Ibid., § 57. The IACtHR reads the right to a healthy environment into ACHR, Article 26, stating that state parties need to adopt measures for the progressive realisation of economic, social, and cultural rights. For critical remarks cf. A. Papantoniou, ,Advisory Opinion on the Environment and Human Rights' (2018) 112 *American Journal of International Law* 460, 463; E. Benz and V. Kahl, ,Das Urteil im Fall Lhaka Honhat: Die Ausweitung der direkten Justiziabilität von DESCA und die unerfüllte Hoffnung der Konkretisierung des Rechts auf eine gesunde Umwelt' (2021) 59(2) *Archiv des Völkerrechts* 119, 210–15.

122 M.A. Tigre, 'Indigenous Communities of the Lhaka Honhat (Our Land) Association v. Argentina' (2021) 115(4) *American Journal of International Law* 706; P. Siwior, above n. 119, 177, 184.

123 E. Benz and V. Kahl, above n. 121, 164, 170; M.A. Tigre and N. Urzola 'The 2017 Inter-American Court's Advisory Opinion: changing the paradigm for international environmental law in the Anthropocene' (2021) 12(1) *Journal of Human Rights and the Environment* 24, 48.

124 Advisory Opinion, above n. 118, §§ 47, 59.

125 Ibid., § 59.

126 Ibid., § 35; P. Siwior, above n. 119, 177, 185 et seq.

127 *Indigenous Communities of the Lhaka Honhat (Our Land) Association v. Argentina*, IACtHR Judgment, 6 February 2020, Series C No. 400, (hereinafter: *Lhaka Honhat*), § 203. Cf. M.A. Tigre, above n. 122, 706–13.

128 *Lhaka Honhat*, § 289: the Court specified that the right to a healthy environment requires not only an obligation to respect but also a positive duty to guarantee environmental protection according to ACHR, Article 1(1).

129 Ibid., § 203.

the livestock and logging activities by the state and non-indigenous settlers have caused significant damage to nature,[130] the IACtHR unfortunately does not consider nature as a victim in the case.[131] While the decision marks a significant milestone for the protection of indigenous peoples' rights, it remains behind the development of the Advisory Opinion.[132] However, the development is still in its infancy, and the IACtHR faces a major challenge in setting more precise standards for the autonomous right to a healthy environment as a result of its physiocentric approach. It is a transition that must be made carefully, as nature as a potential victim, as defined by the ACHR, significantly changes the fundamental ground of the Inter-American System of Human Rights, the protection of human dignity,[133] and thus its consistently practiced *pro homine* principle. According to the latter principle, the ACHR must be interpreted in such a way that it offers human beings the greatest possible protection.[134]

This innovation at the Inter-American human rights level also reflects the growing trend in Latin America to recognise nature as a subject of rights,[135] as expressed in the Constitution of Ecuador[136] or the Bolivian Law on Mother Earth.[137] This has a bottom-up effect in favour of the RoN idea. The IACtHR sets itself at the forefront of the development of non-human rights for nature. But apart from this isolated example in the Inter-American Human Rights System, there is a tendency that RoN have not yet been seriously considered in the context of human rights.[138] This development can serve as a blueprint and could also have a spillover effect on the European human rights system, as human rights courts 'work consciously to co-ordinate their approaches'[139]

---

130 Ibid., §§ 280 et seq.

131 Ibid., § 309.

132 In the Advisory Opinion OC-23/17, above n. 118, 'it had clearly stated that the autonomous rights to a healthy environment aims to protect nature per se, but in the case of the Lhaka Honhat communities, in line with its previous jurisprudence, it aims to protect indigenous peoples' enjoyment of their collective property and related rights': J.J. Faundes Peñafiel, C. Carmona Caldera and P.P. Silva Sánchez, 'La Corte Interamericana de Derechos Humanos. Hermenéutica del derecho al medio ambiente sano, a la identidad cultural y a la consulta, a la luz de la sentencia *"Lhaka Honhat (neustra tierra vs. Argentina" (2020)*' (2020) 10(2) *Revista Brasileira de Políticas Públicas* 644, 668, own translation.

133 D.M. Zambrano, 'Antropocentrismo y ecocentrismo en la jurisprudencia de la Corte Interamericana de Derechos Humanos' (2021) 23(46) *Araucaria* 506, 524. This is also expressed in the ACHR, cf. preamble: 'rights of man'; ACHR, Article 1(2): 'For the purposes of this Convention, "person" means every human being'.

134 *Benjamin et al. v. Trinidad and Tobago*, IACtHR Judgment (Prelimary Objections), 1 September 2007, Series C No. 81, § 70.

135 M. Feria-Tinta and S. Milnes, above n. 119, 69 et seq.

136 Cf. Constitution of the Republic of Ecuador 2008, see above, n. 7.

137 Cf. La Ley de Derechos de la Madre Tierra, see above n. 7.

138 E. Jones, above n. 4, 76, 88.

139 R. Higgins, 'A Babel of Judicial Voices? Ruminations from the Bench' (2006) 55(4) *International and Comparative Law Quarterly* 791, 798.

and there is certainly evidence of convergence in the case law and a cross-fertilisation of ideas between the different human right systems.[140] The ECtHR describes the ECHR as a 'living instrument, which [...] must be interpreted in the light of present-day conditions'[141] and this underlying dynamic interpretation allows thinking outside the anthropocentric framework and opening up to physiocentric implications.

3 RIGHTS OF NATURE AS HUMAN RIGHTS – *QUO VADIS*?

The idea of dehumanisation of human rights is not entirely new to the European human rights system, as it is already practiced in the field of corporate human rights,[142] that is also subject to criticism.[143] In light of the new dogmatic structures resulting from the *Verein KlimaSeniorinnen* ruling, which will continue to develop in the coming decisions, it seems unlikely that RoN will be implemented soon. However, the phenomenon of RoN and a potential inclusion of nature as non-human human rights subject is faced with scepticism[144] and poses some challenges for future research, which will be outlined here.

3.1. Justification of RoN

The IACtHR offers a hybrid justification, focusing on the one hand on the benefits to humankind, but also emphasising the intrinsic value of nature on the other. The intrinsic value is not determined by a particular property, such as the ability to reason or sentience. For the implementation of RoN, the IACtHR

140 *Caesar v. Trinidad and Tobago*, IACtHR Judgment, 11 March 2005, Series C No. 123, Separate Opinion of Judge Trindade, § 7.

141 *Tyrer v. United Kingdom*, no. 5876/72, 25 April 1978, § 31, Series A no. 26.

142 For a comprehensive survey, see M. Emberland, *The Human Rights of Companies: Exploring the Structure of ECHR Protection*, Oxford, Oxford University Press, 2008. For the reasoning the Court refers to the rule of law, cf. e.g. *Société Colas Est and Others v. France*, no. 37971/97, 16 April 2002, § 41: the Court concludes that the registered office, branches and other business premises of a company fall within the scope of protection of ECHR, Article 8. This is an expression of the principle of rule of law, as business premises cannot otherwise be protected against arbitrary state interference.

143 So called 'no-corporate-rights approach', A. Scolnicov, 'Human rights and derivative rights' in T. Kahana and A. Scolnicov (eds), *Boundaries of State, Boundaries of Rights: Human Rights, Private Actors, and Positive Obligations*, Cambridge, Cambridge University Press, 2016, pp. 194 et seq.

144 H. Kersten, ‚Eigenrechte der Natur: Lichtblick oder Irrlicht für einen verstärkten rechtlichen Schutz der Natur?' (1990) 29(3) *Der Staat* 415; K. Hilpert, 'Rechte der Natur. Zur Problematik der Ausweitung der Menschenrechtsfigur auf die Natur' in H.-R. Reuter (ed), *Ethik der Menschenrechte: Zum Streit um die Universalität einer Idee*, Tübingen, Mohr Siebeck, 1999, pp. 321–49; H. Bielefeldt, 'Moving Beyond Anthropocentrism? Human Rights and the Charge of Speciesism' (2021) 43 *Human Rights Quarterly* 515.

offers a new reasoning alongside traditional human rights justification, which regularly refers to human dignity.[145]

3.2. *Dogmatic Challenges*

The IACtHR has linked the RoN to the right to a healthy environment, which is included in the economic, social and cultural rights under ACHR, Article 26. A comparable implementation in the ECHR, relating to civil and political rights, is not conceivable. Also, the counterpart (the European Social Charter (ESC))[146] does not recognise a right to a healthy environment. However, the living instrument doctrine could be a starting point for a more far-reaching interpretation of ECHR, Article 1, for instance. The term 'everyone' could then include both living and non-living entities, such as nature.

3.3. *Who Speaks for Nature?*

Since nature cannot speak for itself, it needs a 'human face'.[147] There is a concern not to flood the ECtHR with RoN lawsuits and thus limit standing to certain associations. A look at national legal mechanisms is instructive: here a distinction is made between a universal legal standing and the guardianship approach.[148] Within the framework of the European system, it is also conceivable to limit the legal standing to associations whose objective is nature conservation. They can take actions against environmentally destructive or unsustainable developments on public interest grounds. That would benefit society, not just individual victims. Therefore, it may be possible to apply the dogmatic construction of the legal standing of associations in the *Verein KlimaSeniorinnen* judgment. The procedural changes are the game-changers and have the potential to unlock cross-border remedies for the victims – whether human or non-human – of environmental degradation.[149]

145 Cf. C. McCrudden (ed), *Understanding Human Dignity*, Oxford, Oxford University Press, 2013; P. Gilabert, *Human Dignity and Human Rights*, Oxford, Oxford University Press, 2018.

146 European Social Charter, 18 November 1961 (ETS 35).

147 Te Awa Tupua (Whanganui River Claims Settlement) Act 2017, Article 18(2), above n. 7.

148 A. Bleby, 'Rights of Nature as a Response to the Anthropocene' (2020) 48(1) *University of Western Australia Law Review* 33, 53–57. Cf. for a universal standing clause: Constitution of the Republic of Ecuador, Article 71(2), above n. 7, and for a guardianship clause: Te Awa Tupua (Whanganui River Claims Settlement) Act 2017, Articles 18–20, above n. 7.

149 M. Feria-Tinta and S. Milnes, above n. 119, 64.

3.4. *What Kind of Rights?*

The intrinsic value of nature has yet to be brought to life. It is obvious that the right to a healthy environment in its autonomous reading needs an ecological interpretation as the constitution of a healthy environment is bound to suffer from uncertainty.[150] Points of reference for the specifications of rights are also provided by the judgments of the Constitutional Court of Ecuador on the Los Cedros Forest,[151] the Aquepi River[152] or the Monjas[153] River.[154] The concept of health implies a value judgment and therefore leaves the ECtHR room for its own interpretation, reformulation, and expansion of the respective rights.[155]

3.5. *Collision between Human Rights and RoN*

The exciting question is how to proceed in the case of a collision between human rights and RoN. These are practical issues relating to the burden of proof and the balancing criteria. Should the principle '*in dubio pro natura et clima*'[156] be applied in case of collision?

3.6. *State Measures*

It is of relevance which state measures are associated with the implementation of RoN. Are there significant changes to the anthropocentric approach? How can states comply with their obligation to respect, protect, and fulfil the RoN?

---

150 A. Boyle, 'The Role of International Human Rights Law and the Protection of the Environment' in A. Boyle and M.R. Anderson (eds), *Human Rights Approaches to Environmental Protection*, Oxford, Oxford University Press, 1996, pp. 43, 50.

151 *Municipality of Cotacachi v. Ministry of Environment*, no. 1149-19-JP/20, 10 November 2021 (Constitutional Court of Ecuador).

152 *Realpe Herrera v. SENAGUA*, no. 1185-20-JP, 15 December 2021 (Constitutional Court of Ecuador).

153 *Monge v. Quito Municipality*, no. 2167/21-EP, 19 January 2022 (Constitutional Court of Ecuador).

154 A summary of the judgments can be found in: C.M. Kauffman and P.L. Martin 'How Ecuador's Courts Are Giving Form and Force to Rights of Nature Norms' (2023) 12(2) *Transnational Environmental Law* 366.

155 D. Shelton, above n. 5, 103, 117.

156 M. Carducci, S. Bagni, V. Lorubbio, E. Musarò, M. Montini, A. Barreca, C. Di Francesco Maesa, M. Ito, L. Spinks and P. Powlesland, 'Nature's rights: Towards an EU Charter of the Fundamental Rights of Nature', Brussels, 13 December 2019, p. 81.

4 CONCLUSION

These are defined research questions that need to be explored further. This chapter gives an overview about the weaknesses of the strong and weak anthropocentric approach of the European human rights system and a possible solution that can be seen in the coming decades in a physiocentric approach that considers nature in its sphere of protection.

> The Convention […] has repeatedly proved itself capable of adapting to new human rights challenges […]. This adaptability will be crucial in helping the continent to face emerging challenges to individuals' rights linked to […] threats to the natural environment.[157]

It therefore remains to be seen how the ECtHR will approach 'new frontiers of human rights law'[158] – also against the background that RoN are also gradually blossoming within Europe as proven in Spain[159] and the Netherlands.[160]

---

157 '70th anniversary of European Convention on Human Rights: a convention for the people', *Council of Europe: Newsroom*, 29 January 2020 <https://www.coe.int/en/web/portal/-/70th-anniversary-of-european-convention-on-human-rights-a-convention-for-the-people>.

158 J. Viljanen, 'The Role of the European Court of Human Rights as a Developer of International Human Rights Law' (2011) 62/63 *Cuadernos Constitutucionales de la Cátedra Fadrique Furió Ceriol* 249, 250.

159 The Spanish Parliament voted in favour of a new law on the recognition of the legal personality of the Mar Menor Lagoon, cf. L. Krämer, 'Rights of Nature in Europe: The Spanish Lagoon Mar Menor Becomes a Legal Person' (2023) 20(1) *Journal for European Environmental & Planning Law* 5; A. Putzer and J. Zenetti, 'Die Rechte des spanischen Mar Menor' in M. Kramm (ed), *Rechte für Flüsse, Berge und Wälder: Eine neue Perspektive für den Naturschutz?*, above n. 115, pp. 55–60.

160 In the Netherlands, the Frisian municipality of Dongeradeel adopted a motion that grants special rights to the Wadden Sea, cf. T. Lambooy, J. van de Venis and C. Stokkermans, 'A case for granting legal personality to the Dutch part of the Wadden Sea' (2019) 44(6–7) *Water International* 786.

CHAPTER 6

HOW SOON IS NOW? THE FUTURE OF REPETITIVE CASES

Ezgi Özlü

1 INTRODUCTION

The number of individual applications to the European Court of Human Rights (ECtHR) increased rapidly in the late 1990s, coinciding with the significant expansion of Council of Europe membership to include Central and Eastern European states.[1] Following the entry into force of the European Convention on Human Rights (ECHR) Protocol No. 11 in 1998, the massive influx of new applications became increasingly evident,[2] contributing to the backlog of the Strasbourg Court.[3] By 2010, the ECtHR had jurisdiction over 47 Council of Europe Member States, encompassing a total population of approximately 800 million. The Court was receiving around 60,000 applications per year and issuing approximately 1,500 substantive judgments annually, making it the international court with the largest caseload.[4]

To prevent the collapse of the system, the ECtHR undertook a process of reform. Some measures focused on deterring inadmissible applications. In this regard, efforts to reinforce the Court's filtering capacity included the introduction of a single-judge system and further restrictions on the admissibility criteria under ECHR, Article 35, such as the adoption of the 'significant disadvantage' criterion[5] and the reduction of the six-month time limit to four months.[6] Other measures were aimed at accelerating proceedings. These included the adoption of a priority policy, the practice of issuing pilot

---

1. P. Leuprecht, 'Innovations in the European System of Human Rights Protection: Is Enlargement Compatible with Reinforcement?' (1998) 8 *Transnational Law and Contemporary Problems* 313, 328.
2. ECtHR, 'Analysis of statistics 2016', January 2017, p. 7, Chart 1. The ECHR is the Convention for the Protection of Human Rights and Fundamental Freedoms, 4 November 1950 (ETS 5).
3. ECtHR, above n. 2, p. 7, Chart 2.
4. ECtHR, 'Analysis of statistics 2010', January 2011, p. 6.
5. Ibid.
6. Protocol No. 15 amending the Convention on the Protection of Human Rights and Fundamental Freedoms, Strasbourg, 24 July 2013 (ETS 213), Article 4.

judgments, and the establishment of three-judge committees for cases already covered by well-established case law.[7]

The concept of repetitive cases is frequently referenced in the documents of the Council of Europe. However, neither the ECHR nor the Rules of Court[8] define this term. Additionally, the ECtHR does not provide information on the categorisation of cases, either on a general basis or by country.[9] In other words, no precise definition or criteria exist for determining what constitutes a repetitive case. In academic scholarship, repetitive cases have often been regarded as a contributing factor to the backlog crisis at the ECtHR and are typically examined in the context of pilot judgments or other potential solutions to this crisis.[10]

Mathilde Kamal conducted an analytical examination of the term 'established case law' as used by the ECtHR, arguing that its application offers several benefits to the Court: it helps protect the Court's autonomy and authority, stabilises its case law, and facilitates the acceleration of judgment delivery.[11] However, Kamal does not explicitly address 'repetitive cases' in her analysis. Furthermore, there appears to be some confusion surrounding the relationship between repetitive cases, simple cases, and well-established case law (WECL) cases.

A 2013 PACE Resolution provides a relatively clear delineation of the relationship between repetitive cases and WECL cases. It asserts that:

> the Court is […] overloaded with a large number of repetitive cases […] [m]ost of [which] relate to structural issues identified by well-established case law.[12]

This claim suggests that the term 'repetitive' is broader than 'well-established', with well-established case law encompassing certain types of repetitive cases.

7 Protocol No. 14 to the Convention for the Protection of Human Rights and Fundamental Freedoms, Amending the Control System of the Convention, Strasbourg, 13 March 2004 (ETS 194).

8 Registry of the Court, 'Rules of Court', 15 September 2025 <https://www.echr.coe.int/documents/d/echr/rules_court_eng>

9 J.-L. Sauron and A. Stepanova, *Guide pratique de procédure devant la Cour européenne des droits de l'homme*, Paris, LGDJ, 2018, para. 197.

10 See e.g. S. Szemesi, 'Repetitive Cases before the Strasbourg Court: The Pilot Judgment Procedure at the European Court of Human Rights' (2014) 2(1) *Hungarian Yearbook of International Law and European Law* 243; D. Reichel and J. Grimheden, 'A Decade of Violations of the European Convention on Human Rights: Exploring Patterns of Repetitive Violations' in W. Benedek, P. Czech, L. Heschl, K. Lukas and M. Nowak (eds), *European Yearbook on Human Rights 2018*, Cambridge, Intersentia, 2018, pp. 267–86; E. Wagner, 'Repetitive Cases: European Court of Human Rights (ECtHR)' in H. Ruiz Fabri (ed), *Max Planck Encyclopedia of International Procedural Law*, Oxford, Oxford University Press, 2019.

11 M. Kamal, 'Les «Jurisprudences Établies» de La Cour Européenne Des Droits de l'homme' (2019) 2 *RDLF* 1 <https://revuedlf.com/cedh/les-jurisprudences-etablies-de-la-cour-europeenne-des-droits-de-lhomme/>.

12 PACE Resolution 1914 (2013) Final version of 22 January 2013, 'Ensuring the viability of the Strasbourg Court: structural deficiencies in States Parties', para. 3.

A senior lawyer at the ECtHR Registry has used the term 'simple cases/ repetitive cases' in a scheme addressing awards for legal costs and expenses, though she does not clarify the connection between the terms or whether they can be used interchangeably.[13]

According to one scholar, WECL cases constitute a subgroup of repetitive cases, with WECL cases being those where the Court has firmly established the grounds for finding a violation.[14] However, this scholar does not explain what non-WECL repetitive cases are, leaving the distinction unclear. Conversely, another scholar argues the opposite, suggesting that repetitive cases are a subset of WECL cases.[15] Similarly, yet another scholar contends that repetitive cases refer to well-founded complaints.[16]

This chapter aims to reflect on the future of repetitive cases. It argues that, in the absence of a precise definition or criteria, the ECtHR exercises broad discretion in interpreting the term. In other words, what is included in or excluded from this category of cases is not static but dynamic, evolving over time. The sections that follow outline the categories of repetitive cases (see below section 2) and highlight their growing significance by examining the procedures applied in such cases (see below section 3).

2 DEFINING THE CATEGORIES OF REPETITIVE CASES

This section first argues that the sole criterion for a case to be classified as 'repetitive' is that it must not 'raise a new legal issue' for the ECtHR (see below section 2.1). It then examines the stage at which the ECtHR determines whether a given case raises a new legal issue (see below section 2.2).

2.1. The Core of the Concept

Any case that does not raise a new legal issue can be defined as repetitive. The Steering Committee for Human Rights (CDDH) describes repetitive applications as those arising from systemic or structural issues at the domestic level. The term 'repetitive' implies that the Court has already addressed the

13 K. Reid, *A Practitioner's Guide to the European Convention on Human Rights*, 6th ed., London, Sweet & Maxwell, 2019, p. 1277.

14 E. Wagner, above n. 10, para. 7.

15 E. Kindt, 'The Pilot Judgment Procedure at the European Court of Human Rights: an Evaluation in the Light of Procedural Efficiency and Access to Justice', University dissertation, Ghent, Ghent University Faculty of Law and Criminology, 2018, p. 116.

16 L.R. Glas, *The Theory, Potential and Practice of Procedural Dialogue in the European Convention on Human Rights System*, Cambridge, Intersentia, 2016, p. 44.

underlying legal issue in a prior judgment.[17] The Department for the Execution of Judgments of the ECtHR further defines a repetitive case as one that pertains to a structural and/or general problem already addressed by the Committee of Ministers in one or more leading cases.[18] This body also distinguishes WECL cases as those where a judgment on the merits is rendered by a Committee of three judges, provided that the issues raised are already covered by the Court's well-established case law under ECHR, Article 28(1)(b).[19]

In such cases, the Court has already identified the legal issue in its previous judgments. Consequently, these cases do not contribute to the further development of the Convention.[20] The Court does not engage in interpreting new legal questions arising under the Convention but instead reiterates its established findings. In this respect, repetitive cases are a specific category of cases characterised by a shared factual background and consistent findings on the merits.[21] For this reason, they are largely identical to one another.[22]

Repetitive cases are not confined to a specific type of violation. Publicly accessible Council of Europe documents provide concrete examples of repetitive cases.[23] These include instances such as 'excessive length of judicial proceedings leading to ineffective protection of a wide range of substantive rights'.[24] Excessive delays in proceedings constitute a breach of Article 6(1) of the ECHR and, in certain cases, also violate the right to an effective remedy under Article 13 of the ECHR.[25] Repetitive cases also encompass issues like the 'chronic non-enforcement of domestic decisions'[26] that can result in violations of ECHR, Article 6(1), Article 13, and Protocol No.1, Article 1. Another recurring example pertains to ownership disputes stemming from the transitions of former Soviet states. In such cases, applicants often seek compensation for

---

17 Steering Committee for Human Rights (CDDH), 'Report containing conclusions and possible proposals for action on ways to resolve the large numbers of applications arising from systemic issues identified by the Court', 11 July 2013, CM(2013)93 add6, § 4.

18 Department for the Execution of Judgments of the ECtHR, 'Glossary', *Council of Europe* <https://www.coe.int/en/web/execution/glossary#{%2215005454%22:[24]}>.

19 Ibid.

20 J.-L. Sauron and A. Stepanova, above n. 9, para. 199.

21 E. Wagner, above n. 10, para. 3.

22 J.-L. Sauron and A. Stepanova, above n. 9, para. 199.

23 C. Pourgourides, PACE, 'Implementation of judgments of the European Court of Human Rights', 20 December 2010, Doc. 12455, para. 5.

24 PACE Resolution 1787 (2011) of 26 January 2011, 'Implementation of judgments of the European Court of Human Rights', para. 5.1.

25 *Rumpf v. Germany*, no. 46344/06, 2 September 2010; *Vassilios Athanasiou and Others v. Greece*, no. 50973/08, 21 December 2010; *Dimitrov and Hamanov v. Bulgaria*, nos. 48059/06 and 2708/09, 10 May 2011; *Finger v. Bulgaria*, no. 37346/05, 10 May 2011; *Michelioudakis v. Greece*, no. 54447/10, 3 April 2012; *Glykantzi v. Greece*, no. 40150/09, 30 October 2012; *Rutkowski and Others v. Poland*, nos. 72287/10, 13927/11 and 46187/11, 7 July 2015; *Gazsó v. Hungary*, no. 48322/12, 16 July 2015.

26 PACE Resolution 1787 (2011) of 26 January 2011, above n. 24, para. 5.2.

property lost, nationalised, or otherwise restricted by domestic authorities.[27] Additionally, the general ban on prisoners' voting rights represents another category of repetitive cases. This blanket and automatic disenfranchisement has been deemed incompatible with ECHR, Protocol No. 1, Article 3.[28]

Grave violations are not excluded from the typology of 'repetitive cases'. For instance, the Court has applied the WECL procedure in cases where detention conditions amount to inhuman or degrading treatment under Article 3 of the ECHR.[29] Examples include prison overcrowding, where national authorities fail to ensure minimum living space per prisoner, requiring some prisoners to sleep on the floor, as well as the lack of natural light, basic hygiene, or adequate mental health care.[30] Another category of repetitive findings involves 'unlawful detention and excessive length of detention on remand'.[31] Even more severe violations are also found among repetitive cases, such as 'ill-treatment by law enforcement officials – sometimes resulting in death – and a lack of effective investigations thereof', as well as enforced disappearances.[32]

The following section examines how a case becomes repetitive – in other words, how a legal question becomes stabilised (section 2.2).

2.2. When Does a Case Become 'Repetitive'?

Neither the Convention nor the Rules of Court specify the point at which a legal issue becomes stable. However, the Convention employs the term 'well-established case law' (WECL) when defining the competence of Committees. Article 28 of the ECHR entrusts Committees of three judges with the authority to deliver judgments in cases governed by well-established case law. To elaborate, a Committee may render a 'judgment on the merits' if the

---

27 *Burdov v. Russia (No. 2)*, no. 33509/04, 15 January 2009; *Olaru and Others v. Moldova*, nos. 476/07, 22539/05, 17911/08 and 13136/07, 28 July 2009; *Yuriy Nikolayevich Ivanov v. Ukraine*, no. 40450/04, 15 October 2009; *Gerasimov and Others v. Russia*, nos. 29920/05, 3553/06, 18876/10, 61186/10, 21176/11, 36112/11, 36426/11, 40841/11, 45381/11, 55929/11 and 60822/11, 1 July 2014; *Burmych and Others v. Ukraine (striking out)*, nos. 46852/13, 47786/13, 54125/13 et al., 12 October 2017; *Béláné Nagy v. Hungary*, no. 53080/13, 13 December 2016.

28 *Hirst v. United Kingdom (No. 2)*, no. 74025/01, 6 October 2005, ECHR 2005-IX; *Greens and M.T. v. United Kingdom*, nos. 60041/08 and 60054/08, 23 November 2010 (extracts); *Frodl v. Austria*, no. 20201/04, 8 April 2010; *Söyler v. Turkey*, no. 29411/07, 17 September 2013; *Anchugov and Gladkov v. Russia*, nos. 11157/04 and 15162/05, 4 July 2013; *Kulinski and Sabev v. Bulgaria*, no. 63849/09, 21 July 2016.

29 L.A. Sicilianos and M.A. Kostopoulou, *The Individual Application Under the European Convention on Human Rights*, Strasbourg, Council of Europe Publishing, 2019, pp. 104, 105.

30 *Ananyev and Others v. Russia*, nos. 42525/07 and 60800/08, 10 January 2012, §§ 143–48; *Torreggiani and Others v. Italy*, nos. 43517/09, 46882/09, 55400/09 et al., 8 January 2013, §§ 70–79.

31 PACE Resolution 1787 (2011) of 26 January 2011, above n. 24, para. 5.4.

32 L.A. Sicilianos and M.A. Kostopoulou, above n. 29, pp. 104, 105.

underlying question in a case – relating to the interpretation or application of the Convention or its Protocols – is already covered by the Court's well-established case law. Consequently, cases handled by this judicial formation can be classified as repetitive cases.

The category of repetitive cases is dynamic. A 2018 CDDH report describes the concept of WECL as:

> case-law in which the particular issue has been addressed, in relation to the State concerned, by a Grand Chamber judgment, or – at Chamber level – by a pilot judgment or a leading judgment.[33]

Pascal Dourneau-Josette, Head of Division at the Registry, offers a similar interpretation, asserting that WECL refers to follow-up cases stemming from Chamber or Grand Chamber judgments. This encompasses situations where there is 'clear and stable jurisprudence on a legal question', indicated by a series of judgments identifying the same violation, or where there is a leading judgment, such as a pilot judgment or a Grand Chamber judgment.[34] Jean-Luc Sauron and Anna Stepanova, aiming to guide practitioners, propose broader conditions for the term WECL than those suggested by the aforementioned authors. While a judgment delivered by a Committee of three judges is one indicator, WECL is not limited to such cases. A Chamber applying consistent case law on a legal matter might also signal a WECL case. Other indicators include the Court having already issued a pilot or leading judgment on the legal question. Applicants should investigate whether the Court has rendered multiple judgments on a similar legal question involving other states. Finally, they should also consider the existence of a Grand Chamber decision or judgment addressing the same legal issue.[35]

To summarise the three perspectives outlined above, the following common points can be deduced: a legal issue becomes well-established only with respect to the respondent state. For example, a blanket ban on voting rights was recognised as a repetitive case against the United Kingdom in 2005.[36] However, this judgment did not have an automatic effect on other Member States with similar blanket bans on voting rights.[37] The Court applied the WECL procedure exclusively to

---

33 ECtHR, 'Follow-up to the CDDH Report on the Longer-Term Future of the system of the European Convention on Human Rights', 19 January 2018, DD(2018)60, para. 12.

34 P. Dourneau-Josette, 'Les adaptations procédurales ou l'accélération du traitement des equêtes' (2020) 1 *Revue Trimestrielle des Droits de l'Homme* 121, 129, 130.

35 J.-L. Sauron and A. Stepanova, above n. 9, para. 198.

36 *Hirst v. United Kingdom (No. 2)*, above n. 28.

37 However, aiming to guide the practitioners, Jean-Luc Sauron and Anna Stepanova also express the conditions for a case to be considered as WECL. In this respect, 'applicants or their representatives should make a research on the ECHR case law concerning the same respondent State': J.-L. Sauron and A. Stepanova, above n. 9, para. 198.

cases of disenfranchisement brought against the United Kingdom. That said, legal issues addressed by the Grand Chamber tend to become straightforward for the respondent state. At the Chamber level, however, the threshold is higher. In such cases, the Court must first address the legal issue in a leading or pilot judgment before it can be treated as well-established.

The Court aims to expand the use of the WECL procedure. To achieve this, the concept of 'broader WECL cases' has been developed to extend the scope of WECL.[38] In June 2017, the Plenary Court resolved to increase its capacity by adopting a broader definition of WECL cases.[39] Under this new approach, a recent (and final) Chamber judgment addressing the specific issue in the respondent state would suffice to establish well-established case law. Equally significant, the revised interpretation allows for the recognition of well-established case law based on at least three recent and relevant judgments involving different states.[40] Consequently, various types of cases may now qualify as WECL. These include high-priority cases, cases concerning key or core Convention rights, cases that are factually complex or raise multiple Convention grounds, and cases communicated at the Chamber level prior to the adoption of this policy.[41] This redefinition is expected to lead to an increased use of the WECL procedure.

Another way to understand repetitive cases is by examining the procedural approach applied to these cases (see below section 3).

3 REPETITIVE CASES AND CASE PROCESSING

There are common trends that apply to all repetitive cases (see below section 3.1). In contrast, certain specific procedures are applicable only to particular types of repetitive cases (see below section 3.2).

3.1. Common Trends

Once a case is classified as WECL or broader WECL, it falls within the competence of Committees rather than Chambers, and the application of the WECL procedure becomes the standard practice. The WECL procedure is characterised by distinctive working methods, including the adoption of simplified procedures introduced by ECHR, Protocol No. 14. Under its original

---

38 CDDH, 'Securing the long-term effectiveness of the supervisory mechanism of the European Convention on Human Rights: the Court's action in 2018–2019', 14 June 2019, CDDH(2019)25, para. 32.

39 Ibid., para. 32.

40 ECtHR, above n. 33, para. 12.

41 Ibid., para. 12.

provisions, Committees of three judges were authorised to decide on both the admissibility and merits of applications where the underlying legal issue was covered by established case law (the WECL procedure).[42] This mechanism was Protocol No. 14's response to the recurring problem of repetitive or clone cases on similar subject matters, which constitute a significant portion of the Strasbourg Court's docket.[43] To further accelerate the processing of repetitive applications, a fast-track version of the WECL procedure (the WECL fast-track procedure) was introduced in 2015.[44] At that time, the WECL fast-track procedure covered over 80% of pending repetitive cases, with the remaining 20% being addressed through other simplified methods.[45] Since its introduction, the WECL fast-track procedure has been used increasingly extensively, further streamlining the processing of repetitive cases.[46]

In repetitive cases, the observation stage is limited to verifying the factual issues raised by the applicant. This limitation arises from the fact that such applications fall under well-established case law, and the Registry and the Rapporteur are already convinced that these complaints are well-founded. However, this conviction is based solely on the applicant's account of the facts. Consequently, the Court communicates the case to the respondent state to determine whether the government possesses information indicating that no violation has occurred. For example, in cases concerning detention conditions, the government may challenge whether the applicant truly had less than $3m^2$ of personal space or whether the prolongation of proceedings was actually requested by the applicant.[47] The Court, however, does not expect the government to submit observations containing legal objections regarding the admissibility or merits of the case, as these matters have already been definitively resolved in a leading or pilot judgment.[48] Should the government nonetheless submit such observations, the Court will inform the applicant accordingly.[49] Even in this circumstance, the Court does not require applicants to respond to the government's observations.[50] In addition to the limited observation stage,

---

42 Protocol No. 14, above n. 7, Article 8.

43 D. Harris, M. O'Boyle, E. Bates and C. Buckley, *Harris, O'Boyle and Warbrick: Law of the European Convention on Human Rights*, 4th ed., Oxford, Oxford University Press, 2018, p. 127.

44 ECtHR, 'The Interlaken Process and the Court (2016 Report)', 1 September 2016, para. 8.

45 Ibid., para. 8.

46 CDDH, above n. 38, para. 28.

47 CDDH, 'Encouraging resolution of the Court's proceedings through a dedicated non-contentious phase of the proceedings', 27 February 2019, CDDH(2019)09, para. 7 (fn. 2).

48 D. Harris, M. O'Boyle, E. Bates and C. Buckley, above n. 43, p. 128; J.-L. Sauron and A. Stepanova, above n. 9, para. 199.

49 D. Harris, M. O'Boyle, E. Bates and C. Buckley, above n. 43, p. 128.

50 R. Muscat and C. Palomares, 'Internal Organisation of Regional Human Rights Courts: The European Court of Human Rights and the Inter-American Court of Human Rights' in P. Pinto de Albuquerque and K. Wojtyczek (eds), *Judicial Power in a Globalized World: Liber Amicorum Vincent De Gaetano*, Cham, Springer, 2019, pp. 313–30, p. 323.

the WECL procedure typically excludes claims for just satisfaction. However, there is some ambiguity in this regard. Pascal Dourneau-Josette states that in cases without government observations, the Court invites applicants to 'present their claims for just satisfaction'.[51] Conversely, other authors assert that the Court determines just satisfaction awards based on the amounts set in the leading judgment.[52]

The Court typically examines repetitive cases jointly. These cases are communicated to governments in groups and presented in a table format.[53] This table includes the essential factual elements of each case. Following this automated process, Registry lawyers and administrative assistants conduct the legal analysis and perform a quality check.[54] The resulting drafts are then submitted to the relevant judicial formation for decision – namely, a specific Committee of three judges within one of the Court's five sections.[55] The Committee examines the applications collectively and issues a single judgment or decision.[56]

In addition to these standard features, there are also certain particularities.

3.2. *Resolution of Repetitive Cases*

Repetitive cases can follow different procedural paths. They may be addressed through repatriation (see below section 3.2.1), resolved via friendly settlement decisions (see below section 3.2.2), or concluded with simplified judgments (see below section 3.2.3).

3.2.1 Repatriation of Cases

Repatriation is one possible outcome for pending repetitive cases that follow a pilot judgment. Repatriation occurs when the respondent state resolves the underlying structural issue by introducing a domestic remedy accessible to individuals in the same position as the applicant in the pilot case. This domestic remedy must be retrospectively applicable, enabling applicants with pending cases to benefit from it. Paul Mahoney, former Registrar of the Strasbourg

---

51 P. Dourneau-Josette, above n. 34, 130, fn. 12.

52 J.-L. Sauron and A. Stepanova, above n. 9, para. 203; D. Harris, M. O'Boyle, E. Bates and C. Buckley, above n. 43, p. 128.

53 D. Harris, M. O'Boyle, E. Bates and C. Buckley, above n. 43, p. 128.

54 H. Bakirci, 'Case Management: European Court of Human Rights (ECtHR)' in H. Ruiz-Fabri (ed), *Max Planck Encyclopedia of International Procedural Law*, Oxford, Oxford University Press, 2019, para. 31.

55 Ibid.

56 *Oprea and Others v. Romania*, nos. 54966/09, 57682/10, 20499/11, 41587/11, 27583/12, 75692/12, 76944/12, 77474/12, 9985/13, 16490/13, 29530/13, 37810/13, 40759/13, 55842/13, 56837/13, 62797/13, 64858/13, 65996/13, 66101/13 and 15822/14, 18 June 2015, § 5.

Court, illustrates the essence of the pilot judgment procedure with reference to the *Broniowski* case:

> The *Broniowski* judgment essentially contained two elements on the issue of execution. The Government were told: firstly, you have to eliminate the source of the violation – that is for the future – and secondly, you must provide a remedy for past prejudice that has been suffered by not only the individual applicant but also all the other 80,000 Bug River claimants adversely affected by the systemic violation found.[57]

In such scenarios, once a new domestic remedy is introduced, the Court typically declares all similar pending applications inadmissible for non-exhaustion of domestic remedies (under Article 34) or strikes these cases from its list (under Article 37). This requires applicants to pursue the newly established remedy.

The repatriation of cases raises multifaceted concerns regarding the interests of applicants with pending cases. Antoine Buyse argues that freezing parallel applications adversely affects the interests of applicants whose cases are pending before the Strasbourg Court. He notes that:

> Especially when it concerns complaints about trials that have taken too long, freezing an application at the international level would be ironic, to say the least.[58]

In 2003, the CDDH expressed concerns regarding the 'obligation for the state to create retroactive domestic remedies for repetitive cases'.[59] Interestingly, in the same document, the CDDH did not analyse the legal implications – such as those related to legal certainty – of compelling applicants to exhaust these retroactive domestic remedies.

The Court defends its practice on a normative basis, citing Article 1 of the ECHR, which obliges states to ensure the protection of Convention rights. The practice is also justified on grounds of judicial efficiency and the effective administration of justice. The CDDH has reflected on this issue, acknowledging that in certain cases, it may be more appropriate to establish new remedies solely for future applicants. However, the report does not specify the circumstances under which this approach should be adopted. According to the CDDH, allowing applicants already before the Court to seek redress

---

57 'Discussion Following the Presentation by Luzius Wildhaber' in R. Wolfrum and U. Deutsch (eds), *The European Court of Human Rights Overwhelmed by Applications: Problems and Possible Solutions*, Heidelberg, Springer, 2009, pp. 77–92, p. 85.

58 A. Buyse, 'The Pilot Judgment Procedure at the European Court of Human Rights: Possibilities and Challenges' (2009) 57 *Nomiko Vima (The Greek Law Journal)* 1890, 1913.

59 CDDH, 'Guaranteeing the long-term effectiveness of the European Court of Human Rights – Implementation of the Declaration adopted by the Committee of Ministers at its 112th Session (14–15 Mar 2003), Interim Activity Report', CDDH(2003)026 Addendum I Final, 26 November 2003, para. 20.

in Strasbourg would not negatively impact the Court's caseload if it could facilitate a faster resolution for applicants, particularly where the government agrees to a friendly settlement or an accelerated procedure before the Court.[60]

The Committee of Ministers has also addressed the implications of pilot judgments, noting that the Court may, in certain cases, invite applicants with similar complaints to pursue the new national remedy. In such instances, the Strasbourg Court could declare the pending cases inadmissible. However, the Committee emphasises that repatriation is not always appropriate. Compelling applicants to bear the additional burden of exhausting domestic remedies – particularly when those remedies would only become available after legislative changes – may be deemed inappropriate in specific circumstances.[61]

Contributing to the discussion on pilot judgments, it is worth emphasising the issue of compensation for pending cases. In some pilot cases, the Court chose not to reserve the question of determining compensation. Instead, it proceeded to analyse the pending cases and awarded just satisfaction.[62] In *Burdov (No. 2)*, which concerned the non-enforcement or delayed enforcement of domestic judgments, the Court based its argument on the principle of fairness. It held that:

> it would be unfair if the applicants [of the applications lodged before the delivery of the present judgment], who have allegedly been suffering for years of continuing violations of their right to a court and sought relief in this Court, were compelled yet again to resubmit their grievances with the domestic authorities, be it on the grounds of a new remedy or otherwise.[63]

Similarly, in *Vassilios Athanasiou*, the Court continued examining pending cases until Greek authorities introduced domestic remedies. Its reasoning echoed that in *Burdov*:

> Indeed, the Court does not wish for the time required by the Greek Government to implement general measures to be to the detriment of the timely examination of pending applications with the same subject matter.[64]

---

60 CDDH, 'Guaranteeing the long-term effectiveness of the control system of the European Convention on Human Rights. Addendum to the final report containing CDDH proposals (long version)', 9 April 2003, CDDH(2003)006 Addendum Final, p. 11.

61 CoE Committee of Ministers, 'Appendix to the Recommendation on the improvement of domestic remedies', 12 May 2004, REC(2004)6, paras. 13–19.

62 In *Manushaque Puto v. Albania*, the Court awarded just satisfaction and it kept dealing with the remaining cases submitted until the *Manushaqe Puto* judgment became final: *Manushaqe Puto and Others v. Albania,* nos. 604/07, 43628/07, 46684/07 and 34770/09, 31 July 2012.

63 *Burdov v. Russia (No. 2)*, above n. 27, § 144. Also in *Gerasimov and Others v. Russia*, above n. 27, § 230.

64 *Vassilios Athanasiou and Others v. Greece*, above n. 26, § 58.

In this case, the Court also aimed to exert pressure on the government to expedite the introduction of such measures, noting that

> further examination of similar cases through the normal procedure will serve as a regular reminder to the Greek authorities of their obligations under the Convention, and particularly of the present judgment.[65]

Should a Member State establish a national compensation scheme, the Court may lower the threshold for its compensation awards. National compensation amounts may be lower than those fixed by the Court in similar cases. The Court grants a wide margin of appreciation to domestic authorities in determining compensation, provided the assessment aligns with the States Parties' domestic legal systems and traditions and reflects the standard of living in the relevant country.[66] While accepting a lower threshold, the compensation awarded is not entirely beyond the Court's scrutiny. In pilot cases concerning detention conditions, the Court adopted a stricter approach to evaluating the adequacy of national compensation remedies and refrained from adjourning pending cases.[67] This policy reflects the fundamental nature of Article 3 of the ECHR. As noted in *Varga and Others v. Hungary*, this principled approach to Article 3 issues is justified by 'the fundamental nature of the right protected by Article 3 [...] and the importance and urgency of complaints about inhuman or degrading treatment'.[68]

In these cases, the Court has consistently criticised the unreasonably low compensation levels set by domestic authorities when compared to its own awards in similar cases. For instance, in *Ananyev and Others v. Russia*, the Court emphasised that:

> the right not to be subjected to inhuman or degrading treatment is so fundamental and central to the system of the protection of human rights that the domestic authority or court dealing with the matter will have to provide exceptionally compelling and serious reasons to justify their decision to award lower or no compensation in respect of non-pecuniary damage.[69]

The Court has also rejected financial constraints as a valid justification for inadequate compensation. It clarified that a state's scarcity of resources does

---

65 Ibid., § 58.

66 *Csaba Domján v. Hungary*, no. 5433/17, 14 November 2017, § 27.

67 *Ananyev and Others v. Russia*, above n. 30. Apart from this case, see also *Neshkov and Others v. Bulgaria*, nos. 36925/10, 21487/12, 72893/12, 73196/12, 77718/12 and 9717/13, 27 January 2015, § 291; *Varga and Others v. Hungary*, nos. 14097/12, 45135/12, 73712/12, 34001/13, 44055/13 and 64586/13, 10 March 2015, § 115; *Rezmiveş and Others v. Romania*, nos. 61467/12, 39516/13, 48231/13 and 68191/13, 25 April 2017, § 115.

68 *Varga and Others v. Hungary*, above n. 67, § 116.

69 *Ananyev and Others v. Russia*, above n. 30, §§ 230, 117.

not mitigate its obligations and is irrelevant in determining damages under compensatory criteria.[70] For example, in *Shilbergs v. Russia*, the applicant was awarded RUB 1,500 – equivalent to less than €50 – for detention in an extremely cold and humid cell, without adequate lighting, food, or a personal sleeping place. The Court held that:

> [t]he Court finds it anomalous for the domestic courts to decrease the amount of compensation to be paid to the applicant for a wrong committed by the State by referring to the latter's lack of funds.[71]

The Court justifies the practice of adjourning and repatriating pending cases on several grounds. First, it highlights the differing roles of national courts and the ECtHR. As a supranational court, the Strasbourg Court's role is subsidiary. The primary responsibility for addressing the structural malfunctions identified by the Court rests with the contracting states. Once the Court points out a systemic issue, it becomes the responsibility of national courts to provide individual redress. This approach aligns with a broader theoretical debate on the role of the Strasbourg Court – whether it should prioritise individual justice or adopt a constitutional role. From the mid-2000s, the future role of the ECtHR was increasingly framed within the dichotomy of 'constitutional justice' versus 'individual justice'. Some scholars observed a 'tension' between the Court's aim to safeguard individual rights ('individual justice') and its objective to establish an authoritative interpretation of human rights standards ('constitutional court of Europe').[72] According to this perspective, while providing individual justice risks reducing the Court to a mere compensation body, repatriating pending cases allows the Court to reaffirm its constitutional role under Article 19 of the ECHR 'to ensure the observance of the engagements undertaken by the High Contracting Parties in the Convention and the Protocols thereto'.[73] Additionally, the Court defends repatriation on grounds of efficiency. In *Załuska and Rogalska v. Poland*, the Court held that the purpose of repatriation is:

> on the one hand, to reduce the threat to the effective functioning of the Convention system deriving from repetitive cases that originate in systemic problems and, on the

---

70 Ibid., §§ 117, 118.

71 *Shilbergs v. Russia*, no. 20075/03, 17 December 2009, § 78, §§ 71–79.

72 J. Christoffersen, 'Individual and Constitutional Justice: Can the Dynamics of ECHR Adjudication Be Reversed?' in J. Christoffersen and M.R. Madsen (eds), *The European Court of Human Rights between Law and Politics*, Oxford, Oxford University Press, 2011, p. 184. S. Greer and A. Williams, 'Human Rights in the Council of Europe and the EU: Towards "Individual", "Constitutional" or "Institutional" Justice?' (2009) 15(4) *European Law Journal* 462; S. Greer and L. Wildhaber, 'Revisiting the Debate about "constitutionalising" the European Court of Human Rights' (2012) 12(4) *Human Rights Law Review* 655.

73 E. Kindt, above n. 15, p. 50.

other, to facilitate the most speedy and effective resolution of a systemic dysfunction affecting the protection of Convention rights in the national legal order.[74]

Similar to repatriation, repetitive cases may also be resolved through friendly settlements.

3.2.2 Friendly Settlements

Friendly settlements serve as a procedural case-management tool designed to simplify and expedite proceedings.[75] Within the WECL procedure, the Court has the discretion to propose friendly settlements at any stage of the process.[76] During various high-level conferences, states have been encouraged to facilitate the use of friendly settlements and unilateral declarations in repetitive cases. The Interlaken Declaration specifically called on states to promote friendly settlements and unilateral declarations to address such cases effectively.[77] Building on this, the Izmir Follow-up Plan further invited states to prioritise the use of friendly settlements and unilateral declarations when resolving repetitive cases.[78]

The Registry may utilise friendly settlements and unilateral declarations as complementary tools to pilot judgments, often referred to as 'follow-up friendly settlements'. In such cases, the Registry may allow the state to resolve pending cases through friendly settlements or unilateral declarations. This approach is employed in various circumstances. One example arises when a Member State resolves a systemic problem but does not apply the solution retroactively, leaving applicants in pending cases unable to obtain redress through the national remedy. The Court may also prefer friendly settlements over repatriation for other reasons. In certain instances, as part of the general measures under Article 46 of the ECHR, the Court has emphasised that applicants in pending cases should not be required to return to the domestic system to receive compensation. Instead, it has obligated the state to provide redress to these applicants within a specified time frame on an ad hoc basis. Compensation in such cases may be offered through a national compensation scheme or a friendly settlement procedure facilitated by the Court.[79]

---

74 *Załuska and Rogalska v. Poland*, nos. 53491/10 and 72286/10, 20 June 2017, § 29.

75 P. Dourneau-Josette, above n. 34, 130; H. Bakirci, above n. 54, para. 32.

76 Explanatory Report to Protocol 14 to the Convention for the Protection of Human Rights and Fundamental Freedoms, amending the control system of the Convention, 13 May 2004 (ETS 194), §§ 92–93.

77 High Level Conference on the Future of the European Court of Human Rights: Interlaken Declaration, Interlaken, 19 February 2010 (hereafter: the Interlaken Declaration), Action Plan, Article D(7)(a).

78 High Level Conference on the Future of the European Court of Human Rights: Izmir Declaration, Izmir, 27 April 2011, Follow-up Plan, Article E.

79 E.g. *Gerasimov and Others v. Russia*, above n. 27, §§ 230–32. A similar solution can be found again later: *Rutkowski and Others v. Poland*, above n. 26.

The Court employs friendly settlements and unilateral declarations extensively. In 2019, it introduced an additional measure (the 'non-contentious phase of proceedings') aimed at facilitating friendly settlements and unilateral declarations.[80] During this phase, the Registry prepares a specific friendly settlement proposal while communicating the application, unless the Court considers the case unsuitable for such a proposal.[81] Unlike the WECL or WECL fast-track procedures, this mechanism is not restricted to repetitive cases. The Court applies this procedure to all applications except those deemed inadmissible at the initial stage.[82] Significantly, the Court stipulates that this procedure is not excluded for Chamber cases that raise new issues concerning the interpretation and application of the Convention. Indeed, it can be used for cases involving novel legal questions.[83] According to a 2019 CDDH document, exceptions to the rule of making a specific friendly settlement proposal include the following:

1. cases that appear to be 'borderline' in light of the Court's jurisprudence;
2. cases that raise new issues never previously examined by the Court;
3. applications that are politically and/or media sensitive;
4. cases where it is challenging to determine a friendly settlement amount due to the existence of pecuniary damage requiring complex or speculative calculations; and
5. all other instances where specific circumstances – such as respect for human rights – lead the Rapporteur, the President, or the Chamber to decide against making a concrete settlement proposal.[84]

Another procedure applicable to repetitive cases under the WECL procedure is the use of simplified judgments.

3.2.3 Simplified Judgments

If a state fails to implement a pilot judgment, the Court may decide to address all other similar cases through the fast-track WECL procedure. A notable example is the *Ivanov*-type cases against Ukraine, which concerned the non-enforcement of domestic decisions and the absence of an effective remedy.

---

80 ECtHR, 'Comment from the European Court on Human Rights on the CDDH contribution to the evaluation of the Interlaken reform process', 11 February 2020, DD(2020)34E, para. 11.

81 Ibid., para. 11. For the new non-contentious phase, the Registry prepares and sends an enclosed declaration of friendly settlement to both parties. ECtHR, 'Information to applicants: Procedure following communication of an application non-contentious phase', 30 July 2020.

82 The exceptions of this non-contentious phase are indicated as 'the cases raising novel issues' or 'for any specific reason it may be inappropriate to propose a friendly settlement'.

83 ECtHR, above n. 80, para. 11.

84 CDDH, above n. 37, para. 11.

The first relevant case was *Kaysin and Others v. Ukraine*, where the legal issue pertained to the applicants' right to an invalidity pension unpaid by their employer.[85] Although the parties reached a friendly settlement, the underlying systemic problem remained unresolved. As a result, the Strasbourg Court continued to receive applications concerning the same legal issue. After identifying similar violations in over 300 cases, the Court applied the full pilot judgment procedure to address this issue, selecting *Yuriy Nikolayevich Ivanov v. Ukraine* as the pilot judgment.[86] In *Ivanov*, the Court noted that it had delivered judgments in more than 300 cases against Ukraine between 2004 and 2009, with approximately 1,400 additional applications pending at that time, all concerning similar problems. Moreover, the Committee of Ministers identified the non-enforcement of domestic judicial decisions as an ongoing structural issue in Ukraine.[87]

With this case, both pending applications ('applications lodged before the delivery of the present judgment') and new applications ('applications lodged after the delivery of the present judgment') were adjourned for a period of one year.[88] The Court emphasised that if:

> the respondent State fails to adopt [the necessary measures] and continues to violate the Convention, the Court will have no choice but to resume the examination of all similar [pending applications and] to ensure effective observance of the Convention.[89]

Following an initial extension of the time period, it became evident that the government had failed to execute the *Ivanov* pilot judgment. A second request for an extension was refused. Hoping to compel the Member State to take action, the Court resumed its assessment of the adjourned pending cases, which were collectively referred to as '*Ivanov*-type cases'.[90] The Committee of three judges applied the WECL procedure when processing these applications until the Grand Chamber overturned this approach in the *Burmych* case.[91]

A comparable situation arose in the well-known Italian length-of-proceedings cases. At the time of the *Bottazzi* case, approximately 14,000 similar cases were pending before the Court.[92] The initial length-of-proceedings cases in Italy eventually led to the enactment of the Pinto Law (Italy's Law 89/2001), designed

85 *Kaysin and Others v. Ukraine*, no. 46144/99, 27 January 2000.

86 A retired soldier who had not been paid the lump-sum pension to which he was entitled. *Yuriy Nikolayevich Ivanov v. Ukraine*, no. 40450/04, above n. 27.

87 Ibid., §§ 83 and 88.

88 Ibid., §§ 97, 98.

89 Ibid., § 100.

90 *Burmych and Others v. Ukraine (striking out)*, above n. 27, § 16.

91 Ibid.

92 *Bottazzi v. Italy*, no. 34884/97, 28 July 1999, § 22, ECHR 1999-V.

to address the issue by awarding compensation to the affected individuals. The transitional provisions of the Pinto Law allowed applicants who had already brought their cases before the Court, but whose cases had not yet been declared admissible, to return to the Italian system to claim compensation. This provision was subsequently utilised by the Court to declare new cases inadmissible on the grounds of non-exhaustion of domestic remedies, effectively repatriating these cases back to the national system.[93] The issue, however, returned to the Court in the form of a quasi-pilot case, *Scordino (No. 1) v. Italy*, in which the Court found that the compensation provided under the Pinto Law was inadequate and that the Pinto Law was ineffective in addressing the underlying problem of excessive length of proceedings in Italy.[94]

As an example, in the 'Hungarian pension cases' the Court adopted a different approach. In this instance, the ECtHR received nearly 8,000 individual applications against Hungary concerning the pension rights of former law enforcement officers who had benefitted from early retirement. These cases raised essentially identical issues, primarily stemming from the enactment of Hungary's Law No. 167 of 2011 on the Termination of Old-Age Pension before Retirement Age, on Benefit Prior to Retirement Age, and on Service Allowance. This law replaced the applicants' non-taxable retirement pensions with a taxable allowance subject to a 16% tax rate.

The applicants argued that this constituted a violation of their right to peaceful enjoyment of their possessions and was discriminatory compared to other groups. They based their complaints on ECHR, Protocol No.1, Article 1 and ECHR, Article 14.[95] The Court selected a limited number of applications to be examined as leading cases and did not take procedural steps for the remaining pending applications. Instead, it requested a reorganisation of similar cases. Specifically, it invited the relevant trade unions to resubmit grouped applications, accompanied by lists of individual applicants' names and details, enabling the Court to register and process them more efficiently. During this process, the Court did not correspond with individual applicants or respond to their enquiries. Instead, it published information related to the leading cases online at appropriate intervals.[96]

93 D. Haider, *The Pilot-Judgment Procedure of the European Court of Human Rights*, Leiden, Brill, 2013, p. 19.

94 *Scordino v. Italy (No. 1)*, no. 36813/97, 29 March 2006, § ECHR 2006-V.

95 ECtHR, 'European Court Registrar calls for special measures to deal with influx of Hungarian pension cases', 11 January 2012, ECHR 009(2011), p. 1.

96 Ibid.

4 CONCLUSION

The future of repetitive cases arguably appears bright for several reasons. Repetitive cases expose systemic issues within domestic legal systems. When combined with challenges in the execution of ECtHR judgments, as illustrated by the example of *Ivanov*-type cases, and the overwhelming volume of individual applications, these systemic issues compel the ECtHR to develop new solutions. These solutions often involve the adoption of innovative procedural measures that expand the scope of the WECL procedure and redefine the boundaries of repetitive cases.

CHAPTER 7

THE EU DIRECTIVE ON CORPORATE SUSTAINABILITY DUE DILIGENCE: MAKING OR BREAKING HUMAN RIGHTS PROTECTION IN EUROPE?

Francesca Mussi*

1 INTRODUCTION

The decade of the 1970s was a critical turning point in the development of the corporate social responsibility (CSR) movement. The term CSR – which generally refers to 'voluntary activities undertaken by firms in environmental or social areas'[1] – was first coined in 1953 but did not become widely used until the 1970s. Beginning with the 'Guidelines for Multinational Enterprises' adopted by the Organisation for Economic Co-operation and Development (OECD) in 1976,[2] international organisations adopted non-binding guidelines with the aim of protecting individuals from human rights violations and other abuses committed by corporations.

Despite said voluntary initiative, human rights violations as a consequence of corporate conduct continued to occur frequently, leading to increased calls for binding 'hard law' remedies.[3] In 2011, the United Nations' (UN's)

---

* This chapter has been researched for and written within the project: 'Le nuove frontiere della responsabilità sociale d'impresa: verso una crescita verde, sostenibile ed inclusiva', funded by the European Union – FSE-REACT-EU, PON Research and Innovation 2014–2020.

1 In this sense, see P.C. Godfrey, C.B. Merrill and J.M. Hansen, 'The relationship between corporate social responsibility and shareholder value: an empirical test of the risk management hypothesis' (2009) 30(4) *Strategic Management Journal* 425, 427.

2 See OECD, 'Guidelines for Multinational Enterprises', 21 June 1976, last updated in 2023 and renamed 'OECD Guidelines for Multinational Enterprises on Responsible Business Conduct'. For an overview on the 'Guidelines for Multinational Enterprises', see J. Letnar Černič, 'Corporate Responsibility for Human Rights: A Critical Analysis of the OECD Guidelines for Multinational Enterprises' (2008) 4(1) *Hanse Law Review* 71.

3 In this sense, see S. Khoury and D. Whyte, 'Sidelining corporate human rights violations: The failure of the OECD's regulatory consensus' (2019) 18(4) *Journal of Human Rights* 363, 364–66.

'Guiding Principles on Business and Human Rights' (UNGPs or Principles)[4] were adopted and unanimously endorsed by the UN Human Rights Council in an attempt to proclaim a legal framework aiming to guide corporations to respect human rights. The UNGPs operationalise the UN's 'Protect, Respect and Remedy Framework' for business and human rights, developed in 2008 by the then Special Representative of the UN Secretary General, Professor John Ruggie, and are based on a twofold assumption. First, the Framework recognises that states have the duty under international human rights law to protect everyone within their territory and/or jurisdiction from human rights abuses committed by business enterprises. Second, it states that all business enterprises have the responsibility to respect human rights wherever they operate and whatever their size or industry.

Despite being merely a soft law instrument, the UNGPs have become universally accepted norms of conduct.[5] They are based on three fundamental pillars – protect, respect and remedy – each defining concrete, actionable steps for businesses to meet their duties and responsibilities to prevent human rights abuses in company operations and to provide remedies if such abuses take place. The main element of relevance is the introduction of the concept of human rights due diligence (HRDD), which is defined as an ongoing management process seeking to identify, prevent, mitigate and account the impacts on human rights that they have caused or contributed to, as well as those directly linked to their operations, products or services through their business relationships, whether contractual or non-contractual.[6] This process

---

4 See J. Ruggie, UN Human Rights Council, 'Guiding Principles on Business and Human Rights: Implementing the United Nations "Protect, Respect and Remedy" Framework', 21 March 2011, UN Doc. A/HRC/17/31, Annex; UN Human Rights Council, 'Human rights and transnational corporations and other business enterprises', 6 July 2011, UN Doc. A/HRC/RES/17/4.

5 See J.G. Ruggie and J.F. Sherman III, 'Adding Human Rights Punch to the New *Lex Mercatoria*: The Impact of the UN Guiding Principles on Business and Human Rights on Commercial Legal Practice' (2015) 6 *Journal of International Dispute Settlement* 455, 459. The authors construe the UNGPs as 'global norms': see also J.G. Ruggie and J.F. Sherman III, 'The Concept of "Due Diligence" in the UN Guiding Principles on Business and Human Rights: A Reply to Jonathan Bonnitcha and Robert McCorquodale' (2017) 28(3) *European Journal of International Law* 921, 923.

6 See UNGP 17. On the notion of HRDD, see J. Bonnitcha and R. McCorquodale, 'The Concept of "Due Diligence" in the UN Guiding Principles on Business and Human Rights' (2017) 28(3) *European Journal of International Law* 899; J. G. Ruggie and J. F Sherman III, 'The Concept of "Due Diligence" in the UN Guiding Principles on Business and Human Rights: A Reply to Jonathan Bonnitcha and Robert McCorquodale', above n. 5; A. Rasche and S. Waddock, 'The UN Guiding Principles on Business and Human Rights: Implications for Corporate Social Responsibility Research' (2019) 6(2) *Business and Human Rights Journal* 227, 228–29; L. Chiussi Curzi, *General Principles for Business and Human Rights in International Law*, Leiden, Brill, 2020, p. 225; C. Macchi, *Business, Human Rights*

should include four core components, namely: identification and assessment of actual or potential adverse human rights impacts; integration of findings from impact assessments across relevant activities of the company; tracking the effectiveness of measures and processes to address adverse human rights impacts; and communicating, in particular to affected stakeholders, how these impacts are being addressed and what policies are being implemented.[7] In terms of material scope, according to the UNGPs, the corporate responsibility to respect human rights refers to all internationally recognised human rights arising under international instruments, not just those binding via domestic law in any one jurisdiction.[8]

In response to the above-mentioned developments at the OECD and UN levels, most recently the concept of HRDD has been endorsed at the European level. In 2016, the Council of Europe adopted a Recommendation that, reflecting the approach and concerns of the UNGPs, calls for governments to implement the Principles and to review their compliance periodically across areas such as company regulation, state-owned enterprises and public procurement, trade agreements, investment promotion and access to justice.[9] Further, in the Recommendation, it has called for Member States to 'apply such measures as may be necessary'[10] to encourage or require business enterprises to apply HRDD 'throughout their operations'.[11]

In the European context, however, it is the European Union (EU) that has played the key role in articulating expectations on businesses to manage human rights risks and other sustainability issues that are becoming increasingly more detailed, demanding and widespread. Indeed, the EU has adopted a whole range of ambitious legislative measures over the last few years, establishing mandatory sustainability due diligence requirements encompassing stronger protection for human rights and, in some cases, broader environmental and governance objectives for certain industry sectors and value chains.[12] In addition, after

---

and the Environment: The Evolving Agenda, The Hague, TMC Asser Press, 2022, p. 91; R. McCorquodale, *Business and Human Rights*, Oxford, Oxford University Press, 2024, p. 120.

7 UN General Assembly, 'Working Group on the issue of human rights and transnational corporations and other business enterprises', 16 July 2018, UN Doc. A/73/163, para. 10.

8 See UNGP 11.

9 See Recommendation CM/Rec(2016)3 of the Committee of Ministers to Member States on human rights and business, 2 March 2016.

10 Ibid., Appendix, para. 20.

11 Ibid.

12 See, among others, Regulation (EU) 995/2010 of the European Parliament and of the Council of 20 October 2010 laying down the obligations of operators who place timber and timber products on the market [2010] OJ L295/11; Regulation (EU) 2017/821 of the European Parliament and of the Council of 17 May 2017 laying down supply chain due diligence obligations for Union importers of tin, tantalum and tungsten, their ores, and gold originating from conflict-affected and high-risk areas [2017] OJ L130/1; Regulation (EU) 2023/1115 of the European Parliament and of the Council of 31 May 2023 on the making

a legislative process lasting more than two years that was marked by difficulties, setbacks, and a healthy dose of sabotage, in 2024, the Council of the EU finally adopted the Corporate Sustainability Due Diligence Directive (CSDDD or the Directive),[13] which represents a fundamental milestone at the global level and marks the most recent step in the long legal evolution of the concept of HRDD. Indeed, the Directive establishes the obligation for EU Member States to introduce within their domestic legal systems a binding set of rules aimed at identifying and, where necessary, preventing, ending, and remediating actual or potential adverse human rights and environmental impacts connected with large European and non-European companies' own operations and those of their business partners across global chains of activities, as well as ensuring that those affected by a failure to respect this duty have access to justice and legal remedies.[14] The adoption of an HRDD legislation for businesses in the EU could represent an innovative tool, suitable – if correctly applied – to strengthen the protection of human rights by corporations along global chains of activities. However, this potentially historic development could easily turn into a missed opportunity if the legislation in question fails to deliver on its ambitious promise or to align with the extant standards developed at the international level.

After illustrating the torturous road that led to the adoption of the CSDDD, the present chapter examines two major deficiencies of the Directive pertaining to effectively preventing and remedying human rights harm,[15] namely the

---

available on the Union market and the export from the Union of certain commodities and products associated with deforestation and forest degradation and repealing Regulation (EU) No 995/2010 [2023] OJ L150/206, Article 25; Regulation (EU) 2023/1542 of the European Parliament and of the Council of 12 July 2023 concerning batteries and waste batteries, amending Directive 2008/98/EC and Regulation (EU) 2019/1020 and repealing Directive 2006/66/EC [2023] OJ L191/1, Article 85.

13 Directive (EU) 2024/1760 of the European Parliament and of the Council of 13 June 2024 on corporate sustainability due diligence and amending Directive (EU) 2019/1937 and Regulation (EU) 2023/2859 [2024] OJ L1760/1 (the CSDDD or the Directive). On the Directive, see A. Bonfanti, 'Corporate Sustainability Due Diligence Directive: A Human Rights-Based Assessment' (2024) 4 *Rivista del Commercio Internazionale* 857; N. Bueno, N. Bernaz, G. Holly and O. Martin-Ortega, 'The EU Directive on Corporate Sustainability Due Diligence (CSDDD): The Final Political Compromise' (2024) 9(2) *Business and Human Rights Journal* 294; V. McCullagh, 'The EU Corporate Sustainability Due Diligence Directive: Real Change or More of the Same?' (2024) 35(5) *European Business Law Review* 603; A. Schall, 'The CSDDD: Good Law or Bad Law?' (2024) 21(3) *European Company Law* 56; M. Thorens, N. Bernaz and O. Hospes, 'Advocating for the EU Corporate Sustainability Due Diligence Directive Against the Odds: Strategies and Legitimation' (2024) 63(2) *Journal of Common Market Studies* 606.

14 CSDDD, preamble, para. 16.

15 According to the normative structuring of the CSDDD, another deficiency is represented by the limited number of companies that are directly obliged to exercise due diligence. Indeed, according to CSDDD, Article 2, paras. 1 and 2, the CSDDD applies only to large EU companies employing more than 1,000 employees and generating a net worldwide annual

limited boundaries of the rights that are sought to be protected, and the delimitation of the due diligence that is sought to be carried out. The aim of the chapter is to assess the implications of the said normative features of the Directive in order to verify whether – and, if so, to what extent – the CSDDD will effectively be able to transform businesses' practices and in turn make a meaningful contribution to the protection of human rights within EU borders. Since the present contribution was finalised before the EU Commission announced, in February 2025, the 'Omnibus' legislative package – a set of amendments significantly revisiting the CSDDD –, the analysis undertaken in the present chapter centers on the original text of the CSDDD of 13 June 2024, and does not take into account the changes introduced thereafter.

2 THE LONG WAY TOWARD THE ADOPTION OF THE CSDDD

In the aftermath of the adoption of the UNGPs, several European states adopted legislation on mandatory due diligence to 'harden' the Principles.[16] France, Germany, Norway, the Netherlands and Switzerland have passed such laws, but with great differences in terms of scope, due diligence standards and enforcement mechanisms.[17] The proliferation of these hard

turnover of €450 million or above in the last financial year, regardless of the sector in which they operate, as well as to non-EU companies generating a net turnover of more than €450 million or above in the EU.

16 O. Martin-Ortega, 'Human Rights Due Diligence for Corporations: From Voluntary Standards to Hard Law at Last?' (2014) 32(1) *Netherlands Quarterly of Human Rights* 44; R. McCorquodale, 'Human rights due diligence instruments: evaluating the current legislative landscape' in A. Marx, G. Van Calster, J. Wouters, K. Otteburn and D. Lica (eds), *Research Handbook on Global Governance, Business and Human Rights*, Cheltenham, Edward Elgar, 2022, pp. 121–42.

17 On the legislations adopted by different European states see, among others, S. Cossart, J. Chaplier and T. Beau de Lomenie, 'The French Law on Duty of Care: A Historic Step Towards Making Globalization Work for All' (2017) 2 *Business and Human Rights Journal* 317; N. Bueno and C. Kaufmann, 'The Swiss Human Rights Due Diligence Legislation: Between Law and Politics' (2021) 6(3) *Business and Human Rights Journal* 542; M. Krajewski, K. Tonstad and F. Wohltmann, 'Mandatory Human Rights Due Diligence in Germany and Norway: Stepping, or Striding, in the Same Direction?' (2021) 6(3) *Business and Human Rights Journal* 550; E. Savourey and S. Brabant, 'The French Law on the Duty of Vigilance: Theoretical and Practical Challenges Since its Adoption' (2021) 6(1) *Business and Human Rights Journal* 141; A.-C. Mittwoch and F.L. Bremenkamp, 'The German Supply Chain Act – A Sustainable Regulatory Framework for Internationally Active Market Players?' (2023) 55(4) *Review of European and Comparative Law* 189; D. Weihrauch, S. Carodenuto and S. Leipold, 'From voluntary to mandatory corporate accountability: The politics of the German Supply Chain Due Diligence Act' (2023) 17(4) *Regulation & Governance* 909; S. Ciacchi and C.W. Cerqua, 'Frontrunners vs Free Riders? Mapping the Institutional Implementation of Human Rights Due Diligence in France and the Netherlands' (2024) 35(3–4) *European Business Law Review* 503.

law regulatory initiatives on sustainability due diligence at the national level played a significant role in the decision of the European institutions to develop EU legislation on the matter. Indeed, it became clear that in the absence of EU-level harmonisation on sustainability due diligence, the field would likely be plagued by legal fragmentation.[18]

The first concrete steps towards the development of legislative intervention in the area of sustainability due diligence date back to 2020, with the launch of the Sustainable Corporate Governance Initiative by the EU Commission.[19] As the name suggests, the Initiative was originally geared towards intervening in the legal framework for corporate governance, looking to regulate two different dimensions of the latter. The first dimension was represented by the need to hold companies accountable for negative impacts on the environment and human rights deriving from their economic activity, including through their global value chain. The second dimension regarded the integration of sustainability in corporate governance, looking at directors' incentives and duties. Over time, the focus was eventually recentred on due diligence requirements through value chains in order to identify, prevent, mitigate and account for abuses of human rights and environmental damage.[20] Indeed, the Inception Impact Assessment, launched by the EU Commission between 30 July and 8 October 2020 to inform citizens and stakeholders about its plans and allow them to provide feedback on the said Sustainable Corporate Governance Initiative as well as to participate effectively in future consultation activities, highlighted the need for a more specific EU legal framework on due diligence.[21] Additionally, the Inception Impact Assessment mentioned the need to catch up with the above-mentioned proliferation of hard law normative initiatives on sustainability due diligence in different EU Member States.[22]

The same year, the EU Commission launched public consultations to gather stakeholders' inputs on the goals and plans of the Sustainable Corporate

---

18 European Commission, 'Proposal for a Directive on Corporate Sustainability Due Diligence', 23 February 2022, COM(2022) 71 final, Explanatory Memorandum, p. 3, available at <https://eur-lex.europa.eu/legal-content/EN/TXT/HTML/?uri=CELEX:52022PC0071>.

19 See 'Sustainable corporate governance: About this initiative', *European Commission* <https://ec.europa.eu/info/law/better-regulation/have-your-say/initiatives/12548-Sustainable-corporate-governance_en>. For a deeper analysis on the EU Sustainable Corporate Governance Initiative, see S. Ciacchi, 'The newly-adopted Corporate Sustainability Due Diligence Directive: an overview of the lawmaking process and analysis of the final text' (2024) 25 *ERA Forum* 29, 32 <https://link.springer.com/article/10.1007/s12027-024-00791-y>.

20 In this sense, see again S. Ciacchi, above n. 19, 33.

21 European Commission, 'Proposal for legislation fostering more sustainable corporate governance in companies: Inception Impact Assessment – Sustainable Corporate Governance', 30 July 2020, Ares(2020)4034032 <https://eur-lex.europa.eu/legal-content/EN/TXT/?uri=pi_com%3AAres%282020%294034032>.

22 Ibid.

Governance Initiative, receiving more than 400,000 public responses and 855 replies to targeted questionnaires.[23] Respondents included a broad range of stakeholders, such as, inter alia, business organisations, investors, local community representatives, trade unions, environmental organisations and non-governmental organisations (NGOs). The highlights of the summary report of the consultations once again reflected a broadly favourable response to the idea of a horizontal sustainability due diligence obligation, over a sector-specific or thematic duty.[24] The responses on corporate governance matters – specifically on introducing a directors' duty of care[25] – were more divided, with opposite reactions coming from NGOs and business organisations: the former responded favourably whilst the latter expressed disagreement and concern.[26] During this time, the Commission's plans to intervene in matters of corporate governance were heavily criticised on the basis of the dubious academic validity of the background studies – in particular, a study conducted by the accounting firm Ernst & Young[27] – that the Commission had relied on to prepare the consultation document.[28] This negative backlash focused on the questionable legitimacy of the Commission's assumption of 'short-termism' – namely, an approach based on immediate business goals rather than long-term objectives – as a major roadblock to more sustainable corporate governance and the need to identify the root causes of short-termism in order to develop possible solutions to align corporate governance with the long-term objectives

---

23 European Commission, 'Sustainable corporate governance initiative: Summary report – public consultation', 2021, Ares(2021)3297206, pp. 2–3, available at <https://ec.europa.eu/info/law/better-regulation/have-your-say/initiatives/12548-Sustainable-corporate-governance/public-consultation_en>.

24 Ibid., p. 4.

25 Ibid., p. 5. The introduction of a directors' duty of care would have imposed an obligation to identify stakeholders' interests, to manage the risks for the company in relation to stakeholder interests, and to identify the opportunities, as well as to set up adequate procedures and measurable science-based targets to ensure impacts on stakeholders.

26 Ibid., p. 6.

27 Ernst & Young for the European Commission DG Justice and Consumers, 'Study on directors' duties and sustainable corporate governance: Final report', July 2020 <https://op.europa.eu/en/publication-detail/-/publication/e47928a2-d20b-11ea-adf7-01aa75ed71a1/language-en>.

28 See for instance the critique of M.J. Roe, H. Spamann, J. Fried and C. Wang, 'EC Corporate Governance Initiative Series: "The European Commission's Sustainable Corporate Governance Report: A Critique"', *Faculty of Law Blogs: University of Oxford*, 20 October 2020 <https://blogs.law.ox.ac.uk/business-law-blog/blog/2020/10/ec-corporate-governance-initiative-series-european-commissions>; European Company Law Expert Group (ECLE), 'EC Corporate Governance Initiative Series: Comment by the European Company Law Experts Group on the European Commission's Consultation Document "Proposal for an Initiative on Sustainable Corporate Governance"', *Faculty of Law Blogs: University of Oxford*, 9 December 2020 <https://blogs.law.ox.ac.uk/business-law-blog/blog/2020/12/ec-corporate-governance-initiative-series-comment-european-company>.

of the UNGPs.[29] Perhaps also due to this backlash, the short-termism angle was eventually dropped as the Sustainable Corporate Governance Initiative shifted its focus away from intervention in corporate governance and toward the introduction of laws mandating sustainability due diligence on companies.[30]

In March 2021, the EU Parliament recommended a Directive covering all large companies, all publicly listed companies, all high-risk small- and medium-size companies and a strict corporate civil liability in case of harm arising out of potential or actual adverse impacts on human rights, the environment or good governance that they, or undertakings under their control, have caused or contributed to by acts or omissions.[31] On 23 February 2022, in response to the EU Parliament's request, as well as the Council of the EU's call for an 'EU legal framework on sustainable corporate governance' including 'cross-sector corporate due diligence along global value chains',[32] the European Commission adopted a Proposal for a Directive on corporate sustainability due diligence.[33] According to the Proposal, only very large companies (500 employees/€150 million turnover) and other large companies (250 employees/€40 million turnover) in high-risk sectors were subject to due diligence obligations and could be held liable for harm based on fault liability.[34]

29 According to many scholars, the reasoning of the Commission was based on unsupported assertions – managers and investors are short-termist and corporate law is responsible for it – rather than rigorous demonstrations. In this sense see, among others, J.M. Fried and C.C.Y. Wang, 'Short-termism, shareholder payouts and investment in the EU' (2021) 27(3) *European Financial Management* 389.

30 In this sense see again S. Ciacchi, above n. 19, 33.

31 European Parliament Resolution of 10 March 2021 with recommendations to the Commission on corporate due diligence and corporate accountability (2020/2129(INL)) [2021] OJ C474/11, Annex, Articles 2 ('Scope') and 19 ('Civil liability').

32 Council of the EU, 'Council Conclusions on Human Rights and Decent Work in Global Supply Chains', 1 December 2020, para. 46.

33 European Commission, 'Proposal for a Directive on Corporate Sustainability Due Diligence', above n. 18. On the Proposal, see S. Velluti, 'Labour standards in global garment supply chains and the proposed EU Corporate Sustainability Due Diligence Directive' (2024) 15(4) *European Labour Law Journal* 822; R. Greco, 'Corporate Human Rights Due Diligence and Civil Liability: Steps Forward Towards Effective Protection' (2023) 17(1) *Diritti umani e diritto internazionale* 5; S. Brabant, C. Bright, N. Neitzel and D. Schönfelder, 'Due Diligence Around the World', *Verfassungsblog*, 15 March 2022 <https://verfassungsblog.de/due-diligence-around-the-world/>; S. Gibbons, 'Some initial thoughts on the proposed EU Due Diligence Directive', Cambridge Core blog, 25 February 2022 <https://www.cambridge.org/core/blog/2022/02/25/some-initial-thoughts-on-the-proposed-eu-due-diligence-directive/>; C. Patz, 'The EU's Draft Corporate Sustainability Due Diligence Directive: A First Assessment' (2022) 7(2) *Business and Human Rights Journal* 291.

34 European Commission, 'Proposal for a Directive on Corporate Sustainability Due Diligence', above n. 18, Articles 2 ('Scope') and 22 ('Civil liability').

After the Council and Parliament adopted their negotiating positions in December 2022[35] and June 2023[36] respectively, trilogue negotiations between the Commission, the Council and Parliament commenced on 6 June 2023 and a political agreement was eventually reached on 14 December 2023.[37] However, following indications that Germany would abstain from confirming the agreement reached in December in a Committee of Permanent Representatives (COREPER) meeting initially scheduled for 9 February 2024, a number of other Member States – notably Austria, Finland and Italy – also indicated that they may abstain or vote against the deal.[38] This led to a reopening of negotiations among Member States to try to secure a qualified majority enabling the CSDDD to proceed through the remaining stages of the legislative process. Only after intense political work behind the scenes, with some horse-trading between Germany and Italy,[39] and with a significant reduction of the scope of the CSDDD, was it possible to secure the Council vote on a new proposal on 15 March 2024, which was later confirmed by the European Parliament Committee on Legal Affairs on 19 March 2024. The agreement reached in March 2024 departs from that of December 2023 in several key respects, including a heavy compromise on the personal scope, further amendments to the civil liability provision and changes in the definition of supply chains. Indeed, the latter are now labelled as 'chains of activities' and include most upstream activities (such as those related to the production of goods or the provision of services by a company, including the design, extraction, sourcing, manufacture, transport, storage and supply of raw materials, products or parts of products and the development of the product or the service), as well as certain elements of the downstream segments (including distribution, transport

35 European Commission, 'Proposal for a Directive of the European Parliament and of the Council on Corporate Sustainability Due Diligence and amending Directive (EU) 2019/1937 – General Approach', 30 November 2022, 15024/1/22 REV 1 <https://data.consilium.europa.eu/doc/document/ST-15024-2022-REV-1/en/pdf>.

36 Amendments adopted by the European Parliament on 1 June 2023 on the proposal for a directive of the European Parliament and of the Council on Corporate Sustainability Due Diligence and amending Directive (EU) 2019/1937, 1 June 2023, P9_TA(2023)0209 <https://www.europarl.europa.eu/doceo/document/TA-9-2023-0209_EN.html>.

37 'Corporate sustainability due diligence: Council and Parliament strike deal to protect environment and human rights', *European Council*, 14 December 2023 <https://www.consilium.europa.eu/en/press/press-releases/2023/12/14/corporate-sustainability-due-diligence-council-and-parliament-strike-deal-to-protect-environment-and-human-rights/>.

38 B. Sjåfjell and J. Mähönen, 'The story behind the torturous road towards the EU's Corporate Sustainability Due Diligence Directive', University of Oslo-Blogging for Sustainability, 24 May 2024 <https://www.jus.uio.no/english/research/areas/sustainabilitylaw/blog/2024/story-behind-road-towards-eu-csddd.html>.

39 E. Riebeling, 'Media reports: Deal to block PPWR agreed by Germany's finance minister and Italy', *EUWID Recycling and Waste Management*, 16 February 2024 <https://www.euwid-recycling.com/news/policy/media-reports-deal-to-block-ppwr-agreed-by-germanys-finance-minister-and-italy-160224/>.

and storage, but not sales or product disposal). This notwithstanding, it was adopted in a plenary session of the European Parliament on 24 April 2024 and formally approved by the Council on 13 June 2024. The CSDDD was published in the Official Journal of the European Union on 5 July and entered into force on the 20th day following its publication, namely on 25 July 2024.

3 THE BOUNDARIES OF THE RIGHTS PROTECTED UNDER THE CSDDD

3.1. Human Rights Violations and Impacts

It is well-known that the duty to protect human rights lies with states. Under international law, states are obligated to respect, protect and fulfil human rights within their territory and/or jurisdiction, so that individuals' rights can be enforced against states and remediated where harms occur. If one individual's human rights abut another's, their mediation proceeds via the state's monopoly of power. This means that it is the state that, if necessary, must protect one individual against the other, for example by keeping businesses from depleting indigenous peoples' natural resources. The CSDDD seems to revolutionise the traditional conception of states as the main duty-bearers when it comes to human rights protection, by making companies bearers of human rights responsibilities as well.[40] Since the adoption of the Proposal for a Directive on corporate sustainability due diligence by the European Commission, such an approach has prompted significant reflection on the extent to which businesses can have a concrete and practical duty to protect the rights of every individual with whom they may come into contact.[41] The process has additionally sparked criticism among scholars around the idea of adopting a Directive that elevates social norms already set out in voluntary initiatives of CSR into a legal context and that seems to replace states with companies as subjects of duty.[42]

---

40 In this sense, see C. Macchi, above n. 6, p. 96.

41 C. Methven O'Brien and J. Christoffersen, 'The Proposed European Union Corporate Sustainability Due Diligence Directive: Making or breaking European Human Rights Law?' (2023) 40(2) *Anales de Derecho* 177, 186.

42 In this sense, see M. Rask Madsen, 'From boom to backlash? The European Court of Human Rights and the transformation of Europe' in H.P. Aust and E. Demir-Gürsel (eds), *The European Court of Human Rights: Current Challenges in Historical Perspective*, Cheltenham, Edward Elgar, 2021, pp. 21–42. On the attribution of responsibility to multiple duty-bearers (including enterprises) and its distribution among them in a policentric governance, see also G.E. Türkelli, 'Extraterritorial human rights obligations and responsibility under international law' in M. Gibney, G.E. Türkelli, M. Krajewski and W. Vandenhole (eds), *The Routledge Handbook on Extraterritorial Human Rights Obligations*, Abingdon, Routledge, 2022, pp. 40–52.

To overcome the above-mentioned conceptual obstacle, the CSDDD defines its material scope by making use of the notion of 'adverse human rights impacts', with a meaning different from the one originally indicated in the Proposal for a Directive on corporate sustainability due diligence drafted by the EU Commission in 2022. Indeed, in Article 3(c) of the Proposal, the EU Commission defined 'a negative impact on human rights' as:

> an adverse impact on protected persons resulting from the violation of one of the rights or prohibitions listed in the Annex, Part I, Section 1, as enshrined in the international conventions listed in the Annex, Part I section 2,

thus admitting that a negative impact presupposes a violation of a right. The explicit reference to a 'violation of [...] rights' has been subsequently deleted from the text of Article 3(1)(c)(i) of the final text of the Directive, which defines 'adverse human rights impact' as follows:

> an impact on persons resulting from [...] an abuse of one of the human rights listed in Part I, Section 1, of the Annex to this Directive, as those human rights are enshrined in the international instruments listed in Part I, Section 2, of the Annex to this Directive.

The shift from 'violation' to 'abuse' is welcome if one considers that authoritative interpretive guidance from the UN Office of the High Commissioner for Human Rights (OHCHR) has clarified that the term 'human rights abuse' is used to refer to abuses committed by non-state actors, including business enterprises, distinguished from 'violations', which are breaches of international law by states.[43] However, such a change does not correspond to known legal terminology. Notably the UNGPs do not use the concept of 'abuse' to define an 'adverse human rights impact', framing the latter as any action or omission that removes or reduces the ability of an individual to enjoy his or her human rights.[44] Recital 32 of the Directive explains that the word 'abuse' should be 'interpreted in line with international human rights law', without however providing further guidance. This is not a particularly meaningful indication on a twofold ground. On the one side, the concept of 'abuse of rights' is used in a different sense under international human rights law and international law.[45]

---

43 UN Office of the High Commissioner for Human Rights (OHCHR), 'Access to Remedy in Cases of Business-related Human Rights Abuse: An Interpretive Guide', 2024, pp. 23–24 <https://www.ohchr.org/sites/default/files/2024-11/access-to-remedy-bhr-interpretive-guide-en.pdf>.

44 See in particular UNGPs 5 and 11.

45 The concept of 'abuse of rights' finds its origins in private domestic law, reflecting the idea that rights are conferred on people with specific social aims and come with inherent limits, i.e. a right should be exercised in conformity with the aim for which the right was created and to exercise a right otherwise would constitute an abuse. In this sense see P. de Morree, *Rights*

On the other side, the clearest articulation of the principle of an abuse of rights in international human rights law is found in so-called 'abuse clauses' in various international human rights instruments prohibiting states or persons from engaging in activities or performing acts aimed at the destruction or limitation of the rights and freedoms in the instrument. Such provisions are found in both the International Covenant on Civil and Political Rights[46] and the International Covenant on Economic and Social Rights,[47] but are not included in any of the other instruments listed in the Annex.[48]

If the CSDDD has rightly rephrased the notion of 'adverse human rights impacts', the term 'abuse' still remains unclear, thus creating uncertainty not only for rightsholders, but also for companies trying to determine the scope and extent of their due diligence. In addition, the decision to give content to the concept of 'adverse human rights impacts' by listing only certain human rights and international human rights instruments departs from the expectation that companies consider impacts on 'all human rights' in two main ways.[49] They concern a limited coverage of rights, on the one side, and the establishment of a convoluted set of conditions under which a company carries due diligence obligations, on the other side.

3.2. *The Limited Scope of Rights*

To determine whether a company has due diligence obligations in relation to the rights covered by the Directive, Part I of the Annex first lists in section 1 a number of selected rights the violation of which more often occurs in practice, while in section 2 it outlines human rights and fundamental freedom instruments.

Section 1 lists 16 rights, around half of which are construed as prohibitions, for example, the prohibition of arbitrary or unlawful interference with a person's privacy (number 4) or the prohibition of unequal treatment in employment (number 14). Several of the listed rights are organised in clusters, for example the right to freedom of association and assembly and the rights to organise and

---

and Wrongs under the ECHR: The prohibition of abuse of rights in Article 17 of the European Convention on Human Rights, Cambridge, Intersentia, 2016, pp. 141–42. The status of the doctrine of 'abuse of rights' under international law is generally accepted in practice but there remains debate on its scope and nature. In the context of international human rights law, the doctrine of abuse of rights is less established: see again P. de Morree, ibid., pp. 135 and 142.

46 International Covenant on Civil and Political Rights, 19 December 1966, 999 UNTS 171 (ICCPR). See Article 5(1).

47 International Covenant on Economic, Social and Cultural Rights, 19 December 1966, 999 UNTS 3 (ICESCR). See Article 5(1).

48 Generally, such 'abuse of rights' clauses can only be applied in conjunction with the substantive provisions of the relevant instrument elaborating the right in question. In this sense, see P. Janig, 'Abuse of Rights' in C. Binder, M. Nowak, J.A. Hofbauer and P. Janig (eds), *Elgar Encyclopedia of Human Rights*, Cheltenham, Edward Elgar, 2022, pp. 13–20.

49 See UNGP 14.

collective bargaining (number 13) that is specified to include: the right to join or form a union; the right to join or form a union not to be used as the basis for discrimination or retaliation; the right of the union to freely operate without interference; and the right to strike. Similarly, number 8 on the list covers five distinct rights for the protection of children's health, access to education and well-being. A particularly noteworthy inclusion is the right to enjoy 'just and favourable conditions of work, including a fair wage and an adequate living wage for employed workers and an adequate living income' for self-employed workers and smallholder farmers; decent living, safe and healthy working conditions and reasonable working hours (number 6), a much advocated for right that, together with the obligation to take appropriate measures to alter purchasing practices in Articles 10 and 11, holds real economic redistributive potential not only for business suppliers in global value chains but specifically for (self-employed) workers. The listed rights must be interpreted according to international law, regardless of the potentially different – and often diminished – levels of implementation granted within the domestic jurisdictions of some of the countries where the chain of activities operate. This means that companies and implementing authorities will need to take international jurisprudence and recommendations of treaty bodies into account and will be obliged to require their subsidiaries and business partners operating in the territory of states where the level of protection is not in line with the international human rights standards, to nevertheless comply with them. Despite this approach not being fully in line with the UNGPs – according to which human rights that are likely to be potentially violated by corporations cannot be identified in a closed list[50] – it may be suitable in order to grant corporations a higher level of certainty.[51] Numbers 15 and 16 in section 1 of the Annex build a bridge between the human rights and environmental normative scope of the Directive as they cover human rights harms induced by environmental degradation.

At first glance, the Annex appears relatively comprehensive, as it contains many of the key and fundamental international human rights instruments adopted at the universal level.[52] This is undoubtedly laudable, given the inclusion of non-European companies in the scope of application of the Directive. However, on

---

50 See the Commentary to UNGP 1: '[…] business enterprises can have an impact on virtually the entire spectrum of internationally recognized human rights'.

51 In this sense, see A. Bonfanti, above n. 13, 863.

52 These are the ICCPR; the ICESCR; the Convention on the Rights of the Child, 20 November 1989, 1577 UNTS 3; the International Labour Organisation (ILO) Conventions No. 87 (Freedom of Association and Protection of the Right to Organise Convention, 9 July 1948), No. 98 (Right to Organise and Collective Bargaining, 1 July 1949), No. 29 (Forced Labour Convention, 28 June 1930) and its 2014 Protocol, No. 105 (the Abolition of Forced Labour Convention, 5 June 1957), No. 138 (the Minimum Age Convention, 26 June 1973), No. 182 (the Worst Forms of Child Labour Convention, 17 June 1999), No. 100 (the Equal Remuneration Convention, 29 June 1951), and No. 111 (the Discrimination (Employment and Occupation) Convention, 25 June 1958).

closer inspection, there are serious lamentable absences such as the International Convention on the Protection of the Rights of All Migrant Workers and Members of their Families,[53] the Convention against Torture and Other Cruel, Inhuman or Degrading Treatment or Punishment,[54] the Convention on the Elimination of All Forms of Discrimination against Women[55] and the International Convention on the Elimination of All Forms of Racial Discrimination,[56] as well as a reference to international humanitarian law. Further, particularly worrisome is the fact that the Annex does not refer to key European human rights instruments including the European Convention on Human Rights (ECHR)[57] and the EU Charter of Fundamental Rights (CFR).[58] The CFR enjoys the same legal status as the EU's founding treaties while EU Member States are required to give effect to it when implementing EU law. As regards the ECHR, this is recognised as part of the common constitutional tradition in Europe,[59] with special significance in EU law. All EU Member States are parties to it which is furthermore a requirement for joining the EU. The duties of the EU itself, Member States and third parties under the ECHR and CFR have been extensively examined in the case law of the Luxembourg and Strasbourg courts. All new EU legislation must respect the ECHR and the EU Commission has adopted a strategy to secure this goal.[60] Since the CSDDD explicitly acknowledges in the preamble that:

> the Union is founded on the values of respect for human dignity, freedom, democracy, equality, the rule of law and respect for human rights as enshrined in the Charter of Fundamental Rights of the European Union,[61]

it is then hard then to see how duties established in the Directive might be interpreted by the Court of Justice of the EU or Member States as not referring

---

53 International Convention on the Protection of the Rights of All Migrant Workers and Members of their Families, 18 December 1990, 2220 UNTS 3.

54 Convention against Torture and Other Cruel, Inhuman or Degrading Treatment or Punishment, 10 December 1984, 1465 UNTS 85.

55 Convention on the Elimination of All Forms of Discrimination against Women, 18 December 1979, 1249 UNTS 13.

56 International Convention on the Elimination of All Forms of Racial Discrimination, 7 March 1966, 660 UNTS 195.

57 Convention for the Protection of Human Rights and Fundamental Freedoms, 4 November 1950 (ETS 5).

58 Charter of Fundamental Rights of the European Union [2012] OJ C326/391.

59 In this sense, see Case 4/73, *J. Nold, Kohlen-und Baustoffgroßhandlung v. Commission of the European Communities*, ECLI:EU:C:1974:51.

60 Directorate-General for Communication, 'Incorporating fundamental rights into EU legislative process', *European Commission* <https://commission.europa.eu/aid-development-cooperation-fundamental-rights/your-rights-eu/eu-charter-fundamental-rights/application-charter/incorporating-fundamental-rights-eu-legislative-process_en>.

61 CSDDD, recital 1.

to the ECHR and CFR.[62] It is also unclear what arguments might be made to justify their omission, especially regarding impacts (whether by EU or foreign-registered companies) occurring inside the EU.[63]

Besides it being difficult to understand the rationale behind the inclusion of some international human rights instruments and the exclusion of others, such an approach makes the material scope of the CSDDD necessarily partial and not inclusive of the full range of rights the actions of business enterprises may affect. In this regard, it is, however, important to note that the European Commission has the power, via Article 3(2) of the CSDDD, to amend the list of instruments included in the Annex by means of a delegated act, which is an act of executive lawmaking by the Commission supplementing or amending certain non-essential elements of the underlying law, in this case the CSDDD. Recital 32 specifies that once ratified by all Member States, the Commission shall add the ILO Occupational and Health Convention, 22 June 1981 (No. 155) and the ILO Promotional Framework for Occupational Safety and Health Convention, 15 June 2006 (No. 187) to the list of instruments.

3.3. *The Conditions for Due Diligence Obligations*

As anticipated, the second deviation from the expectation that companies consider impacts on 'all human rights' relates to the fact that the human rights a company is required to consider are not only limited but also subject to complex conditions. In this regard, Article 3(1)(c)(ii) of the CSDDD provides that human rights that are enshrined in the international instruments listed in Part I, section 2 of the Annex are relevant provided that: the right concerned can be abused by a company or legal entity; the abuse directly impairs a legal interest protected in the human rights instrument; and the company could have reasonably foreseen the risk that such human right may be affected, taking into account the circumstances of the specific case.

As far as the first condition is concerned, in its General Approach, the Council of the EU had originally proposed a different wording, namely that 'the human right can be abused by a company or legal entity other than a Member State […]'.[64] This seems to be, once again, a clear reference to distinctive state

62 See I. Jędrzejowska-Schiffauer, Ł. Szoszkiewicz, J. Wilde-Ramsing, K. Booth, P. Barraud de Lagerie and B. Faracik, 'Towards EU-wide Mandatory Human Rights and Environmental Due Diligence for Business: A Breakthrough in Europe and Beyond?' (2022) 42 *Polish Yearbook of International Law* 245, 268.

63 Similar concerns were expressed also with regard to the Proposal for a Directive on corporate sustainability due diligence: see C. Methven O'Brien and J. Hartmann, 'The European Commission's proposal for a directive on corporate sustainability due diligence: two paradoxes', *EJIL: Talk!*, 19 May 2022 <https://www.ejiltalk.org/the-european-commissions-proposal-for-a-directive-on-corporate-sustainability-due-diligence-two-paradoxes/>.

64 European Commission, above n. 35, Article 3(c)(ii).

obligations under international human rights law, such as the protection and the fulfilment of human rights. While, according to the UNGPs, businesses are not expected to take on these state obligations, Principle 12 highlights that companies can have an impact on the entire spectrum of internationally recognised human rights. This means they also can contribute to or be linked to human rights violations resulting from a state's failure in relation to its obligation to fulfil a human right. It is, therefore, to be welcomed that the wording of the first condition has not followed the General Approach of the Council.[65] Also, as previously said, according to recital 32, the notion of 'abuse' is to be interpreted in line with international human rights law. According to international standards, human rights abuse relates to harm that a business has caused, contributed to or is linked to.

The second condition set out in Article 3(1)(c)(ii) is much more problematic. The phrase 'directly impairs a legal interest protected in the human rights instruments' is unclear – especially how or why a 'legal interest' can be differentiated from a right in any of the international human rights conventions.[66] Regarding the requirement that the abuse directly impairs such a 'legal interest', it must be borne in mind that the CSDDD establishes a clear, overarching obligation on companies to undertake due diligence across their own operations, those of their subsidiaries, and those of their business partners in order to prevent, mitigate and bring to an end adverse human rights impacts (Article 1(1)(a)); and to ascertain their level of involvement (causing, or jointly causing) when doing so (Article 8(1)). Considering this overarching obligation on companies to undertake due diligence across the chain of activity, the phrase 'directly impairs a legal interest' must be taken to apply to any abuse by the company, its subsidiaries and its business partners.

Finally, the third condition generates considerable legal uncertainty for companies, as some human rights will be foreseeably affected in some contexts, for some companies, but not in others. It is, therefore, highly context specific. The requirement that 'the company could have reasonably foreseen the risk that such human right may be affected' is a significantly lower threshold than reasonable foresight of the right actually being abused.[67] First, foresight of risk is far easier to satisfy than foresight of an actual right being impacted; second, it is only necessary to show foresight of a right being affected as opposed to abused. Rights can be affected in a myriad of nuanced ways; abuse is far more targeted and specific. Whereas 'abuse' is specified to be interpreted in accordance with international human rights law, 'affected' is not specified. The

---

65 In this sense see also N. Meyer and C. Patz, 'Dividing the Indivisible', *Verfassungsblog*, 1 June 2024 <https://verfassungsblog.de/dividing-the-indivisible-human-rights-under-the-eu-corporate-sustainability-due-diligence-directive/>.

66 Ibid.

67 Ibid.

obligation on companies to undertake meaningful stakeholder consultation, as well as the right and ability of stakeholders to notify the company of risks and actual impacts to their human rights will undoubtedly play a key role in increasing companies' foresight of human rights affected and henceforth the normative human rights scope per se.

4 THE DELIMITATION OF THE DUE DILIGENCE THAT IS CARRIED OUT IN THE CSDDD

The process of due diligence outlined in the CSDDD broadly aligns with expectations under the international standards developed at the UN and OECD levels. Under Articles 5–16 of the CSDDD, states are obliged to ensure that relevant companies conduct risk-based HRDD. In this regard, the said provisions set out a series of concrete duties that imply the attribution of obligations of means on companies. Indeed, businesses must develop an HRDD policy and integrate it into their activities. In addition, companies must identify actual or potential adverse impacts; prevent and mitigate potential ones; bring actual adverse impacts to an end; minimise their extent and provide remediation; carry out meaningful engagement with stakeholders;[68] establish and maintain a notification mechanism and a complaints procedure; monitor the effectiveness of the due diligence policy and measures; and publicly communicate. The implementation measures include making the necessary financial or non-financial investments, modifications of, or improvements to, the business plan, overall strategies and operations, such as the purchasing, design, distribution, trading, procurement and pricing practices.[69] In addition, the Directive establishes that companies shall be required to seek to obtain contractual assurances from business partners as regards the respect of human rights within the latter's activities.[70]

The recourse to contractual clauses as an instrument to guarantee respect for human rights has represented a controversial issue during the Directive's negotiation process. Indeed, through the exercise of negotiating autonomy, companies could bypass the respect of their due diligence duties, charging with them the business partners.[71] In order to avoid such risk, the text of the Directive specifies that contractual assurances shall be designed to

---

68 On this specific aspect see C.O. Lichuma, 'Harmonization Pains but Stakeholders' Gain', *Verfassungsblog*, 25 May 2024 <https://verfassungsblog.de/harmonization-pains-but-stakeholders-gain/>.

69 Recital 41 of the CSDDD.

70 Articles 10–11 of the CSDDD.

71 See broadly R. Mares, 'The Unintended Consequences of Mandatory Due Diligence', *Verfassungsblog*, 13 June 2024 <https://verfassungsblog.de/csddd-the-unintended-consequences-of-mandatory-due-diligence/>.

ensure that responsibilities are shared appropriately by the company and the business partners and, when they are obtained from a small- and medium-sized enterprise (SME), the terms used shall be fair, reasonable and non-discriminatory.[72] Appropriate measures of assistance and support shall be granted by the company to the SMEs and the costs of independent third-party verification shall be borne by the former.[73] The contractual assurances shall be accompanied by appropriate measures to verify compliance.[74]

Among the most significant innovations introduced about management of the business partners, the Directive provides that, should a violation of human rights occur within the activities of one of them, the company shall nonetheless be required to 'responsibly exit' the business relationship. This means that, before suspending or terminating a business relationship, the company shall assess whether the adverse impacts of such a decision would be higher, and eventually either decide not to suspend or terminate the contract or to take the appropriate steps to prevent, mitigate or bring to an end the impacts arising from the suspension or termination.[75] Therefore, EU Member States will be required to reform their contract laws accordingly, in order to grant the companies the possibility of temporarily suspending or terminating the business relationship and performing the required responsible exit.

The inclusion of the HRDD duties into contracts is the object of a corporate duty *de negotiando*: the Directive clearly recognises that 'the company should only be obliged to seek the contractual assurances, as obtaining them may depend on the circumstances'.[76] Despite this clarification, as a matter of fact, the conclusion of HRDD-aligned contracts with business partners certainly represents a relevant instrument, even though it does not automatically exonerate companies from civil liability.

As it has been rightly observed, a contract disregarding the aforementioned requirements – for example, a contract providing for unreasonable commercial terms and pricing conditions and putting on the SME involved as the business partner the overall duty to respect human rights, without adequately assisting or supporting it – due to the pressure exercised by the company during the contracts' negotiation, or not correctly implemented due to its misconduct, should be considered inadequate to demonstrate the company's effective compliance with its HRDD duties.[77]

As anticipated, the CSDDD requires that a company's due diligence covers not only a company's operations and the operations of its subsidiaries, but also

---

72 Articles 10–11 of the CSDDD.

73 Articles 10(5) and 11(6), and recital 46 of the CSDDD.

74 Article 10(5) of the CSDDD.

75 Article 11(7) of the CSDDD.

76 Recital 46 of the CSDDD.

77 In this sense see A. Bonfanti, above n. 13, 876.

that of its business partners in its so-called 'chain of activities'. The wording of the provisions referring to the extension of the HRDD duties to the activities performed by the business partners has represented one of the most highly debated issues during negotiation. Indeed, despite a generic convergence of the European institutions regarding the idea – essential to the concept of HRDD as conceived by the UNGPs – that the newly introduced duties should have included the activities of the contractual partners, their positions significantly diverged when dealing with the coverage of the indirect partners and of both the upstream and downstream value chains.

After removing the Commission's limitation to the only 'established' business relationships – namely, to the only long-term and not ancillary commercial relationships[78] – the Directive provides that the company must exercise its due diligence duties in a way that covers the activities of all partners within its chain of activities, without any limitation. If, on the one hand, the attained solution comes to include the activities of all direct business partners (i.e. those 'with which the company has a commercial agreement related to the operations, products or services of the company or to which the company provides services')[79] and of all indirect business partners (i.e. 'not [...] direct business partner[s] but which perform [...] business operations related to the operations, products or services of the company'),[80] on the other hand, the reference to the notion of 'chain of activities' has the effect of limiting the duties' coverage to some specific portions of the global value chain. Indeed, according to Article 3(1)(g), the 'chain of activities' includes the activities of upstream business partners that relate to the products and services of the company in question, and activities of downstream business partners, but are limited to the distribution, transport and storage of products provided that these activities are carried out for the company or on its behalf, therefore with the exception of their disposal. These limitations undoubtedly represent a departure from the UNGPs,[81] which expect due diligence to be conducted along the full value chain. However, since, as a matter of principle, the activities of both direct and indirect business partners are covered, to avoid imposing excessive burdens on companies the Directive allows them to prioritise the most severe and foreseeable identified adverse impacts.[82] Therefore, when companies are unable to contain all impacts, they are allowed to give priority to the most serious

78 European Commission, 'Proposal for a Directive on Corporate Sustainability Due Diligence', above n. 18, Articles 1(1)(a) and 3(f).

79 Article 3(1)(f)(i) of the CSDDD.

80 Article 3(1)(f)(ii) of the CSDDD.

81 On this aspect, see B.F. Hogan and J. Reyes, 'Downstream Human Rights Due Diligence: Informing Debate Through Insights from Business Practice' (2023) 8(3) *Business and Human Rights Journal* 434.

82 Article 9 of the CSDDD.

and most probable negative ones.[83] This selection relies on a diligent mapping of the impacts, taking into account the relevant risk factors and based on the preliminary identification of general areas where negative impacts are more likely to occur and to be more serious.[84] Once the most severe and most likely adverse impacts are addressed within a reasonable time, the company shall address less severe and less likely adverse impacts.[85]

Said limitations have important implications for financial undertakings, such as banks. Indeed, following intense lobbying, the final text of the Directive includes the financial sector within scope of the CSDDD, but in a limited way: financial institutions are required to conduct due diligence on their own operations and their supply chain, rather than being required to consider the impacts of investments, loans, insurance or other financial services (i.e. their 'downstream' activities). As these areas are both at the core of the business activities of financial institutions and where they have the most risk of negative human rights impacts, this is a critical shortcoming of the CSDDD and a missed opportunity to include a key player in the transition to a more sustainable global economy. This is unfortunate as financial institutions are uniquely placed to exercise leverage and improve the human rights practices of thousands of real economy companies. There are good emerging HRDD practices from the sector, and many institutions have voiced their support for finance being fully included in the CSDDD.[86] However, as recent studies on financial institutions have showed, the sector struggles to demonstrate respect for human rights.[87] At the same time, it is among the larger companies that a range of strategies to address the root causes of adverse human rights impacts and work more collaboratively with their business partners can be found.[88] These include the use of human rights impact assessments, making investments in management or production processes and creating business models that

---

83 Ibid.

84 Article 8 of the CSDDD.

85 Article 9(3) of the CSDDD.

86 See the document 'Investor Statement of Support for an Ambitious and Effective European Directive on Corporate Sustainability Due Diligence', 24 November 2022, signed by 145 financial institutions <https://investorsforhumanrights.org/sites/default/files/attachments/2022-11/Investor%20Statement%20of%20Support%20for%20an%20Effective%20EU%20Directive%20on%20CSDD%2011.24.22.pdf>.

87 S.A. Lysgaard, S. Tansey and I. Tuta, 'Documenting respect for human rights in the financial sector', 12 December 2023, *Danish Institute of Human Rights* <https://www.humanrights.dk/files/media/document/Documenting%20Respect%20for%20Human%20Rights%20in%20the%20Financial%20Sector%20%E2%80%93%20A%202023%20Snapshot%20of%20Danish%20Financial%20Institutions_accessible.pdf>.

88 See G. Holly 'The EU Corporate Sustainability Due Diligence Directive: Maximising Impact through Transposition and Implementation', 24 April 2024, *Danish Institute of Human Rights*, p. 18 <https://www.humanrights.dk/files/media/document/DIHR_The%20EU%20Corporate%20Sustainability%20Due%20Diligence%20Directive_0.pdf>.

better respect human rights, encouraging long-term collaboration and capacity building with partners and working at the sectoral level.

As has been observed,[89] translating the normative expectations of soft law instruments into hard law obligations is challenging for any legislature. On the one hand, obligations must have a precise and definite nature to enable companies to understand their duties and other stakeholders to monitor the efforts of companies. On the other hand, prescribing a closed list of measures a company must take may stifle innovation and encourage 'check-box compliance' rather than a risk-based approach to due diligence.[90] The CSDDD uses several mechanisms to guard against this possibility. First, the Directive clarifies several qualifying reservations attached to some duties whose vague formulation could frustrate its desired objectives. For example, companies must take 'appropriate measures' and take into account specific factors when designing them. 'Appropriate measures' are defined in Article 3(1)(o) as measures:

> capable of achieving the objectives of due diligence by effectively addressing adverse impacts in a manner commensurate to the degree of severity and the likelihood of the adverse impact, and reasonably available to the company, taking into account the circumstances of the specific case, including the nature and extent of the adverse impact and relevant risk factors.

Article 3(1)(u) of the CSDDD specifies that 'risk factors' include geographic and contextual factors and factors specific to a product, service and business operations. Introducing an effectiveness requirement for such measures should encourage targeted measures to effectively address specific impacts on human rights, rather than being focused solely on compliance. Arguably, this requirement should also rule out mere contractual delegation of due diligence measures. When determining the appropriate measures to prevent or end adverse impacts, companies should also take into account whether an impact is or may be caused by the company; caused jointly by the company and a subsidiary or business partner; or caused only by a business partner, and what influence the company has over the business partner.[91] This formulation departs from the language of the UNGPs concerning a company's involvement in an impact (cause, contribute, and direct linkage), but these levels of involvement

---

89 See again N. Bueno, N. Bernaz, G. Holly and O. Martin-Ortega, above n. 13, 3.

90 Ibid., p. 4. Similar concerns were expressed also with regard to the Proposal for a Directive on corporate sustainability due diligence: see G. Quijano and C. Lopez, 'Rise of Mandatory Human Rights Due Diligence: A Beacon of Hope or a Double-Edged Sword?' (2021) 6(2) *Business and Human Rights Journal* 241, 254; I. Jędrzejowska-Schiffauer, Ł. Szoszkiewicz, J. Wilde-Ramsing, K. Booth, P. Barraud de Lagerie and B. Faracik, above n. 62, 247.

91 Articles 10(1)(a) and 11(1)(a) of the CSDDD.

should be interpreted in line with the international framework. In the same vein, the CSDDD requires 'meaningful' engagement with stakeholders. The latter notion is defined – even if in a broad sense – in Article 3(1)(n), and includes companies' employees, employees of its subsidiaries, trade unions and workers' representatives, consumers and other affected individuals, groups and communities but also national human rights institutions. Both this wide definition and the specific obligations of meaningful engagement and consultation with stakeholders in all steps of the due diligence process were demanded by civil society and scholars and were included relatively late in the negotiating process.[92]

5 CONCLUSIONS

The protection of human rights from corporate abuses will be greatly strengthened by the Directive's domestic implementation. For the time being, it is possible to conclude that, at least potentially, the positive impacts in terms of corporate respect of human rights and accountability are undeniable. The implementation of the HRDD duties along the chain of activities and the establishment of civil liability on companies for human rights violations occurring throughout their chains of activities will make the companies falling within its scope of application improve their business models, strategies, procurement policies, corporate governance and investments, and, in some cases, lead to substantive improvements in terms of corporate conduct. However, an HRDD legislation can be efficacious only if it is appropriately tailored. In this regard, despite the great expectations, the Directive is designed in a way that poses a series of hurdles that need to be overcome in order to facilitate the concrete strengthening of human rights protection in Europe and the countering of an adverse impact on this protection at the hands of businesses.

An initial obstacle is represented by the fact that the EU co-legislators have not followed international standards and ensured that the CSDDD covers all internationally recognised human rights, or at the very least provided a clearer and more comprehensive list of pertinent rights missing as listed above. Instead, the Directive's normative human rights scope is the obvious result of a political compromise. Though co-legislators were aiming to increase legal certainty for companies, the outcome is a lack of clarity and a complicated test whether due diligence obligations actually arise for individual companies in specific instances. To overcome these challenges, Member States and the Commission should improve the language and ensure clarity in their transposing national laws and in the forthcoming Guidelines (under Article 19) respectively. The

92 Article 13(3) of the CSDDD.

uncertainties related to the use of the term 'abuse' in the definition of 'adverse human rights impacts', as well as the absence of a number of important human rights instruments – notably those applicable at the regional level, such as the ECHR and the CFR – are serious and must be rectified at the EU level during the first review of the CSDDD. Given the status of the law as a Directive, Member States also have the freedom to add these missing instruments during national transposition, and hopefully they will do so at a later stage in order to further honour their commitments under the UNGPs.

A second hurdle to the CSDDD's desired strengthening of human rights protection is the (at least sometimes) unclear nature of the concrete duties in which the due diligence process is articulated. Indeed, on the one hand, the Directive tightens companies' duties (compared to the UNGPs) by specifying legal duties, but on the other hand these legal duties are, compared to the UNGPs, weakened by various restrictions. In this regard, suffice it to mention the not always clear formulation of the implementation measures set out in Article 5(1) of the Directive. Therefore, it will be necessary for any forthcoming guidance on the implementation of the CSDDD to emphasise the need to interpret its requirements in line with the expectations of the UNGPs.

PART III.

Novel Approaches to Human Rights Research

CHAPTER 8
'THE REVOLUTION WILL BE LIVE-STREAMED': NARRATING THE TENSIONS AROUND THE RIGHT TO POLITICAL EXPRESSION IN THE PRIVATISED DIGITAL PUBLIC SPHERE

Tomáš Morochovič

The revolution will not be right back
After a message about a white tornado
White lightning, or white people
You will not have to worry about a dove in your bedroom
The tiger in your tank, or the giant in your toilet bowl
The revolution will not go better with Coke
The revolution will not fight germs that may cause bad breath
The revolution will put you in the driver's seat

Gil Scott-Heron, 'The Revolution Will Not be Televised' (1970)

1 INTRODUCTION

When the hashtag '#blacklivesmatter' started circulating widely on Facebook and Twitter (now known as X) in 2013, one could have hardly foreseen the impact of the phrase on political discussion over the following decade. The decentralised racial justice and anti-discrimination movement that was triggered by the slogan not only had a profound influence on the global discussion around race, but it also changed society's understanding of the role of social media within politics – 'slacktivism' and performative allyship were overshadowed by sustained movements for social and cultural change.[1] However, it was not the first time that the political

[1] The terms 'slacktivism' and 'performative allyship' are intended as pejorative terms used to describe an uncommitted participation 'in a social movement by liking or sharing social media posts promoting a particular cause'. See J. Bowman Williams, N. Mezey

effects of social media were brought to public scrutiny. Two years earlier, activists gathering in Cairo's Tahrir Square widely used social media platforms to circulate on-the-ground accounts of protests and instantaneously reach a global audience.[2]

In roughly the decade since these movements started, the landscape in which the interaction between political expression and the online world occurs has changed considerably. The internet, and social media platforms in particular, have become indispensable tools for political campaigning. Political candidates have used the immediacy of social media for rapid-fire, impactful, and at times vacuous messaging,[3] while simultaneously taking advantage of the personalised nature of online advertising for political microtargeting of prospective voters.[4] Tech companies have been mutual beneficiaries from this development, too, as tailored political messaging works symbiotically with the popularity-based algorithms used by social media platforms, maximising user engagement while at the same time polarising society.[5] Yet, in many ways, the growth of the digital public sphere[6] has also made participation in political life far more accessible. Fischli and Muldoon point to a significant body of literature that suggests digital technology has facilitated public participation in political decision-making, for example by using online spaces to enable large-scale public deliberation or policy crowdsourcing by political parties.[7] Similarly, Sarah Joseph highlights that, despite legitimate concerns about censorship and

---

and L. Singh, '#BlackLivesMatter – Getting from Contemporary Social Movements to Structural Change' (2021) 12 *California Law Review Online* <https://www.ssrn.com/abstract=3860435>.

2 See e.g. S. Joseph, 'Social Media, Political Change, and Human Rights' (2012) 35(1) *Boston College International and Comparative Law Review* 145, 153.

3 There is hardly a better example of this behaviour than the US President Donald Trump.

4 B. Sander, 'Democratic Disruption in the Age of Social Media: Between Marketized and Structural Conceptions of Human Rights Law' (2021) 32(1) *European Journal of International Law* 159, 165.

5 P.M. Barrett, J. Hendrix and J. Grant Sims, 'Fueling the Fire: How Social Media Intensifies U.S. Political Polarization – And What Can Be Done About It', New York, NYU Stern Center for Business and Human Rights, 2021, p. 8 <https://bhr.stern.nyu.edu/wp-content/uploads/2024/03/NYUCBHRFuelingTheFire_FINALONLINEREVISEDSep7.pdf>; E.J. Finkel, C.A. Bail, M. Cikara, P.H. Ditto, S. Iyengar, S. Klar, L. Mason, M.C. McGrath, B. Nyhan, D.G Rand, L.J. Skitka, J.A. Tucker, J.J. Van Bavel, C.S.Wang and J.N. Druckman, 'Political sectarianism in America' (2020) 370 *Science* 533, 534.

6 The notion of a 'digital public sphere' is a term predominantly taken from international relations theory – see e.g. M. Eisenegger and M.S. Schäfer, 'Editorial: Reconceptualizing public sphere(s) in the digital age? On the role and future of public sphere theory' (2023) 33(2–3) *Communication Theory* 61; M.S. Schäfer, 'Digital Public Sphere' in G. Mazzoleni (ed), *The International Encyclopedia of Political Communication*, 1st ed., Hoboken, Wiley, 2016 <https://onlinelibrary.wiley.com/doi/10.1002/9781118541555.wbiepc087>. The UN Special Rapporteur on the promotion and protection of the right to freedom of opinion and expression has conceptualised the term in terms of a 'public forum'. Throughout the chapter, these terms are used interchangeably.

7 R. Fischli and J. Muldoon, 'Empowering Digital Democracy' (2024) 22(3) *Perspectives on Politics* 819.

surveillance, social media platforms have largely played the role of 'passive facilitators' with respect to pro-democracy revolutions.[8]

Indeed, the two political movements mentioned at the outset of this chapter both underline the participatory potential of social media. One slogan that was used by activists within both movements references the song 'The Revolution Will Not be Televised' by poet and civil rights activist Gil Scott-Heron. At first sight, it might appear as a counter-intuitive choice for two movements that relied so heavily on modern technology and the screens of mobile phones, computers, and, indeed, televisions to get their message across. However, Scott-Heron's message within the song is more assertive, and has more layers, than the title suggests. In the last two verses, Scott-Heron emphasises that 'the revolution will put *you* in the driver seat [...] the revolution will be *live*'. In this sense, it can also be understood as a rally for a proactive, unmediated engagement with politics – something that the prevalence of political expression online may contribute to. Arguably, it is this latter meaning of the song that really encapsulates the mobilisations seen from Cairo to Ferguson, Missouri.

By paraphrasing the last verse of Scott-Heron's song in this chapter's title, the aim is to engage the 'empowering' interpretation that it carries in order to question the tensions that have characterised the expansion of political expression in the online sphere. Although politics on social media platforms often appears exactly as the sort of entertainment consumer content that Scott-Heron railed against,[9] the ability to use the online space for political purposes also provides a unique tool for empowering dissidents, mobilising protesters, and even organising revolutions. Moreover, as an inherently public category of discourse, questions arise about how to reconcile this social function with the private structuring of the technologies – whether the internet at large or, more specifically, major online platforms. Critically analysing how political expression online is construed becomes increasingly pressing as these private spaces become our contemporary public squares. An analysis of how the right to political expression online is being construed in light of these two sets of tensions – between empowering/disruptive effects and public/private functions – can prove crucial in understanding the future transformations of political expression in the digital public sphere. In particular, the approach adopted here makes one attentive to the political qualities and values that governance actors prioritise in construing this as yet emerging space for public deliberation.

---

8 S. Joseph, above n. 2, 185.

9 There is hardly a better example of the problems with the populist and consumerist aspects of political expression online than Elon Musk's activity on X (formerly known as Twitter) and his purchase of said platform. See e.g. A. Chakrabortty, 'Elon Musk is the king of trolls in an age of troll politics. Time to stop feeding him', *The Guardian*, 26 April 2022 <https://www.theguardian.com/commentisfree/2022/apr/26/elon-musk-king-of-trolls-purchase-twitter-dangerous>.

The chapter adopts an approach that is focused on the interpretation of political expression online as part of human rights discourse. It traces the narrative construction of the internet and social media platforms within decisions of two dispute settlement mechanisms – the European Court of Human Rights (ECtHR) and the Facebook/Meta Oversight Board (OB or the Board). After the introduction in section 1, section 2 sketches out the contours of political expression online and the limits of this intervention. After explaining the understanding of the two sets of tensions, the chapter discusses the merits of focusing on dispute settlement mechanisms as relevant 'narrators' of political expression online (see below section 2.1), provides justifications about why seeing the issue as one of human rights is warranted (see below section 2.2), and elaborates on the narrative approach used to study decisions (see below section 2.3). Subsequently, section 3 turns to the analysis of the construction of political expression online. Beginning in section 3.1, the chapter discusses how the two dispute settlement bodies selected embody the dichotomy between public and private visions of the digital public sphere. Finally, section 3.2 of the chapter turns to the analysis of individual cases and assesses how the two bodies construct the internet and social media platforms as spaces for political expression. By focusing on two narrative elements – the 'scene' in section 3.2.1 and 'agent' in section 3.2.2 – the chapter draws insights about the normative contours that the Court and the Board use to interpret this space, pointing out divergences and similarities in the approach of the two bodies and the different ways of resolving the two sets of tensions between empowering/disruptive effects and public/private functions.

2 THE CONTOURS OF THE DIGITAL PUBLIC SPHERE – NARRATING ONLINE POLITICAL EXPRESSION AS A HUMAN RIGHTS ISSUE

It has become a truism to say that the internet, and social media platforms more specifically, are essential means of communication and expression for billions of people around the world. People get their news online, keep in touch with relatives, and exchange views with strangers. Regardless of how uncomfortable it may feel, today the notion of being 'live' is intimately coupled with being connected to the world through the internet. And just as the rest of one's life, politics have moved there, too. Online spaces are transformed into quasi-public fora, proving essential for social engagement, expression, and assembly.[10] Journalists point out that elections are now decided by candidates' ability to have

[10] See e.g. UN Human Rights Council, 'Report of the Special Rapporteur on the promotion and protection of the right to freedom of opinion and expression', 30 March 2017, UN Doc. A/HRC/35/22; UN Human Rights Council, 'Report of the Special Rapporteur on the

a dominant presence on social media platforms such as TikTok, Facebook, or X.[11] The importance of the internet for political expression is acutely present in both liberal and illiberal regimes – perhaps more so in the latter, where using the internet to pursue political agendas can prove an effective way to avoid censorship and governmental oversight of non-conforming speech.[12]

Inevitably, such a reconfiguration of the realm of public discourse also has the potential to negatively disrupt existing practices of political participation. The introduction of this chapter (see above section 1) already highlighted some of the challenges. These range from relatively minor issues, such as the difficulties in monitoring campaigning moratoria in the immediate run-up to an election day,[13] all the way to major concerns about the governmental surveillance of opposition figures[14] or protesters,[15] the erosion of the voting process through disinformation,[16] and the facilitation of polarisation within society along political 'wedge' issues.[17] Where governments have the necessary level of control over technological infrastructure, the embedding of politics into the online world generates opportunities for the amplification of propaganda

---

promotion and protection of the right to freedom of opinion and expression', 6 April 2018, UN Doc. A/HRC/38/35; UN Human Rights Committee, 'General Comment No. 37 (2020) on the right of peaceful assembly (article 21)', 17 September 2020, UN Doc. CCPR/C/GC/37.

11 A. Kalia, C. Barr and A. Giuffrida, 'Revealed: how Italy's populists used Facebook to win power', *The Guardian*, 17 December 2018 <https://www.theguardian.com/world/2018/dec/17/revealed-how-italy-populists-used-facebook-win-election-matteo-salvini-luigi-di-maio>.

12 S. Joseph, above n. 2.

13 Council of Europe, 'Study on the Use of Internet in Electoral Campaigns', 2018, DGI(2017)11, p. 17.

14 R. Dixon, 'Russia's surveillance state still doesn't match China. But Putin is racing to catch up.', *Washington Post*, 17 April 2021 <https://www.washingtonpost.com/world/europe/russia-facial-recognition-surveillance-navalny/2021/04/16/4b97dc80-8c0a-11eb-a33e-da28941cb9ac_story.html>.

15 A. Greenberg and L.H. Newman, 'How to Protest Safely in the Age of Surveillance', *Wired*, 8 January 2020 <https://www.wired.com/story/how-to-protest-safely-surveillance-digital-privacy/>; A. Funk, 'How Domestic Spying Tools Undermine Racial Justice Protests', *Freedom House*, 22 June 2020 <https://freedomhouse.org/article/how-domestic-spying-tools-undermine-racial-justice-protests>; R.P. Yu, 'The Emergence of Surveillance Culture: The Relationships between Facebook Privacy Management, Online Government Surveillance, and Online Political Expression' (2021) 65(1) *Journal of Broadcasting & Electronic Media* 66.

16 Digital, Culture, Media and Sport Committee, 'Disinformation and "Fake News": Final Report', 18 February 2019, HC 1791, especially paras. 241 et seq.; see also C. Cadwalladr, '"Plucky little panel" that found the truth about fake news, Facebook and Brexit', *The Observer*, 28 July 2018 <https://www.theguardian.com/politics/2018/jul/28/dcms-committee-report-finds-truth-fake-news-facebook-brexit>.

17 Council of Europe, above n. 13; P. Barrett, J. Hendrix and G. Sims, 'How tech platforms fuel U.S. political polarization and what government can do about it', *Brookings*, 27 September 2021 <https://www.brookings.edu/blog/techtank/2021/09/27/how-tech-platforms-fuel-u-s-political-polarization-and-what-government-can-do-about-it/>.

and censorship of 'undesirable' political opinion.[18] At a more fundamental level, the reduction of political expression into soundbites or posts meant to be shared instantaneously should cause additional apprehension – indeed, Scott-Heron's song criticises exactly this sort of impersonal, consumerist repackaging of politics in the context of broadcast media.

Thus, there is an apparent, and quite fundamental, paradox operating here. The internet is at once a tool facilitating political engagement in unprecedented ways, empowering communities and giving a voice to the disenfranchised, but also the biggest threat to democracy, being misused at the hands of authoritative governments and cynical tech company executives chasing profits. Moreover, one can also observe a notable tension between the 'publicness' of political expression and the private underpinning of the platform economy that serves as the avenue for such expression. As Sander notes, this has resulted in 'the privatization, commodification and datafication of the digital public sphere'[19] in a manner that is unprecedented in comparison to traditional media. What remains a cross-cutting understanding throughout these two sets of tensions, however, is the fact that the internet and social media *are* consequential for the governance of political expression and the public sphere.[20] This consequentiality of the internet operates as a starting premise for the inquiry in this chapter and the two sets of tensions – between public/private notions of online political expression and between its empowering/disruptive effects – are its two analytical focal points.

2.1. Dispute Settlement as Norm Stabilisation – Two Modes of Reasoning

The tension between public/private manifests already in the selection of the two specific dispute settlement mechanisms that are actively involved in the governance of political expression online through the language of human rights. More broadly, however, it is appropriate to ask why one should narrow down on dispute resolution mechanisms instead of other actors, such as the private corporations that develop the framework of rules and content moderation guidelines through which expression is regulated online. This chapter argues that a focus on narrative construction by dispute settlement bodies can counterbalance a potentially one-sided and self-interested construction of freedom of political expression by operators who, at present, are mostly left to self-regulate. Although this may sound counterintuitive with respect to

18 As Titus Chen highlights in relation to China, such efforts can go hand-in-hand with neoliberal market reforms – see T.C. Chen, *The Making of a Neo-Propaganda State: China's Social Media under Xi Jinping*, Leiden, Brill, 2022, pp. 4–7.

19 B. Sander, above n. 4, 192.

20 For an illustration of how the internet is theorised as a public sphere in Habermasian terms, see e.g. R.S. Geiger, 'Does Habermas Understand the Internet? The Algorithmic Construction of the Blogo/Public Sphere' (2009) 10(1) *Gnovis: A Journal of Communication, Culture, and Technology* 1, 29.

the OB, this chapter suggests that the specific type of interpretative authority linked with dispute resolution processes mitigates against purely utilitarian constructions that are associated with unmediated self-regulation.

This is particularly important given the absence of a robust legal framework that would operationalise the protection of political rights and freedoms in the digital public sphere. The concern here is not that human rights, including those concerning political expression, would lack applicability online – this notion runs counter to explicit statements by states and other actors to the contrary.[21] However, where authoritative statements by traditional governance actors about *how exactly* human rights should be translated into the online space are absent, corporations can use the regulatory space to step in with their own interpretations. As De Gregorio and Radu contend,

> [o]nline platforms are, *de facto*, free to define and interpret users' fundamental rights according to their legal, economic and ethical frameworks, since there are limited laws or regulations currently in place to prevent them from doing so.[22]

In the absence of other modes of legal governance, dispute resolution bodies can significantly contribute to the legalisation and transformation of international discourses[23] into concrete normative expectations that would counteract the utilitarian interpretations by corporate actors. This is not to suggest that a reliance on dispute resolution bodies is a panacea for a lack of democratic rulemaking. I recognise that the legitimacy of normative formulations issued by such bodies, especially those established by a restricted group of stakeholders and embedded in private logics of governance, is a point of contention. Nevertheless, echoing the work of von Bogdandy and Venzke, this chapter suggests that the process of norm stabilisation in which dispute resolution bodies are involved is valuable even if the legitimacy question remains unsettled. The modus of justifying decisions,[24] when courts and dispute resolution mechanisms weigh up different normative claims rather than simply finding and applying the applicable rule, has the benefit of bringing to the table and contrasting various narrative constructions of norms.

---

21 M.N. Schmitt (ed), *Tallinn Manual 2.0 on the International Law Applicable to Cyber Operations*, 2nd ed., Cambridge, Cambridge University Press, 2017, Chapter 6; D. Dror-Shpoliansky and Y. Shany, 'It's the End of the (Offline) World as We Know It: from Human Rights to Digital Human Rights – a Proposed Typology' (2021) 32(4) *European Journal of International Law* 1249.

22 G. De Gregorio and R. Radu, 'Digital constitutionalism in the new era of Internet governance' (2022) 30(1) *International Journal of Law and Information Technology* 68, 78.

23 A. von Bogdandy and I. Venzke, 'In Whose Name? An Investigation of International Courts' Public Authority and Its Democratic Justification' (2012) 23(1) *European Journal of International Law* 7, 40.

24 Ibid., 15.

By contrasting the different narrative interpretations of the right to political expression undertaken by the Meta Oversight Board, a private body, and the ECtHR, Europe's foremost human rights institution, one can get insights about two quite different ways of construing the digital public sphere. Both bodies are engaged in a process of norm stabilisation through reasoning which weighs up the validity of competing normative interpretations. However, their differing structural setup – in the case of the ECtHR, one firmly embedded in democratic governance structures in the European public space, and in the case of the OB, one intended to pursue a private logic of self-regulation – are wont to produce very different views of online political expression. As the chapter highlights below, the analysis of select decisions by each of these actors can help to identify some attributes of the internet as a public space for political deliberation, and especially with respect to the two sets of tensions.

2.2. Political Expression Online – A Human Rights Issue?

Perhaps unexpectedly, much of the discourse around political expression online has been framed through the lens of human rights protection. This is even though such online expression can be analysed from various theoretical perspectives, many of which might be more adept at unpacking the relationship between political expression online and the democratic process. For example, De Gregorio approaches the issue through a constitutionalist lens,[25] whereas Marshall and Drieschova focus on the turn to a 'post-truth politics', which is triggered by the move of political life online.[26] For the purposes of this chapter, however, I propose a framing of the issue that is based on the understanding of political expression as a norm of international human rights law (IHRL). In doing so, this chapter follows other legal scholars who have already approached the issue from the same perspective.[27]

One major reason why the topic merits a human rights-centred analysis is that it is already being consistently framed in terms of the *human right* to freedom of expression by actors involved in internet governance, both internally

---

[25] See G. De Gregorio, *Digital Constitutionalism in Europe: Reframing Rights and Powers in the Algorithmic Society*, Cambridge, Cambridge University Press, 2022, Chapter 5.

[26] H. Marshall and A. Drieschova, 'Post-Truth Politics in the UK's Brexit Referendum' (2018) 26(3) *New Perspectives* 89.

[27] See e.g. R.F. Jørgensen (ed), *Human Rights in the Age of Platforms*, Cambridge (MA), The MIT Press, 2019; T.D. Oliva, 'Content Moderation Technologies: Applying Human Rights Standards to Protect Freedom of Expression' (2020) 20(4) *Human Rights Law Review* 607; S. Joseph, above n. 2; B. Sander, above n. 4; M. Zalnieriute, 'Human Rights Rhetoric in Global Internet Governance: New ICANN Bylaw on Human Rights' (2020) 10 *Harvard Business Law Review Online* 1.

and externally.[28] Here, the term 'internal' refers to private actors who control or own the technical infrastructure of the internet (be it hardware or software) and use the language of international human rights law to guide their internal rules and governance processes. One example of such internal framing is the Internet Corporation for Assigned Names and Numbers (ICANN), which is a private entity tasked with the management of domain names and the existing internet protocol. In 2019, ICANN adopted a new set of Bylaws mandating the corporation to respect 'internationally recognized human rights',[29] and has been utilising the rhetoric of human rights, including freedom of expression in particular, when discussing its governance responsibilities.[30] Another example would be Facebook's Corporate Human Rights Policy,[31] or the extensive reference by the OB to human rights norms in its decisions, which will be described in detail in the following sections.

The term 'external' is intended to refer to regulatory actors on the national, international, or transnational level who use the language of human rights when constructing governance mechanisms applicable to online expression. This has been extensively done by a variety of actors, such as the UN Special Rapporteur on the promotion and protection of the right to freedom of opinion and expression[32] or the African Commission on Human and Peoples' Rights.[33] International courts are also active in framing online expression along human rights terms, with the ECtHR a prominent example explored in the analysis below. While some authors, such as evelyn douek, have cautioned against the framing of online expression as a human rights issue, questioning the value of what IHRL can bring to the table in terms of regulatory guidance,[34] governance actors appear to be actively adopting human rights as the dominant language for online expression despite potential shortcomings.

---

28 See e.g. M.K. Land, 'Regulating Private Harms Online: Content Regulation under Human Rights Law' in R.F. Jørgensen (ed), above n. 27, pp. 285–316; N.S. Levinson, 'Idea entrepreneurs: The United Nations Open-Ended Working Group & cybersecurity' (2021) 45(6) *Telecommunications Policy* 102142; T.D. Oliva, above n. 27.

29 'Bylaws for Internet Corporation for Assigned Names and Numbers', *ICANN*, 2 June 2022 <https://www.icann.org/resources/pages/governance/bylaws-en>.

30 M. Zalnieriute, above n. 27.

31 Meta, 'Corporate Human Rights Policy', March 2021, available at <https://about.fb.com/wp-content/uploads/2021/03/Facebooks-Corporate-Human-Rights-Policy.pdf>.

32 UN Human Rights Council, A/HRC/38/35, above n. 11: 'The activities of companies in the ICT sector implicate rights to privacy, religious freedom and belief, opinion and expression, assembly and association, and public participation, among others' (para. 5), or 'The founder of Facebook recently expressed his hope for a process in which the company "could more accurately reflect the values of the community in different places". That process, and the relevant standards, can be found in human rights law' (para. 41).

33 African Commission on Human and Peoples' Rights, 'Declaration of Principles on Freedom of Expression and Access to Information in Africa', November 2019; see e.g. Principle 5 mandating the rights to freedom of expression online; or Principle 39 on Internet Intermediaries mandating the mainstreaming of human rights standards in content moderation.

34 E. Douek, 'The Limits of International Law in Content Moderation' (2021) 6(1) *UC Irvine Journal of International, Transnational, and Comparative Law* 37.

2.3. *The Narrative Approach to Analysing Law*

When discussing Scott-Heron's lyrics at the outset of this chapter, the chapter implied that the song can be understood as having multiple layers. Yet even the two interpretations that were briefly outlined are not necessarily conspicuous, and certainly not exclusive. They represent two ways in which the lyrics of the song can be reconstructed to produce a particular meaning, a particular narrative.[35] What this section of the chapter argues is that the production of legal meaning occurs in a similar manner. Legal norms only tell part of the story, and deriving legal meaning from a specific case or set of regulations is a process that involves the narrative organisation of events that revolve around the legal norms in question.[36] While a focus on particular norms can help orientate a narrative, and this chapter uses the IHRL norm of political expression in exactly this way, a narrative approach to law is premised on the understanding that legal rules are only one part of the overall picture.

When a court such as the ECtHR applies a rule in legal proceedings in a particular way, or when a non-governmental organisation (NGO) publicises a human rights violation, they are not simply engaged in a neutral exercise based exclusively on legal logic. In assembling what they consider the relevant facts that will eventually lead to the finding of a legal breach, they do not simply represent reality, but they rather *construct* it.[37] Certain facts of a legal situation are emphasised (or understated), brought into a relation with a legal norm such as freedom of expression (or uncoupled). What the law, understood as a social phenomenon, *is* in a particular situation can vary, be 'something else depending on our concrete collaborations with it'.[38] In thinking about how the assemblages of facts and norms and circumstances occur in a legal context, this chapter draws upon the work of law and literature scholars who understand legal meaning as organised in a narrative, a legal story.[39]

---

35 Here this draws on the work of Lianne Boer who traces the presence of legal scholars in their texts through the narrative device of the 'plot', and the way in which this impacts a reader's perception of what is or is not law. See L.J.M. Boer, 'Narratives of Force: The Presence of the Writer in International Legal Scholarship' (2019) 66(1) *Netherlands International Law Review* 1.

36 P. Brooks, 'Narrative Transactions – Does the Law Need a Narratology?' (2006) 18(1) *Yale Journal of Law & the Humanities* 1; J. Bruner, 'A Narrative Model of Self-Construction' (1997) 818(1) *Annals of the New York Academy of Sciences* 145.

37 Referencing here J. Bruner, 'The Narrative Construction of Reality' (1991) 18 *Critical Inquiry* 1, 5.

38 I. van Oorschot, *The Law Multiple: Judgment and Knowledge in Practice*, Cambridge, Cambridge University Press, 2021, p. 15.

39 See e.g. M. Minnow, M. Ryan and A. Sarat (eds), *Narrative, Violence, and the Law: The Essays of Robert Cover*, Ann Arbor, University of Michigan Press, 1992; W.J.T. Mitchell (ed), *On Narrative*, Chicago, University of Chicago Press, 1981; A.G. Amsterdam and J. Bruner, *Minding the Law*, 1st Harvard University paperback ed., Cambridge, Harvard University Press, 2002; F. Di Donato, *The Analysis of Legal Cases: A Narrative Approach*, 1st ed., London, Routledge, 2019; P. Brooks, above n. 36.

Thinking about storytelling in law should not come as a surprise, as:

> [e]very legal case starts with a story – the client's story – and it ends with a legal decision that, in effect, offers another version of that story, one cast into a legal framework.[40]

The value of thinking about law more broadly in narrative terms is connected to the fact that storytelling is a universal, 'innate',[41] way of structuring human experience. Human beings organise experiences around narratives, stories that a person tells oneself and that also allow one to communicate with others – consequently:

> narratives constitute a version of reality that is conventionally acceptable, plausible and constructed in accordance with the laws of narrative, rather than with empirical verifiability and logical correctness.[42]

Approaching law through the lens of narrative hence repackages legal reality into a form that is inherently accessible but, importantly, also underlines the 'falsely contingent'[43] nature of legal phenomena, the fact that they are simultaneously bound and unbound by the actors, norms, facts, and contexts in which they are construed. Thus, drawing on Bruner, this chapter contends that legal knowledge[44] 'is never "point-of-viewless"'.[45]

Rediscovering the positioned nature of legal storytelling serves as the starting point for the analysis that will follow in section 3 of the chapter. Indeed, this is why the chapter suggested earlier that the public/private tension around political expression online is already manifest in the selection of the two institutions whose decisions are analysed below. Their rooting in different governance structures (and logics) will necessarily impact the narratives that these bodies construct. At the same time, however, the purpose here is not to map or trace narratives around freedom of political expression online. Trying to reassemble a coherent narrative would represent, at least to some extent, an artificial post hoc exercise in rationalisation.

Instead, adopting an analytical lens inspired by narrative theory and that focuses on distinct *elements* that constitute a narrative allows a better understanding of the discursive construction of the online space in which the right to political expression is exercised. By identifying and comparing

40 C. Rideout, 'Storytelling, Narrative Rationality, and Legal Persuasion' (2008) 14 *Legal Writing: J. Legal Writing Inst.* 53, 54; J.B. White, *Heracles' Bow: Essays on the Rhetoric and Poetics of the Law*, Madison, University of Wisconsin Press, 1989.

41 C. Rideout, above n. 40, 55.

42 F. Di Donato, above n. 39, p. 25.

43 S. Marks, 'False Contingency' (2009) 62(1) *Current Legal Problems* 1.

44 In the sense of knowing what is the 'legal reality' applicable to a particular context.

45 J. Bruner, above n. 37, 3.

narrative elements in existing decisions by dispute settlement bodies that engage human rights, one can sketch out the contours of the discourse and assess where actors have converging or diverging interpretations, and how they mediate the two sets of tensions. By narrative elements, I more specifically mean the five questions identified by Amsterdam and Bruner to which a legal narrative provides some kind of answer: what was done ('act'), when or where it was done ('scene'), who did it ('agent'), how (s)he did it ('agency') and why ('purpose').[46] Deconstructing these elements and treating them as individual building blocks of the plot can be valuable, and enable one to 'analyse how facts are shaped within a legal dispute, by whom and by what means'.[47]

For the purposes of this chapter, the analysis will narrow down on two narrative elements. First, on the notion of *scene*, i.e. the quasi-material and temporal context in which a particular dispute concerning freedom of political expression has been set. Second, attention turns to how the *agent* of a dispute is construed, and what degree of actor-hood is attributed to the various entities involved with the case. For each narrative element, the analysis is limited to one case decided by the ECtHR and the OB respectively. Narrowing down the scope to the two dispute settlement bodies, the narrative elements of scene and agent, and to the issue of political expression online as a human rights matter have been the primary filters for case selection. Additionally, case selection was driven by a focus on situations that concern expression on social media platforms specifically, or at least to online services that can be plausibly considered as an open space for expression (i.e. there is an emphasis on such a function by the service provider, contributions are not pre-filtered before they can be posted).

The approach inspired by narrative theory described above recalibrates how one evaluates legal phenomena. Instead of focusing on questions such as what the applicable legal rule is, whether it was violated in a particular case, and who can be held responsible for the violation, the chapter shifts attention to matters that are usually not regarded as legally relevant but are rather treated as background information, providing the factual context in which the legal rules are applied. Asking about who is the actor in a particular legal situation or what are the contours of the space in which the legally relevant occurrence has happened pushes one to look at law 'sideways, or upside down'.[48] This can generate novel insights about how law operates that can be particularly relevant in circumstances where the dynamics of governance are still being negotiated in response to new phenomena, such as in the case of online political expression.

---

46 A.G. Amsterdam and J. Bruner, above n. 39, as quoted in F. Di Donato, above n. 39, p. 29.

47 F. Di Donato, above n. 39, p. 55.

48 Here this evokes the approach of the edited volume M. Constable, L. Volpp and B. Wagner (eds), *Looking for Law in All the Wrong Places: Justice Beyond and Between*, New York, Fordham University Press, 2019.

3 HOW DO DISPUTE SETTLEMENT MECHANISMS NARRATE POLITICAL EXPRESSION ONLINE? CASE STUDIES FROM THE PUBLIC AND THE PRIVATE REALM

The earlier parts of the chapter have hinted at the fact that a variety of governance actors – whether they are private or public, international or transnational – are using human rights language to construe narratives about the internet and social media platforms as avenues for the exercise of the right to political expression. In this chapter, the analysis is focused on two dispute resolution mechanisms – the ECtHR and the Meta Oversight Board. As becomes clear from the analysis below, the choice of these two institutions embodies the tension between the public and private conceptions of the digital public sphere.

3.1. Materialising the Public and the Private – Online Political Expression before the European Court of Human Rights and the Meta Oversight Board

On the one hand, the ECtHR arguably represents an ideal model of an independent external public regulator within the human rights sphere, empowered to act to the benefit of the citizens subject to its jurisdiction and in a manner that is binding on the states that have devised its mandate. In fact, as is explained below, it is primarily the ECtHR that has substantiated the protection of *political* expression as a distinct, and distinctly valuable, typology of expression in the European human rights sphere. On the other hand, the OB is the result of a distinctly private logic of self-regulation according to which platforms themselves are best placed to create and incorporate rules that affect their users, regardless of whether such governance impacts human rights or issues of key public importance. Although ostensibly independent from Meta and Facebook, and authorised to issue decisions that are binding on the corporation, its grounding in private regulatory structures triggers scepticism about the sources of legitimacy for its decision-making.[49] Such concerns become only more pressing in the context of political expression due to its strong association with the public interest.

Section 2.1 of this chapter has suggested that the practice of dispute settlement bodies is key for transforming international normative discourse into concrete standards of behaviour. One can see this process of stabilising normative expectations in relation to freedom of political expression quite clearly with the first of the bodies selected: the ECtHR. The living document

49 See e.g. J. Mazur and B. Gramblicková, 'New Regulatory Force of Cyberspace: The Case of Meta's Oversight Board' (2023) 17(1) *Masaryk University Journal of Law and Technology* 3; B. Haggart and C. Iglesias Keller, 'Democratic legitimacy in global platform governance' (2021) 45(6) *Telecommunications Policy* 102152.

doctrine[50] has enabled the Court to interpret the provisions of the European Convention on Human Rights (ECHR)[51] in light of present-day conditions, and in a sense to 'read-in' considerations that are not explicitly mentioned in the ECHR text. In fact, this is the case with regard to the protection of freedom to political expression in general, and not just in the digital sphere. Although the ECHR does not explicitly provide for political expression as a separate category of protected speech, the ECtHR proactively accorded a privileged status of protection to political speech within its case law due to the particular public interest that is inherent in this kind of expression.[52]

This line of jurisprudence by the ECtHR not only resulted in the recognition of political expression as a distinct category of speech but also in the assertion that 'speech that is expressed in a political context should be especially protected'.[53] The ECtHR accords such special protection to political expression because of its importance for public debate and, more generally, for matters in the public interest. Notably, in the landmark case of *Lingens v. Austria*, the court said that 'freedom of political debate is at the very core of the concept of a democratic society which prevails throughout the [ECHR]'.[54]

The close relationship between political expression and the public interest has since been consistently reaffirmed by the ECtHR,[55] and increasingly so in the context of political expression online.[56] Given the ECtHR's centrality to the specification of protection of political speech within European human rights discourse and its increasing engagement with the exercise of the right online, the Court and its decisions represent a valuable example of how political expression online is construed from a more public-interest aligned perspective.

The selection of the OB as the second body to be analysed might appear more contentious. While some have called the OB Facebook's 'Supreme Court',[57] there is scepticism about whether the establishment of the OB is intended as anything more than a PR exercise by Facebook/Meta and whether

---

50 First promulgated by the ECtHR in *Tyrer v. UK*, no. 5876/72, 25 April 1978, Series A no. 26.

51 Convention for the Protection of Human Rights and Fundamental Freedoms, 4 November 1950 (ETS 5).

52 See e.g. D. Murray, 'Freedom of Expression, Counter-Terrorism and the Internet in Light of the UK Terrorist Act 2006 and the Jurisprudence of the European Court of Human Rights' (2009) 27(3) *Netherlands Quarterly of Human Rights* 331, 336.

53 V. Ferreres Comella, 'Freedom of Expression in Political Contexts: Some Reflections on the Case Law of the European Court of Human Rights' in W. Sadurski (ed), *Political Rights Under Stress in 21st Century Europe*, Oxford, Oxford University Press, 2006, p. 85.

54 *Lingens v. Austria*, no. 9815/82, 8 July 1986, § 42, Series A no. 103.

55 *Perinçek v. Switzerland*, no. 27510/08, 15 October 2014, § 197; *Ceylan v. Turkey*, no. 23556/94, 8 July 1999, § 34.

56 See e.g. *Cengiz and Others v. Turkey*, nos. 48226/10 and 14027/11, 1 December 2015; *Delfi AS v. Estonia*, no. 64569/09, 16 June 2015.

57 K. Klonick, 'Inside the Making of Facebook's Supreme Court', *The New Yorker*, 12 February 2021 <https://www.newyorker.com/tech/annals-of-technology/inside-the-making-of-facebooks-supreme-court>.

it can actually provide accountability to the users of the platform. However, as shall be discussed below, this does not take away from the fact that the OB *is* actively shaping the limits of political expression in the digital public sphere through its decisions.

The essential function of the OB is to serve as an appellate body for content moderation decisions taken on Meta's platforms (Facebook, Instagram, and Threads), whether these result from automated, algorithm-based processes or those taken by humans. In doing so, the OB refers to Meta's own content policies and values and, importantly, international human rights norms protecting freedom of expression. The latter in particular allows the OB to engage more robustly with political expression as a distinct category of speech. The independence of the OB from Facebook/Meta is guaranteed through a separate trust fund, which finances the operation of the OB and its administration. Thus, the institutional setup of the OB and its procedures strongly resemble an adversarial dispute resolution process. In addition to being modelled as a court, the OB extensively invokes human rights norms such as the ICCPR or the UN Guiding Principles on Business and Human Rights in its content moderation decisions.

The particulars of which human rights norms are entangled in OB's decisions and how merits a separate discussion, and other authors have already provided valuable accounts of this issue.[58] For the purposes of the argument here, suffice it to say that there have been multiple decisions where the OB drew on various provisions of IHRL that specifically concern the protection of political expression.[59] What matters from the perspective of this chapter is the fact that the OB *engages* human rights norms in its decision-making *as if* it were a human rights court. Thus, similarly to the ECtHR, the OB, through its decision-making, performs a norm stabilising function but from a distinctly private structural standpoint. This creates a unique interpretation of freedom of political expression in the digital public sphere as narrated by the OB, whose legitimacy is both constrained through the body's private

---

58 See, e.g. the work of Stefania Di Stefano on this issue – S. Di Stefano, 'The Emergence of "Platform Law": Implications, Challenges, and Law "Beyond the State"' in *Multiple Legalities: Conflict and Entanglement in the Global Legal Order*, virtual conference, 13–15 January 2021; S. Di Stefano, 'The Facebook Oversight Board and the UN Guiding Principles on Business and Human Rights: A Missed Opportunity for Alignment?' in J. Andrew and F. Bernard (eds), *Human Rights Responsibilities in the Digital Age: States, Companies and Individuals*, Oxford, Hart Publishing, 2021.

59 E.g. UNHRC General Comment No. 34 in Facebook Oversight Board, 'Case decision 2021-007-FB-UA: Myanmar Bot', 11 August 2021 <https://www.oversightboard.com/decision/FB-ZWQUPZLZ/>; UNHRC General Comment No. 25 in Facebook Oversight Board, 'Case decision FB-0TGD816L: Australian Electoral Commission Voting Rules', 9 May 2024 <https://www.oversightboard.com/decision/bun-ij9kg9e9/>.

embedding[60] and enhanced by virtue of the process of reasoned decision-making.[61] This conceptual closeness to a dispute resolution mechanism makes the OB an interesting parallel to the ECtHR, and its positioning within private governance structures and a mandate tied to corporate interests provide a unique comparator from the perspective of the public/private tension identified earlier.

3.2. *Deconstructing Narratives of the Right to Political Expression*

Breaking down cases from the ECtHR and the OB into narrative elements can illuminate the disposition of the online world as a space for political expression. What sort of space does the digital public sphere represent – one that fosters or undermines political discussion, is oriented towards the public interest, or is restrained by its private structure? What are the various roles that users, platform moderators, and the technology itself perform in this respect? Is the algorithm itself an actor? These are but some of the questions that a narrative approach can answer – however, the insights one gains will depend on the narrative element that is in focus. As indicated earlier in section 2.3, this chapter narrows down on the narrative elements of 'scene' and 'agent' to inform the analysis.

3.2.1 The Element of 'Scene'

As explained earlier in the chapter, the narrative element of scene provides insights about where or when a particular act was performed. When applied to the online world, the question is loaded with significance as the internet and social media are spaces that are digital – and hence immaterial. Yet, as demonstrated below, they are imbued with particular qualities by the dispute settlement mechanism that provides these digital spaces with a strong resemblance to analogue (and perhaps idealised) visions of the public sphere. Arguably, with a digital space, the importance of discursive construction of its limits and contours is even greater than in the case of tangible, 'real' counterparts (this is not to ignore the actual technical limits of the online world determined by physical infrastructure, however). The analysis in this subsection is even more interesting as it concerns cases that were relatively similar in terms of the geopolitical and temporal context in which they have occurred, notably during pre-election periods in Russia.[62]

---

60 B. Haggart and C. Iglesias Keller, above n. 49, 8; J. Mazur and B. Grambličková, above n. 49; generally also E. Douek, 'Facebook's "Oversight Board:" Move Fast with Stable Infrastructure and Humility' (2019) 21(1) *North Carolina Journal of Law & Technology* 1.

61 B. Haggart and C. Iglesias Keller, above n. 49, 8.

62 However, note that the OB case was not concerned with expression that would directly relate to elections but was rather prompted by protests in support of the Russian opposition leader Alexei Navalny who was jailed after returning to the country. See A. Roth, 'Alexei Navalny

The ECtHR case that this subsection turns to is *Savva Terentyev v. Russia*,[63] in which the claimant was jailed after posting a comment under a blog post containing insults targeted at the police. The blog post was uploaded by the head of an NGO in Russia on his personal site, hosted by a blogging platform, where he criticised a heavy-handed search of the office of a local newspaper in Syktyvkar, Komi Republic. The police search was conducted during a regional election and the authorities confiscated computers belonging to the newspaper on the premise that the software installed on the computers was counterfeit. In reaction to the blog post, Mr. Savva Terentyev wrote a comment in which he called the police 'pigs', 'hoodlums', 'lowbrows', and suggested that people should burn them in 'an oven, like at Auschwitz'.[64] Because of the comment, he was found guilty of publicly inciting hatred and enmity by a Russian court.

In contrast, the decision appealed to the OB was quite tame. Case decision 2021-004-FB-UA (Case 2021-004)[65] concerned Facebook's decision to remove a comment in which a supporter of the Russian opposition leader Alexei Navalny called another Facebook user 'a cowardly bot' as part of a discussion under a post on the social media platform. The post in question shared information about protests held in Saint Petersburg and across Russia that the poster of the infringing comment attended in person. The comments to the post included a lively discussion, as part of which some personal insults were exchanged. The infringing comment was taken down after being reported by the user to whom it was targeted, as the term 'cowardly' was considered to be a negative character claim against a private person and thus violated Facebook's Bullying and Harassment Policy.

Both cases were treated as concerning the right to freedom of expression, and specifically to political speech in an online environment. In both instances, the relevant dispute mechanism established that the right had been violated. In *Savva Terentyev*, the criminal conviction was considered disproportionate and adjudged to have violated the right to freedom of expression of the applicant under ECHR, Article 10. In Case 2021-004, the removal of the comment represented the impugned behaviour and Facebook was compelled by the OB to reinstate the comment on its platform. However, there are marked differences in how the respective dispute resolution bodies construe the narrative.

---

protests: Moscow in lockdown as police detain thousands'*The Guardian*, 1 February 2021 <https://www.theguardian.com/world/2021/jan/31/russian-protests-continue-for-second-weekend-in-support-of-jailed-kremlin-critic-alexei-navalny>.

63 *Savva Terentyev v. Russia*, no. 10692/09, 28 August 2018.

64 Ibid., § 13.

65 Facebook Oversight Board, 'Case decision 2021-004-FB-UA: Pro-Navalny Protests in Russia', 26 May 2021 <https://www.oversightboard.com/decision/FB-6YHRXHZR>.

Looking first at the general construction of the online space as a domain for political expression, one could be forgiven for having the impression that the ECtHR and the OB are reflecting on two completely different versions of the internet. In the ECtHR's approach, there is a relatively mixed conception of the internet that echoes the paradox that was described at the beginning of this chapter – while 'user-generated expressive activity on the Internet provides an unprecedented platform for the exercise of freedom of expression',[66] it is simultaneously

> true that the risk of harm posed by content and communications on the Internet to the exercise and enjoyment of human rights and freedoms is certainly higher than that posed by the press, as unlawful speech, including hate speech and calls to violence, *can be disseminated as never before*, worldwide in a matter of seconds, and sometimes remain persistently available online.[67]

Thus, the internet as seen by the ECtHR is both a boon and a threat at the same time. The ECtHR positions the key tension between the empowering and disruptive constructions of the digital public sphere at the centre of its understanding of the online space as an avenue for a political expression, without making much of an attempt to lean towards either side of the dichotomy. It is also interesting to note that, despite the recognition of the political context in which the speech occurred, the ECtHR does not construe the internet primarily along the lines of political expression but rather in light of its role for exchange of information and insults. This suggests a narration in which the ECtHR is relatively ambivalent about any 'public deliberative' value of the internet and certainly does not seem to construe the online world as a quasi-public space for political debate. Thus, while for the ECtHR in this case the more pedestrian, private elements of life might have been embedded online, the ECtHR shows a degree of ambivalence about construing this space in a way that would lean towards one or the other end of the empowering/disruptive tension.

The approach of the OB in Case 2021-004 is markedly different. Where the ECtHR showed ambivalence, the OB concluded that 'political speech is central to the value of "Voice"', which is how Facebook frames the notion of freedom of expression in its Community Standards. It is also the paramount value of the social media platform *tout court* and can be seen as the most influential principle of the Community Standards that bears an oversized influence on how expression is moderated on the platform. By emphasising political speech as being central to 'Voice', the OB deliberately construes Facebook as a place that is fundamental for public discussion, and fundamentally about

66 *Savva Terentyev v. Russia*, above n. 63, § 79.

67 Ibid. (emphasis added).

such discussion. Indeed, the OB doubles down on its construction of the social media platform as a quasi-public space by pointing to the context of the political speech:

> In relation to political matters, 'Voice' is *particularly important in countries where freedom of expression is routinely suppressed.* The Board considered well-documented instances of pro-government actors in Russia engaging in anti-opposition expression in online spaces. *While there is no evidence of government involvement in this case,* the general efforts of the Russian authorities to manipulate online discourse and drown out opposition voices provides *crucial context* for assessing Facebook's decision to limit 'Voice' in this instance.[68]

The OB reiterates this point again in another part of its decision (when discussing necessity and proportionality).[69] That the OB considered the importance of political speech so paramount that it mandated the inclusion of contextual background about political expression in Russia that had only a very tenuous link to the decision (and no immediate effect on the facts of the case) is quite telling. It highlights a significantly different narration of the online space (or at least of the digital public space on Facebook more narrowly) than was provided by the ECtHR. The narration provided by the OB does not indicate a neutral scene but looks to be imbuing Facebook with a strong responsibility to promote freedom of political expression and thus construing an online digital sphere that is fundamentally empowering. Interestingly, the OB's depiction of Facebook seems to posit the platform as an *actor* with an obligation to facilitate political speech, and especially so in oppressive, fraught contexts. This notion of platforms as actors becomes even more prominent when turning the focus of analysis to the narrative element of agent.

3.2.2. The Element of 'Agent'

In contrast to the narrative element of scene, a consideration of the agent element turns the analysis from the context to actors in seeking an answer to the archetypal 'who did it' question. Within the legal context, this will normally point attention towards the usual participants in legal proceedings – applicants and respondents, victims and perpetrators. However, the notion of agency is more complicated than simply considering the interested parties, not least by the role of the dispute resolution mechanisms themselves who, by organising the facts and norms of a case into a narrative discourse, *act* upon

---

68 Facebook Oversight Board, above n. 65 (emphasis added).

69 Ibid.

a particular legal situation and acquire the status of agents.[70] What becomes clear is that the agent question fundamentally relates to the problematisation of the relationship between an actor and an action that has occurred as part of a legal narrative.[71] How one understands an agent is often inferred from the role that they perform in relation to the plot of a narrative or how central their acts are to the story.

In the ECtHR context, this is particularly visible in the judgment in *Sanchez v. France*,[72] a case in which a relatively complex factual background triggered an expansive assessment of the agent question. The applicant, Mr. Julien Sanchez, was a politician and elected mayor representing the *Front national* party in France. When the conduct at the heart of the case occurred, Mr. Sanchez was standing for election to the French parliament. He made a sarcastic post on his publicly accessible Facebook profile, mocking the campaign of his political rival and sitting member of the European Parliament, Mr. F.P. Reacting to the Facebook post, two further users, S.B. and L.R., posted multiple comments that vilified the Muslim population of France. In the comments, S.B. and L.R. criticised Mr. F.P. for the increase in the size of this social group in Nîmes. One can already see from these facts that the agent question is multifaceted and the relationship between the applicant, Mr. Sanchez, and the 'act' of incitement of hatred against a minority for which he was charged is not straightforward. The agent-action nexus is most clearly established with regard to the commenters whose actions directly triggered the dispute within this legal narrative.

Nevertheless, Mr. Sanchez, S.B., and L.R. were charged and convicted for incitement to hatred or violence against a group of people by the Nîmes Criminal Court, and their sentence was upheld by the appeal tribunal. The reasoning of the French courts is notable. According to the first instance court, Mr. Sanchez failed to act promptly to stop the spread of the hateful comments and was guilty as the producer of the public communication – the original Facebook post – on which the comments circulated. What is particularly interesting from the perspective of this chapter is the fact that the Nîmes Court of Appeal placed special weight on Mr. Sanchez' status as a political figure. The court suggested that this increased the level of vigilance he ought to exercise over content posted on his Facebook page. Mr. Sanchez subsequently challenged the conviction before the ECtHR, claiming that the

---

70 Peter Brooks illustrates this notion well by emphasising the language used by a judge in the US case *Rusk v. State* when retelling the facts of the case. In Brooks' view, the language 'eschews narrative precision in favor of an arch rendering of the story from a normative narrative standpoint which is that of the judge': P. Brooks, above n. 36, 11. It is also reminiscent of the 'hidden' agency that international legal scholars have through their texts, see L.J.M. Boer, above n. 35.

71 R. Barthes and L. Duisit, 'An Introduction to the Structural Analysis of Narrative' (1975) 6(2) *New Literary History* 237, 258.

72 *Sanchez v. France*, no. 45581/15, 15 May 2023.

sentence amounted to an interference with his right to freedom of expression under ECHR, Article 10.

In a landmark judgment, the Grand Chamber of the ECtHR concurred with the French courts, holding that the criminal sentence did not violate the rights of the applicant under the ECHR. Importantly, the majority of the ECtHR judges also agreed with the assertion that the political status of the applicant required him to exercise a higher degree of control over the content that others post on his social media page. This is an interesting illustration of how the political, public-interest nature of an expression in the digital sphere can be construed to amplify the legal responsibility of its producers. There was no doubt about the status of S.B. and L.R. as agents in this context, as they were responsible for comments that the ECtHR considered to be 'clearly unlawful'.[73] Such an inference was not possible for Mr. Sanchez, however, as he did not write any comments; he did not 'do' anything per se. Interestingly, this omission, coupled with Mr. Sanchez' public, political position, was exactly the vehicle for the ECtHR's construction of the applicant's agency when it echoed:

> [I]n general, a politician has duties and responsibilities [...], in addition to the fact that a degree of notoriety and representativeness necessarily lend a certain resonance and authority to the person's words or deeds. *Owing to a politician's particular status and position in society*, he or she is more likely to influence voters, or even to incite them, directly or indirectly, to adopt positions and conduct that may prove unlawful, *thus explaining why he or she can be expected to be 'all the more vigilant'*, to use the words of the Nîmes Court of Appeal.[74]

The narrative appears almost counterfactual – Mr. Sanchez is responsible for the comments not despite but *because* he did not do anything. His agent status is tied to his lack of action *via* the characterisation of his activities as political and part of public discourse. Such a construction of Mr. Sanchez' responsibility was contingent on other considerations that formed part of the narrative – his political status – and that show more about how the ECtHR understood the nature of the online platform with respect to political expression. By making the narrative link between Sanchez' omission and his agentivity possible by virtue of his status as a politician, the ECtHR is reiterating the public-interest value of the platform and grounding it firmly as a component of democratic public discourse.

Interestingly enough, there are prominent similarities to how the OB has construed the agentivity of actors in Case decision 2021-001-FB-FBR

---

[73] Ibid., § 177.

[74] Ibid., § 187 (emphasis added).

(Case 2021-001).[75] Probably the most widely publicised OB decision to date, it concerned the actions of then-US President Donald Trump with respect to the violent storming of the US Capitol on 6 January 2021.[76] Due to a number of posts by Mr. Trump that were perceived as encouraging the violent behaviour, his Facebook and Instagram accounts were blocked for an indefinite period.[77] Reading the OB decision, one can clearly see how the Board construed a strong link between Mr. Trump and the actions, asserting his status as narrative agent. The Board started the discussion of the background of the case with the following:

> Elections are a crucial part of democracy. On January 6, 2021, during the counting of the 2020 electoral votes, a mob forcibly entered the Capitol Building in Washington, D.C. This violence threatened the constitutional process. Five people died and many more were injured during the violence. *During these events*, then-President Donald Trump *posted two pieces of content*.[78]

Considering the way in which this paragraph is structured and given its positioning right at the start of the case, one immediately gets a sense that Mr. Trump shares responsibility for the violence even without knowing what the content of the comments was. The dramatised assembly of the facts by the OB leaves space for no other conclusion. Mr. Trump's status as narrative agent is clearly linked to the action underlying the case and his agentivity is primarily defined in lieu of his role rather than, say, his function or character traits.

Interestingly, however, later in the decision, the OB interprets Mr. Trump's agency through the prism of particular attributes that he possessed, just as the ECtHR has done in *Sanchez*. Notably, the Board considered that his status as a political leader created additional risks for how his social media posts might be interpreted, highlighting strong similarities with the political responsibility that featured in *Sanchez*. While this would suggest a public-interest-leaning narrativisation of political expression on the platform, the OB actually appears to swing the other way by pointing to another agentive attribute that can trump the relevance of political status. Both in relation to Mr. Trump but also as a matter of general recommendation to Facebook's

---

75 Facebook Oversight Board, 'Case decision 2021-001-FB-FBR: Former President Trump's Suspension', 5 May 2021 <https://www.oversightboard.com/decision/FB-691QAMHJ>.

76 D. Smith, 'America shaken after pro-Trump mob storms US Capitol building' *The Guardian*, 7 January 2021 <https://www.theguardian.com/us-news/2021/jan/06/trump-mob-capitol-clash-police-washington>.

77 Mr. Trump's Facebook and Instagram accounts were eventually reinstated in early 2023, with additional monitoring measures remaining in place. Any remaining restrictions were removed in July 2024.

78 Facebook Oversight Board, above n. 75 (emphasis added).

policy, the Board concludes that the *reach* of an actor can influence the risk that their expressions can trigger:

> The Board believes that it is not always useful to draw a firm distinction between political leaders and other influential users. [...] What is important is the *degree of influence* that a user has over other users.[79]

The contestation about which attribute should influence agent status and how is notable, as it highlights a change in how one understands agency in the digital world – formal political status is trumped by the actual reach and influence that actors possess. Reflecting on what this means for the public/private tension around online political expression, one can certainly say that the approach taken in Case 2021-001 recognises the impact of online political expression on public discourse. The comments by Mr. Trump on the platform are positioned as an important part of political developments in the USA, underlining the public function that Facebook plays in this regard. Simultaneously, however, the deliberations by the OB show how the notion of 'publicness' is changing in the new digital context. The emphasis placed on actual reach rather than formal political function suggests that the private structuring logic of the social media network – adopting the lens of online engagement, a data and numbers-focused assessment of influence that an act of political expression can have – is forcing a reassessment of how the 'public' character of the digital public sphere may look. In this regard, the narrative construction of agency performed by the ECtHR in *Sanchez* appears more conservative, with its emphasis on the formal political function of the applicant from which the 'publicness' of his actions was derived. Yet, it is interesting that both bodies have a fundamentally similar approach to how they construe the status of narrative agents – it represents an amalgam between the relationship of the actor and the action, but also of particular attributes that are assigned to the actor.

4 CONCLUSION

The profound changes brought about by the internet have affected both the private and public dimensions of people's lives. Unsurprisingly, political expression has become an important aspect of people's online presence and governance actors are becoming increasingly more aware that it represents a peculiar and indispensable type of expression, one to which very specific considerations are attached. Yet, the growth of the digital public sphere also entails a reassessment of how political expression appears in the online

79 Ibid. (emphasis added).

world. Key tensions surface about the function that online platforms ought to perform in relation to political discourse and about how the public nature of this type of speech can be squared with the fundamentally private grounding of digital structures and technologies. This chapter has illustrated an alternative approach to analysing international human rights discourse concerning the right to freedom of political expression online, which was inspired by narrative thinking and law and literature theory. Breaking the narrative analysis down to a focus on narrative elements allowed a comparison of how the ECtHR and the OB construe the scene in which political expression is taking place and the agents that are engaged in its exercise. In some respects, one could see a marked difference in how the two bodies approached social media – such as the contrast between a very emancipatory, politically-driven understanding of scene provided by the OB and the much more ambivalent interpretation by the ECtHR, which expressed wariness about both the positive and disruptive impacts of the digital world for political expression. But the analysis also highlighted remarkable similarities, with both bodies problematising the notion of agency through a focus on the relationship between actor-action but also on the specific attributes that were possessed by the agent. While, in this context, both the ECtHR and the OB recognised the public role of online political expression, their different assessments of the relevance of an agent's attributes highlight how the private underpinning of online platforms can impact the understanding of public discourse. Where the ECtHR adopted a conservative approach that emphasised the formal political function of an agent, the OB's focus on reach and engagement provided a novel understanding of political expression seen through the lens of a privatised market logic that prioritises data.

As seen from the cases covered in section 3.2, the normative dimensions of the online world are still being contested and renegotiated by governance actors. This unsettled state allows greater room for reflecting on how the engagement with these rules and laws can impact the eventual construction of the normative space. The narrative approach used here is valuable in that seeing decisions by dispute settlement mechanisms, such as the ECtHR or the OB, as legal narratives can uncover aspects of law that would normally stay hidden and thus make the familiar strange again. Such a move towards unfamiliarity is particularly important as society tries to map existing normative paradigms onto a digital online space that, in many respects, is fundamentally different from its live counterpart.

CHAPTER 9

EDUCATION, PERCEPTION AND THE FUTURE OF EUROPEAN HUMAN RIGHTS

Samuel White*

1 INTRODUCTION

One of the most frequently cited threats to the human rights movement in Europe, and across the world, comes from what is often termed a backlash against human rights.[1] Equally serious is the general tendency to accept the existence of this threat as a fact. However, evidence calls this into question. Surveys carried out over the past decades demonstrate that the public are generally supportive of human rights and the institutions that protect them. Nevertheless, the perception that there is no support for instruments such as the European Convention on Human Rights (ECHR) and institutions such as the European Court of Human Rights (ECtHR) have been used by governments to justify proposals that may weaken human rights protection, such as the recently threatened overhaul of the Human Rights Act 1998 in the United Kingdom (UK).[2]

---

* The author is grateful to the editors for their extremely helpful comments on this chapter, to all those who attended the workshop in Cologne for their questions and comments, and to Dr. Susannah Paul for comments on an earlier draft of this work. All errors remain the author's.

1 Some have argued that this is a new transitional phase of human rights protection, characterised by states ejecting themselves from the international human rights framework, see F. Klug, 'Key challenges to human rights in democracies at a time of transition: Where to now?' in K. McCall-Smith, A. Birdsall and E. Casanas Adam (eds), *Human Rights in Times of Transition*, Cheltenham, Edward Elgar, 2020, pp. 16–40. At the same time, some have suggested that this is now the 'endtimes' of human rights: S. Hopgood, *The Endtimes of Human Rights*, New York, Cornell University Press, 2013. Others still refer to a time of crisis for human rights or the crossroads that human rights find themselves at, see e.g. A. Bullard (ed), *Human Rights in Crisis*, Farnham, Ashgate, 2008; M. Goodale, *Human Rights at the Crossroads*, Oxford, Oxford University Press, 2015.

2 Although the proposed replacement of the Human Rights Act 1998 with a British Bill of Rights fell by the wayside, the fact that the proposals advanced as far as the introduction of the Bill in the House of Commons by the Lord Chancellor illustrates how serious these proposals were.

This chapter argues that the key to engendering greater, more effective and more vocal support for human rights in Europe is through education. What evidence there is about the public's views on and support for human rights suggests that there is a strong link between positive perceptions of human rights and knowledge and awareness of the same. This chapter therefore asserts that this correlation needs to be harnessed to support the case for greater human rights education within European states.

In examining these claims, this chapter focuses on the UK. The UK has been chosen as it is a country that has historically been engaged with European human rights in a positive way, but that, in recent times, has witnessed increasing attacks on the institutions that protect these rights. As such, it provides a clear example of the need to deliver public education on human rights, and the lessons learned in this context may be applicable elsewhere.

This chapter starts by examining the UK's current human rights framework and maps the results of surveys in the UK, which show that the public is generally supportive of this framework, by contrast with politicians' assertions that this is not the case. Next, it draws a link between education and positive views on human rights. In doing so, it illustrates that where people have an understanding of their rights and the protections offered to them, they are more likely to view rights treaties and their institutions positively. Finally, it looks ahead to the next 20 years, calling for a concerted and coordinated effort by organisations like the Council of Europe and its Member States to develop a greater understanding of the impact of education on human rights protection and to ensure that effective, high-quality education on human rights is made available to all.

2 THE UK EXPERIENCE

This section provides an overview of the UK's framework of human rights protection, putting this into its wider historical context. It outlines how the framework currently operates, demonstrating how recently, in terms of UK law, the concept of judicially enforceable rights has developed. It then turns to look at the existing polling data on public attitudes to the protection of human rights in the UK, illustrating that this is much more positive than is often claimed, particularly by politicians. Finally, it comments on the causes for concern that emerge from the polling data, noting that there is a demonstrable lack of knowledge of human rights amongst the UK public.

2.1. *Human Rights Protection in the UK*

The UK is often described as a country with a long history of human rights protection,[3] but this distorts the truth. Rather, the UK had a long history of liberty, allowing individuals to act freely as long as the law did not prohibit the action. This period was also characterised by limitations on the executive branches of the state, which were prohibited to act without legal authorisation.[4] Many argued that these liberties were more than enough to allow individuals to live their lives freely and without unnecessary interference from the state. Indeed, Jennings went so far as to assert that:

> In Britain we have no Bill of Rights; we merely have liberty according to the law; and we think – truly I believe – that we do a better job than any country which has a Bill of Rights or a Declaration of the Rights of Man.[5]

Nonetheless, it became increasingly clear that this was not the case. The experience of mass detention without trial in the UK during both World Wars was a clear example of the weakness of this system when faced with an overbearing executive branch;[6] the courts too were slow to step in to protect the individual in these circumstances.[7]

As the calls for international protection of human rights grew and took shape following the end of World War II, the UK played a role in the development of the ensuing treaties.[8] Indeed, the UK was heavily involved in the drafting of, and was one of the first signatories to, the ECHR.[9] Despite

---

3 Indeed, Sieghart argues that it 'has a good claim to be considered the cradle of human rights […] From at least Magna Carta in 1215 [it] has contrived to excuse principles of "civil rights" and "civil liberties" from the interstices of a succession of internal political or economic power struggles': P. Sieghart, 'Foreword' in P. Sieghart (ed), *Human Rights in the United Kingdom*, London, Pinter Publishers, 1988, pp. 2–3.

4 Historically, these restrictions were on the power of the Crown to act (for example, Magna Carta 1215 and the Bill of Rights 1689) but later also applied to government (for example in *Entick v. Carrington* [1765] EWHC J98 (KB); 95 ER 807).

5 W.I. Jennings, *The Approach to Self-Government*, Cambridge, Cambridge University Press, 1956, p. 99.

6 This is discussed in A.W.B. Simpson, *In the Highest Degree Odious: Detention without Trial in Wartime Britain*, Oxford, Clarendon Press, 1994.

7 See, for example, the decision of the House of Lords in *Liversidge v. Anderson* [1941] UKHL 1; [1942] AC 206, where the only exception to the acceptance was the powerful dissent by Lord Atkin.

8 Although this role, and the motivation behind it, was often ambiguous, see G. Marston, 'The United Kingdom's Part in the Preparation of the European Convention on Human Rights, 1950' (1993) 42 *International and Comparative Law Quarterly* 796; E. Bates, *The Evolution of the European Convention on Human Rights*, Oxford, Oxford University Press, 2010.

9 A.W.B. Simpson, *Human Rights and the End of Empire: Britain and the Genesis of the European Convention*, Oxford, Oxford University Press, 2004.

this early involvement on the international stage, however, the protection of rights domestically lagged behind quite significantly. Between the entry into force of the ECHR in 1953 and the full entry into force of the Human Rights Act in 2000, almost 50 years elapsed. During this period, the impact of the ECHR on UK domestic law was limited. This is in part because the UK is a 'strongly dualist' legal system,[10] requiring domestic legal action to incorporate international legal norms into law enforceable before UK courts. Prior to the Human Rights Act no such action had been taken.

In addition to the absence of any legal mechanism by which to assert rights at the domestic level, no real culture of human rights knowledge or awareness existed amongst the public.[11] Some commentators and jurists, such as Lord Bingham, suggested that the ECHR had exerted a:

> pervasive influence on judicial decision-making in [the UK, in particular] affecting the interpretation of ambiguous statutory provisions, guiding the exercise of discretions, [and] bearing on the development of the common law'.[12]

Nevertheless, the extent of this pervasive influence was not enough to curb the rising number of cases before the ECtHR that the UK lost from the first case in 1975.[13]

In 1998, the landscape of UK human rights protection changed completely.[14] The Human Rights Act was introduced to incorporate the ECHR into the UK's domestic law and bring 'home' the rights contained in the ECHR.[15] Part of the justification for this was the fact that the lack of justiciability of ECHR rights in UK law made it costly and time-consuming to enforce these rights against the state; indeed in 1997, it took an average of five years and £30,000 to bring a case to the ECtHR.[16] But more than this, a major issue was that the ECHR

---

10 J. Crawford, *Brownlie's Principles of International Law*, 8th ed., Oxford, Oxford University Press, 2012, p. 63.

11 This is clear from the tenor of the Government White Paper that preceded the Human Rights Act 1998: Secretary of State for the Home Department, 'Rights Brought Home: The Human Rights Bill', 1997, Command Paper No. Cm 3782.

12 *R. v. Lyons* [2002] UKHL 44; [2003] 1 AC 976, para. 13.

13 See S. White and J. Hartmann, 'Submission to the Independent Review of the Human Rights Act', 3 March 2021, para. 4 <https://discovery.dundee.ac.uk/ws/portalfiles/portal/69758784/Samuel_White_Jacques _Harmann.pdf>. See also A. Donald, J. Gordon and P. Leach, 'Research Report 83: The UK and the European Court of Human Rights', London, Equality and Human Rights Commission, 2012. The UK was first before the ECtHR in *Golder v. United Kingdom*, no. 4451/70, 21 February 1975; the UK lost the case.

14 McGoldrick described the Act's significance 'as enormous to the point of revolutionary': D. McGoldrick, 'The United Kingdom's Human Rights Act 1998 in Theory and Practice' (2001) 50(4) *International and Comparative Law Quarterly* 901, 945.

15 Secretary of State for the Home Department, above n. 11, para. 1.19.

16 Ibid., para. 1.14. Adjusted for inflation using the Bank of England's inflation calculator, this was the equivalent to £57,477 in August 2024.

rights were 'no longer actually seen as British rights'.[17] In other words, there was a strong perception that there was no public ownership of these rights.

The Human Rights Act allows individuals to challenge public authorities directly where their ECHR rights have been breached. It provides the courts with a number of tools to remedy these situations. Section 2 of the Act requires the UK courts to 'take into account' the jurisprudence of the ECtHR, ensuring that the UK courts keep pace with the ECtHR's decision-making and interpretation of the ECHR.[18] Meanwhile, section 3 of the Act creates a powerful rule of interpretation. The section reads:

> So far as it is possible to do so, primary legislation and subordinate legislation *must be read and given effect* in a way which is compatible with the Convention rights.[19]

At the time of the Act's introduction, the government of the day's senior law officer, the Lord Chancellor, indicated that this section was intended to mean that:

> if it is possible to interpret a statute in two ways – one compatible with the convention and one not – the courts [would] choose the interpretation which is compatible.[20]

The section 3 power allows the courts broad discretion in interpretation, however in situations where section 3 cannot be used to remedy the wording of a statute, section 4 provides the courts with a power to make a non-binding declaration of incompatibility.[21] This is effectively a statement that the court considered the legislation in question to be in breach of the ECHR and that it cannot be interpreted into compliance.[22] Whilst section 4 may appear to

---

17 Ibid.

18 Following *R. (AB) v. Secretary of State for Justice* [2021] UKSC 28, the UK Supreme Court has said that the UK courts must not go further in their interpretation of ECHR rights 'than they can be fully confident than the [ECtHR] would go', para. 57 (per Lord Reed).

19 Human Rights Act 1998, section 3 (emphasis added).

20 HL Deb. 3 November 1997, vol. 582, col. 1230. In fact, as cases such as *Ghaidan v. Godin-Mendoza* [2004] UKHL 30; [2004] 2 AC 557 have illustrated, the courts have used this power broadly to read words into statute (as happened in *Ghaidan*) and to adopt approaches that might be considered linguistically strained (as suggested by Lord Steyn in *R. v. A* [2001] UKHL 25; [2001] 3 All ER 1).

21 Under the UK's constitution, the doctrine of parliamentary sovereignty means that courts do not have the power to overturn acts of Parliament. For more discussion see C. O'Cinneide, 'Human Rights and the UK Constitution' in J. Jowell and C. O'Cinneide (eds), *The Changing Constitution*, 9th ed., Oxford, Oxford University Press, 2019. The section 4 power is limited to the higher courts, that is the High Court, Court of Appeal and Supreme Court in England and Wales and their equivalents in Scotland and Northern Ireland.

22 Sections 3 and 4 characterise what Gardbaum terms the 'new Commonwealth model of constitutionalism', which attempts to find a path between the traditional dichotomy between legislative and judicial supremacy models for addressing these questions. See S. Gardbaum, *The New Commonwealth Model of Constitutionalism*, Cambridge, Cambridge University Press, 2013.

be a weaker remedy than section 3, it has proven itself effective. Indeed, despite the fact that it may not create a legal requirement that the government acts, commentators such as Kavanagh suggest that the political weight of a section 4 declaration, coupled with the fact that the domestic courts consider a violation of the ECHR to have occurred, makes it a powerful tool.[23] Although these have been vital tools in allowing the courts and Parliament to further the protection of human rights, they have also been the source of much of the discomfort of those who believe that the Human Rights Act has moved too much political decision-making into the area of the courts.[24]

The Human Rights Act has proved successful in improving the protection of human rights in UK law, becoming 'an integral part of UK public law'.[25] As can be seen, the tools provided to the courts to do this are effective, and even a cursory examination of the UK's rate of success before the ECtHR illustrates the effectiveness of these measures at reducing the rate at which the UK has lost before the Court. Accepting that this kind of analysis is something of a blunt instrument in assessing success, it is still clear from looking at the number of cases that the UK lost before the ECtHR that there is a consistent, downward trend from around 20 judgments finding violation in 2000 (when the Act entered into force) to around two a year by 2020.[26] The consistent downward trend across this period is hard to attribute to any other factor than the Human Rights Act.

Part of the justification for introducing the Human Rights Act was to engender a sense of ownership of the ECHR amongst the UK public (by bringing rights 'home'), and to allow the courts to remedy breaches of the ECHR more quickly and effectively. Nevertheless, these powers have often been cited by those seeking the repeal of the Human Rights Act as a reason for a lack of public support for and trust in the Act.[27] They argue that it 'places unjustified restraint' on Parliament, at the same time affording courts, in particular the ECtHR, too much power.[28] These commentators often argue that their side is supported by public sentiment. As will be illustrated, such claims seem ill-founded but remain persistent.

---

23 See A. Kavanagh, 'What's so weak about "weak-form review"? The case of the UK Human Rights Act 1998' (2015) 13(4) *International Journal of Constitutional Law* 1008.

24 See e.g. P. Sales and R. Ekins, 'Rights-Consistent Interpretation and the Human Rights Act 1998' (2011) 127 *Law Quarterly Review* 217.

25 C. O'Cinneide, above n. 21, p. 67.

26 See Joint Committee on Human Rights, 'Human Rights Act Reform', 23 April 2022, HC 1033, HL Paper 191, para. 15. See also the ECtHR's statistics ('Statistical reports', *European Court of Human Rights* <https://www.echr.coe.int/statistical-reports>).

27 See, for example, S. Braverman, 'Suella Braverman: People we elect must take back control from people we don't Who include the judges.', *Conservative Home*, 27 January 2020 <https://www.conservativehome.com/platform/2020/01/suella-braverman-people-we-elect-must-take-back-control-from-people-we-dont-who-include-the-judges.html>. See also the work of the Judicial Power Project.

28 C. O'Cinneide, above n. 21, p. 60.

2.2. *Anti-Human Rights Rhetoric in the UK*

Despite the evidence pointing to the success of the Human Rights Act when it comes to allowing individuals to vindicate their rights, commentators, particularly politicians but more recently former judges, have been calling for its replacement almost since its entry into force.

Former Prime Minister Tony Blair, whose government led the incorporation of the Convention into UK law, became 'an angry critic' of the Human Rights Act, especially after the growth of global terrorism in the early 2000s.[29] In 2006, Prime Minister David Cameron – who once infamously said that he felt 'physically ill' at the thought of giving prisoners the vote[30] – suggested that he would abolish the Human Rights Act and replace it with a British Bill of Rights.[31] Abolition soon became a recurrent theme in UK politics, and this policy was reannounced in 2014.[32] The reasoning was explained by Dominic Raab, then a junior justice minister. He said: 'Our aim is to protect fundamental rights, prevent the abuse of human rights law and restore some common sense to the system'.[33] Particularly in the increasingly Eurosceptic last decade, political rhetoric targeting the Human Rights Act and the ECHR has grown. In 2016, then Prime Minister Theresa May received 'sustained applause' when, at her party conference, she attacked 'activist left wing human rights lawyers' who 'harangue and harass the bravest of the brave: the men and women of our armed forces'.[34] This rhetoric was harnessed when she made clear her intention to campaign to withdraw the UK from the ECHR.[35]

---

29 J. Norman and P. Oborne, *Churchill's Legacy: The Conservative Case for the Human Rights Act*, London, Liberty, 2009, pp. 6–11.

30 H. Mulholland and A. Stratton, 'UK may be forced to give prisoners the vote in time for May elections', *The Guardian*, 1 February 2011 <https://www.theguardian.com/society/2011/feb/01/prisoners-vote-may-elections-compensation-claims>.

31 David Cameron's speech to the Centre for Policy Studies on 26 June 2006: 'Balancing freedom and security – a modern British Bill of Rights', *The Guardian*, 26 June 2006 <https://www.theguardian.com/politics/2006/jun/26/conservatives.constitution>.

32 O. Wright, 'David Cameron to "scrap" Human Rights Act for new "British Bill of Rights"', *Independent*, 1 October 2014 <https://www.independent.co.uk/news/uk/politics/conservative-party-conference-cameron-announces-plans-to-scrap-human-rights-act-9767435.html>.

33 HC Deb. 6 May 2016, vol. 609, col. 515.

34 S. Osborne, 'Theresa May speech: Tory conference erupts in applause as PM attacks "activist left wing human rights lawyers"', *The Independent*, 5 October 2016 <https://www.independent.co.uk/news/uk/politics/theresa-may-tory-conference-speech-applause-attacks-activist-left-wing-human-rights-lawyers-a7346216.html>.

35 W. Worley, 'Theresa May "will campaign to leave the European Convention on Human Rights in 2020 election"', *Independent*, 30 December 2016 <https://www.independent.co.uk/news/uk/politics/theresa-may-campaign-leave-european-convention-on-human-rights-2020-general-election-brexit-a7499951.html>.

For a time, the urgencies of Brexit seemed to take priority for the UK government, but in 2020 Boris Johnson's government instigated an Independent Human Rights Act Review (IHRAR). The terms of reference for the IHRAR noted that: 'There is a perception that, under the HRA, courts have increasingly been presented with questions of "policy" as well as law'.[36] No evidence was provided for this assertion, but it carried with it the implication that the public was unhappy with this change. Implicit in these calls for reform and repeal is the idea that such a policy is a vote winner; politicians clearly believe that the public does not approve of the current UK human rights regime.

When the IHRAR published its final report in late 2021 it recommended only minor changes to the Human Rights Act.[37] Nevertheless, the government swiftly indicated that it intended to press ahead with replacing the Act with a new Bill of Rights.[38] Part of the justification for this overhaul of the system, which had been opposed not only by the IHRAR but also by the Parliamentary Joint Committee on Human Rights and the vast majority of those who provided evidence to both bodies, was that 'public trust in the human rights framework has been undermined' in the UK.[39] Yet again, no evidence was adduced to support such a conclusion.

Despite this, in June 2022, Dominic Raab, by then Secretary of State for Justice, introduced a Bill of Rights in Parliament. Introducing the Bill, Raab made reference to the 'goalposts on human rights' shifting over time, blaming expansive judicial interpretations both domestically and at the ECtHR.[40] Key, however, was the assertion at the end of the statement that the proposed reforms, which many argued would significantly reduce the scope of human rights protection in the UK,[41] would be 'essential for commanding greater public confidence'.[42] Once again, in this statement and the wider Bill documents, the underlying assumption that there was a crisis of public confidence in either human rights or their judicial protection remained

---

36 UK Government Independent Human Rights Act Review (IHRAR), 'Independent Human Rights Act Review: Call for Evidence', 2021, p. 10 <https://assets.publishing.service.gov.uk/government/uploads/system/uploads/attachment_data/file/962423/Call-for-Evidence.pdf>.

37 Secretary of State for Justice and IHRAR, 'The Independent Human Rights Act Review', December 2021, CP 586.

38 Secretary of State for Justice, 'Human Rights Act Reform: A Modern Bill Of Rights – A consultation to reform the Human Rights Act 1998', December 2021, CP 588.

39 Ibid., p. 6, para. 8.

40 HC Deb. 22 June 2022, vol. 716, cols. 845–47.

41 In a letter to Dominic Raab, the then chair of the UK Parliament's Joint Committee on Human Rights described the effect of the Bill as leading to 'an unfortunate regression in rights protection'. See letter from Joanna Cherry QC MP to Rt. Hon. Dominic Raab MP, 30 June 2022.

42 HC Deb. 22 June 2022, vol. 716, col. 847.

unproven. This was picked up on by the Joint Committee on Human Rights in its legislative scrutiny report on the Bill, which noted that although it agreed:

> that public confidence in the human rights framework is important, we think the Government has failed to [...] provide evidence that there is a lack of public confidence in the [Human Rights Act].[43]

The Bill was quietly retired from Parliament in 2023 following a change of Prime Minister, yet Raab's successor Alex Chalk noted that while the Bill would not proceed, the 'Government remain[ed] committed to a human rights framework that is up to date, fit for purpose and works for the British people'.[44] Once again, the suggestion that the current framework was unfit for purpose and did not work for the general public was made without support, and met with little challenge in Parliament.

Despite the fact that politicians have wielded the greatest threat to existing human rights protections in the UK, the voices calling for reform have included many academics and, increasingly, some former judges. Whilst these two groups have made more nuanced, and perhaps principled, arguments than many politicians,[45] they have also failed to demonstrate that there is a clear public antagonism towards human rights generally and the current framework in particular.

2.3. *Public Opinion of Human Rights in the UK*

Part of the problem with combatting this narrative of waning or limited public support for the Human Rights Act, and by extension the ECHR, is that these claims are often uncontested, as noted above. However, a significantly greater difficulty in contesting these claims, in the UK at least, is the lack of up-to-date data aimed at measuring public support for human rights and the measures that protect them. Very little research has been carried out that examines these claims directly and there is a notable lack of polling data that directly asks the public for their views on human rights and the instruments that protect these.

The most in-depth study of UK attitudes to human rights is now over 15 years old. It was commissioned by the UK's Equality and Human Rights Commission in 2009 with the aim of building 'a strong evidence base' that

---

43 Joint Committee on Human Rights, 'Legislative Scrutiny: Bill of Rights Bill, 25 January 2025, HC 611, HL Paper 132, para. 332.

44 HC Deb. 27 June 2023, vol. 735, col. 145.

45 See e.g. Lord Sumption's Reith Lectures in 2019 that argued inter alia that the ECHR and Human Rights Act allowed courts to usurp the function of politics. This also links with the work of the Judicial Power Project. Although it should be noted that it has been convincingly argued that Sumption selectively presented the case in his lectures, see e.g. J. Rozenberg, *Enemies of the People? How Judges Shape Society*, Bristol, Bristol University Press, 2020.

could assist the Commission in its work.[46] Another limitation of this data is the focus on only one of the jurisdictions of the UK (England and Wales); more recent polling carried out in Scotland suggests that it is nevertheless a good indicator of the public's attitudes.[47]

The 2009 study broadly demonstrates that the UK public appears to be supportive of human rights generally, and their legal protection in particular. Indeed, this study showed that nearly two thirds (64%) of respondents 'disagreed' with the claim that 'human rights are meaningless to me in everyday life'. Only 21% 'agreed' with the statement.[48] When asked for their views on the statement 'It is important to have a law that protects human rights in Britain', 85% either said they 'strongly agree' (40%) or 'tend to agree' (44%).[49] This suggests that the public both value human rights as an ideal and agree that these rights need to be protected by effective domestic legislation.

The 2009 study is undoubtedly the most detailed recent poll of public attitudes, but a range of smaller polls have been carried out. In 2012, research into public attitudes towards human rights in the UK suggested that 26% of the public were 'opposed' to human rights, 22% 'supportive', 41% 'conflicted' and 11% were simply 'uninterested'.[50] However, these results do not fit with the narrative of the 2009 study or a with a 2013 poll carried out by ComRes on behalf of rights charity Liberty. In the 2013 poll, when answering the question 'How important or unimportant do you think it is that there is a law that protects rights and freedoms in Britain?', 98% of respondents said 'important'.[51]

These data illustrate clearly that there does not appear to be an overwhelming public antagonism towards human rights. There is certainly not enough

---

46 K. Kaur-Ballagan, S. Castell, K. Brough and H. Freimert, 'Public perceptions of human rights', Equality and Human Rights Commission, 2009, p. iii. The study was carried out by Ipsos Mori on behalf of the Equality and Human Rights Commission. The quantitative research adopted a face-to-face omnibus poll among a representative sample of 1,994 British adults aged 16 or over. The qualitative research made use of deliberative workshops carried out over three hours with 23 members of the public. The research was carried out between 14 and 21 August 2008. See ibid., pp. 3–5 for detailed discussion of the methods used.

47 See Scottish Human Rights Commission (SHRC), 'Attitudes to Human Rights in Scotland', December 2023. This study grouped respondents into four categories based on how they felt about human rights: 'supportive, 'conflicted', 'disengaged', and 'opposed'. Supporters made up the largest group (48%) and those opposed to human rights the smallest (10%). This showed a growth in support since the last report in 2017 (SHRC, 'Building a human rights culture in Scotland', February 2018).

48 K. Kaur-Ballagan, S. Castell, K. Brough and H. Freimert, above n. 46, p. 15.

49 Ibid., p. 23.

50 They sampled 2,280 adults in England, Scotland and Wales between 25–29 May 2012. See Equally Ours (formerly Equality and Diversity Forum), 'Telling the Story of Everyone's Rights, Every Day', 2013 <https://web.archive.org/web/20140719130027/https://www.disabilityrightsuk.org/sites/default/files/pdf/TelltheStory.pdf >.

51 Cited in A. Wagner, '"A Bad Name in the Public Square": Does It Matter What People Think about Human Rights?' (2016) 21(1) *Judicial Review* 58.

evident hostility to justify the oft-repeated political stance that human rights lack public support in the UK. Summarising the existing polling in 2016, Adam Wagner noted that 'people are generally supportive of rights in principle' and that while there appear to be some who favour reform of the current system, there is by no means a majority who favour such change.[52]

In Scotland, two sets of polling support Wagner's assertion, and may even suggest that it under-represents the case. Whilst these relate only to Scotland, there is no reason to believe that the results are at any significant variance with wider UK attitudes, save for the fact that the Scottish government has arguably had a more progressive approach to human rights protection and education.[53] This polling showed that there was a 6% growth of support for human rights (from 42% to 48%) between data collection exercises in 2017 and 2023.[54] Similarly, those 'opposed' to human rights in this survey reduced from 13% to 10%.[55] Concerningly, however, the 'conflicted' group, who had previously been characterised as the group most likely to respond to education and positive stories about human rights,[56] remained at 30% of the population.[57]

The recent IHRAR provides another insight into how the public perceives the UK's human rights framework, built upon the Human Rights Act and the ECHR. In early 2021, the IHRAR issued a public call for evidence to 'all interested parties'.[58] Although this does not equate to a public opinion poll, it provides valuable insight into the perception of those who respond, which is likely to include both those who support the status quo and those who oppose it.

The final report of the review indicated that:

> The vast majority of submissions received by IHRAR spoke strongly in support of the HRA. They pointed to its impact in improving public administration for individuals, through developing a human rights culture.[59]

In relation to the subject of public support, the report suggested that the Human Rights Act did not:

> in some quarters, enjoy the level of settled public acceptance that it should command to be secure as an enduring feature of the UK's constitutional landscape,[60]

---

52 Ibid., 61.
53 See section 3.1 below.
54 SHRC, 'Attitudes to Human Rights in Scotland', above n. 47, p. 13.
55 Ibid.
56 SHRC, 'Building a human rights culture in Scotland', above n. 47, pp. 12–13.
57 SHRC, 'Attitudes to Human Rights in Scotland', above n. 47, p. 13.
58 IHRAR, above n. 36, p. 2.
59 Secretary of State for Justice and IHRAR, above n. 37, para. 46.
60 Ibid., para. 47.

however a clear reason was presented for this. The report quoted Cowell, who suggested that the Human Rights Act had faced unprecedented and escalating attacks, which were designed not only to undermine the legislation but also to strike at the heart of the concept of human rights.[61]

The Review concluded that:

> The fact and persistence of hostility to the HRA is noteworthy. It may be that these views are less widespread than might first appear but are disproportionately fuelled and ventilated by negative media and political coverage. However, even if such is the case, it seems clear to the Panel that much work needs to be done to understand the basis of and challenge this negative perception of the HRA, and also to increase the sense of public ownership of the HRA, so serving to reduce what was described as a sense of 'disempowerment'.[62]

This evidence serves to show that, despite the claims that the UK's human rights framework lacks public support or even engenders public hostility, it is very hard to point to any data that substantiate this. On the contrary, what limited data does exist suggest that the opposite is true and that support may, in fact, be growing.

2.4. *Areas for Concern*

Whilst the extant data suggest that the public is broadly positive about the Human Rights Act, and the ECHR,[63] there are some areas with which the public consistently express concern. Moreover, the data also consistently show that there are gaps in public understanding and awareness of these systems and their operation. This is arguably illustrated by the high levels of response illustrating uncertainty about issues of human rights and their protection.

One issue about which the UK public seem exercised when human rights are discussed are their perceived use by those intent on taking unfair advantage

---

61 F. Cowell (ed), *Critically Examining The Case Against The Human Rights Act*, Abingdon, Routledge, 2018, p. 16; quoted in Secretary of State for Justice and IHRAR, above n. 37, para. 47.

62 Secretary of State for Justice and IHRAR, above n. 37, para. 48.

63 Limited polling directly related to this question has been carried out, but that which has does not point to an overwhelming antipathy to the UK's membership of the ECHR. A 2016 poll, carried out by YouGov, asked 'Do you think Britain should or should not remain a member of the European Convention on Human Rights?'. Here, 42% believed the UK should remain a member compared with 35% who believed it should not. 23% of respondents did not know how to react to this question, suggesting no strong feeling either way. Interestingly a more recent survey suggested support for remaining a member of the ECHR had risen to 54% with only 23% arguing for withdrawal and 23% remaining unsure. See 'Do you think Britain should remain a member of the European Convention on Human Rights or should we withdraw from it?' *YouGov*, 6 June 2024 <https://yougov.co.uk/topics/international/survey-results/daily/2024/06/06/df96f/2>.

of the system. The 2009 poll illustrates the extent of this concern. In that study, 80% of respondents believed that 'some people take unfair advantage of human rights'.[64] Alston has also noted this concern, saying that:

> the majority in society feel that they have no stake in the human rights enterprise, and that human rights groups really are just working for 'asylum seekers', 'felons', 'terrorists', and the like.[65]

Interestingly, polling suggests that this view was held more strongly by those who read tabloid newspapers.[66] This further underscores the concern expressed in the IHRAR report about the impact of negative media coverage on the public perception.[67]

Although the supposed abuse of human rights appears to be the main concern for the public, another, more general, trend that emerges from the data is the lack of understanding and awareness of the Human Rights Act, ECHR and human rights protection more widely.[68] In many cases, respondents to surveys did not know how to respond to questions on human rights,[69] or had more favourable views when the workings or positive outcomes of these systems of protection were explained to them.[70]

When asked about their knowledge and awareness, the public appeared to validate this concern. In the 2009 study, 58% of respondents said they knew: 'Not very much' (50%) or 'nothing at all' (8%) about human rights.[71] When asked similarly about the Human Rights Act, 66% indicated that they knew 'not very much' (50%) or had 'heard of, but knew nothing about' the Act (16%).[72] More recently, in 2021, the IHRAR report asserted that public engagement with the Review 'was strongly suggestive of public interest in human rights and an appetite to discuss and engage with the issues'.[73] Nevertheless, it noted that

---

64 K. Kaur-Ballagan, S. Castell, K. Brough and H. Freimert, above n. 46, p. 16.

65 P. Alston, 'The Populist Challenge to Human Rights' (2017) 9(1) *Journal of Human Rights Practice* 1, 6.

66 K. Kaur-Ballagan, S. Castell, K. Brough and H. Freimert, above n. 46, p. 16.

67 Secretary of State for Justice and IHRAR, above n. 37, para. 48.

68 This trend is not only evident amongst the public, Lord (Kenneth) Clarke, a former UK Secretary of State for Justice, claims that the lack of understanding of the system also permeates politics. He said that 'Right-wing members of [the Conservative Party] often believe that these are creations of the European Union and are fiercely opposed to the Court's jurisdiction over the United Kingdom': K. Clarke, *Kind of Blue*, London, Pan Macmillan, 2016, p. 457.

69 For example, in the YouGov poll cited above ('Do you think Britain should remain a member of the European Convention on Human Rights or should we withdraw from it?', above n. 63) where nearly a quarter of respondents did not know how to answer a binary question.

70 SHRC, 'Building a human rights culture in Scotland', above n. 47, pp. 10–17.

71 K. Kaur-Ballagan, S. Castell, K. Brough and H. Freimert, above n. 46, p. 17.

72 Ibid., pp. 21–22.

73 Secretary of State for Justice and IHRAR, above n. 37, para. 52.

'there is much room for increasing understanding of the UK's constitution, and particularly, of the HRA, of the Convention and the ECtHR'.[74]

Looking at the existing data, the evidence suggests that there is an important place for the role of education on human rights and the frameworks and institutions that protect them. This chapter now turns to examine the link between education and positive attitudes towards human rights and asks whether this holds the key to protecting the future of public support for human rights.

3 UK HUMAN RIGHTS EDUCATION, PERCEPTION AND THE FUTURE

3.1. Human Rights Education and Perception in the UK

The data show that the public appears to be broadly supportive of human rights but does not profess to know a huge amount, yet the same polling appeared to indicate that support for human rights increased following discussion and education.[75] The 2018 Scottish study on attitudes towards human rights proves instructive in this regard, and offers more commentary than its 2023 counterpart.[76]

This study grouped participants into four categories according to their attitudes on human rights: 'supporters', 'conflicted', 'disengaged' and 'opposed'. First, 'supporters' (42%) were those who 'agree with positive messages about human rights, and disagree with negative messages about human rights'.[77] Perhaps most tellingly, this group was described as tending to have a greater general knowledge of human rights.[78] In the other three groups, the study suggests a common theme: a lack of any significant knowledge of human rights and the way these are protected. Thus, the 'conflicted' group (30%) agree with some positive and some negative portrayals of human rights, but also have 'very little knowledge about human rights'.[79] The report suggests that those

74 Ibid., para. 53.

75 K. Kaur-Ballagan, S. Castell, K. Brough and H. Freimert, above n. 46, pp. 33–34, although the size of the sample upon which this conclusion was drawn was not large enough to be statistically significant.

76 SHRC, 'Building a Human Rights Culture in Scotland', above n. 47. The more recent report illustrates the growth in support for human rights in Scotland but does not offer the same analysis of the groups surveyed, SHRC, 'Attitudes to Human Rights in Scotland', above n. 47.

77 SHRC, 'Building a Human Rights Culture in Scotland', above n. 47, p. 10.

78 Ibid.

79 Ibid., p. 12.

in this group 'have the potential to become supporters of human rights with more information'.[80]

The 'disengaged' group (14%) were characterised as being remote from issues of human rights, and not in possession of firm views on the topic.[81] The study suggested that 'their knowledge of human rights and the Human Rights Act is low or non-existent', but that they were a little more positive in their outlook on human rights than those in the conflicted group.[82] Given this, it seems plausible to suggest that a programme of education aimed at illustrating the benefits of human rights, and the frameworks that protect them, might help re-engage members of this group and encourage them to become supporters.

The final group were those 'opposed' to human rights (13%). This group is described as being those who 'disagree with positive messages and agree with negative messages about human rights'.[83] In common with the trend noted earlier, this group is likely to believe that human rights are abused by some people.[84] Importantly:

> However, when given information, this group did agree that human rights sound good in theory. They would be more supportive if they were to hear about the benefits of human rights from individuals or groups who have experienced human rights breaches.[85]

From this snapshot, it seems fair to suggest that education on human rights and their protection is an important factor in support for human rights amongst the Scottish public. Looking at the UK more broadly, the IHRAR panel also argued that education played an important role in engendering public ownership of and support for human rights generally, and the Human Rights Act in particular.[86] The panel therefore recommended to the government that:

> serious consideration is given by Government to developing an effective programme of civic and constitutional education [...] Such a programme should, particularly, focus on questions about human rights.[87]

Part of the problem with harnessing education in an effective manner, however, is the profile of those most likely to support human rights and those most likely to oppose them. The 2023 Scottish study, for example, consistently suggested

80 Ibid., p. 13.
81 Ibid., p. 16.
82 Ibid., p. 17.
83 Ibid., p. 14.
84 Ibid.
85 Ibid.
86 Secretary of State for Justice and IHRAR, above n. 37, p. 20.
87 Ibid., p. 21.

that younger people are generally more supportive of human rights, while those characterised as opposed to human rights are more likely to be older.[88] This trend is also broadly supported by the earlier Equality and Human Rights Commission study.[89] This suggests that whilst human rights education in schools is an important part of ensuring support for human rights, it is easier to target this towards those who are generally already most supportive of human rights but more difficult to ensure that those whose views are most likely to be changed by education are able to receive this.

A second issue raised by this correlation between age and support for human rights is the correlation between age and voter turnout in the UK. A report by the House of Commons Library on the turnout in the 2019 UK General Election notes that there is a body of data that suggests that nearly three quarters of over-65s (74%) vote in the election, compared with under half of those in the 18–24 bracket (47%).[90] Thus, those who appear most antagonistic to human rights also appear to be most likely to vote. This, in turn, suggests that attacking human rights (as the IHRAR report was occurring in the UK) may be a vote winner amongst the group of voters most likely to turn out. The data are not available for the most recent general election in July 2024 but there does not seem to be any reason to think that this has changed.

Whilst the age profile of those who are most likely to be disengaged from, conflicted about or opposed to human rights means that they are less likely to benefit from changes to school curricula or university syllabi, this does not mean that it is impossible to design a programme of public education that can benefit all. However, more research is needed before this can be done effectively. Moreover, it is true that these are simplifications and that there will be many in both groups who do not fall within these generalisations, therefore the provision of human rights education in schools, for example, remains important.[91]

Although there appears to be a clear link between education and support for human rights in the UK, a number of points should be made. First, as the IHRAR report cautioned, a core consideration 'is whether increasing public or civic education will itself be sufficient to enhance public ownership of [human rights]' in the UK.[92] While it may be an important factor in engendering

---

88 SHRC, 'Attitudes to Human Rights in Scotland', above n. 47.

89 K. Kaur-Ballagan, S. Castell, K. Brough and H. Freimert, above n. 46, pp. 15–16. Those over 55 were more likely to agree that human rights were meaningless in their day-to-day lives and that people take unfair advantage of human rights.

90 R. McInnes, 'General Election 2019: Turnout', *House of Commons Library Insight*, 7 January 2020 available at <https://commonslibrary.parliament.uk/general-election-2019-turnout/>.

91 Indeed, as noted in A.E.C. Struthers, 'Human rights: A topic too controversial for mainstream education?' (2016) 16(1) *Human Rights Law Review* 131, views antagonistic to human rights can become entrenched even before secondary school.

92 Secretary of State for Justice and IHRAR, above n. 37, p. 20.

positive public attitudes towards and ownership of human rights and the frameworks that protect them, it must be accompanied by other measures aimed at increasing political ownership of human rights and challenging those who deliberately incite the unprecedented and escalating attacks that make use of incorrect or deliberately misleading information on human rights.[93]

Secondly, as the data examined show, there is little up-to-date or in-depth polling on public attitudes towards human rights in the UK. In order to strengthen the case for better education on issues of human rights, contemporaneous and detailed study of these issues throughout the UK is required to understand the shifts that have occurred during the last decade.

Finally, there is a degree of regional disparity in the UK in attitudes to human rights amongst governments. In general, the devolved governments in Scotland and Wales have shown themselves to be more progressive on matters of human rights. For example, in relation to education, the Equality and Human Rights Commission noted that:

> The Scottish and Welsh Governments have introduced some measures which encouraged schools to adopt [human rights education ... but] in England [...] a lack of government support made it more challenging.[94]

Other examples of this disparity include the additional incorporation of the United Nations Convention on the Rights of the Child (UNCRC),[95] which was partially incorporated in Wales by way of the Rights of Children and Young Persons (Wales) Measure 2011. A similar attempt to incorporate the UNCRC in Scotland failed as the act of incorporation was ruled to be *ultra vires* by the Supreme Court,[96] however an amended Act was passed in 2024.[97] Although this may colour the results of any future study, it does not suggest that the need for human rights education is any less great, and a joined-up UK approach would be desirable.

---

93 For example, the 'catgate' affair, where then Home Secretary Theresa May falsely claimed that an individual could not be deported because of his pet cat. This incident, and its direct impact on immigration and human rights law, is discussed in D. Campbell, '"Catgate" and the challenge to parliamentary sovereignty in immigration law' [2015] *Public Law* 426.

94 L. Culhane and E. McGeough, 'Respect, equality, participation: exploring human rights education in Great Britain', Equality and Human Rights Commission, November 2020, p. 9.

95 Convention on the Rights of the Child, 20 November 1989, 1577 UNTS 3.

96 *Reference by the Attorney General and the Advocate General for Scotland – United Nations Convention on the Rights of the Child (Incorporation) (Scotland) Bill* [2021] UKSC 41.

97 United Nations Convention on the Rights of the Child (Incorporation) (Scotland) Act 2024.

3.2. *What Does this Mean for the Future of UK Human Rights?*

In the UK, despite claims to the contrary, there appears to be a reasonable level of support for human rights. Despite this, based on current data, large proportions of the UK public are conflicted about or disengaged from human rights. Importantly, the data suggest that, given exposure to education and information about human rights, the people have the potential to become supporters and advocates of human rights and the systems that protect them.

The existing support for human rights in the UK does not, however, appear to be enough to protect the frameworks that have been developed to safeguard them. The recent history of human rights in the UK has seen a Bill of Rights, which would have significantly weakened human rights protection, make it as far as the House of Commons, in the face of direct opposition from an independent review designed to inform reform of the law in that area. Whilst that threat has now diminished, voices from the Europhobic Reform UK party are now to be heard in Parliament with Nigel Farage MP using his maiden speech to call for a referendum on continued membership of the ECHR.[98] Similarly, in 2024 the Conservative Party, now in opposition, held (yet) another leadership contest with candidates openly calling for the UK to depart from the ECHR. Indeed, the initial frontrunner in the leadership election, Robert Jenrick, invoked the spirit of Winston Churchill, arguing that the late Prime Minister would 'turn in his grave' if he could see the impact of the ECHR on today's UK.[99] Most recently, the then Secretary of State for Justice made a speech to the Council of Europe, which suggested that the result of the current approach of the ECtHR and the UK courts in respect of ECHR rights was 'legal outcomes [that] feel disconnected from public reasonableness'.[100] Once again, this harnesses the rhetoric of public perceptions of human rights to justify an overhaul of the current system.

This suggests that the next battle for human rights protection in the UK may be that on its relationship with both the ECHR and ECtHR. Although that seems unlikely under the current government, the growth of this rhetoric appears to have started and to be gaining greater mainstream acceptability. In order to challenge this human rights backsliding, one must understand better how the public perceives human rights, how education affects this and what works most effectively in terms of this education. Given the current antagonism

98 HC Deb. 23 July 2024, vol. 752, col. 570. As noted above, however, Mr Farage may be in for a surprise if that referendum were run given the current level of public support for the UK's membership of the ECHR.

99 C. Calgie, '"Churchill is rolling in his grave!" Robert Jenrick tears into the ECHR in new attack', *Express*, 30 September 2024 <https://www.express.co.uk/news/politics/1955186/Robert-Jenrick-ECHR-churchill-is-rolling-his-grave>.

100 S. Mahmood, 'Lord Chancellor speech at the Council of Europe, *Gov.UK*, 18 June 2025, <https://www.gov.uk/government/speeches/lord-chancellor-speech-at-the-council-of-europe>.

towards the ECHR from sections of Parliament, this is likely to have to come from other sources in order to build the case that human rights matter to the majority of the public and that weakening the frameworks designed to protect these rights can no longer be regarded as a vote winner.

4 CONCLUSION: THE NEXT 20 YEARS

The post-World War II consensus on human rights in Europe is in a state of flux. Increasingly, states that had previously been supportive of this consensus have entered what Klug has termed the 'ejection phase'.[101] In countries such as Hungary and the UK (to a greater or lesser extent as the party of government has changed), governments have appeared intent on rolling back the progress achieved by these rights and the institutions charged with protecting them. As society enters this difficult phase, it becomes more important than ever to ensure that there is a clear understanding of how to improve the public perception of human rights, and instruments that protect them like the ECHR. This should be done by focusing on the good that they do and the harms that they prevent, so that this can be brought to bear in domestic politics. Evidence from the UK suggests that tools such as human rights education may provide a way to do this.

The UK is not alone in facing this challenge. The situation in Denmark, for example, another historic supporter of the ECHR currently at a crossroads, is remarkably similar to that of the UK.[102] The increasing framing of issues such as mass migration and climate change as questions of human rights may cause increasing friction between states and institutions such as the ECtHR.[103] This friction is likely to increase further as more avowedly nationalist parties grow in power or take key roles in coalition governments across Europe. The recent history of the UK in this field has been characterised by the decision to withdraw from the European Union,[104] a threat to replace the Human Rights Act 1998, and, most worryingly, the increasing calls from opposition parties, in the form of the Conservative Party and a strengthening Reform UK Party, to withdraw from the ECHR. If lessons can be learned in the UK in order to

---

101 F. Klug, above n. 1.

102 For a more detailed comparison of this see J. Hartmann, 'Misdiagnosing the Human Rights Malaise: Possible Lessons from the Danish Chairmanship of the Council of Europe' in G. Ziccardi Capaldo (ed), *The Global Community Yearbook of International Law and Jurisprudence 2018*, Oxford, Oxford University Press, 2019; J. Hartmann and S. White, 'The alleged backlash against human rights: Evidence from Denmark and the UK' in K. McCall-Smith, A. Birdsall and E. Casanas Adam, above n. 1.

103 For example, see responses to the ECtHR's recent decision in *Verein KlimaSeniorinnen Schweiz and Others v. Switzerland*, no. 53600/20, 9 April 2024.

104 Of which many in the UK believe that the ECHR forms a part, see K. Clarke, above n. 68.

prevent threats to European human rights protection, an understanding of what might work in the UK is likely to prove instructive for other countries as voices opposed to human rights grow in strength, encouraged by what is happening across Europe.

Although by no means the only option, education is clearly an important means of encouraging support for, and re-engaging the public with, human rights. However, in order to properly harness it as a tool, more needs to be known not only about human rights education[105] but also about what the public actually thinks about human rights. Additionally, it is necessary to understand how the many variable factors (such as age, income, and education) impact on this. There thus remains a wealth of research still to be carried out in order to better understand these factors. If this research bears out what has been seen so far in the UK, further work will also be required to convert this understanding into effective and meaningful education that helps tell the positive stories of human rights and provides the public with the ability to articulate and enforce their rights.

With particular regard to the ECHR, the Council of Europe itself would be well placed to lead the charge in coordinating Member States in developing public awareness and education programmes. In doing this, it could build on the work already being carried out by its Education Department.[106] The Department engages in capacity building across states parties aiming to ensure that they have the tools and coordination required to deliver consistent and appropriate education, not just about human rights but also on issues related to democracy and democratic process.

Given the increasingly localised challenges posed by anti-ECHR rhetoric within states, such as Reform UK in the UK, it seems likely that the capacity building function of the Department is likely to be increasingly important: empowering non-governmental organisations (NGOs) and other actors to step in to fill the gap left by states in providing well-rounded and positive education on the impact and effectiveness of human rights. This could be done at the same time as the development of country-specific educational resources, which could be rolled out in educational institutions or in the form of freely available online training coordinated by national human rights institutions (NHRIs), who would be well placed to identify interested stakeholders.

---

[105] Although much work has already been done to look at how this works in schools, see for example A.E.C. Struthers, above n. 91; A.E.C. Struthers, 'The underdeveloped transformative potential of human rights education: English primary education as a case study' (2017) 9(1) *Journal of Human Rights Practice* 68; C. Robinson, 'Translating human rights principles into classroom practices: Inequities in educating about human rights' (2017) 28(1) *The Curriculum Journal* 123.

[106] See more detail on the current work of the Department at 'Human Rights Education in the Council of Europe', *Council of Europe* <https://www.coe.int/en/web/human-rights-education-youth/hre-coe>.

Linked with the work of the Education Department, the Council of Europe could further its work in this field by updating or overhauling the Charter on Education for Democratic Citizenship and Human Rights Education (2010).[107] This ought to place a greater emphasis on the need for high-quality education on the positive impact that human rights have had, and the difference the ECHR has made, at the same time as addressing misconceptions about the ECHR and ECtHR that abound. As was demonstrated by the IHRAR report, discussed above, disinformation remains a key factor in damaging public perceptions on human rights; therefore, education that includes a focus on media literacy may be particularly important in teaching individuals how to identity and call out 'fake news'.[108]

The 2022 draft report on the implementation of the 2010 Charter suggests that there remains much work to be done by Member States to ensure that there is a strong provision of education at all levels, noting that 'a systemic approach specifically addressing [human rights education] is still absent in most education policy frameworks'.[109] Thus, it is vital that the Council of Europe works to encourage and support Member States in developing such an approach, particularly recognising the importance of this education for the future good health of the ECHR system itself. However, in doing so, there needs to also be a recognition that this work must be underpinned by up-to-date research on both public attitudes towards human rights in Member States, as well as on the impact of education at all levels of human rights perception; areas that are currently under-studied.

Finally, in its coordination role, the Council of Europe ought to encourage states to share best practice and facilitate cross-country cooperation. This does not, and indeed, should not, be limited only to Member States or even states; rather it should bring interested parties from around the world to develop a response to the growing challenge of misinformation about the effect of human rights and the institutions that protect them and public support for the same.

Based on what is evident from the UK experience, this coordinated approach to human rights education seems likely to deliver a number of benefits for engagement with and perception of human rights. This, in turn, should encourage a sense of ownership and pride in these rights and the

107 Recommendation CM/Rec(2010)7 of the Committee of Ministers to member states on the Council of Europe Charter on Education for Democratic Citizenship and Human Rights Education, 11 May 2010.

108 See e.g. T.D. Adjin-Tettey, 'Combating fake news, disinformation, and misinformation: Experimental evidence for media literacy education' (2022) 9(1) *Cogent Arts & Humanities* 2037229.

109 Council of Europe, 'Third Review of the implementation of the Council of Europe Charter on Education for Democratic Citizenship and Human Rights Education', 16 September 2022, CP-YD/ETD (2022) 207, p. 5.

mechanisms that protect them. The IHRAR noted the importance of education in engendering public ownership of rights, and the Scottish experience demonstrated not only that there was a direct correlation between education and support for human rights, but also that education offered a means by which to re-engage those who were disengaged.[110] One key challenge remains how to get those who are not in formal education to take part in education activity. This is likely to be an area in which NGOs, states and NHRIs need to play part, responding to the particular needs and paradigms at a state level to harness the benefits of good, positive human rights education.

Looking to the next 20 years, although the future of human rights may be less certain than it was 20 years previously, there are many clear examples of their power to make the world a better place, particularly in areas of enormous global significance such as climate change.[111] By creating a public who are engaged, enthusiastic and enlightened about human rights, education is a powerful means by which to ensure that these challenges can be met head-on and guarantee that European human rights protection in the 2040s is strong, successful but, above all, supported.

---

110 Secretary of State for Justice and IHRAR, above n. 37, and SHRC, 'Attitudes to Human Rights in Scotland', above n. 47.

111 See for example P. Siwior, 'The Potential of Application of the ECHR in Climate Change Related Cases' (2021) 23(2–3) *International Community Law Review* 197.

CHAPTER 10

MAPPING THE ACTORS IN A HUMAN RIGHTS TRAJECTORY BEFORE THE EUROPEAN COURT OF HUMAN RIGHTS: HOW PROCEDURAL OPENINGS ENABLED THE EXCEPTIONAL WIN OF A HIJABI WOMAN IN *LACHIRI V. BELGIUM*

Cathérine Van de Graaf*

1 INTRODUCTION

In Belgium, as in many other European countries, there is a 'manifest or latent hostility towards the growing visibility of Muslims'[1] that hinders constructive engagement. The fact that the ultimate marker of 'Muslimness' – the veil – is worn by women contributes to the fact that more complaints of Islamophobia are made by women than by men.[2] Sami Zemni argued in this regard that, in the eyes of legislators, the Islamic headscarf has become 'the typifying content of Islam'.[3] As argued by Eva Brems, Saila Ouald-Chaib, and Katrijn Vanhees, 'when confronted with a manifestation of Islamic veiling, banning seems to be

* This chapter is written as part of the project 'Who is the Court for? Bringing the Human (Back) into Human Rights Research', supported by the Volkswagen Foundation under its funding framework 'NEXT: Law between Normativity and Reality'.

1 N. Fadil, F. El Asri and S. Bracke, 'Belgium' in J. CESARI (ed), *The Oxford Handbook of European Islam*, Oxford, Oxford University Press, 2014, pp. 222, 239.

2 E. Bayrakli and F. Hafez (eds), *European Islamophobia Report 2017*, Istanbul, SETA, 2016, p. 88; E. Mescoli, 'Forgotten Women: The impact of Islamophobia on Muslim women in Belgium', Brussels, ENAR, May 2016, p. 21; Muslims' Rights Belgium, 'Islamophobie en Belgique Francophone: Rapport annuel – 2014', Brussels, 2014 pp. 14–15.

3 Here, S. Zemni, 'The shaping of Islam and Islamophobia in Belgium' (2011) 53(1) *Race & Class* 28, 29 referring to S. Žižek, 'Multiculturalism, or, the Cultural Logic of Multinational Capitalism' (1997) 225 *New Left Review* 28, 29.

the default option in Belgian society'.[4] Acts of discrimination against Muslims are linked to their identification as the cultural and religious 'other', and surface arbitrarily in all kinds of contexts: when applying for a job, when trying to graduate from secondary school, when going for a dip in a local swimming pool and – as apparent in the case discussed in this chapter[5] – even when trying to access the courtroom.[6] Ideally, members of religious minority groups can rely on the European Court of Human Rights (ECtHR or Court) to fulfil its role as a counter-majoritarian protector of human rights.[7] Ideally, the Court corrects the:

> inherent inegalitarian effects of a democratic system where people belonging to minority groups by definition have less weight in the scale and a voice less heard.[8]

Yet, reality shows that – often by referring to the margin of appreciation awarded to Member States – the Court has often failed to fulfil this role.[9] Scholars like Kristin Henrard have argued that by granting this wide margin to states, it has enabled governments to push religious minorities out of the

---

4 E. Brems, S. Ouald-Chaib and K. Vanhees, '"Burkini" bans in Belgian municipal swimming pools: Banning as a default option' (2018) 36(4) *Netherlands Quarterly of Human Rights* 270, 274. See also: T. Heirwegh and C. Van de Graaf, 'The local swimming pool as a space of rights contestation – an analysis of "burkini" policies in Belgian local public swimming pools' (2019) 51(2) *The Journal of Legal Pluralism and Unofficial Law* 233.

5 *Lachiri v. Belgium*, no. 3413/09, 18 September 2018.

6 E. Mescoli, 'Countering Islamophobia in Belgium' in I. Law, A. Easat-Daas, A. Merali and S. Sayyid (eds), *Countering Islamophobia in Europe*, Cham, Palgrave Macmillan, 2019, pp. 253–87, pp. 253, 256; K. Van Acker, 'Flanders' Real and Present Threat: How Representations of Intergroup Relations Shape Attitudes Towards Muslim Minorities', PhD thesis, Leuven, Katholieke Universiteit Leuven, 2012; E. Brems, 'Discrimination against Muslims in Belgium' in M. Saral and Ş.O. Bahçecik (eds), *State, Religion and Muslims: Between Discrimination and Protection at the Legislative, Executive and Judicial Levels*, Leiden, Brill, 2020, pp. 65–108.

7 J.H. Ely, *Democracy and Distrust*, Cambridge (MA), Harvard University Press, 1980, p. 103; S. Mancini, 'The Crucifix Rage: Supranational Constitutionalism Bumps Against the Counter-Majoritarian Difficulty' (2010) 6 *European Constitutional Law Review* 6, 20, 25. See also P.T. Lenard, *Trust, Democracy, and Multicultural Challenges*, University Park, Pennsylvania State University Press, 2012, pp. 2–3. See also S. Ferrari, 'The Strasbourg Court and Article 9 of the European Convention of Human Rights: A Quantitative' in J. Temperman (ed), *The Lautsi Papers: Multidisciplinary Reflections on Religious Symbols in the Public School Classroom*, Leiden, Martinus Nijhoff Publishers, 2012, p. 31. Ferrari argues that 'finding satisfactory balance between dictatorship of majority and a fundamentalist conception of human rights, is the condition upon which an effective protection of religious freedom is dependent'.

8 S. Ouald Chaib, 'Belief in Justice. Towards More Inclusivity in and through the Freedom of Religion Case Law of the European Court of Human Rights', PhD thesis, Ghent, Ghent University, 2015, p. 29.

9 E. Benvenisti, 'Margin of Appreciation, Consensus and Universal Standards' (1999) 31(4) *New York University Journal of International Law and Politics* 843.

public space.[10] Yet, on 18 September 2018, the ECtHR ruled that the exclusion of Mrs. Lachiri from the courtroom for wearing a hijab was a violation of her freedom of religion as protected by Article 9 of the European Convention on Human Rights (ECHR or Convention).[11]

The relevance of this judgment is captured by a statement of Julie Ringelheim: 'with Lachiri, the Court for the first time, finds a violation in a case where the wearing of a headscarf by a Muslim woman was at stake' and did not refer to the margin of appreciation.[12] Although – read in its entirety – the judgment did not leave an undivided positive impression and perhaps gives little guidance as to the limits of prohibiting religious dress,[13] it leads to measurable change quite fast through a legislative amendment as part of the requested general measures during the execution process. What a further study of this case makes quite clear is that its outcome is not self-evident but depends on how a variety of actors engaged with human rights.[14] As such, in order to understand how such a success came about it is necessary to go beyond the judgment of the Court and look into which civil society actors engage with human rights in the pre-trial and post-trial phase and what conditions made their impact on human rights law's capacity to produce or inhibit social change more likely.[15] While this mapping exercise will involve a big network of actors, it will focus on two actors in depth as they appeared in the trajectory because of institutional openings to civil society foreseen in the Court and execution proceedings, namely by way of third-party interventions and Rule 9(2) submissions.[16]

---

10 K. Henrard, 'Integration reasoning at the ECtHR: Challenging the boundaries of minorities' citizenship' (2020) 38(1) *Netherlands Quarterly of Human Rights* 55. More information: M.-C. Foblets, 'Islam under the Rule of Law in Europe: How Consistent is the Human Rights Test?' (2021) 12(10) *Religions* 857.

11 Convention for the Protection of Human Rights and Fundamental Freedoms, 4 November 1950 (ETS 5).

12 J. Ringelheim, 'Lachiri v. Belgium: Headscarf Ban Imposed on a Civil Party in a Courtroom in Violation of Religious Freedom', *Strasbourg Observers*, 23 November 2018 <https://strasbourgobservers.com/2018/11/23/lachiri-v-belgium-headscarf-ban-imposed-on-a-civil-party-in-a-courtroom-in-violation-of-religious-freedom/>. Interestingly, however, the margin is mentioned in the dissenting opinion of Judge Mourou-Vikström. See P. Kaushik, '*Lachiri v Belgium* and Bans on Wearing Islamic Dress in the Courtroom: An Emerging Trend' (2019) 21(1) *Ecclesiastical Law Journal* 48, 53.

13 Ibid.

14 E. Desmet, 'Analysing users' trajectories in human rights: a conceptual exploration and research agenda' (2014) 8(2) *Human Rights & International Legal Discourse* 121, 125.

15 S. Talesh and J. Pélisse, 'How Legal Intermediaries Facilitate or Inhibit Social Change' (2019) 79 *Studies in Law, Politics, and Society* 111, 112.

16 Article 36(2) of the Convention. More information about Rule 9(2) can be found here: 'EIN Publications: Rule 9 Submission Guide', *European Implementation Network* <https://www.einnetwork.org/rule-9-submission-guide>.

The chapter has been structured in the following way. First, the contribution begins by briefly sketching how and why to approach a human rights trajectory from an actor- or user-based perspective (see below section 2). Second, the chapter continues with a chronological illustration of this actor-based approach from the period before the judgment (see below section 3), a reflection on the judgment (see below section 4) and then the period after the judgment (see below section 5). Finally, a brief conclusion (see below section 6) is offered at the end of the chapter.

2 METHOD AND METHODOLOGY

The current section of the chapter will first elaborate on the approach and second on how this research was carried out. Ellen Desmet's article 'Analysing users' trajectories in human rights' was central in this undertaking.[17] Desmet stressed that to adopt a users' perspective on human rights demands a different way of thinking and asking.[18] As such, in the present case, the interest lies not in which obligations rest on a Council of Europe Member State regarding a hijabi woman's right to enter a courtroom (although the approach of the ECtHR will certainly be disclosed in the present chapter). Instead, the interest is in finding out which civil society actors engage with human rights in the pre-trial and post-trial phase and what they add to the human rights trajectory in this specific context. The social constructivist starting point of such research is that '[t]he outcome of a case is neither self-evident nor inherent in the logic or structure of human rights law, but determined by how human rights are used'.[19] The amendment of the Belgian Judicial Code after the finding of a violation in Strasbourg was anything but a self-evident consequence of the continuing dismissal of hijabi women from the courtroom. Rather, both the amendment and the violation judgment were the result of mobilisations of individual actors (and organisations) that 'push' and 'pull' in various directions.[20] Talesh and Pelisse have rightly stressed that more research is needed on the role that a variety of actors play in 'facilitating and inhibiting social change across a wide "variety" of social institutions'.[21] An important additional question that needs answering is how it is possible for certain key actors to be as impactful

17 E. Desmet, above n. 14.
18 Ibid., 124.
19 Ibid., 125.
20 W. van Rossum, 'The roots of Dutch strategic human rights litigation: comparing "Engel" to "SGP"' in M. van den Brink, S. Burri and J. Goldschmidt (eds), *Equality and Human Rights: Nothing but Trouble? Liber amicorum Titia Loenen*, Utrecht, Netherlands Institute of Human Rights (SIM), 2015, pp. 387–400, 387.
21 S. Talesh and J. Pélisse, above n. 15, 113

as they are.[22] In this context, it has been signalled that it is important to reflect both on the type of actors but also on the factors on which they depend and that are often out of their control.[23]

Throughout the human rights trajectory, having various actors or users was inevitable for the obtaining of the above-mentioned result. In mapping out the human rights users involved, a central importance is attributed to the rights claimants and their representation on the one hand and the Court (and the component judges) as an institutional user of human rights on the other hand.[24] Yet, these are expected users in any litigation effort before the ECtHR and one would rather add to the knowledge on what Van Rossum describes as the 'hidden driving forces' behind Court cases.[25] As such, the focus of the chapter will lay on the category of 'supportive human rights users' or 'supportive organisations',[26] their relation to the ECtHR and how they managed to have impact in the present case.[27]

For the purpose of this chapter, the case of *Lachiri v. Belgium* will be investigated, drawing on the ethnographic extended case method (ECM).[28] Documents will primarily comprise the ECtHR judgment[29] and case files,[30]

---

22 T. Havinga and J. Hoevenaars, 'Éliane Vogel-Polsky en de realisatie van vrouwenrechten: een actor als factor' in R. Baas, T. Havinga, M. Laemers and H. Den Tonkelaar (eds), *Rechtspleging en Rechtsbescherming: Liber amicorum voor Prof. Dr. Leny E. De Groot-van Leeuwen*, Deventer, Wolters Kluwer, 2015, p. 96.

23 Ibid.

24 In other research, the focus has been on lawyers and applicants that bring cases to the Court. For example: L. Hodson, 'Activists and Lawyers in the ECtHR: The Struggle for Gay Rights' in D. Anagnostou (ed), *Rights and Courts in Pursuit of Social Change: Legal Mobilisation in the Multi-Level European System*, Oxford, Hart Publishing, 2014, pp. 207–28; L. Lavrysen, '"Strasbourg Was Something New, It Was an Adventure": A History of the Belgian Cases before the European Court of Human Rights in the 1960s, 1970s and 1980s' (2018) 86(3–4) *Tijdschrift voor Rechtsgeschiedenis/Revue d'histoire du droit/The Legal History Review* 482, 547; M.-B. Dembour, 'What it takes to have a case: the backstage story of Muskhadzhiyeva v. Belgium (illegality of children's immigration detention' in E. Lambert-Abdelgawad (ed), *Preventing and Sanctioning Hindrances to the Right of Individual Petition to the European Court of Human Rights*, Cambridge, Intersentia, 2011. Others scholars have focused on the actors involved in the execution of judgments specifically. For example: A. Donald and A.-K. Speck, 'The dynamics of domestic human rights implementation: lessons from qualitative research in Europe' (2020) 12(1) *Journal of Human Rights Practice* 48, 70.

25 W. van Rossum, above n. 17, p. 392.

26 Ibid., p. 388.

27 This is a term used by Ellen Desmet in her article: E. Desmet, above n. 17.

28 On the ECM, see, e.g. M. Burawoy, 'The Extended Case Method' (1998) 16(1) *Sociological Theory* 4, 33; T.M.S. Evens and D. Handelman (eds), *The Manchester School: Practice and Ethnographic Praxis in Anthropology*, New York, Berghahn Books, 2006; D.D. Barata, 'Extended Case Method' in A.J. Mills, G. Durepos and E. Wiebe (eds), *Encyclopedia of Case Study Research*, Thousand Oaks and London, SAGE, 2010, pp. 375–76.

29 These are accessible through the HUDOC database. 'HUDOC', *European Court of Human Rights* https://www.echr.coe.int/hudoc-database.

30 Case files are made available by the Court Archives upon request. The application form is available at <https://app.echr.coe.int/Contact/EchrContactForm/English/1>.

including parties' submissions and correspondence with the Court, but also relevant legal scholarship. By consulting case files, one will gain an initial understanding of the main agents involved. This document-based reconstruction will be empirically complemented by data gathered through semi-structured, qualitative interviews with agents of litigation, such as individual applicants, legal representatives, third-party interveners, national equality bodies, NGO representatives, (former) ECtHR judges and other Council of Europe officials.[31] Because the trajectory of human rights that is being uncovered is very context-specific and depends on the subject, topic and region, the current analysis will also be tailored to this specific context.[32]

3 BEFORE THE JUDGMENT

3.1. Issue in Belgian Courts

The *Lachiri v. Belgium* case was the result of the experience of one woman, Hagar Lachiri, who was told she could not enter the courtroom unless she removed her headscarf. While Lachiri was the first woman to take this all the way to the European Court of Human Rights, what happened to her was not a one-off or stand-alone example. For years prior to Lachiri's application to the Court (and during the process as well), women and their lawyers had been reporting similar incidents to the Belgian national equality body (Centre Unia).[33] Since 2007, numerous cases had been reported to Unia of individuals who were refused entry into the courtroom, both for religious as well as other reasons.[34] Besides many women with headscarves, a man who refused to remove a bonnet he was wearing for medical reasons was convicted for insulting a magistrate and another man was excluded from the courtroom for refusing to take off his kippah.[35] Yet, in an interview, the relevant case officer stated that the majority of reports came from Muslim women and that – although they wanted to make a record of these incidents – none of the women

---

31 Interviews will be conducted online and in-person depending on the informant, their availability and preferences.

32 See also: E. Desmet, above n. 17, 124.

33 Interview with the relevant case officer at Unia, conducted and transcribed in French on 19 April 2024.

34 Communications submitted by Unia during the execution process at the Committee of Ministers, 1348th meeting in June 2019: 'Règle 9.2 Communication du Centre interfédéral pour l'égalité des chances et la lutte contre le racisme et les discriminations (UNIA) (08/03/2019) relative à l'affaire Lachiri c. Belgique (requête no. 3413/09) [French only]', 26 June 2019, DH-DD(2019)329, para. 2 <https://hudoc.exec.coe.int/eng?i=DH-DD(2019)329F>.

35 Ibid.

or their lawyers had wished to make an official complaint against the judges in question at Unia.[36] She explained that:

> in most of these cases, I was not even able to take any action because the women were afraid. They made the report and explained the situation, but did not dare go any further for fear of making an enemy out of the judge.[37]

It was stressed by the case officer at Unia that this was a very problematic situation because the persons in question were already in quite complicated situations, such as complex separations with issues relating to custody of children, financial problems and so on. She stressed that:

> they found themselves in front of a judge who was going to decide their fate, for example custody of the children, and possibly alimony payments by one or the other,

and did not dare to refuse the order.[38] In some cases, the women in question did not make these reports but their lawyers did, stating that these events turned the hearings into an emotional ordeal that had a disproportionate impact on their clients.[39] The problem can only be sketched based on the cases that have been reported, but in its observations Unia stated that these only constitute the tip of the iceberg with many more cases remaining unreported.[40] Based on the various cases that had reached it, Unia had already, in August of 2015, expressed its concerns to the then Minister of Justice Koen Geens and had advocated for a reform of Article 759 of the Belgian Judicial Code.[41] Ever since the early 19th century, the Belgian Judicial Code has included the provision:

> anyone who attends hearings must remain uncovered, respectful and silent; anything that the judge orders to maintain order must be carried out promptly and in a timely manner.[42]

In those days, removing a hat when entering certain spaces was a sign of respect and a recognition of authority.[43] This article was often used by judges as a justification to exclude persons who covered their hair for religious reasons. Yet, Unia's advocacy had not yet yielded any result.

---

36 Ibid., para. 3.

37 See above, n. 33.

38 Ibid.

39 'Règle 9.2 Communication du Centre interfédéral pour l'égalité des chances et la lutte contre le racisme et les discriminations (UNIA) (08/03/2019) relative à l'affaire Lachiri c. Belgique (requête no. 3413/09) [French only]', above n. 34, p. 2.

40 Ibid., para. 3.

41 Ibid., p. 1.

42 At that moment, this provision was still included in Article 88.

43 Wetsontwerp om justitie menselijker, sneller en straffer te maken (Belgian 'Bill to make justice more humane, faster and more rigorous'), p. 21; K. Lemmens, 'Chapeau voor de Antwerpse correctionele rechtbank' (2007) 2 *Nederlands Tijdschrift voor Rechtsfilosofie en*

3.2. *Starting National Proceedings*

On 20 June 2007, Mrs. Lachiri appeared at the Court of Appeal in Brussels as a civil party in the criminal case about the violent death of her brother.[44] This was an appeal against a previous order of the Court of First Instance of Brussels to reclassify the facts as a premeditated assault resulting in death without intent.[45] During the hearing at the Court of Appeal, Mrs. Lachiri was told by the usher (on behalf of the President of the Chamber)[46] that she would not be allowed to enter the courtroom if she did not remove her headscarf.[47] When her representative asked for an explanation for this ban, the President stated that this decision was taken in accordance with Article 759 of the Belgian Judicial Code, which states that anyone who attends hearings must remain uncovered. As the applicant refused to comply, she was not able to attend the hearing. Her presence in the courtroom was especially important because her father and brother, as well as other family members (who were civil parties), relied on her to explain what was being said to them, as she was the only person with a degree.[48] Her representative then hastily drew up handwritten submissions on behalf of the applicant's parents, who were also civil parties, arguing that the exclusion of the applicant from the courtroom was a violation of the principle of equality of citizens before the law, enshrined in the Belgian Constitution, and of Article 6 of the Convention.[49] In a judgment of 12 September 2007, the appeals against the reclassification of the facts were declared admissible but unfounded.[50] On her exclusion from the courtroom, it stated:

> Whereas the document described as a 'submission' by its author [...] merely states that 'the exclusion of [the applicant] from the hearing by the court (...) is a violation of the principle of equality of citizens before the law, enshrined in the Belgian Constitution, as well as of Article 6 of the [Convention]';
>
> Whereas it should be noted that in the present case, this simple statement is not based on any legal reasoning that would make it possible to determine the scope that the civil party intends to attribute to it;

Rechtstheorie 53; T. Scheir, 'De politie van de terechtzitting: "Contempt of court" naar Belgisch recht' (2009) 9 *Rechtskundig Weekblad* 346; B. Van Den Broeck, 'Rechter moet neutraal zijn, burger niet' (2007) 147 *De Juristenkrant* 3.

44 *Lachiri v. Belgium*, above n. 5, § 10.

45 Ibid., § 9.

46 The Chamber that is referred to is the indictment chamber ('*chambre des mises en accusation*').

47 *Lachiri v. Belgium*, above n. 5, § 12.

48 Case file, *Lachiri v. Belgium*, above n. 5, application to the ECtHR, arrived at the Court on 12 January 2009, p. 3.

49 *Lachiri v. Belgium*, above n. 5, § 15.

50 Judgment of the Indictments Chamber of the Brussels Court of Appeal, 12 September 2007.

> That it is therefore a simple argument which in no way constitutes a plea to which the court would be obliged to respond;
> That the court has, moreover, complied strictly with the provisions of Article 759 of the Judicial Code.[51]

The applicant and the other civil parties appealed against this judgment. In support of their appeals, the applicants complained about the application of Article 759 of the Judicial Code in this case,[52] arguing that, in the absence of disrespectful or disruptive behaviour, the circumstances did not justify the application of this provision. The decision taken was unpredictable and a source of legal uncertainty as it had never been invoked in the jurisdiction of the Brussels Court of Appeal to ask 'a Catholic nun, a Jew wearing a kippah or a Sikh wearing a turban' to remove them, nor a Muslim woman to remove her headscarf. They argued that the contested judgment had not responded to their submissions that there had been a violation of the Constitution and the Convention by the discriminatory exclusion of the applicant from the courtroom. In violation of Articles 6(1) and 9 of the Convention, Articles 14 and 18 of the International Covenant on Civil and Political Rights[53] and Articles 10 and 19 of the Constitution, the contested judgment had failed to guarantee respect for the equality of citizens before the law and the impartiality of courts and tribunals, which require that:

> all litigants should be allowed to attend courtrooms in any capacity whatsoever, wearing their traditional dress or dress in accordance with their religion or philosophical belief, as long as their attitudes and behaviour are respectful of the judges and do not disrupt the hearing.

At the hearing before the Court of Cassation, the applicant was allowed to appear wearing her headscarf. In a judgment of 25 June 2008, the Court of Cassation declared the appeals inadmissible and stated that:

> From the mere fact that the characterisation adopted by the council chamber is not the one that the civil party claims to have given to the offence, it does not follow that the decision given by the investigating court in this respect is prejudicial to that party's action.[54]

The proceedings before the trial courts against the defendant in the homicide of the applicant's brother continued and, on 11 May 2010, the Brussels Court of Appeal handed down a judgment sentencing the defendant to seven years'

51 Ibid., § 16.
52 Ibid., § 22.
53 International Covenant on Civil and Political Rights, 19 December 1966, 999 UNTS 171.
54 *Lachiri v. Belgium*, ibid., § 18.

imprisonment.[55] It reserved judgment on the interests of the civil parties. The civil parties lodged an appeal in cassation against the judgment of the Court of Appeal. In a single ground of appeal, they complained that the Court of Appeal's judgment had not taken account of the quantified claim made by the civil parties at the hearing. The appeal was dismissed by the Court of Cassation in a judgment of 24 November 2010 on the grounds that the appeal had been lodged out of time.[56]

3.3. *To the European Court of Human Rights*

After exhausting domestic remedies, Hagar Lachiri and her lawyers (de Beco) submitted an application to the ECtHR, which arrived at the Court on 12 January 2009. In the application, they complained of a violation of Articles 6(1) and 9 of the Convention.[57] The case was communicated on 9 October 2015.[58] The main grief included in the communication was the applicant's complaint about the decision of the President of the Indictments Division of the Brussels Court of Appeal to exclude her from the courtroom on the grounds that she had refused to remove her hijab. Unlike the double complaint in the application to the Court, when communicated, the complaint was requalified as an infringement of her right to freedom of thought, conscience and religion under Article 9 of the Convention alone.[59]

3.4. *Third-Party Intervention (TPI)*

The ECtHR has a procedure that allows a third party to the case to provide information to the Court.[60] Article 36(2) of the Convention states in this regard:

> The President of the Court may, in the interest of the proper administration of justice, invite [...] any person concerned who is not the applicant to submit written comments or take part in hearings.[61]

---

55 Judgment of the 11th Criminal (Correctional) Chamber of the Brussels Court of Appeal (11 May 2010).

56 Judgment of the Court of Cassation (24 November 2010).

57 Application to the European Court of Human Rights, *Lachiri v. the Belgian Government*, arrived at the ECtHR on 12 January 2009, p. 4.

58 *Lachiri v. Belgium* (communicated case), no. 3413/09, communicated on 9 October 2025, available at <https://hudoc.echr.coe.int/eng?i=001-158419>.

59 Ibid.

60 Besides the discussed *amicus curiae*, this procedure is open to States Parties of the applicant's nationality, states that are neither a party to the proceedings (of which the applicant does not have the nationality), the Commissioner for Human Rights and other persons who are also 'concerned' by the proceedings.

61 The procedure is further explained in Rule 44 of the Rules of Court: Registry of the Court, 'Rules of Court', 15 September 2025 <https://www.echr.coe.int/documents/d/echr/rules_court_eng>.

Groups such as national human rights institutions, non-governmental organisations, interest groups, bar associations, and universities can assist it as an *amici curiae* or 'friend of the court' in the process of reaching a decision.[62] The role of these interveners is 'to enlighten the Court with their expertise as to the legal and cultural issues, both national and international'.[63] In the present case, the Human Rights Centre (HRC) of Ghent University requested leave to intervene in the *Lachiri v. Belgium* case.[64] At that point the team, that consisted of six PhD students under the supervision of Prof. Eva Brems, had already intervened in several other cases.[65] They prepared these interventions in a highly voluntaristic manner in cases with a link to their research interests and expertise.[66] The time limit to submit an intervention is always quite short, giving interveners usually no longer than a month. As both the letter granting leave and the submission of the intervention happen by mail, in reality this period is closer to two weeks. In this case, as the letter granting them leave to intervene and setting the deadline arrived at the University over the Christmas break, the team of the HRC asked the Section Registrar for the first time whether the deadline for submitting their intervention could be extended, stating that this would allow them to submit 'a high-quality intervention with unique empirical data'.[67] The request was granted to the interveners of the Human Rights Centre. Indeed, in preparation of the third-party intervention, a small research project was initiated into the practical application of Article 759 of the Belgian Judicial Code by Belgian judges.[68] After verifying the methodological

62 Practice Direction on 'Third-party intervention under Article 36 § 2 of the Convention or under Article 3, second sentence, of Protocol No. 16' issued by the President of the Court in accordance with Rule 32 of the Rules of Court on 13 March 2023, 10. <https://www.echr.coe.int/documents/d/echr/pd_third_party_intervention_eng-pdf>.

63 P. Pastor Vilanova, 'Third Parties Involved in International Litigation Proceedings. What Are the Challenges for the ECHR?' in P. Pinto de Albuquerque and K. Wojtyczek (eds), *Judicial Power in a Globalized World: Liber Amicorum Vincent De Gaetano*, Cham, Springer, 2019, p. 382.

64 The author of this chapter has participated in the writing of many third-party interventions as a member of the Human Rights Centre of Ghent University since 2021. At the time of the *Lachiri* intervention, she was not working at the HRC and thus not involved in the writing process.

65 The team had intervened in eight cases prior to the *Lachiri v. Belgium* case. The first intervention was submitted when it was communicated that the *Konstantin Markin v. Russia* case (*Konstantin Markin v. Russia*, no. 30078/06, 22 March 2012) would be going to the Grand Chamber. A full list of cases in which the Human Rights Centre submitted interventions to the Court can be found here: 'Third-Party Interventions before ECtHR', *Human Rights Centre* <https://hrc.ugent.be/clinic/third-party-interventions-before-ecthr/>.

66 Interview with Eva Brems, conducted and transcribed in Dutch on 29 November 2024.

67 Case file, *Lachiri v. Belgium*, above n. 5, letter by Prof. Dr. Eva Brems to the ECtHR, from 6 January 2016.

68 E. Brems, C. Heri and L. Verdonck, 'Head Coverings in the Courtroom: A Question of Respect for the Judge or of Judicial Tolerance?', 2016 <https://hrc.ugent.be/wp-content/uploads/2019/10/Head-Coverings-in-the-Courtroom.pdf>.

rigour with a colleague sociology professor, an anonymous survey study was conducted among 255 Dutch-speaking and 263 French-speaking judges in Belgium. The survey resulted in five main findings. First, most judges had never applied Article 759 of the Judicial Code.[69] Second, most judges are aware of the *ratio legis* behind the article so they (would) only use it when someone misbehaves in their courtroom.[70] Third, many judges differentiate between religious and non-religious headgear.[71] Yet, some are of the opinion that both types of headgear should be treated equally, either by prohibiting both or by allowing both.[72] Fourth, certain judges who would prohibit religious headgear in the courtroom would differentiate between religions: a Muslim woman would be asked to remove her headscarf but a Catholic nun would not be.[73] Finally, a large number of respondent judges indicated that they want clearer guidelines to avoid an inconsistent application in practice.[74] The results of this survey were picked up by national newspapers such as *De Standaard*[75] and *Het Nieuwsblad*[76] as well as *VTM Nieuws*.[77] Also, the *Juristenkrant* reported on the position towards the headscarf of the various Bar associations in Belgium. The results of the survey provided the Court with information that could not have been obtained anywhere else. Yet, other topics covered in the TPI such as the wider context of headscarf bans in Belgium and the historical background of the provision concerned could also have been relevant. While TPIs are

---

69 Ibid., p. 3. Only 23.5% of the Dutch-speaking and 38% of the French-speaking judges. Only 5% of the of the Dutch-speaking and 8% of the French-speaking respondents had already asked for religious headgear to be removed.

70 Ibid., p. 4.

71 This was justified by one of the participating judges as follows: 'It seems to me that the purpose of this legal provision is to ensure respect and order during the proceedings. I do not think that the fact that a Jew wears a kippah, or the other examples cited, shows any disrespect toward the court. [...] On the other hand, not removing a cap or a beanie – whose wearing reflects neither a conviction nor a necessity – seems to me at best a lack of manners, at worst a lack of respect.' (author's own translation). From Dutch-language version of the report E. Brems, C. Heri and L. Verdonck, 'Hoofddeksels in de rechtszaal: Een kwestie van respect door de rechter of tolerantie door de rechter?', p. 8.

72 The rationale is as follows: banning both (10% of the Dutch-speaking and 25% of the French-speaking judges) or allowing both (18% of the Dutch-speaking and 9.5% of the French-speaking judges).

73 This is true for 2.4% of the Dutch-speaking and 7.4% of the French-speaking judges.

74 Certain judges indicated that they find the provision archaic and that it should either be removed entirely or at least the words referring to the head being uncovered should.

75 '1 op 7 rechters wil geen hoofddoek op zitting', *De Standaard*, 14 January 2017 <https://www.standaard.be/cnt/dmf20170113_02673009>; '1 rechter op 7 heeft probleem met hoofddoek op zitting', *De Standaard*, 14 January 2017 <https://www.standaard.be/cnt/dmf20170113_02673370>.

76 M. Justaert, 'Rechters houden niet van de hoofddoek', *Het Nieuwsblad*, 14 January 2017 <https://www.nieuwsblad.be/cnt/dmf20170113_02673702>.

77 '1 rechter op 7 wil geen hoofddoek in zitting', *VTM Nieuws*, 14 January 2017.

certainly one of the ways in which to influence international courts,[78] it usually remains a mystery to third-party interveners whether or the extent to which their intervention had any effect on the final decision of the Court.[79] Yet, one could argue that an explicit reference by the Court to the observations of the third-party intervener are a good indication of having effectively influenced the judges' deliberations. Such references are found at several points throughout the *Lachiri* judgment.

4 DURING THE JUDGMENT

This chapter does not aim to explore the Court's reasoning nor its position within earlier case law in the greatest detail.[80] Nevertheless, it is necessary to explain how the Court developed its arguments and the extent of the disagreement between judges on these arguments in order to demonstrate the relevance of the intervention. *Lachiri v. Belgium* is a judgment of the Second Section of the European Court of Human Rights of 18 September 2018.[81] Usually, the Court dedicates most of its efforts to the proportionality analysis of the interference. Yet, before that, it goes into the questions whether an interference exists, whether it is prescribed by law and whether it has a legitimate aim. First, it was quite evident that the exclusion from the courtroom for wearing a headscarf constituted a restriction on the right to freedom of religion. Then, the Court assessed the legal basis and the quality thereof. While finding the legal basis in Article 759 of the Belgian Judicial Code was quite straightforward, this is not so for the question of accessibility and foreseeability of the provision. The Court mentioned that it is quite clear from both the arguments raised by the applicants and by the third party that the Belgian courts' application of the invoked legal basis is a source of great legal uncertainty.[82] Yet, the Court did not find it necessary to decide on the question.[83] When looking at the

---

78 D. Cardamone, 'Independence of International Courts' in P. Pinto de Albuquerque and K. Wojtyczek (eds), above n. 60, p. 96; L. Van den Eynde, 'An Empirical Look at the Amicus Curiae Practice of Human Rights NGOs before the European Court of Human Rights' (2013) 31(3) *Netherlands Quarterly of Human Rights* 271.

79 P. Harvey, 'Third Party Interventions before the ECtHR: A Rough Guide', *Strasbourg Observers*, 24 February 2015 <https://strasbourgobservers.com/2015/02/24/third-party-interventions-before-the-ecthr-a-rough-guide/>.

80 An article that discusses in detail the reasoning of the Court (e.g. the stricter proportionality review) and places it within the framework of earlier case law is P. Kaushik, '*Lachiri v Belgium* and Bans on Wearing Islamic Dress in the Courtroom: An Emerging Trend' (2019) 21(1) *Ecclesiastical Law Journal* 48, 53.

81 The judgment of *Lachiri v. Belgium* is only available in French. Thus, all the included citations are the author's own translations.

82 *Lachiri v. Belgium*, above n. 5, § 35.

83 Ibid., § 36.

legitimate aim, it remarked that the Belgian government did not contend that the rights and freedoms of others were at stake. Based again on the results of the investigation by the Third-Party Intervener, the Court concluded that the obligation to appear uncovered before the judge has the intention to avoid conduct that would be disrespectful to the judiciary or would disrupt the smooth running of the hearing. It linked this intention to the legitimate aim of 'protection of public order'.[84]

Then, in the proportionality test, the Court found that the sole basis for prohibiting the applicant from entering the courtroom was the President's interpretation of the disputed provision. It then went on to state that the applicant was 'merely a citizen' and no representative of the state. Thus, she cannot be subjected to an obligation of discretion in the public expression of her religious convictions.[85] In response to the applicant's argument that the Palace of Justice in Brussels is a public space, the Court argued that a courtroom is not a public space comparable to a square as a public space. A court is a public space in which respect for neutrality may take precedence over the exercise of the right to manifest one's religion. In this context, it refers to the 'more comparable' public space of the public educational establishments.[86] Yet, as the preservation of neutrality in the public space did not seem to be the aim pursued, the court only checked whether the measure was justified by the protection (or maintenance) of public order. *In concreto*, the Court found that the facts of the case do not demonstrate that the applicant's behaviour was disrespectful or likely to 'constitute a threat to the proper conduct of the hearing'.[87] As such, the necessity of the restriction on the applicant's right could not be established and a violation of ECHR, Article 9 was found.[88] The judgment was adopted with a majority of six votes to one. Judge Mourou-Vikström dissented, stating that the decision of the judge in question was based on the application of an objective text. She further contended that as Article 9 of the ECHR was not invoked by the applicant's lawyer in the initial proceedings, but merely equality before the law and Article 6 of the Convention, the Court should not have dealt with it. In her opinion, when the Court, however, decided to assess the interference with Article 9, it should have paid attention to the context of the judicial 'ritual' which aims to erase the personal differences of each person 'in order to place the legal and judicial debate at the heart of the trial'.[89] Drawing

---

84 Ibid., § 38. In this regard the Court mentioned the aim of maintaining the authority of the judiciary, which exists only under ECHR, Article 10(2), but then linked it to the protection of public order as mentioned in the main text of this chapter.

85 *Lachiri v. Belgium*, above n. 5, § 44.

86 Ibid., § 45.

87 Ibid., § 46.

88 Ibid., §§ 47–48.

89 Ibid., dissenting opinion of Judge Mourou-Vikström, § 34.

a parallel with *Leyla Sahin v. Turkey*,[90] it is argued by the judge in question that a Court is a public institution where respect for neutrality trumps the right to manifest one's religion. Judge Mourou-Vikström states that parties are not exempt from these obligations. Her opinion concludes with a reference to a lack of consensus and thus a wide margin for the Belgian state to 'assess national needs'.[91]

In the concurring opinion of Judges Griţco and Vučinić, the focus lay in particular on whether or not the disputed provisions of Article 759 of the Belgian Judicial Code actually met the requirements of foreseeability of the law. In the Court's case law, 'law' refers to the text in force as interpreted by the competent courts.[92] The concurring judges find that as the provision was interpreted 'in two diametrically opposed ways' at the level of the Court of Appeal and that of the Court of Cassation, it did not meet the foreseeability requirement.[93] The judges refer again to the results of the survey submitted in the TPI[94] and state there explicitly: 'the Belgian Government has not questioned the data which served as the factual basis for the Court's findings cited above'. Hereby, they indicate the importance of the submitted data to the judgment of the Court. In conclusion, they argue that the Court could have found a violation without further looking into whether the interference pursued a legitimate aim or was necessary in a democratic society.

When looking at the earlier case law of the Court, there is one case that is of great importance: *Hamidović v. Bosnia and Herzegovina*.[95] It is very similar to *Lachiri v. Belgium* in that it is a case about religious dress of a minority religion in the courtroom. In Bosnia and Herzegovina, Islam is not a minority religion but the Salafist community that practices orthodox interpretation of Islam is. Mr. Hamidović belonged to this community. He, as well as Mrs. Lachiri, was asked to remove his skullcap, and, upon refusing to do so, he was expelled from the courtroom and convicted for contempt of court.[96] In this case, the Court again found that there was no indication that the applicant had been disrespectful during the trial. Unlike other members of his religious group, he had appeared before the court when he was summoned and stood up when requested. The Court argued that this showed that he clearly submitted to 'the

90 *Leyla Şahin v. Turkey*, no. 44774/98, 10 November 2005, ECHR 2005-XI.

91 *Lachiri v. Belgium*, above n. 5, dissenting opinion of Judge Mourou-Vikström, §§ 37–39.

92 Among other authorities, *Sunday Times v. United Kingdom (No. 1)*, no. 6538/74, 26 April 1979, § 47, Series A no. 30; *Kruslin v. France*, no. 11801/85, 24 April 1990, § 29, Series A no. 176-A; *Casado Coca v. Spain*, no. 15450/89, 24 February 1994, § 43, Series A no. 285-A; and *Leyla Şahin v. Turkey*, above n. 87.

93 *Lachiri v. Belgium*, above n. 5, concurring opinion of Judges Griţco and Vučinić, § 11.

94 *Lachiri v. Belgium*, above n. 5, §§ 28–29.

95 *Hamidović v. Bosnia and Herzegovina*, no. 57792/15, 5 December 2017.

96 Ibid., § 7. Mr. Hamidović was sentenced to a fine that was later converted into 30 days of imprisonment.

laws and courts of the country'.[97] It argued that by punishing him with contempt of court solely for not removing his skullcap the domestic authorities had exceeded their margin of appreciation and had breached his right to freedom of religion.[98] The Court also pointed out the difference between this situation and those about the wearing of religious symbols by public officials. The latter, the Court argued 'may be under a duty of discretion, neutrality and impartiality, including a duty not to wear such symbols and clothing while exercising official authority'.[99] In a concurring opinion, Judge De Gaetano holds that the examination by the Court could have stopped at whether it was 'prescribed by law'. De Gaetano argued that the applicant was punished based on 'a general and vague provision of law'.[100] With no statutory provision prohibiting the wearing of the skullcap, the applicant could not have reasonably foreseen that this was included in the notion 'dress code applicable to judicial institutions'. The majority argued that there were no strong reasons to depart from the finding of the Constitutional Court that concluded that the interference was lawful, but De Gaetano stated that this constituted 'a vagueness which no amount of circumlocution by the Constitutional Court could effectively veil'.[101] What is important to signal here is that in the section on comparative law in the *Hamidović* judgment, the study conducted by the Human Rights Centre and submitted to the Court by way of third-party intervention in the *Lachiri* case was mentioned, although at that point in time the judgment in the latter case had not been delivered yet.[102] The *Lachiri* judgment would only come out around nine months later and was deliberated in chamber formation by the Second Section while *Hamidović* was deliberated by the Fourth Section.

5 AFTER THE JUDGMENT

Once the judgment became final, the execution process before the Committee of Ministers started. In the first Action Report of December 2019 submitted to the CoM, the Belgian government submitted that by publishing the judgment on the website of the Court of Cassation as well as the targeted dissemination

97 Ibid., § 42.

98 Ibid., § 43. This judgment was adopted with a majority of six votes to one. Judge Ranzoni disagreed with the finding of violation and argued that the ECtHR can only substitute its view for that of the national courts when a Member State has clearly overstepped its margin of appreciation. He argues that in the majority's assessment of the case at hand contains 'only general statements not specifically linked to the particular facts of the present case'. This is not sufficient for holding that the Bosnia and Herzegovina government overstepped its margin of appreciation.

99 Ibid., § 40.

100 Ibid., concurring opinion of Judge De Gaetano, § 3.

101 Ibid.

102 Ibid., § 21.

of the judgment's conclusion among all Belgian judges, it has taken all the general measures necessary for the full execution of the *Lachiri* judgment.[103] The government noted in this Action Report that the modification of Article 759 of the Belgian Judicial Code – although recommended by the judiciary – was not a prerequisite for the closure of the execution process and that the general implementing measures mentioned above were such as to prevent similar violations of the Convention in the future.[104] At that moment, Unia had already submitted a Rule 9(2) communication to the Committee of Ministers indicating that only a legislative amendment could eradicate the legal uncertainty and make sure that courts and tribunals would act in conformity with the *Lachiri* judgment.[105] The next section will demonstrate that this was a correct assumption on Unia's behalf.

5.1. *Intervention of the Belgian National Equality Body*

The case of Hagar Lachiri was never reported to Unia, although – as stated under section 3 – they received countless other reports. Thus, the first time the case officers at Unia heard about the case was when the ECtHR judgment came out.[106] While assuming this would have solved the problem, Unia continued to receive new reports of similar incidents. This triggered a discussion within Unia:

> So, as we received reports following Lachiri confirming that this practice was continuing despite the ruling, we said to ourselves: this is problematic because not complying with a court ruling is already something in terms of discrimination, there are possible criminal proceedings, possible penalty payments, and so on. But this is at a much higher level and it's binding. So, we thought, well, we can't just let this go, and that's why we went to the enforcement committee and asked what we could do.[107]

It is only when getting in touch with a legal officer at the Department for the Execution of Judgments of the ECtHR that they were informed about the possibility of submitting a Rule 9 application to the Committee of Ministers. Unia had never done this before and the case officer explained that for them

---

103 The individual measures to be taken consisted solely of the payment of just satisfaction to the applicant. (1362nd meeting in December 2019, 'Bilan d'action (26/09/2019) – Communication de la Belgique concernant l'affaire Lachiri c. Belgique (Requête no. 3413/09) [French only]', 1 October 2019, DH-DD(2019)1076 <https://hudoc.exec.coe.int/eng?i=DH-DD(2019)1076F>.)

104 Ibid.

105 'Règle 9.2 Communication du Centre interfédéral pour l'égalité des chances et la lutte contre le racisme et les discriminations (UNIA) (08/03/2019) relative à l'affaire Lachiri c. Belgique (requête no. 3413/09) [French only]', above n. 34, paras. 12–13.

106 Interview with the relevant case officer at Unia, conducted and transcribed in French on 19 April 2024.

107 Ibid.

it was 'the first time we've been faced with such a blatant failure to comply'.[108] The case officer at Unia stated that the legal officer in charge of the execution was easily accessible and explained the procedure over the phone, adding that the whole process 'went very smoothly, because it can also be very difficult when you're dealing with international authorities like that'.[109]

Then, Unia submitted a new Communication to the Committee of Ministers explaining the persistence of similar violations in Belgian courts. They stated herein that one year after the dissemination of the judgment, in October 2019, they had received a new report of a woman who was asked to remove her headscarf or leave the courtroom during divorce proceedings before the Family Tribunal. The relevant case officer explained:

> I cannot tell you about the files we have still received following the Lachiri ruling because the women did not want to make it official, but I was able to get the women's consent to tell the ECHR's enforcement committee that there was still a problem. I could not give them the victims' identities because the persons were far too scared. I did explain to the victims that it could be very useful if I could at least share this information anonymously with X of the ECHR's enforcement committee.[110]

In the communication to Committee of Ministers, it was described that the woman in question found herself in a delicate situation where the judge was deciding on the custody of the children and alimony payments, so she did not dare to refuse the order of the judge.[111] Then, it was mentioned that Unia contacted the woman's lawyer and explained the legal framework and, most notably, the recent *Lachiri* judgment. During a new hearing at the same court, the judge made the same order to the woman in question. The judge had responded that she was aware of the case law of the ECtHR but that – based on Article 759 of the Belgian Judicial Code – she nonetheless was the one to decide on how to maintain law and order in her courtroom.[112] Based on the previous interaction at this court, the woman had decided not to attend this second hearing so the judge had insisted that the lawyer would go to fetch his client so that she could explain her request to her. Again, the judge asked the woman to remove the lower part of her headscarf.[113]

---

108 Ibid.

109 Ibid.

110 Ibid.

111 1377th meeting in June 2020, 'Rules 9.3 et 9.6 - Communication of a NHRI (Centre interfédéral pour l'égalité des chances et la lutte contre le racisme et les discriminations (UNIA)) (17/03/2020) concerning the case Lachiri v. Belgium (application n° 3413/09) and response of the authorities (01/04/2020) [French only]', <https://hudoc.exec.coe.int/?i=DH-DD(2020)282-revF>.

112 Ibid.

113 Ibid.

In the communication to the Committee of Ministers, Unia argued that these new reports it had received demonstrated that the only manner in which similar new violations could be prevented (and the *Lachiri* judgment fully executed) is by the amendment of the relevant provision in the Judicial Code.[114]

5.2. *Amendment of the Judicial Code*

What would happen afterwards was surprising to the case officer at Unia:

> I remember that after years of working on these issues, it was really a great victory, and it's so rare that it was really incredible. But what happened after we got back to the Belgian level was that the recommendation that was made was directly followed up.

In a second action plan from early December 2021 submitted to the Committee of Ministers by the Belgian government, it was mentioned that such a legislative amendment had taken place. It was also stated that prior to this, the Judicial Training Institute was asked to incorporate the judgment into the initial and ongoing training of judges in ethics and professional conduct, to remind them that nothing in national law expressly prohibits the wearing of religious symbols by private individuals at court hearings, as the spirit of the Judicial Code is solely aimed at ensuring that they run smoothly.[115] In November 2021, the Belgian Parliament finally reached an agreement on amending the Judicial Code in order to remove the disputed section. This step in the execution process took place quite soon after the adoption of the judgment, although Belgium is usually plagued by indecision and strategic ambiguity when it comes to the headscarf. As stated earlier, the Belgian Judicial Code was amended in order to remove the contested section. Article 23 of the Law of 28 November 2021 removed the word 'uncovered' ('*met ongedekten hoofde*') from Article 759 of the Belgian Judicial Code, which now states that hearings should be attended 'respectfully and silently' ('*eerbiedig en stilzwijgend*') by the audience.[116] This modified provision entered into force on 10 December 2021. In the draft bill, the ECtHR judgment is mentioned, and it is stated that the judge in question reasoned from a literal interpretation of the law, whereas the amendment will bring the text in line with the original purpose of the legislator.

---

114 Ibid.

115 1428th meeting in March 2022, 'Action Plan (01/12/2021) - Communication of Belgium on the case Lachiri v. Belgium (application n° 3413/09) [French only]', <https://hudoc.exec.coe.int/?i=DH-DD(2021)1316F>.

116 Wet van 28 november 2021 om justitie menselijker, sneller en straffer te maken (Law of 28 November 2021 to make the justice system more humane, faster and stronger.)

5.3. *Communication Strategy on Impact*

The removal of a hijabi from the courtroom was not an exceptional occurrence. Yet, what was quite remarkable to the case of Hagar Lachiri was that she was present or wished to be present in that courtroom because of a tragic event, namely the murder of her brother. This is explicitly mentioned in the description of the case on the European Court's impact page. In the background of the case, it is stated that:

> Hagar Lachiri was in court to plead that the man accused of her brother's death should stand trial for murder and not a lesser offence. It was a difficult day for the bereaved family, made worse by the court's attitude towards Hagar's *hijab*, the headscarf she chooses to wear as a practising Muslim.[117]

When looking for 'impact cases' in the context of freedom of religion, this is the first case that pops up across 46 Member States. This chapter does not claim that the selection of 200 examples of judgments whose implementation has improved people's lives across Europe is decisive for the course of justice in the present case. Yet, it is interesting that, first, the *Lachiri* case made it onto that list and, second, that this particular detail was seen as important enough to mention.

6 CONCLUSION

The present chapter set out to explore which civil society actors engage with human rights in the pre-trial and post-trial phase and what they add to the human rights trajectory in this specific context. Through this exploration, the chapter aimed to demonstrate the importance of such a mapping exercise in order to obtain knowledge about the protection of human rights in Europe and beyond and the role that is played by other actors besides courts in this protection. To research case law of supranational and regional human rights courts while remaining in the dark about the complete map of actors that were involved in the process of pushing and pulling human rights and through that contribute to the construction of human rights law is a missed opportunity. The present chapter shed light on the variety of actors that were fundamental while focusing on two actors in particular that were able to leave their mark on the case through a procedural opening provided by the European Court of Human Rights or the Committee of Ministers of the Council of Europe. Several contextual, personal and institutional factors were essential to the creation of an environment in which both actors could add to the human rights trajectory of the case.

117 'Legal code changed after a woman was excluded from a courtroom for wearing a hijab', *Council of Europe* <https://www.coe.int/en/web/impact-convention-human-rights/-/legal-code-changed-after-a-woman-was-excluded-from-a-courtroom-for-wearing-a-hijab>.

CONCLUSION: UNCERTAIN FUTURES OF HUMAN RIGHTS PROTECTION IN EUROPE

Angelika Nußberger, Cathérine Van de Graaf and Yannick Schoog

This volume has explored a series of pressing issues that confront the European human rights project today, ranging from the regulation of memory and historical truth to the challenges of pandemics; from the enduring legacies of empire to the prospects for social and environmental rights; from corporate accountability to the privatisation of the digital public sphere. Read together, the chapters paint a picture of a legal order that is neither settled nor entirely predictable. Rather, the protection of human rights in Europe is best understood as a field in flux: subject to the pressures of geopolitical upheaval, institutional adaptation, technological transformation and social contestation.

While each chapter offers insights into a particular dimension of this evolving landscape, several overarching themes can be drawn from their juxtaposition. What follows is not attempt to provide definitive answers or a unified vision for the future of human rights protection in Europe. Instead, the aim is to trace points of convergence and divergence, to identify the normative and institutional tensions that recur across different fields and to sketch possible directions in which further scholarly and practical engagement may be needed.

1 THE WEIGHT OF THE PAST IN SHAPING THE FUTURE

The future of human rights protection in Europe cannot be disentangled from the ways in which the past is remembered, interpreted, and institutionalised. In Chapter 1, Paula Rhein-Fischer's analysis of mnemonic laws highlights the growing recognition of collective memory as a legal value in itself. This recognition, however, raises fundamental questions about the boundaries of free discourse, the risks of instrumentalising history and the potential fragmentation of European legal space when national approaches diverge.

A similar concern with historical legacies runs through Sergii Masol's Chapter 2, on Russia's fraught relationship with the Council of Europe. The argument that de-imperialisation is a prerequisite for any future re-engagement underscores how unresolved historical trajectories of power and domination continue to shape present possibilities. In this respect, the chapters converge on an important insight: Europe's human rights order is not only forward-looking but also deeply conditioned by how institutions and states grapple with difficult pasts. Whether in the form of memory laws or post-imperial reckoning, the past exerts a gravitational pull that complicates attempts at linear progress.

The question of historical trajectories also concerns the concept of human rights protection itself. From its origins, it was oriented towards the past in that its intention was to overcome the 'untold sorrow' brought upon humanity by war and dictatorship. However, with the assertion of 'never again', it was also future-oriented, using the lessons of the past to create a better future. Nevertheless, this historical mission appears to be sidestepped when the focus of human rights shifts towards 'new' challenges despite the fact that 'old' challenges remain unresolved and resurface. Although this issue is not addressed directly in this volume, it is omnipresent in the discussion about the future of human rights protection in an increasingly hostile 21st century.

2 VULNERABILITY OF RIGHTS IN TIMES OF CRISIS

Several chapters are reminders of the fragility of rights protections when states face crises – whether pandemics, migration flows or security threats. Reza Khabook's contribution in Chapter 3, focusing on states of emergency in the context of pandemics, illustrates the risks of unchecked executive discretion. His call for proportionality-based judicial review echoes a broader concern about ensuring that exceptional measures do not erode the foundations of the rule of law.

This theme resonates with Samuel White's discussion, in Chapter 9, of the politicisation of human rights in national debates, particularly in the UK and Denmark. When political leaders present human rights as obstacles to effective governance in moments of perceived crisis, public support for supranational institutions can rapidly weaken. Both chapters therefore highlight the importance of institutional safeguards – whether through courts or through public education – to ensure that crises do not become pretexts for long-term retrenchment.

3 FRAGMENTATION AND PLURALISM OF LEGAL ORDERS

Another cross-cutting issue concerns the multiplicity of actors and regimes involved in human rights protection. Yannick Schoog shows, in Chapter 4, how the protection of social rights remains fragmented between different instruments (the ECHR, the ESC, the EU Charter and political declarations such as the European Pillar of Social Rights). His cautious assessment suggests that without stronger convergence, social rights will remain the 'poor relation' of civil and political rights in Europe.

In Chapter 10, Cathérine Van de Graaf's mapping of actors in the *Lachiri* case underscores the importance of recognising the roles played by non-judicial actors – civil society organisations, national institutions and transnational networks – in shaping the trajectory of rights protection. Similarly, Ezgi Özlü's analysis of repetitive cases in Chapter 6 highlights how systemic deficiencies within national legal systems spill over into supranational institutions, compelling the European Court of Human Rights to develop new procedural innovations.

Taken together, these chapters draw attention to a fundamental feature of the European human rights landscape: it is multilayered, pluralistic and at times incoherent. The challenge is not only to coordinate among diverse institutions, but also to recognise the legitimacy of actors beyond the courts in shaping the normative order.

4 EMERGING FRONTIERS: ENVIRONMENT, CORPORATE ACCOUNTABILITY AND THE DIGITAL SPHERE

The future of human rights protection in Europe will also be determined by the system's capacity to engage with new frontiers of rights claims. My Hanh Pham's Chapter 5 points to the tentative but growing debates around recognising the rights of nature. While the European Court of Human Rights remains tied to an anthropocentric framework, the gradual emergence of physiocentric approaches in some national and international jurisdictions raises the possibility of doctrinal evolution. Yet, as the chapter makes clear, significant dogmatic and procedural obstacles remain, and the tension between environmental protection and established human rights doctrines is unlikely to be resolved quickly.

Francesca Mussi's contribution in Chapter 7 on corporate sustainability due diligence likewise examines a developing field where expectations are high, but uncertainties abound. The Directive may significantly enhance accountability for corporate human rights abuses, yet its effectiveness will depend on national implementation and the willingness of EU institutions to close normative gaps left by political compromises.

Finally, Tomáš Morochovič's narrative analysis of online political expression in Chapter 8 highlights the privatisation of the digital public sphere as a structural challenge for human rights protection. Here, the tension between emancipatory potential and risks of distortion is acute: online platforms amplify voices but also entrench private control over what counts as public discourse. This chapter illustrates how new technological environments require rethinking traditional assumptions about agency, responsibility and the boundaries between public and private regulation.

5 THE CENTRAL ROLE OF LEGITIMACY AND PUBLIC SUPPORT

Across the chapters, legitimacy emerges as a central concern. Whether the issue is judicial review in times of crisis, the recognition of new rights or the enforcement of corporate due diligence, the durability of human rights protections depends not only on formal rules but also on broader societal acceptance. Samuel White's emphasis on human rights education as a means to counter disinformation and rebuild public trust is particularly salient in this regard.

Indeed, the volume as a whole suggests that the most serious threats to the European human rights system may not come from external shocks but from a gradual erosion of legitimacy within Member States. If citizens and political leaders perceive human rights institutions as disconnected, intrusive or unresponsive to pressing concerns, their willingness to comply with supranational judgments may diminish. Conversely, if human rights protections can be linked to tangible benefits in people's daily lives, they may be seen not as abstract ideals but as essential components of democratic life.

6 REFLECTIONS AND AVENUES FOR FURTHER RESEARCH

The chapters in this volume not only map current debates but also open up avenues for future research. One clear lesson is that the study of the future of human rights in Europe cannot be confined to the doctrinal analysis of legal texts and judgments alone. Several chapters have shown the value of interdisciplinary engagement. Narrative theory, as used by Tomáš Morochovič, or the sociological and anthropological approaches to memory highlighted by Paula Rhein-Fischer, reveal aspects of law that might otherwise remain invisible. Similarly, philosophical inquiry into the possible recognition of nature as a subject of rights, as advanced by My Hanh Pham, demonstrates the need to move beyond traditional legal categories in order to capture new normative possibilities. These contributions are reminders that the law does not operate in isolation but in constant dialogue with broader intellectual traditions and that only by drawing on insights from neighbouring disciplines can human rights scholarship adequately grapple with the transformations under way.

A second dimension that deserves closer attention is the comparative one. Several authors point to developments outside of Europe that may provide useful reference points, particularly the jurisprudence of the Inter-American system concerning the rights of nature and environmental protection. Comparative engagement can be a fruitful way of testing the limits of European approaches and assessing whether alternative models might be adapted to local conditions. At the same time, comparative analysis must be pursued with caution: as Sergii Masol's chapter discusses, the European human rights system is shaped by specific historical and geopolitical legacies, not all of which have direct analogues elsewhere. Future research might thus combine comparative openness with a sensitivity to contextual particularities, recognising both the opportunities and the limits of borrowing from other regions.

Thirdly, the resilience of European institutions in the face of political and structural pressures is a theme that merits sustained scholarly attention. The contributions on repetitive cases, on the strained protection of social rights and on the CSDD Directive all illustrate how supranational institutions are required to navigate complex environments marked by political backlash, limited enforcement capacities and growing caseloads. How these institutions adapt – through procedural innovation, new forms of dialogue or recalibration of their jurisprudence – will determine the future strength of the European system. A careful empirical study of these adaptive strategies and of their reception in Member States, would greatly enrich the understanding of the dynamics of institutional resilience.

Finally, the role of public engagement emerges as a vital but under-explored component of human rights protection. As Samuel White emphasises, legitimacy is not generated by courts and legislatures alone, but also through the ways in which citizens perceive, understand and internalise rights. There is a pressing need for empirical research on public attitudes toward human rights across Europe, examining not only levels of support but also the social, economic, and educational factors that shape such support. Moreover, the link between human rights education and public perception requires further exploration, particularly regarding how educational initiatives can be designed to counter misinformation and disengagement. In this respect, the role of civil society actors, highlighted in Cathérine Van de Graaf's chapter, becomes especially significant: NGOs, grassroots organisations, and national human rights institutions are not merely intermediaries but active participants in sustaining the legitimacy and effectiveness of human rights protections.

In short, the chapters collected in this volume point to a research agenda that is necessarily interdisciplinary, comparative, institutional and societal in scope. Each of these dimensions offers a pathway for scholars to deepen their collective understanding of how the European human rights system might evolve and of what conditions are necessary to ensure that it continues to serve as a meaningful framework for the protection of human dignity in a rapidly changing world in which the individual should remain in the centre.

7 CONCLUDING REMARKS

This volume set out to examine the 'future of human rights protection in Europe', but it would be misleading to suggest that a single, coherent future can be discerned. Rather, the chapters collectively highlight the plurality of futures that are possible – some more optimistic, others more constrained. What unites them is a shared recognition that human rights protection in Europe is neither guaranteed nor static. It is a contested field, shaped by historical legacies, the zeitgeist, institutional choices, societal attitudes and foreseeable and unforeseeable crises.

To study the future of human rights is therefore not to predict outcomes but to map possibilities, highlight tensions and identify where further vigilance and engagement are required. If there is a common message in this volume, it is that the European human rights project will remain viable only if it can continue to adapt, to include new voices and perspectives, and to foster legitimacy both within and beyond the courtroom. The task for scholars, practitioners and citizens alike is to remain attentive to these dynamics, recognising that the future of human rights in Europe will ultimately be determined not by abstract ideals alone but by the choices, struggles and commitments of those who seek to uphold them.

www.ingramcontent.com/pod-product-compliance
Ingram Content Group UK Ltd.
Pitfield, Milton Keynes, MK11 3LW, UK
UKHW051905290926
8980IPUK00017B/1781

9 781839 704413